Television Writing and Selling

Television Writing and Selling

BY

Edward Barry Roberts

WITH AN INTRODUCTION BY
IRA L. AVERY

Boston   THE WRITER, INC.   *Publishers*

The Riverside Press
CAMBRIDGE · MASSACHUSETTS
PRINTED IN THE UNITED STATES OF AMERICA

To the memory of
George Pierce Baker, the teacher,
and to the living, growing forces
his teaching set in motion.

Preface to the Third Edition

As I write these words for the third edition of *Television Writing and Selling*, I must remind myself all over again that television is "show business", and as such is subject to the sudden, unpredictable changes, fluctuations, caprices and aberrations of the entertainment world. I have learned (and should already have known) that it is hazardous to commit one's self to a statement of fixed policy-procedure for any form of show business, particularly for the television form. In the preface to the second edition (turn a few pages and you'll see) I wrote glowingly about the large number of dramatic programs on the air, requiring the skill of many television playwrights. I had in mind at that time the fact that there were between fifteen and twenty hour-length anthology drama programs competing for the services of writers. Swiftly these hour programs went off the air, until at this writing there are only a very few such programs left. (I refuse to name them, because they may go off the air at any time and again make me look a bit silly.)

Various pressures operated to cause the demise of the hour anthology program: They were economic, sociological, political, changes in public taste; or the dramatic anthologies perhaps had run their course for a while. And, lastly, perhaps the showing of so many old Hollywood motion pictures on the air gave the viewing public a surfeit of drama.

Still, as a genre, the original television drama, preferably in the hour or hour-and-a-half length, seems to have been the most enduring favorite with television viewers; and if these dramas have absented themselves for a while from our felicity, they also can return to their one-time favored position, both in number and quality. Those of us who truly have a sense of dedication about television drama of the highest, most provocative character can only hope that the cycle will return by popular demand, to meet the age-old human request, "Tell us a story".

Of course, there have been, are now, and will be the Westerns, in apparently unending number. And the whodunits, the crime stories, the private eyes, the plays of violence and of raw, crude conflict no doubt will continue, for large segments of the viewing public seem to watch them. A bit cynically, I will remark that they are the easiest form of television play to write. Therefore, the hack playwright who formerly may have written for the pulps, or for the B-C-and-downward-to-Z movies, is now having a field day, utilizing a full bag of clichés. Other playwrights will hold fast to the high standards, quality and ideals of a *Playhouse 90*, in spite of its many commercials and station break interruptions. There *is* hope for the future. A television playwright who can create a *Little Moon of Alban,* namely, James Costigan, still can arrive at the top with one prodigious leap of artistic effort. And times *do* change, the world *does* move on; a topflight television producer told me that he doubts if he would now produce a television play of detailed character study which was a classic of the old Philco Theatre. He said that nowadays he's looking for plays presenting "character in action". . . . *action,* but let us strive for and hope for *meaningful* action, not action merely for the sake of motion which can truly interest only the childish, whether it be a child of eight years or one fifty years old, a child in an adult's body.

I have read through the second edition of *Television Writing and Selling.* It is filled with references to drama programs now off the air — *Robert Montgomery Presents, Studio One,* etc. Short of a rewrite of the whole book, to remove these allusions, the text as is must stand. For the principles which these programs illustrate are unchanged; and the substitution of drama programs on the air as of this writing would mean only that in due time these new references, too, would become obsolete. As I remarked earlier, television is show business, and so is subject to unpredictable change. But in relation to the *principles of television playwriting* set forth in this book, I'd like to quote the aphorism from the French: "The more it changes, the more it is the same."

If television is to reach full maturity and complete expression, there is, in my opinion, an important obstacle to be overcome — pre-censorship exercised by powerfully organized pressure groups which operate behind the scenes, unknown to the American people in general. Unfortunately, many people who denounce the "mediocrity" of television programs on the one hand, knowingly or unconsciously allow themselves to become part of a "pressure group" which demands that their point of view and theirs only be expressed on television and in television drama and write angry letters threatening to boycott the sponsor's products. To "play it safe", the sponsor offers still another Western, or another crime series.

Some readers may think that this statement of censorship does not belong in a book on the technique of writing for television. I think it does, for censorship to a large degree determines what can or cannot sell to television, and all the technique in the world is useless if free Americans are not given the chance to say what they think on television. Points of view will inevitably clash, but at least the American people can choose. Television playwrights of the future reflecting on the relationship between censorship and their work might like to recall that Thomas Jefferson said that the American people could be "safely entrusted to hear everything true and false and form a correct judgment between them."

✻   ✻   ✻

Technically, the heavy increase in the use of magnetic tape recording of video, the visual part of television, has been the most interesting development. Practice has shown that scripts to be recorded on tape need not be written in the form of screen plays to be filmed; scripts written in "live" technique also are taped. The important thing for the television playwright to remember is that in a script to be taped, the *time* element is removed so that required costume, make-up and locale (sets) changes no longer must be considered in relation to the all-over time limitations of a "live" telecast. In taping, an actor can be shown in a bathing suit on the beach, and in the next following scene can be seen in evening dress on the dance floor. Taped dramas can be shot out of sequence; or the procedure of taping can be halted while the actor changes costume and/or make-up, and moves to another set. The need for meaningful cover scenes is thereby removed in taped dramas. And magnetic tape recording of video can now be spliced, edited and inter-cut like motion picture film, a tremendously important technical advance. Still, most of the half-hour television dramas are photographed, and television playwrights are therefore required to know motion picture technique, screenplay writing. The television playwright should know in advance, before he starts writing, if possible, how his play is to be presented — "live", taped, or filmed; for the construction of his drama will be vitally affected, depending upon the method of presentation to be used. I still think, however, that it is important that a television playwright first master the most rigorous and demanding (as well as the most interesting and creative) technique of "live" television playwriting techniques.

Some informed individuals believe that Pay Television is imminent. If Pay Television should come, it still must be written employing the techniques of commercially-sponsored television.

Production of television has, as of this writing, largely moved to Hollywood; there are those who say that the television playwright must live and work either in New York or Hollywood. The New York market still has tremendous importance, however; New York is the home of most of the sponsoring corporations which give the final approval to material for network telecasting; and the home offices of the major advertising agencies which have these corporations as clients are largely in New York. Also, the New York literary agents dealing with television material and with television playwrights maintain their importance, and it is my conviction that the New York agents generally are more accessible. I have too often (in New York) been on the receiving end of frantic telegrams and telephone calls from Hollywood to "get us material and writers at once" to believe otherwise. There just is no comparison between the volume of free-lance material submitted in New York (it is immense) and such material originating in Hollywood. Could it be that New York remains the intellectual and creative center of our country, while in Hollywood, that lotus land, even the unknown, unestablished dramatist writes only on assignment?

Recently I had the privilege of helping to conduct the CBS Television Network's Writing Grants Program, in New York. By far the largest number of applicants in this program lived in or near New York City; Hollywood and its environs were a poor second, the Middle West and Southwest a poorer third. These applicants represent the television playwrights of tomorrow; and I wish to say with a bit of amazement that their writing for the most part astounded me with its high quality. There is indeed great hope for the future when these presently "unknown, unestablished" television playwrights find fulfillment — and markets! — for their talents. Since I think it unfair, even immoral, to encourage new writers who have not been able to demonstrate talent *as far as my opinion and judgment are concerned,* I would not presume to express such optimism for the future of television playwriting if I did not believe in this future with my whole heart.

EDWARD BARRY ROBERTS

Acknowledgments

— to the many people who helped so greatly:

Mr. Vic Allan, for his excellent photographs; Mr. Robert Anderson, television playwright; Mr. Walt Arnold, cameraman, Armstrong's Circle Theatre; Miss Kay Arthur, television playwright; Mr. Ira L. Avery, television playwright; Miss Anne Howard Bailey, television playwright; Mr. Joseph W. Bailey, for "Robert Montgomery Presents"; Mr. Max Banzhaf, for Armstrong Cork Company; Mr. Frank B. Barry, for his wise counsel; Mrs. Mildred Emerson Bartels, who typed the manuscript; Mr. Norman H. Bonter, for his friendly help; Mr. Hal Boyle, foreign correspondent, the Associated Press; Mr. Stewart Pierce Brown, television playwright; Mr. Thad H. Brown, for the National Association of Radio and Television Broadcasters; Miss Evelyn F. Burkey, for the Authors League of America; Mr. Rodney Bush, of Twentieth Century-Fox Films, Inc.; Mr. Theodore W. Case, television playwright; Mr. Saxe Commins, for Random House; Miss Mary L. Cummings, for her professional advice; Mr. Frank P. De Felitta, television playwright; Mr. F. Lyman Dewey, for E. I. Du Pont de Nemours & Company; Mr. Ross Donaldson, of the National Broadcasting Company; Mr. John Driscoll, for his invaluable aid; Mr. William Dudley, television playwright; Mr. Herbert J. Patrick Emerson, who helped with the research; Mr. Don Ettlinger, television playwright; Dr. Millard C. Faught, who supplied valuable data; Mr. Hudson Faussett, producer, Armstrong's Circle Theatre; Mr. H. William Fitelson, for the Theatre Guild; Miss Martha Fulton, television playwright; Mr. Roger Garis, television playwright; Mr.

Nelson Gidding, television playwright; Mrs. Betty Grove, editor, Armstrong's Theatre of Today; Miss Doris Halman, television playwright; Mrs. Francis Head, literary agent; Mr. Arthur Heinemann, of the Columbia Broadcasting Company; Mr. C. A. Jackson, Jr., for the American Tobacco Company; Miss Lois Jacoby, television playwright; Mr. Edward Rogers Knowlton, television playwright; Mr. William Koppelman, for Brandt & Brandt, literary agents; Mr. Robert J. Landry, for permission to quote from his important writings; Mr. Norman Lessing, television playwright; Mr. Fred Manchee, executive vice-president, Batten, Barton, Durstine & Osborn, Inc.; Mr. Frederic Manley, television playwright; Mr. Paul Markman, for his sympathetic support; Mr. and Mrs. Frederick P. McDougal, for their wise counsel and material help; Mr. Irving Gaynor Neiman, television playwright; Miss Janice O'Connell, formerly of the Columbia Broadcasting System; Mr. Frank O'Neill, scenarist and television playwright; Miss Joan O'Neill, surely the perfect secretary; Mr. Paul Osborn, playwright, for "On Borrowed Time"; Mr. William White Parish, of the National Broadcasting Company; Mr. Paul Peters, radio playwright; Mrs. Mary Leonard Pritchett, literary agent; Miss Mary Shea, of the National Broadcasting Company; Mr. Garry Simpson, television director, Armstrong's Circle Theatre; Professor Boyd M. Smith, chairman, Department of Drama, Yale University; Mr. John A. Thomas, without whom this book would never have been written; Mr. Jack Tyler, associate on Armstrong's Circle Theatre and director of Armstrong's Theatre of Today; Mr. Turnley Walker, author of "Rise Up and Walk"; Mr. Lawrence Edward Watkin, novelist, for "On Borrowed Time"; Mr. E. Carlton Winckler, Manager of Production, Program Department, Columbia Broadcasting System, for his vast technical assistance; Mr. M. J. Wing, for the Associated Press; Mr. John Winterich, editor, "The American Writer"; Miss Janet Wood, of the Columbia Broadcasting System; Mrs. Elspeth Woodward, for her enthusiastic interest and counsel; Dr. and Mrs. Edward H. Wray, Jr., for their unceasing friendship and support. . . .

. . . thank you!

E. B. R.

Contents

Introduction to the Revised Edition, *Edward Barry Roberts*   xv

Introduction, *Ira L. Avery*   xix

1. Television: the New Playwriting   1

Television defined; its unique qualities. Working conditions of commercially-sponsored television. Playwright's desirable equipment, experience. Challenge of television playwriting.

2. Choosing Your Story   6

Organizing it for writing. Length of play, type of story. A program's format notes, sample script. "Live" television plays: time, studio limitations. Film clips. Unities of Aristotle. Cover scenes defined. Consistency of style. Sub-plots. Filmed television plays: time, setting limitations removed. Over-plotting filmed television plays. Outdoor action. Narrative technique, its hazards. Testing your story: mandatory beginning, middle, end. A short and a long synopsis illustrated. Scene-by-scene breakdown from *Remembrance Island*. The television play: its physical form: *Remembrance Island* opening sequence. Making your intention clear.

3. Settings and Special Effects   33

How they govern stories which can be done "live." Usual special effects now available listed. Motion picture film; film clips; cost of special filming. Theatre-in-the-Round. Usual television studio layout. Time and sequence of producing a "live" television play. The playwright's imagination must inspire new special effects.

4. Camera Directions   45

Camera Directions the television playwright must know and use. Four types of directions usually needed. More common directions illustrated: starting, ending scenes and plays; elapse of time; transitions; dissolves, cuts; *Caprice* examples; reaction shots; glossary of camera terms defined and discussed. Examples of film clips from *Only This Night*. Telling your story visually: example from *Way of Courage;* discussion of effects achieved. Statement by Garry Simpson. Where to begin your television play.

5. Problems of Time   63

In "live" television plays. Point of attack on material. Transitions in "live" television plays: *Way of Courage* example. Close-ups, and excluding other characters; matched dissolves, distort. Transitions in filmed television plays. Transitions through a montage: illustration from *The D. O. Basket* and *Red Tape*. Use of doubles in montages. Montages and their importance in advancing story, covering time lapses. Categories of difficulties with Time in your play.

6. Exposition   78

Its types: from stage plays, radio, motion pictures. Fundamental television principle: Exposition in action with principal characters on camera at once. Example from *The D. O. Basket,* results discussed; from *High Steel,* with discussion; from *Maquisard,* showing use of Narrator; from *Mr. Bemiss Takes a Trip,* stream-of-consciousness, prerecorded. The monologue or soliloquy. Old-fashioned exposition: other characters "expose" principals, wrong way, right way illustrated. Fundamental principle re-stated.

7. Contrasts in Technique   97

On Borrowed Time as a novel, a stage play, a motion picture, a radio play, a television play. Basic story given. Discussion of number of characters and settings in each medium. The Action in each medium compared. Condensation the answer in television playwriting, with your story begun "in medias res."

8. History of a One-Act Play   115

Synopsis of hour-long one-act play: *The Prison in Paradise*. Full text of half-hour television play developed from this one-acter: *Best Trip Ever*: Discussion of problems of transforming long one-acter into television play: Title, Time, Sets, Characters, Dialogue. Master scenes of stage play listed and contrasted with master scenes of television play.

9. The Half-Hour Television Play: "Live"   165

Its severe time limitations when produced "live." Excerpt from *The Runaway Heart*. Sub-plots. Two fundamental principles of structure. Motivation, simplicity of basic situation. "Left field" solutions. Flashbacks, their use and purpose illustrated from *Pilgrimage*. Complete script of *Billy Adams, American;* discussion of its transitions.

10. The Half-Hour Filmed Television Play   225

Complete script of *What Hath God Wrought*, by Richard Blake, produced on film for the Cavalcade of America television program. Discussion of differences between "live" plays and filmed plays as regards possible markets, Time, Characters, Settings, Costumes, Make-up, Transitions, scope of story, specific description of shots, camera techniques.

11. The Fifteen-Minute Television Play   264

Its special requirements. Complete script of *Impersonation*, by Anne Howard Bailey, reproduced. Comment on this script.

12. The Hour-Length Television Play   282

Complete script of *The Inn*, produced "live" on the Kraft Theatre program. Discussion of narrative as opposed to the "Ibsen technique"; Settings, Characters, Time, Transitions.

13. Adaptations   361

Goal of successful adaptations. Selective process of dramatic technique. Elimination of minor characters, sub-plots, for steady emphasis and forward movement on main story. Visual effects replace descriptive passages. Writing out basic story. Listing master scenes of original work. Successive steps in preparing master scene plot of television play. These principles applied to *Rise Up and Walk;* basic story, book's master scenes, television play's master scenes, discussion of differences. Prose passages from book written as play dialogue (pre-recorded). Condensed script of *Wuthering Heights* as a television play given, with key scenes in dialogue. Discussion of creating play out of original novel; amount of story used; Characters, Settings, Transitions. Adapting the short story and the long stage play. Material for adaptations: public domain, copyrighted material, bringing your material to the editor's attention.

Your rights in adaptations. Qualifications on copyrights and adaptor's rights, by Ross Donaldson.

14. The Documentary Television Play   418

Condensed script, with key scenes in dialogue, of *The Thousand-Yard Look,* by Don Ettlinger and Nelson Gidding, based on Associated Press dispatches from Korea by foreign correspondent Hal Boyle; produced "live" on The Pulitzer Prize Playhouse television program. The motion picture newsreel, the Federal Theatre *Living Newspaper* stage plays, the March of Time, *The Ramparts We Watch* and *The House on 92nd Street* (motion pictures) as variations of the documentary play, preceding the television documentary play. Excerpts from the actual AP dispatches inset into body of *The Thousand-Yard Look* as they inspire Story, Characters, Incident. Importance of thorough research.

15, Selling Your Television Scripts   454

Procedure for submitting an unsolicited manuscript to networks, "package producers" and advertising agencies' television editors. Release forms. Getting the information you need about personnel, addresses and requirements of programs. Literary agents, the advantages of having one. Copyright information, procedure; other *protection* techniques. The Writers Guild of America, Inc., information on membership requirements and benefits to members. Television commercials, by Ira L. Avery. Release forms illustrated.

16. The Television Code   470

The Television Code of the National Association of Radio and Television Broadcasters. Excerpts relevant to television writing quoted.

17. The Editor's Grab Bag   477

Highly personal remarks by a practising television editor on relations between playwright and the television editor. Other odds and ends of great importance to the beginning television playwright. Excerpts from a musical variety television program, a highly specialized writing job. Remarks on the future of television.

18. The Television Playwright as an Artist   497

William Faulkner's Nobel Prize for Literature Acceptance

Speech. George Pierce Baker's final remarks to his 1929
Drama 47 Workshop class at the Yale Department of
Drama, New Haven.

Appendix   500

Magnetic Tape Recording of Video — The Important New
Technical Development in Television Playwriting. Some
Copyright Facts

Introduction to the Revised Edition

These are exciting times for the television playwright. At this writing, the market for television drama is open to all. The future is brighter than it ever was.

There are more hour-long dramatic programs than ever before. "Playhouse 90," an hour-and-a-half dramatic program, and a pioneer in this length, has won public and critical success. Soon there will be the two-hour dramatic program. Then the dramatic program of whatever time-period the length of the play requires. It's inevitable that the finest theatre, the finest dramatic writing, will be done on television in the years to come (and not so many years, either).

All of these major dramatic programs are open to the unknown, unestablished television playwright: both CBS and NBC (and presumably any other major network which presents a dramatic program in the future) *will read anyone's work, as long as it is in television play form.* So, a knowledge of television technique is indispensable.

There have been changes in marketing and producing procedures, and there has been one tremendous technical advance. To summarize:

The half-hour dramatic market has moved almost entirely to Hollywood, and half-hour scripts are, at this writing, mostly produced on film. Still, much of the buying for this market is done in New York City. See the chapter on Selling.

The fifteen-minute dramatic market is now mostly day-time

and "live." Television serials of various lengths (in number of episodes, that is) make up the bulk of this market. Writing for these day-time serials is done most usually on assignment; however, a Query Letter directed to the appropriate producer may bring results (see chapter on Selling).

The tremendous technical advance is Ampex, the magnetic tape recording of picture (Video) as well as sound — of *both* Video and Audio. A special Appendix on Ampex appears at the end of this book.

Color is an accepted fact, at least as far as telecasting in color is concerned. To the best of my knowledge, the constantly increasing use of color televison does not influence or change the basic principles of writing for television.

Actual production of television programs has largely moved out of the advertising agencies (for economic reasons) into the networks and "package" producers (organizations which deliver the complete program, from buying scripts to casting and producing the play on the air). However, since there has been a lot of talk about the advertising agencies resuming production, the section which explains how to deal with advertising editors-producers has been left in the chapter on Selling, for your possible future guidance.

If I myself were a beginning (or even a practising and successful) television playwright, I'd bear down hard on learning to write for motion picture filming as well as for "live" production. The reasons, as ever, are practical: I've had many friends, "live" television playwrights, who have sold plays to Hollywood, where their original material has been turned into screen plays for filming. In most cases which I know about, the original "live" playwright has received much less money for his work than has the Hollywood "adaptor"; and not infrequently the Hollywood "adaptor" gets more screen credit than the original author. This situation seems hardly fair to me; the answer is for the original author of the "live" play to learn how to present his material (if he chooses to do the work) in screen play form; then conceivably he'll get all the money and all the screen credit, and rightly so. (Screen and air credits are of enormous importance to the television playwright, as they are evidence of his success.) Permit me to say that I stand in back of the chapter in this book, Chapter Ten: the Half-hour Filmed Television Play, meaning that anyone who learns the technique set forth in Chapter Ten can write for motion pictures of *any* length.

A second important reason for learning screen play technique is: I believe that the television play of the future will be a combination of Ampex (magnetic tape recording of Video) or of some other picture-recording device, and of "live" action; or perhaps the future television play will be recorded entirely by Ampex, or by some comparable system. Since writing for magnetic tape recording of Video is exactly like writing for motion picture filming, *i.e.*, screen plays, the television playwright who has learned motion picture technique will be prepared to cope with the new Ampex technique when it comes into general use; and it is surely coming.

To print an hour-and-a-half long television script in this second edition would add unnecessary bulk to an already large book. Playwrights wanting to write in this length can be told confidently to "keep going" — that is, to write a script in three-act structure with a *maximum* number of 150 pages of manuscript, typed half-way across the page, as all television plays are typed.

The following table of *maximum* number of pages for dramatic scripts is generally accepted by television producers:

15-minute script .   .   .   .   20 pages
Half-hour script .   .   .   .   40 pages
Hour script .   .   .   .   .   . 100 pages
Hour-and-a-half script . . 150 pages

This table is based on typing half-way across the standard 8½″ × 11″ paper, using a typewriter which has "normal" or pica type. If your typewriter has elite (much smaller) type, scale down the number of pages by roughly one-third, since with elite type you get much more on each page.

(Should you wonder why an hour script is not twice the 40 pages of a half-hour script, but is instead 100 pages *maximum*, it's because of the difference in the handling of the commercials and station identification time.)

That's about all, except that I want to express my profound

gratitude and thanks for the wonderful reception this book has received from professional critics, television personnel and individual writers. On several occasions I've had the enormous (there is no other word for it) pleasure of having a new television playwright tell me (when he did not know my identity as the author of this book) that he has learned the technique of writing for television from my book. Could there be a greater reward for the author of a "how to" book? I doubt it.

EDWARD BARRY ROBERTS

Introduction

It's a cinch to find out what's wrong with television. Anybody will tell you. Ask an actor. He'll say, "It's mechanical. The director spends his time directing cameras and lights instead of people." Ask a director. He'll say, "It has all the disadvantages of the movies, radio and the stage with none of the advantages of any of them." An educator will tell you it's corrupting the children. The sponsor says it's too expensive and the returns can't be measured. The critics say it would be fine if the sponsors stayed out of it. The producer says the writers aren't furnishing enough material. The writer says the producer can't tell a good script from an ulcer. The network executive says it's impossible to make a profit. Everybody reaches for the benzedrine and says, "We never realized what a pleasure radio was."

Hardly seems worth it, does it? Well, it wouldn't be if it weren't for one meek little opinion — the opinion of that nobody, everybody's stepchild, the public. The public *likes* television. Why? For different reasons, all contradictory, all depending on different conditioning, different desires, different tastes. And every single one of them saying, "The only real trouble with television is you have to give me a little more of what *I* want!"

The customary first step toward driving a wedge between the public and its spending money is, especially in the case of a dramatic program, to adopt what is known as a "formula." The ideal formula is a magic recipe for pleasing everybody. As it happens, the first three or four shows don't please everybody

after all, so the formula is immediately changed. This plan was
obviously invented by a baby doctor. Then there's another plan
— the ostrich method . . . play safe, don't hurt anybody's feelings.
Home and mother, huckleberry pie, happy endings, the good
guys win, the bad guys lose. (Correction: there aren't really any
bad guys, just misunderstood ones) . . . nobody gets hurt. And
nobody could possibly object!

So what's wrong with that?

Well, there is something wrong with it, and here's why. In
television we have the greatest medium for mass enlightenment
and entertainment the world has ever known. A monster of tech-
nological, ideological, logical and illogical potentialities. In short,
we have a bear by the tail. Now, in the case of the bear, the
thing no one has ever explained satisfactorily is how anybody got
in that fix in the first place. Presumably because he wanted to
catch the bear. Then the only solution is to hang on. Only presumably he now regrets his action. Then the solution is to let
go. Either one is a gamble, but doing both is an impossibility. And
the true gambler's first rule is to gamble decisively — especially in
this case, because the bear isn't going to stand still. And neither is
television.

And if it isn't going to stand still, where is it going to go? All
of the creative forces involved will help to determine that. Television, a mass of cables and cameras and tubes and relays, will
not move of its own accord. Those who will guide its direction
have a staggering responsibility. Not just to their advertisers and
to the public, but to themselves and to their integrity. There are
forward-thinking people in television for whom it is not going to
be enough to satisfy the largest possible group of the public with
every single show, because there's a larger group in the long run
— and a less static one — the group composed of many widely
divergent, restless, demanding segments of the population, *all*
wanting to be genuinely entertained. Entertainment isn't simply
the process of not being offended. It's the process of being
stimulated, soothed, warmed, pleased, excited, emotionally moved
— all *positive* values, none of them to be achieved by compromise.

How then does one set about on this uncompromising course?
Not by trying to be all things to all men all the time but by trying

sincerely and to the best of one's ability to do each thing completely and well. An exciting melodrama must *be* an exciting melodrama. A tear-jerker must *be* a tear-jerker, a comedy must *be* a comedy, and neither the public nor any single period of television time will adjust itself to a melodramatic tear-jerking comedy.

Sometimes a play is unclassifiable as a comedy, fantasy, tragedy or straight drama, and yet it has a unique quality of writing or characterization or an individuality of plot that makes it impossible for the editor to put it down. Why not assume that these same qualities will appeal to a television audience? The only way to find out is to present it as an experiment. Granted, the audience may not like it, after all. It may have been ahead of its time; it may have offended those to whom it did not appeal; it may, after all, have just been plain bad. But at least the public was given its own chance to make the decision. There are two principles of the entertainment business to be remembered here: One is that too much master-minding often destroys itself; the other is that something unmistakably good will often excite controversy.

Who says all this? "Who's going to tell *me* that show was good?"

Here's who. The man in the cigar store. Or the woman next door. Or somebody on the streetcar — somebody who liked it. The two of you will argue until you're blue in the face — and you'll both be right. Last week's show was a clinker because you didn't like it . . . it was also a smash because some people loved it. But it didn't hit half way in between — at least it didn't fall in the category of "nothin' for nobody." Whatever it was, it stood on its own feet and was a credit to somebody's willingness to take a chance.

Now the question is, does this sort of thing work? Isn't it pretty well proved what the public goes for? The answer to that, borne out, not through decades, or even centuries, but through thousands of years, is that nothing is proved in show business, except how to play safe in any given period in history. We know how to play safe in television, but we can't stop there. Viewers will get restless — they already are. There are increasing demands for better and better material. The audience, now that the

novelty has worn off, is becoming sharply critical and articulate
— as always, in all different directions.

The whole point is this: how is the so-called public going to
know whether or not it likes something good unless given a
chance to see it and find out? Saying that such and such a TV play
is good dramatically and artistically, but that the public won't
accept it, is like saying the public won't accept automobiles because they're used to horses. But let's face it . . . these things are
said, and by people in responsible positions — by people who
would rather protect a single week's rating than contribute to
the growth of an industry. These people are by no means to be
condemned. They constitute the majority, because obviously
everyone cannot be a leader. Pioneering requires originality, and
originality, by definition, can hardly be a common characteristic.

Also, pioneering means making mistakes, often big and noisy
ones. However, *even mistakes pay off if properly exploited and
added intelligently to the sum of experience.* The important thing
a pioneer must know to survive is how to profit by a mistake. A
dramatically artistic show may be a failure this year and a howling success three years from now — or vice versa. Guessing wrong
is not necessarily fatal, but guessing wrong consistently requires
an independent income. When we talk about dramatically
artistic shows, by the way, we are not referring to so-called "arty"
productions. The arty and the truly artistic have no more relation than the superstitions of astrology have to the science of
astronomy. What we do mean is that art and long-range commercial soundness are not so incompatible as shallow thinkers
would have us believe. Art is not an ugly word. Cheapness is.

We also do not mean to imply that anything should be crammed
down the audience's throat to indulge an irresponsible whim,
because here another element enters the picture. Television, while
it stimulates the critical faculties of the audience far more than
radio ever did, is nevertheless a medium which must be ap-
proached with much the same care in its selection of story material. A television program of any kind is an invited guest in the
sanctity of the viewer's home, and in order to be invited again
must observe the rules of decorum that any other guest would
observe.

The average American family has, for instance, 2.3 children, and although everybody knows that all children are little monsters except yours and mine, we have no right to outrage a parent because of anything said or done that would misguide, offend or hurt even .3 of one child.

There are also groups of viewers who are highly sensitive to certain types of character portrayals. Some of these groups employ wholesale tactics in their condemnation of all characterizations depending, for example, on dialect. Whether or not the character portrayed possesses human dignity will escape such critics entirely, but the possibility of invoking their displeasure must always guide us to a reasonable degree. It must be remembered, of course, that the motives of some few arbitrary critics are far from sincere and cause true embarrassment among their own fellows. A rule that no one need apologize for is to follow the dictates of good taste.

Thoughtful producers and advertisers in television have adopted a philosophy somewhat as follows. First, that every listener is a potential customer — and that he will tolerate being displeased by a single show, but he will not tolerate a succession of displeasures nor will he stand for being actually offended, even once. Second, that good drama is absolutely compatible with commercial drama and that neither of these ideals should be sacrificed for the other. Third, that the advertiser in television has a threefold responsibility — to the public, to his product and to himself. We use the term "advertiser" because it applies even to an unsponsored program. The network or station advertises itself in every moment of operation.

How do networks, stations, advertisers, producers, know whether they're succeeding or not?

They have three check sources. One is the rating, a figure achieved by a cross section survey which gives a rough estimate of the number of viewers for a given program. But of course if we depended on surveys for results, Tom Dewey would have been President in 1948. The rating, however, is certainly a factor. A second check source is direct audience response by mail and by word of mouth. A third is the advertiser's selling organization, reports on unsolicited comments by dealers and their customers and response to merchandising devices such as offers of free booklets.

There is a fourth measuring instrument not to be overlooked. It's intuition — but the term is an over-simplification. It's the sum of experience in dealing with the public, experience in the field of entertainment and faith in one's own judgment and in the innate good sense of the audience. Two parts experience, one part faith. You can vary the proportions, but you can't vary the ingredients, as you'll be told by any expert martini mixer.

What is actually done is to compare the conclusions in all four of these areas and, as the economists say, evaluate the trend. When the rating is a respectable figure and shows a continual upward slant, when letters are 98% complimentary and when dealers report a growing recognition of a program, then you can hardly blame a producer for modestly admitting that he planned it that way.

The foregoing are random facets of television production that the practising writer must acknowledge. As we see them, they are generally encouraging. There are advertisers, producers and editors who ignore trends, others who follow trends, and still others who create trends. You will undoubtedly write for those in the first two categories; you may be lucky enough to achieve an association with those in the third category. You may be able to choose, or you may not, and as far as that goes, it may not matter to you. In any case, you must know the ground rules as they exist and you can take comfort from the fact that when they're changed in any degree, the heart and sinew of the change will be the writers. A writer, therefore, must learn all that it's possible to learn about why television is the way it is. Several hundred writers have already concluded that Edward B. Roberts is an inexhaustible source of the kind of information and inspiration that leads not only to understanding television but to selling scripts.

You will probably agree.

IRA L. AVERY

Television Writing and Selling

1

Television:
the New Playwriting

WHEN THE TELEGRAPH CABLE was laid from England to India, John Ruskin was informed of the miraculous achievement. He is reported to have said, "Good! Now, what do we cable to the people of India?"

What — and how — shall we write for television?

The question is put in the future tense because it's in the future that television will begin to realize the awesome possibilities it has shown at this writing (the year 1953). Inescapably, this book will have a certain topical flavor, because the conditions of writing for television are developing so rapidly that what is set down today may be (and the author hopes fervently, *will* be, in the best interests of the growth of the art of television) — outdated five years from now. If this book, therefore, conveys a feeling of urgency, even of impatience, it is because the author frets at the present mechanical clumsiness and timorousness of "live" television, and at the ineptness and the tawdriness of most of the filmed television. Yet these characteristics are to be expected at this stage, no doubt, because no man now can quite answer, "What is television?"

The inimitable Beatrice Lillie reputedly quipped, "Television is summer stock in an iron lung." Others, more serious, have declared that television is the greatest means of communication since the invention of printing. Certainly, "live" or on film, it is the most mechanical of any means of communication, requiring the most elaborate and expensive equipment for both transmitting

1

and receiving. It is also, one might say, the most subtle, mechanically, of any means of communication, based as it is on the mysterious (to the non-scientist) laws of electronics. And if television is "subtle," mechanically, its artistic qualities and possibilities lie ahead, equally mysterious, and more than tantalizing and full of promise to the writer-artist who responds to the challenge of John Ruskin's question about the use of the under-seas cable.

I will attempt an answer to the question, "What is television?" *Television is communication that cannot be made as well in any other medium.*

The peculiar and unique characteristic of television is its *immediacy,* which is to say, its *intensity.* This is immediacy of impact, intensity of *impact on the viewer,* not the intensity in light of your television set in operation. Television, particularly "live" television, cancels out time and space. We are *there,* a part of what's happening. The long determined ambition of the playwrights to eliminate the "fourth wall" of the stage is achieved in television.

This quality of immediacy, of intensity, is apparent whether there are only one or two persons on view on your TV screen, or thousands — as in the case of the Republican and Democratic National Conventions of 1952. It is not being merely reportorial to mention these historic "first" television events: it is, on the other hand, of deepest significance that the Democrats, in convention and on television two weeks after the Republicans, learned enough from the first convention radically to re-design the speaker's platform so that the orators were viewed head-on instead of in profile; and that the Democrats placed a card in each delegate's seat warning him, in effect, to "mind your manners, because you're likely to be on television when you least expect it and perhaps don't know it." In short, the Democrats learned swiftly that power of television's immediacy, *as it might reveal character* — good or bad — *but reveal character it would!* If proof were needed, let the incident be recalled of the Republican delegate from Puerto Rico who insisted on being polled. Surely, never before, in the history of the world, have so many people so quickly, *and simultaneously,* been given an insight into the character of an unknown human being!

It is another unique quality of television that it reveals character in quick, intense touches. More than the printed page, more than the stage, more than motion pictures, more — oh, so much more than radio — television, with its immediacy, gets to the heart of the matter, to the essence of the character, to the depicting of the human being who is *there*, as if under a microscope, for our private contemplation, for our approval, our rejection, our love, our hate, our bond of brotherhood recognized.

Of course, it requires the art of the writer so to present this human being under scrutiny by us, as if we were gods judging a soul naked and exposed and unable to escape our X-ray advantage. The movies have their close-ups? Yes, they do; but in television, the human being is there, suffering, rejoicing, experiencing as we watch — so close, we feel we can touch him. The legitimate stage has its intense climactic moments? Of course; but the actor still is remote, on a platform removed from us, *not*, again, so close we feel we are a part of his scene, his life, his action, his thought.

So — it has arrived, the most difficult literary form yet to appear, the New Playwriting — writing for television. This book attempts to lay down some of the principles of the New Playwriting, always with the future looking over the shoulder of the author of this book, as he writes.

Before television, the playwright had only to be concerned with the principles of Aristotle, perhaps; with the poetics of Horace, the criticism of Lessing, the Dramatic Prefaces of Shaw; and with the practices of, say, Sophocles, Shakespeare, Ibsen, Shaw, Chekhov, Wilde, Sardou, Pinero, Rostand, and of such contemporaries as he might admire and be able to see performed on the legitimate stage. His play might be written as his talent and art allowed, without any consideration for the mechanical difficulties. He could, literally, "express himself," within the bounds of decency. He could extend the boundaries of modern playwriting, as some critics declare Tennessee Williams has done; he could write a play to be performed in sections on successive nights, as Shaw did in "Back to Methusaleh"; he could start his play at five in the afternoon, break for dinner, and continue until eleven P.M., as O'Neill did in "Strange Interlude."

The playwright ambitious to write for television is under rigid restrictions. He must concern himself, in addition to the artistry of his play, with budgets, commercials, sponsors, cameras, lighting, special and trick effects, markets — and time. Heavily he must concern himself with time, as will be discussed in a chapter on "Problems of Time." Even if he is writing plays to be filmed for use on television, the time problem is different from that of motion pictures shown in theatres.

And most importantly, the television playwright must concern himself with markets, highly specialized and ephemeral, as will be discussed in the chapter on "Selling."

The television playwright must, of course, be able to write. Experience in any and every form of writing will help. A practiced novelist stands a better chance than a tyro playwright. A professional short story writer has an excellent chance for success, if he will learn the new mechanics. A seasoned playwright, an adept screenwriter, will succeed as he learns to discipline his technique. Radio writers are writing successfully for television as they learn to "see" instead of to "hear."

But everyone is a beginner at writing some time or other. To the individual determined to write and determined to write for television, the author cries "Welcome!" Watch all the television you can. If there are to be adaptations of published works, get those works ahead of time, and read them. Then watch the television shows made from that work. See what was selected, note what was left out. Watch television endlessly. And if the quality is poor, in your opinion, remember what a lot of critics and teachers have said: "You learn more from a bad play than from a good one." A good play is like a smoothly joined mechanism of stainless steel, and the joints, the individual pieces that make it up, are harder to detect than those of a crudely executed mechanism. The faults of a bad television play are even more glaring than those of a bad stage play, because of that immediacy, that intensity, we've talked about; and an amateur critic may spot them — to his profit — if he is a television writer.

If playwriting for television is the most difficult literary form to appear, still it is the most exciting, the most fascinating, and — remembering the tinker toy stage of television's present development — the most full of promise. And it is *only* through good writing that television will grow and fulfill its potential destiny as the most important means ever known of communicating information, entertainment and education.

Daily, the mechanical problems of television are being solved and its tools improved by highly creative technicians. It is the solemn responsibility of highly creative writers to provide the life for these electronic marvels.

2

Choosing Your Story

You MUST DECIDE FIRST whether you intend your play for "live" television, or for a motion picture to be filmed and televised from the film. The techniques and opportunities differ importantly.

(A third technique which television playwrights must be prepared to use is on the horizon: the video tape recorder, developed by the Ampex Corporation. The implications and possibilities of the Ampex system are so immense that at this writing, no man can set them down conclusively. The video tape recorder is so important that a special discussion of it is given in an Appendix at the back of this book. For the moment, let's concern ourselves only with "live" or "filmed" techniques.)

Having decided between "live" and "filmed" techniques for your play, you next must determine its length, in time. Will it be for a fifteen-minute program, a half-hour program, an hour program, an hour-and-a-half program, or — in the years immediately ahead — even longer?

Finally, you must, if possible, decide which television program you are aiming for. Some dramatic programs use only mystery and crime stories. Others won't touch mystery and crime. Still another program may want only stories of high adventure or the supernatural. Still others may be doing only adaptations of famous works of literature.

Since the dramatic television programs are in a state of constant flux, being on the air, then off the air, or changing style, there's only one way to choose the program you want to write for. Watch television enough to become familiar with the program or programs you're aiming for, and, as far as *genre* is concerned, pattern your play on a given program. (Then hope the program doesn't change, or go off the air, before you can get your script in to the editor!)

Every dramatic program has an editor. Sometimes, this editor has available for writers a mimeographed description of his play requirements, the "do's and don'ts," which he probably will send to you if you write and ask him for a copy. Address your request, for example, "Editor, *Name of Program*, care of *Network telecasting the program*, New York, N.Y." You know what this network is from the channel you watch on your own set. Your letter will eventually reach the editor; it may take time to receive a reply. And right here let's say that everything in television takes time; *you must learn to be patient.*

You may receive a description of the program's format; or you may get a notice that the program is not open to new free-lance writers; or you may be advised that only scripts which are submitted through accredited agents will be read.

If a program is receptive to new, unknown writers, probably the editor will send you a release form, for you to fill in and sign, and without which the editor will not read your material.

Better still would be to secure a copy of an actual as-broadcast script of the program you're aiming for; but it is not general practice for an editor to give out scripts unless he knows personally the writer asking for a copy. There are books published, however, showing television scripts in various lengths and formats; it would be most helpful to study these published television plays, which have actually been telecast on a variety of programs (and also helpful and interesting to study these complete scripts in relation to the principles of technique which are explained in this book).

"Live" Television Stories

The first consideration is, can your proposed story be done on "live" television? To take an extreme example: "Live" television produced in a studio could not show your hero mounting a horse and galloping across the prairie, unless this action be photographed as a "film clip," which is a short length of motion picture film to be made especially, at great cost, probably prohibitive, for your play. It *might* be possible to show your hero mounting a horse, a real horse, and *starting* out across the prairie; it would depend on the courage of the producer of your play, and on his ability to find a horse with an amiable disposition which wouldn't suddenly bolt or go into horse hysterics just when your show is on the air; it would also depend on the actor's willingness to mount a horse.

Neither could "live" television show your hero and heroine strolling down a country lane, stopping, and kissing each other goodbye, with the hero then jumping over the fence and walking away from the heroine across the field.

In general, extensive exteriors are difficult in "live" television, although wonderful trick and special effects can be secured. However, when you consider a story to be done "live," bound your imagination by the walls, floor and ceiling of a television studio, which resembles an empty warehouse; and decide whether or not the action required in your story can be done within the available space. If your story demands a climax of two racing cars smashing together as they round the home stretch, it cannot be done "live" without those special, *expensive* film clips, the cost of which probably would bar your play from favorable consideration by a sensible producer.

The rather discouraging remarks about the use of film clips or of motion picture film integrated with the "live" action apply to the majority of dramatic programs as of this writing. However, there are dramatic programs such as "Playhouse 90" and the "United States Steel Hour" which constantly use film integrated with the "live" action, and quite successfully.

We have said already that it is better to aim your television play for a specific program. It has been suggested that you watch this program, and study its techniques, before beginning to write your play. Then, as far as film clips and extensive use of integrated motion picture film are concerned, do as the program you're aiming for does. It would seem impossible to generalize with any degree of accuracy on the use or non-use of integrated motion picture film in a "live" production. Each case is special. It *can* be said positively, however, that motion picture film which has to be especially made to include the principal actors in your "live" play is very expensive, and its use should be avoided.

The setting of a play for "live" television, then, is the first consideration. Unless the setting can be encompassed within the four walls of a warehouse-like room, the television studio, possibly also using film clips which can be bought from a film library, (Stock Shots: see Chapter Four) lay this story aside as one which must be done on film, as a motion picture.

Immediately you have decided that your story can be done "live" within the rigid length limitations (fifteen-minute, half-hour, hour, hour and a half, or, eventually, longer), you are confronted with the special requirements of a "live" play. Perhaps "confronted" is a bad word; it may have an ominous connotation. It might be better to say that you have ahead of you the fascinating task of putting together a play under conditions of writing which demand the best a playwright can offer.

The more your "live" play can conform to the Unities of Aristotle, the better it is likely to be. These Unities are those of Time, Place and Action. They simply mean that you should choose, preferably, a story with a tightly-knit plot, which takes place in not too many settings, and in as short a period of time as possible. It is not always desirable that you have only *one* setting, unless it be extensive and elaborate; visual monotony and "talkiness" might be the result because the camera wouldn't have as much opportunity to tell your story visually. On the other hand, if your proposed story requires a great many sets, it means in all likelihood that it's broken up into a lot of little narrative bits so that you get a play lacking in dramatic impact. If you have to write a lot of short scenes, you don't have the chance really to get underway and develop drama with "sock," to speak colloquially.

Also, if you attempt a play with a lot of scenes to be done "live," you run into problems of costume and make-up changes, as well as perhaps unwanted "cover scenes" which are difficult to prevent being mere padding.

Right here, let's define a "cover scene": a cover scene is a scene which keeps the action going, and which *should* advance the plot, without the presence of one or more of the principal characters who must appear in an immediately following scene in different costume and/or make-up; and, in the case of "live" television, in a different set which may be as far away as fifty feet across the studio from the preceding set. In short, a "cover scene" is just what its name says: it "covers up" changes in costume, make-up or physical position in the sets by one or more characters in your play. And in television, "live" or on film, "cover scenes" must pay their way; they must advance the plot. With Time as short as it is, at best, you simply cannot be extravagant and waste any of this precious Time on a scene which doesn't advance the plot.

To sum up on Cover Scenes: In a "live" television play, the sets are already prepared. The actors have only to move from one set to another. But costume and make-up changes must be made *while the play is in progress, on the air, within the time limit unchangeably fixed:* and so cover scenes in "live" television plays require greater ingenuity in their construction. *Television cover scenes cannot be "padding"; they must be an essential part of the play's progression toward the climax and denouement.* There is, at best, little enough Time to tell a proper story; every second must be made to count.

Furthermore, in a story of extended action, whether you have few scenes or many, there is the damnable necessity for opening each new scene with exposition to tell the audience what has happened between scenes, in the time lapse. So again, you are squandering valuable Time in expository scenes when you should be acting out your story (i.e. dramatizing it) in front of your audience.

Consider your story material with greatest care, and see if it can't be re-cast, should it go over a long period of Time, so that in a more condensed form you can achieve the same story values but in a drama of less extended Action, resulting in stronger impact.

Your proposed television play must be consistent in style, more so than a play for any other medium. The intimacy, the intensity of television demands a dramatic simplicity, as far as style is concerned. We must believe what we see on television more completely than anything we see in whatever medium. A tragedy with comic interludes would enrage us, because it would confuse us. (Just as to this day many critics violently object to the Porter scene in *Macbeth*.) A television play offering believable, human characters in a comedy drama of a true-to-life story which suddenly drifts off into fantasy almost inescapably becomes unbelievable, and audiences fret, even if they don't turn to some other channel for their entertainment.

This is not to say that fantasy cannot be "believable." It can and must be believed *on its own terms, on its own premise*. From the start of your play, you, the playwright, must signal ingeniously to the audience that it's a fantasy they're going to see; and then, unless the viewer has a violent dislike for fantasy, with your premise accepted, you are likely to find a willing audience. But even fantasy, within the experience of one editor, must have a realistic application to life; should, in effect, "point a moral" or have meaning over and above the fantastic elements. As an example of a fantasy one editor did not believe, there was the play which told of an angel sent down from heaven to shoot a woman who baked especially good chocolate cake: it seemed the inhabitants of heaven liked chocolate cake, and took the direct way to establish a good baker in the heavenly region. This one editor frankly did not believe the premise of this particular fantasy, and so for him the play was a failure.

Tragedy must be tragedy and nothing else, then, on television; farce must be farce; comedy must be comedy; consistency, named a jewel by Shakespeare, must direct the style in which your television play is written. And you must at once, as soon as possible, through every means available — setting, costume, lighting, music, dialogue, pantomime, sound effects — let the viewer realize the style of your play; the mood, if you prefer, which you're creating.

Sub-plots in television plays are hard to handle, because there isn't time to develop them within the limitation of the half-hour or hour lengths. Every second, every minute you take away from your principal characters in your main story means that much less development of all-important characterization of your principals, and the truncating of your main story. As television plays increase in length, it may be possible to work in a meaningful sub-plot; but for practical purposes, until such time that television plays may be as long in time as the story demands, it's best to avoid sub-plots.

It will be said elsewhere in this book, but it bears constant repeating: Here is a rule which cannot be broken if a good play is to result: *Keep the action on your principal characters!* If you *cannot* keep the action on your principals, if you need a sub-plot to fill out even the brief, allotted time, you have a rickety, sparse main story which probably is not worth the telling, and your sub-plot is nothing but padding. On the other hand, successful keeping of the action on your principals for the full time available automatically guarantees that you have a full-bodied main story to tell because you *can* fill the allotted time with what the principals *must* do in order to finish the story.

It's a good test of your story, then: If you have room for a sub-plot, your main story is thin, or else you have failed fully to realize your material and/or to present your principal characters in rich characterizations so that we, the viewers, know them thoroughly and can accept them for what they may be: whole, believable people, good, evil, or a mixture of the two.

Filmed Television Stories

Much of what has been written so far in this chapter applies also to stories chosen for filming. It still is preferable in filmed television plays that the Action not be extended too far, or broken up into many short narrative scenes, because you have the same problem of beginning each new scene with exposition of what has happened in between. It still is necessary to maintain a consistent style. Sub-plots are not desirable in filmed television plays for the same reason: there isn't time to develop them, except at the expense of your main story and of your principal characters.

However, in filmed television plays, you are at once free of the restrictions of Time and Place (or Setting). Filmed television plays are made like motion pictures, in separate scenes, one at a time, which are physically glued together in the laboratory. Your heroine can change her dress as often as she likes or as the story may demand; she doesn't have to make the change while your play is actually in progress, on the air. Your hero can grow a beard, or put on a false one, at his leisure: he has as much time as the movie production chief is willing to allow him. And as far as settings go, your story may be told in a raging storm at sea, or on the race track with thousands of people on hand. If your movie producer is agreeable, the entire troupe can journey to Paris to film part of the story; then it can go on to China for some more, and back to Grand Rapids for the rest.

Time and *Place* (*Setting*) as restricting factors do not exist in filmed television plays. Nor does *Action* restrict the playwright insofar as its nature is concerned: *Now* your hero can mount a horse and gallop across the prairie, and your swain can kiss his sweetheart, leap over the fence, and disappear out of sight across the fields.

But that phrase, "out of sight," is a clue to the extent or scope of scenes you, the playwright, write in as a part of your filmed television play. It is known to all that the viewing screens of home television sets still are small. Accordingly, since everything is in proportion, i.e. people in relation to their setting, the vaster your setting in view, the smaller your people. The motion picture camera, therefore, filming your play for television, must work in *closer* than it does for conventional-size movies. "Long shots" taking in miles of terrain are dangerous on television, unless they are used briefly as "establishing" shots. Chases, the trademark of "westerns," are meaningless unless we are close enough to identify who is chasing whom; and action for the sake of action quickly bores all but the very young and the moronic.

The special temptations into error in writing a television play for filming are three. The first of these is planning a play with *too much plot*. Since the playwright is free of the limitations of Time, Place and Action (or so he decides in the first exhilarating sunburn of being out of the television studio); since he can have

scenes *anywhere* he wants, *whenever* he wants; since he can, if he
chooses, take his heroine from cooing babyhood to serene old age
as she circles the earth three times, he is apt to try it. We know,
because many playwrights trying it have had such overblown
plays filmed and telecast. These playwrights also may have won-
dered at the snorts from the critics about the low state of television
drama; or they may have performed their sausage-stuffing in the
light, cynical mood that anything is good enough for a television
play, on film, since it is nothing after all but a midget-size, bastard
movie.

To no one's surprise, they are right. Such over-plotted, overstuffed filmed "television" plays *are* midget-size, bastard movies,
and their fathers frequently have good cause not to acknowledge
their offspring. Prominent in this category are "mystery" and
"crime" plots; once the puzzle (the plot) is propounded, there is
no choice but to see it through to the end. The man going over
Niagara Falls in a barrel can't stop halfway down. He is committed to landing; and so are supposed "television playwrights"
who set a mechanical plot in motion, in a race against time to reach
the end. Such plots are truly a "bed of Procrustes"; characterization, believability, identification of the viewer with the play, are
chopped and hewn and stretched and tugged, for the purpose of
the swollen plot. The dictionary defines "Procrustes" as "a fabled
robber of ancient Greece who stretched or mutilated his victims
to make them conform to the length of his bed." For "victims"
read "plots"; for "bed" read "time" — the time, rigidly limited, that
you have in which to present your play. Let all such playwrights
remember what Galsworthy said: "Character is the basis of all
plot." What people are determines what people do. And let us
remind ourselves here that the unique quality of *all* television is
its ability to reveal character more compellingly than any other
medium of expression. Doesn't it follow that the best television
plays are those which start from character rather than from plot,
i.e., from a situation?

It is also a great temptation in writing television plays to be
filmed to include scenes of far-flung outdoor action, in competition with such scenes remembered and loved from motion pictures; it is a temptation which must be resisted until such time as

the viewing screen on home television sets can compete in size with the motion picture screen.

Since a playwright is "free" of Time and Place, it is also a temptation, and an insidious one, to write a play intended for filming with *many* scene changes, i.e., in the "narrative technique." This temptation, if yielded to, brings its own punishment: a story which is as much exposition as it is dramatic portrayal acted out before our eyes; sketchy characters whom we barely know (there isn't time to illustrate their characteristics *in action*); casual motivation of scenes and action or maybe no motivation at all. (I recall seeing a Bret Harte classic done — and literally "done" — on film, in approximately 24 minutes. At the end of one climactic scene, the heroine in effect told the hero that she hated him. There was a FADE OUT-FADE IN, perhaps six seconds in elapsed time, and in the new scene we saw the heroine in the hero's arms, behaving very affectionately. What induced this flip-flop in the heroine was never explained. There wasn't *time* to explain it, because the whole story had been so broken up into small scenes necessary to tell the far too complex story, that if the play were to finish in the allotted time, the Time purchased by the sponsor on the air, everything had to be jam-packed in, in a hurry, and the devil take such things as motivation and credibility!)

It is a far, far better thing in television plays intended for filming to hew as closely as possible to Aristotle's Unity of Action, just as one must in successful "live" television plays.

The virtues of filming plays for television, then, are: one is out of the warehouse-like studio, with its four-walls limitations on sets and kinds of action; and one doesn't have to make costume and make-up changes *against a deadline, while the play is actually on the air.*

Testing Your Story — Your Mandatory "Beginning, Middle and End"

You've decided on a story. Can you write it out to show the "bare bones" of the structure; can you test it to make sure that you have the material needed at all stages of the story's progression?

Here is a story written out in briefest form. From this synopsis a successful half-hour television play was written. (*The Checkerboard Heart,* by Kay Arthur.) This synopsis is about 350 words long.

THE BEGINNING

A gay, pert, plucky, pretty, smart, self-made girl of 20 is engaged to a man, 30, who has begun to criticize her and make her over. She tries desperately to suit him perfectly, to enter the life of this educated, polished man, not because she's a "social climber" but because she thinks she really loves him. He really loves her; merely wants her to be perfect. Hence his attempts to change her.

THE MIDDLE

The girl tries so hard to please her sophisticated fiance that her self-confidence is undermined and she is miserable. A friend tries to tell her he's not the last man on earth, that tomorrow she might sit next to someone on the bus who'd be *it*. She disagrees; this is the only man for her. But she finally can't stand it any more, breaks it off when her fiance forbids her to chew gum. She cries on the shoulder of another man she knows. This one is 24, more like herself in personality and background, and he loves her *as she is*. She hasn't given him a tumble, not because of his lack of polish, but because she's had eyes only for the older man who represents an ideal she has set for herself. The shoulder of the younger man is, however, awfully reassuring and comfortable. So, bang, she falls in love with him on the rebound, after she's broken with her fiance. However, her fiance refuses to give her up.

THE END

Having let herself become engaged to the younger man, the girl now can't resist making *him* over. He complains that she herself is doing the very things she criticized her former fiance for — telling him what to do, because she wants him to be perfect. Finally he can't take it any longer, says, "Look, baby, I'm walking out on you." She's hoist on her own petard. At this point, the older man, the original fiance, steps in with his more mature point of view to try and save the girl's happiness. She ends up

accepting the younger man completely *as he is*. They go off together gaily, both chewing gum like mad. The older man, the
fiance, looks after them philosophically, slowly folds a nice fresh
stick of gum into his own mouth.

(End of synopsis)

Here is a longer, more detailed synopsis spelling out the master
scenes of a play in more detail. Characterization and incident are
clear and interesting. From this synopsis, also, a successful half-
hour television play was written (*Price Tag*, by Doris Halman,
produced on Armstrong's Circle Theatre.)

THE BEGINNING

Hylie Jones has a date with a man.

The man is the office wolf in the firm where, just out of High
School, she has her first job as a file clerk. When he asks her on
Thursday to go out with him Saturday night, she doesn't know
that he has lost a bet — and this is the payment thereof; for Hylie
in her cheap little plain black dress is shy and quiet and scared,
and the glamour boys pass her up.

She is thrilled, till she realizes that she has to have something
to wear — and all she can spend is ten dollars.

At this point she is rescued by a sympathetic fellow file clerk
who tells her about Small's. . . .

Small's is downtown, a wonderful rat-trap composed of a block
of ancient mouldering brownstones hurled together to make a
store. It sells clothes, and it sells them cheap by eliminating sales-
ladies and by stocking leftovers and garments in which slight
errors have been made. Its goods are displayed on racks all over
the floor — long rows of racks with narrow aisles between for
the customers to navigate in as best they can. If you want to buy
something, you see it, you grab it, you fight off somebody who
wants to grab it from you; you rush with it to a cashier in a
corner booth, you stand in line, you pay what's on the price tag
plus tax, you get your box from the adjacent bundle wrapper and
depart in triumph. If you don't want to keep what you risked
your neck to buy, you can return it within five days and no questions asked. Small's has a magic all its own, although some people
never go there because it makes their heads ache. . . .

Hylie Jones is inducted into the mysteries of Small's on that Thursday after work by her sympathetic friend. The store stays open on Thursday until nine P.M.; they reach it at quarter to six. So do droves of other office workers. The shoving and grabbing in the narrow aisles between the racks is terrific; recriminations fly.

The dress — the perfect dress for Saturday — is $10.95. A dollar too much. Hylie feels she shouldn't pay it, and goes on down the racks of stuff her size — on down to the end and around the corner, where there are more racks. There is nothing to touch that dress — and now she knows she has to have it and, deciding she can dispense with a couple of lunches, she hurries back for it, — and it's *gone.* It is, in fact, just disappearing on the arm of a well-dressed woman into a place marked DRESSING ROOMS, where you try on stuff in open cubicles so you won't be tempted to steal.

If the woman decides not to take the dress, it is returned to the rack. This is done every hour on the hour by a stock boy wheeling his heterogeneous load from rack to rack. . . .

THE MIDDLE

At six, Rinty O'Meara, a stock boy, arriving at the size 12's, first sees Hylie Jones. She doesn't see him. Her pleading eyes are fixed on the dresses he slings by their hangers to the racks. She is there with another, slightly impatient girl.

At seven, when Rinty comes round again, Hylie Jones is still blocking traffic, but she is by herself. Her eyes are now frantic. He has to ask her to get out of the way. The dress isn't with him. When he turns toward the size 14's, Hylie runs after him. Is he sure he's brought out *all* the 12's from the dressing rooms? She describes the one she's been waiting for all that time. She watched the cashier's booth, but it never went there. The granite-faced woman in charge of the floor approaches to bawl Rinty out for philandering when he has work to do — so he beats it. But presently he comes back with his empty wheeler and the news that the service desk now has the dress and is holding it till this evening for the woman who tried it on. Hylie is stricken, so Rinty tries to cheer her up by telling her that the woman may change her mind and not come back for it after all, since no deposit was paid.

Hylie, tired and hungry but desperate, haunts Small's that evening. Rinty, passing her at seven and again at eight, winks at her; and she smiles wanly back at him. At eight-thirty, the woman who left the dress at the service desk comes back and buys it!

Rinty has been watching, too, from behind the scenes. He sees Hylie get up from the chair which he found for her hours ago, and turn blindly for the exit to the stairs. On the stairs he catches up with her; there's still hope, the woman has five days in which to return the dress, she may do it by Saturday!

On Friday during the noon hour something is back at Small's — but it's Hylie. She feels worse than ever, because she has discovered the same dress hanging around unwanted and unloved in a size 20 which would fall right off her. She shows it to Rinty who, a man, though very young, cannot see for the life of him why she doesn't buy something else in a 12 and call it a day. But she is right about the dress: It's a good one, not cheap and frilly, and it was there — as the size 20 is there — because of some minor imperfection noted on the price tag as "Slightly Irregular." She tries to make Rinty understand this, and he can't; but he promises that, if the dress is returned during the afternoon, he'll stick his neck out and save it till she gets there just before closing time.

THE END

On Friday afternoon, at the firm where Hylie works, the man who won the bet with the office wolf gets stuck with a double date. The wolf is released from the bet on condition that he come along. He means to tell Hylie, of course, but something comes up and he doesn't just then. And when he finally gets round to it, it's a minute or so past closing time, and she has raced off — to Small's!

The dress hasn't come back — but there's all day tomorrow . . . Only now, Rinty doesn't really believe it will be returned, and his young heart is torn for Hylie, an old friend. By this time he has learned about her wonderful date with a walking personification of romance. Rinty wants her to go to that date all shining and beautiful, as she wants to go, and therefore. . . .

On Saturday morning, early, Rinty O'Meara, stock boy, has a session with Mr. Small, boss. For years Mr. Small's kindness to the poor and unfortunate has been proverbial. So a phone call is made to a manufacturer; and after this Rinty gets an hour off from the store. When he comes back he has a brand new, perfect size 12 dress which he bought at retail in a department store with his own money ($19.95) — and this dress is then fixed up with a price tag marked "Slightly Irregular — $10.95," and put on the rack at noon!

For Hylie. And when Rinty sees her face as he dumps the dress in her arms, he is *not* sorry he did it. . . .

That evening, as the store is closed and as Rinty remembers how Hylie once mentioned that she lives at a certain club for girls who work, Rinty goes to reap his full reward — to see Hylie come out in all her glory, escorted by the glamorous date he himself could never hope to rival! She doesn't come out in anything with anybody; that is, not till after a long, long while, when Rinty O'Meara goes *in* and learns that the wolf never showed — and Rinty takes her, looking so lovely, to a movie!

And you know what? When she got ready for the wolf, she found herself wishing that it was *Rinty* who'd come, not the wolf — because she thinks Rinty is *nicer!*

There again she's right. The last we see of them, Hylie is saying it's funny, but when the dress came back all the rips were sewed up in it — and Rinty is saying that dame musta mended it before she decided not to keep it. Rinty is *nice.*

(End of synopsis)

If you can write out your story in short or long form, like a road map, as it were, and see for yourself that you have the material needed for each natural division, the beginning, the middle, the end, you are ready to go on to the next step: a detailed scenario, or a scene-by-scene breakdown, in which the action of each character in each scene is delineated.

Here is such a scene-by-scene breakdown, prepared as the final step before the actual writing of dialogue, to produce another successful two-act, half-hour television play (*Remembrance Island*, by Anne Howard Bailey).

ACT I. *Scene One*

Open on Exterior Shot of terrace of the Stanley estate. A high wind is blowing and Peter Dixon is hammering on the French doors trying to get inside. Shoot Through to show Alison Stanley in her wheel chair, looking out at him, but making no move to admit him. Finally Dr. Andrews enters the room and admits Peter. We find out that Peter is Alison's fiancé, and that he has been trying desperately to see her and talk to her since she has retreated to her mother's lonely shore estate, following the automobile accident which robbed her of the use of her legs. Alison refuses to listen to Peter's pleas that she marry him. She seems to be living in a dream world. She wheels herself out.

Peter and the doctor talk. Peter admits that although he is sure Alison loves him, she had stalled their marriage even before the accident. The doctor says that actually she could walk now, if she wishes; that subconsciously she prefers to be an invalid, as an excuse to keep from going through with the marriage. They talk for a moment about the influence Alison's dead mother had had upon her. Mrs. Stanley was unhappily married to Alison's father — there is some strange tragedy in her background — and the doctor fears that her mother's unhappiness has warped and affected Alison. The doctor says he is sure that something malignant is influencing her. He suggests that the only thing to do is to try and let Alison work it out. Peter leaves, after promising to come back soon.

ACT I. *Scene Two*

Cut to Alison in the summer house, a rustic shelter overlooking the ocean from a high cliff. Alison sits alternately staring off towards Remembrance Island, and reading from a worn old book which looks like a diary.

Ezra Anchor, the old gardener, comes up and begins to talk. He tells Alison he knew her mother, and hints that he knows a lot about the mother's mysterious and tragic love affair. Alison questions him, and we learn that Alison's mother had a brief and tempestuous love affair with a young fisherman, Jeb, who killed himself over her. Ezra leaves, as the fog begins to roll in. Alison sits dreaming to herself, and conjures up Jeb. (To Alison and to the audience, when she is alone with Jeb, he is a real person. When others of the cast appear, Jeb vanishes.) Alison is re-living her mother's experience, and when she and Jeb meet, it is as if time had rolled backward. They talk about things that her mother and Jeb might have talked about on the occasion of their first meeting. Jeb promises to return. Fade Out.

ACT I. *Scene Three*

Fade In. Interior of the house, a few days later. Alison is again reading her mother's diary, but when Dr. Andrews enters she furtively hides it. She is nervous about the doctor's visit, keeps glancing at the clock. Apparently it is nearly time for her rendezvous with Jeb in the summer house. The doctor excuses himself for a phone call; and Alison quickly wheels herself out to the summer house.

ACT I. *Scene Four*

Dissolve to summer house. Jeb materializes as Alison wheels herself into the scene, and they talk. Clearly there have been several meetings, and they are falling in love. Suddenly, as Jeb is on the point of declaring his love, the doctor's voice is heard. Jeb vanishes, and the doctor comes to find Alison weeping stormily. Fade Out.

(END OF ACT I)

ACT II. *Scene One*

Fade In on the summer house, where Alison is sitting staring out at Remembrance Island. Ezra arrives, warns of a nor'easter blowing up with the fog, tries to persuade Alison to let him wheel her in. At Alison's insistence, Ezra talks more of her mother's tragic romance; it was just such a night as this that her mother and Jeb were to meet. But her mother's future husband, later to be Alison's father, arrived unexpectedly; and her mother could not get away to warn Jeb when he arrived, expecting her. He had misunderstood her absence, had flown into a rage of fury and despair, and rushed away in the fog. Alison's mother had run after him, but Stanley had stopped her. She saw Jeb leap over the cliff to certain death. Alison is almost on the point of hysteria, and demands that Ezra leave her alone. He goes.

Jeb materializes. He tells Alison he loves her and cannot live without her. They have a passionate love scene, interrupted by the insistent, monotonous ringing of the telephone in the house. The phone will not stop; Alison realizes she had better answer it. She wheels into the house, promising to come back, as Jeb disappears.

ACT II. *Scene Two*

It is Peter on the phone. He has learned of the nor'easter, is afraid for her, is horrified by her strangeness. He says he is coming to the house as fast as he can. Alison's violent reaction frightens him and he hangs up, saying he is on his way to the house. Fade Out.

ACT II. *Scene Three*

Fade In, interior the house. Peter has arrived, can't find Alison, is frantic. Almost at once, the doctor arrives, calms Peter, shows him the diary he has found. Together they piece out the story: they realize that Alison is re-living her mother's experience. They figure out the parallel, and the doctor warns Peter that tonight may well be the climax, since it is the same kind of night that Jeb plunged to his death in the roaring breakers below the cliff. They go out together to look for Alison.

ACT II. *Scene Four*

Cut to the summer house. The storm is howling. Peter and the doctor find Alison there, having an impassioned conversation with the non-existent Jeb. She doesn't see Peter and the doctor. Peter starts to go to her, but the doctor holds him back. They listen to Alison re-living the whole scene, and finally they see her struggle to her feet and start to go after Jeb, to "stop" him, even as her mother had tried with the real Jeb, as the imaginary Jeb presumably rushes away in the fog toward the cliff. At this point the doctor releases Peter, who hurries to stop Alison. He holds her back from the cliff's edge. But the words Alison says to Peter are not the words her mother had said to John Stanley when he held her back from trying to stop her lover. For at the crucial moment Alison's own mind had taken over and in her semi-conscious state she had realized that she *wanted* to be stopped from following "Jeb" over the cliff. She faints in Peter's arms. Fade Out.

Act II. *Scene Five*

Fade In, interior the house. When Alison regains consciousness, later, Peter is there to explain gently to her the transference her mind has made. He tells her how she had lived out the parallel of her mother's romance, until the moment when her own true feelings were at stake. At that moment, she had deviated from following her mother's pattern of behavior. She finally understands that it is Peter she loves, and has loved all along. Peter tells her that the whole experience was important because it has cleared the last barrier between them. What is that, Alison asks. Gently Peter tells her that in the stress of the moment, she had *walked*. Alison looks at him, amazed . . . then again struggles to her feet, to walk to the arms of the man she really loves. Fade Out.

(End of scene-by-scene breakdown,
End of Play)

THE PLAY ITSELF: Its Physical Form

The playwright proceeds from his scene-by-scene breakdown into the play itself. Reproduced in following is the opening of Miss Bailey's *Remembrance Island,* from the detailed scenario immediately preceding.

Let it be said here that the first consideration of the playwright is *clarity,* the making sure that the reader, and eventually the producer, the director, scene designer, the actors, and all technicians concerned with the play's production *understand clearly* the playwright's *intention* at all times.

For instance, the listing of the cast: it helps the producer in casting to know the physical appearance of the characters as the playwright sees them. The sort of detailed description Miss Bailey gives of her characters is also of great help to the actor in creating his characterization. Similarly, the description of the sets is valuable to the scene designer. Notice that the author makes a special point of indicating that the sets must be built so as to permit the camera angles she has written into the script, for the special dramatic effects she sees as an integral part of the story.

Finally, observe the method of typing the camera directions and the dialogue, on one half of the page only. This technique is purely practical: on the other, blank half of each page, the television director will write in, usually in longhand, the stage business he devises, the number of the camera photographing that particular shot (Camera One, Camera Two, Camera Three, etc.), the measure of the camera lens he will use on that shot, determining the *kind* of shot it will be (Long Shot, Medium Shot, Close-Up, etc.), cues for sound effects, music, and any other information he may want to record for his convenience in directing the show. It is the accepted convention that all material excepting dialogue be typed in CAPITAL LETTERS.

Not all television scripts are typed on the *left* half of the page. Some directors prefer the *right* half. Some networks want the "video," i.e., the action which is visual, on one half of the page, and the "audio," the dialogue, music and sound effects, on the other half. However, *never* type the video and audio directly opposite each other, as in the example immediately following. It is too hard to read and to integrate. It is the accepted convention that video precedes on a page the audio with which it is associated. That is, first you read about what you are going to see and then you read what you hear.

WRONG WAY

VIDEO	AUDIO
SHE LEANS ACROSS HER CHAIR ARM TO RETRIEVE HER BOOK, BUT STOPS, ARRESTED BY THE SIGHT OF A PAIR OF FEET IN WORN, BROKEN OLD SHOES THAT STAND AT THE THRESHOLD OF THE SUMMER HOUSE. SLOWLY SHE STRAIGHTENS, FORGETTING THE BOOK. SHE AND EZRA STARE AT EACH OTHER. HIS	EZRA (HOARSELY) Gor. . . Y' gu' me a turn. I thought 'twas Miss Alison settin' there. ALISON I'm Alison Stanley. EZRA Th' other 'un. What's dead now.

```
FACE IS THAT OF A MAN SEEING                ALISON
A GHOST.                            My mother.
                                    (SOUND:  A FOG HORN IN
                                    THE DISTANCE BLOWS
                                    ONCE, MOURNFULLY)
                                    (MUSIC:  SNEAK IN
                                    GHOST THEME)
```

RIGHT WAY

(That is, if the network wants Video on the left, and Audio on the right, instead of in a single column down one-half of the page)

```
          VIDEO                              AUDIO
SHE LEANS ACROSS HER CHAIR
ARM TO RETRIEVE HER BOOK,
BUT STOPS, ARRESTED BY THE
SIGHT OF A PAIR OF FEET IN
WORN, BROKEN OLD SHOES THAT
STAND AT THE THRESHOLD OF
THE SUMMER HOUSE.  SLOWLY
SHE STRAIGHTENS, FORGETTING
THE BOOK.  SHE AND EZRA
STARE AT EACH OTHER.  HIS
FACE IS THAT OF A MAN SEEING
A GHOST.

                                        EZRA (HOARSELY)
                                    Gor. . . Y' gu' me a
                                    turn.  I thought 'twas
                                    Miss Alison settin'
                                    there.
                                        ALISON
                                    I'm Alison Stanley.
                                        EZRA
                                    The other 'un.  What's
                                    dead now.
                                        ALISON
                                    My mother.
                                    (SOUND:  A FOG HORN IN
                                    THE DISTANCE BLOWS
                                    ONCE, MOURNFULLY)
                                    (MUSIC:  SNEAK IN
                                    GHOST THEME)
```

However, you are perfectly safe in typing your play in a single column down the left half of the page, putting the VIDEO and STAGE DIRECTIONS and SPECIAL EFFECTS NOTATIONS in CAPITAL LETTERS, and the dialogue in upper and lower case letters, the normal way of typing.

Now, here's the beginning of *Remembrance Island:*

REMEMBRANCE ISLAND
CAST

ALISON STANLEY —	a hauntingly attractive girl of about 24. Since becoming invalided in a wheel chair, she has retreated from all reality — and finds refuge only in the vague imaginings of her own dream world.
PETER DIXON —	Alison's fiance. A likable young man of perhaps 28 or 30, whose extroverted personality does not get in the way of sensitive understanding.
DOCTOR ANDREWS —	Alison's doctor. A spare, wiry little man of near 50, whose acid tongue is his only defense for a large and tender heart.
JEB BOLIN —	the young fisherman, loved by Alison's mother — re-created in Alison's imagination. (Although he obviously must take corporeal form for his scenes with Alison, lighting and camera effects should cloak him with an atmosphere of unreality.) Dark, powerfully built, vital — about 26.
EZRA ANCHOR —	an old salt. A garrulous old man in his mid 60's whose life is made up of the lore and the gossip centered around Remembrance Island.

HOUSEKEEPER (BIT) — a motherly woman in her fif-
                   ties who has been hired to
                   look after Alison.

SETS

1. INT. Living Room of the Stanley House. It is
   typical of the parlors of those old crumbling
   shore estates that infest the New England coast
   line. Heavy period furniture, horsehair sofa,
   dank, dark draperies, intricate candelabra,
   worn Persian rugs, and peeling portraits on the
   wainscoted walls. The only redeeming virtue of
   the room is the tremendous set of French doors,
   with large open-work panes, which give out on
   the terrace which leads directly to the sea
   cliff.

2. EXT. Terrace and Summer House. The terrace is
   flag-stoned, for a short space, and leads to a
   short strip of grass, to a latticed summer
   house, octagonal in shape, with crude rustic
   benches running around the sides. It is completely open to the sea view — and from it, one
   may peer directly over the cliff to the rocks
   far below, and out to sea where Remembrance Island can be seen offshore.

NOTE: (The sets should be so constructed that
       the camera will be able to shoot from within
       the L.R. towards the terrace and summer
       house. It must also be possible to take an
       exterior shot, from the terrace, of the
       French doors and the interior of the L.R.)

FILM CLIPS: Shot of house high on cliff overlooking
             the sea.
             Shot of small island offshore.
             Several shots from cliff height of the
             sea in various stages, calm, raging,
             violent.

SPECIAL EFFECTS: Fog — High wind.

REMEMBRANCE ISLAND
ACT ONE
OPENING SHOT:
EXT: THE TERRACE
OPEN: THE ANGLE SHOT FROM THE TERRACE,
SHOWING THE FRENCH DOORS, AND A PORTION
OF THE ROOM INSIDE.   ALISON SITS IN HER
WHEEL CHAIR, A LIGHT QUILT THROWN OVER
HER LEGS.   HER CHAIR IS DRAWN UP QUITE
CLOSE TO THE FRENCH DOORS -- SHE GAZES
OUT WITH A DREAMY, WISTFUL STARE.   A
HIGH WIND IS BLOWING, IT HOWLS ACROSS
THE OPEN EXPANSE AND WHIPS BRANCHES
AGAINST THE GLASS DOORS.   THE SCENE IS
SEMI-DARK, SUGGESTING A HALF TWILIGHT,
GREY WITH AN APPROACHING STORM.
AT FADE IN, A MAN, PETER DIXON, BURSTS
ABRUPTLY INTO THE FRAME, AT A HALF RUN.
HE WEARS A TAN TRENCH COAT, UNBUTTONED,
WHICH FLAPS IN THE STIFF WIND.   HE
RUSHES TO THE FRENCH DOORS, STOPS SHORT
AT THE SIGHT OF ALISON GAZING OUT.   HIS
WORRIED EXPRESSION RELAXES AT SIGHT OF
HER.   HE SMILES, AND JOGGLES THE HANDLES
OF THE DOOR.   THE DOOR IS LOCKED.
ALISON BY NEITHER MOVE NOR LOOK ACKNOWL-
EDGES THAT SHE RECOGNIZES HIM.
PETER AGAIN JOGGLES THE DOOR HANDLES,
AND RAPS ON THE GLASS.
            PETER (SHOUTING OVER THE WIND)
Alison! Alison! -- it's me! Peter! (HE
BEATS ON THE GLASS.   AN EXPRESSION OF
ANNOYANCE CROSSES THE GIRL'S FACE.   SHE
SIGNALS FOR HIM TO GO AWAY)
(THIS INTENSIFIES HIS DETERMINATION TO
GET IN.   HE SHAKES THE DOOR VIOLENTLY.)
                        PETER
Alison! Let me in!
(SHE SHAKES HER HEAD, AND BEGINS TO
BACKWHEEL HER CHAIR AWAY FROM THE
DOORS.)

PETER (FRANTICALLY)

Alison!

(AS THE GIRL IS ABOUT TO REACH THE EXIT
FROM THE LIVING ROOM, A MAN IN HAT AND
RAINCOAT, CARRYING A BLACK MEDICAL BAG,
ENTERS. HE GLANCES FROM THE GIRL TO THE
MAN BEATING ON THE DOORS. HE FROWNS AT
ALISON, SAYS SOMETHING REPROVING WHICH
ARRESTS HER FLIGHT, THEN STRIDES QUICKLY
TO THE DOORS. HE OPENS THE BOLT, AND
THROWS THEM OPEN.)

CUT TO: INT. LIVING ROOM.

(PETER BURSTS INTO THE ROOM, HE BRUSHES
PAST THE DOCTOR, IGNORING HIS RAISED
HAND OF WARNING, AND HASTENS TOWARD THE
GIRL IN THE CHAIR.)

PETER (ANXIOUSLY)

Darling. . . .!

(ALISON TWIRLS HER CHAIR, AND WHEELS IT
AWAY FROM PETER'S ADVANCE, PUTTING A
TABLE BETWEEN HERSELF AND HIM.)

ALISON (QUIETLY)

It's over, Peter. Why won't you believe
me?

PETER

You could have left me a note -- a message.

It's taken me a week to find you.

ALISON

I did not mean for you to find me.

(PETER TURNS ACCUSINGLY TO THE DOCTOR)

PETER

You let her do this! You should have
called me!

DOCTOR

She says she doesn't want to marry you,
Peter. I have no medicine for this.

(PETER'S FACE WORKS. IT IS CLEAR THAT
HE CANNOT ACCEPT THE TRUTH. HE TURNS,
ALMOST HELPLESSLY, IN ALISON'S DIREC-
TION. HE MAKES A FUTILE LITTLE GESTURE
TOWARDS HER.)

                    PETER (BROKENLY)
But I -- I love you, Alison.
(SHE LOOKS AT HIM STONILY FOR A MOMENT.
THEN HER BREATH CATCHES.)
                    ALISON (HOPELESSLY)
Like this?
                    PETER (EXPLOSIVELY)
Yes!

                    ALISON
Look around you, Peter. There are so
many attractive people in the world.
Beautiful women. Who can walk.
                    DOCTOR (ACIDLY)
You can see she's a woman of decision.
She knows what's best for you.
                    PETER (ANGRILY)
Can't you let me talk to her alone for
a moment?
                    ALISON (QUICKLY)
No!

                    DOCTOR (STOPPING HER)
Certainly. But it won't do any good.
Don't you remember the martyr who lived
on a pillar of stone in the desert for
three and thirty years? (HE BARKS A
SHORT HARSH LAUGH AT HIS OWN JOKE, TURNS
TO THE DOOR AND OPENS IT. THE FORCE OF
THE WIND TEARS IT FROM HIS HAND, AND IT
BANGS.) (HE EXITS)
(PETER GLARES AFTER HIM. THEN HE TURNS
TO ALISON WHO LOOKS DISTRESSED AT BEING
LEFT ALONE WITH HIM.)
                    PETER (FIRMLY)
I've come to take you home, darling.
We'll fold up your chair, and put it in
the back of the car -- and we'll be in
New York before midnight.
                    ALISON
This is home, Peter. It was my mother's
-- and all my life I've waited to come
back to it. I intend to stay here.

              *   *   *   *

I have not changed one word of the playwright's opening, to make it possibly conform to a hard-and-fast rule of camera shot and camera angle specifications. As you master the camera terms and uses and your imagination goes to work on the scene you intend to portray, you will instinctively "direct" the camera to secure the effect you want. There *is* no hard-and-fast rule, except one:

Make your intention entirely clear at all times, so that the technicians producing your play will be able completely to fulfill that intention.

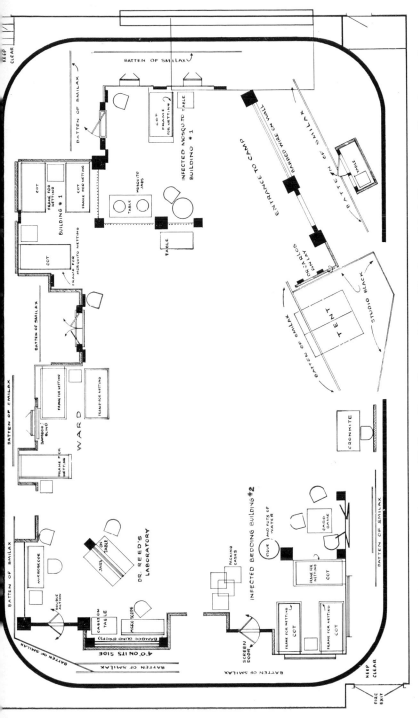

Floor plan: layout of sets for production, "Yellow Fever," telecast on the "You Are There" program. With the sets arranged around the four walls of the studio, this is practically an ideal layout, since the whole center area is free for the movement of cameras, sound booms, actors and technicians. The heavy black line surrounding the sets denotes a sky cyclorama which, when lighted, serves as an all-protective backing for camera shots from almost any angle. *CBS Television Network Production.*

The TV camera and the actress, two of the components of a show. The third is your script. This is a pedestal camera, moved manually by the cameraman, who also changes from one lens to another (four in all) by turning a handle in back of the camera. *CBS Television Network Production.*

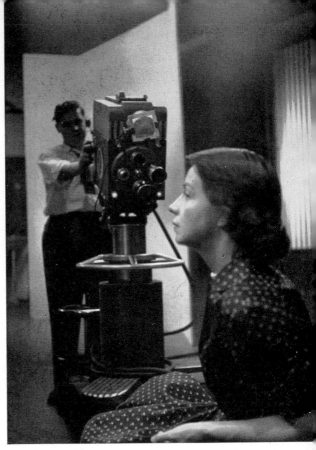

A TV camera mounted on a crane, in turn mounted on a dolly. The crane can be raised or lowered, moved from side to side, and, conceivably, in a circle. The cameraman rides the crane, and a technician pushes or pulls back the dolly, as required. *CBS Television Network Production.*

This is a photograph of a rear-projection taken from the rear of the screen. It shows the skyline of New York, and, also projected on the same screen, a picture of the Zeiss Projector used on the program, "Adventure." The dramatic action takes place in *front* of the screen. *CBS Television Network Production.*

The actor stands in *front* of the rear-projection screen onto which this wintry scene is projected by the technique shown in the photograph above. *CBS Television Network Production.*

Faye Emerson rides a "prop" steamboat, "Maid of the Mist," in front of a roaring Niagara Falls, an effect achieved by rear-projected motion picture film. On the air, the shadow on Niagara Falls would not show, as lighting technicians take expert care of such details. *CBS Television Network Production. Set design by Kathleen Ankers.*

Rear-projection gives this sea effect of scudding clouds and moonlight rippling on the waves, all moving slowly as the "prop" sailing ship is "rocked" back and forth by studio stagehands. *CBS Television Network Production. Set design by Kathleen Ankers.*

A romantic setting for a ballet is created by set pieces (detached portions of scenery placed artistically against a background) and a huge "sky cyclorama" which, when lighted, gives the effect of limitless space. A "horizon piece" of mountains increases the illusion of space and distance. The studio floor is painted. *CBS Television Network Production. Set design by Kathleen Ankers.*

Artificial trees and foliage (suspended from battens), plus the suggestion of a rail fence and a light concealed behind a "horizon piece" create the illusion of a country road stretching ahead for miles. A grass (artificial) ground cloth heightens the illusion. *CBS Television Network Production.*

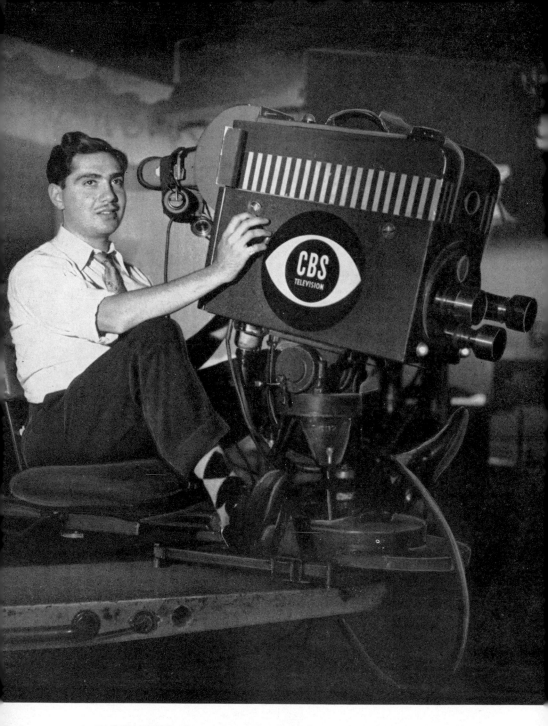

A CLOSE SHOT of a cameraman riding the crane of a TV camera mounted on a dolly so that the TV camera can be moved in three dimensions. When he is operating the camera, the cameraman watches the scene being photographed through the close-fitting aperture seen directly opposite his eyes. *CBS Television Network Production.*

The sound technician operates the sound boom mounted on a wheeled tripod. The microphone is at the end of the boom, and can be moved instantly in any one of three dimensions by a system of levers controlled by the sound technician. The tripod is moved around manually. The object, of course, is to keep the microphone close to the actor speaking. At the same time, the microphone must be kept out of camera range, and it must be so handled as to avoid a "microphone shadow." *CBS Television Network Production.*

In the master control room, the show being telecast is watched by the engineers on the monitors. Only *one* camera may be on the air, but *all* cameras are "live" during a telecast, and the Technical Director in charge cuts from one "live" camera to another, as the Director orders. *CBS Television Network Production.*

A former legitimate theatre is being converted into a television studio. Cable, TV camera, sound boom with microphone, a portion of a set, technicians are shown in the normal confusion of preparing the studio. *CBS Television Network Production.*

An exterior street scene, with the sets built in perspective so that they give an illusion of distance, backed up finally by a painted backdrop of faraway trees and sky. Overhead are lights; to the left, a switchboard. The snakelike cable across the floor is typical (visitors must *not* step on it!). *CBS Television Network Production.*

A typical box-like interior set with a photo-mural backdrop outside the window which helps to set the locale through its representation of a community of small-income homes. Out of camera range are overhead lights, while the microphone is seen above and to the right, on the very end of the sound boom. The dark streak, lower right, is more cable. *CBS Television Network Production.*

A beautiful exterior set achieved very simply by the use of a few set pieces arranged against a cyclorama and a horizon piece representing distant mountains. Because of skillful lighting and photography, on the air you would not see the seam in the cyclorama which you see here. The floor is painted. More typical snaky cable! *CBS Television Network Production.*

A miniature three-dimensional shadow box of an observatory, which, when photographed in a CLOSE SHOT, would have life-size proportions. The miniature is resting on an average-size table. Such a device is used to establish a locale. *CBS Television Network Production. Set design by Kathleen Ankers.*

A backdrop painted in careful perspective and photographed under expert lighting creates an illusion of great distance. The actors will perform in and around the area marked off by the realistically built archway and balcony balustrade. *CBS Television Network Production.*

FULL SHOT of a telecast, with everybody doing his job. This photograph is taken from a catwalk in the grid, and shows well the overhead clutter (normal) of battens, lights, rigging, etc., etc. The scene is a street exterior. The sound man is riding the tripod being pulled manually by another technician, who must keep his cables from fouling the wheels of the tripod. The actors are in place. One cameraman, operating a pedestal camera, is moving into position for the next shot. Undoubtedly he is listening to directions being given through his ear phones by the Director, in the control room. *CBS Television Network Production.*

Another FULL SHOT showing the marvelous and normal orderly confusion of sets built adjoining each other, actors, technicians, lights, sound booms and cameras. If any illustration in this book could be picked as most typical of a television studio in action, this one would be it. *CBS Television Network Production.*

This is a CLOSE SHOT of an actual television studio monitor, showing a girl "walking around" on the hand of a man. The photograph below shows how it's done, through the technique described in the text (Chapter Three) as the Electronic Matting Amplifier. This is a photograph of a rehearsal; the man has not yet put on his checked shirt. *CBS Television Network Production.*

You see here that a full-scale set is built, showing a backdrop painted to represent the man's shirt, while his sleeve and hand are also built full-scale (in relation to the girl). Two cameras are used; through the Electronic Matting Amplifier technique, the actual girl walks around on the full-scale hand and it seems as if she is walking on the actual man's hand. (Here, the man in rear of the girl is standing against the backdrop only to show its proportions; he is not at this point a "part of the act.") *CBS Television Network Production.*

Here is a typical legitimate theatre box-like set (except for the ceiling most stage sets have). The two white marks on the floor are to indicate rehearsed positions for either cameras, actors, or sound boom tripods. The more difficult positions are usually marked on the floor. Note that the walls of the set extend well above possible camera range. *CBS Television Network Production.*

A beautiful set combining interior and exterior effect, with the distant slopes painted on a backdrop. Artificial vines in the middle distance and the potted plants in the foreground immeasurably heighten the illusion of distance. Here's an excellent example of floor painting. *CBS Television Network Production.*

This last illustration has the third component — your script — in the picture. In a choked voice, the actress reads the letter of farewell with which you have provided her, while camera and sound boom telecast the whole cooperative effort to the world. *CBS Television Network Production.*

3

Settings and
Special Effects

IN THE PRECEDING CHAPTER we discussed the choice of your story
from the standpoint of the producer's being able to stage the show
"live" within the four walls of a warehouse-like studio. We named
certain impossibilities for "live" production such as an actor's
mounting a horse and galloping away across the plains.

If in this chapter we seem sometimes to contradict ourselves, it
is because some of the startling new techniques described in following are still in the experimental stage. Also, not all networks
and indeed not all studios of a given network will have the special
techniques available. For instance, in one huge studio of a network operation certain things can be done which are impossible
in the adjoining, smaller studio. This circumstance frequently
makes necessary special knowledge about the television program
you're aiming for. In general, you can be guided by following the
production practice you have observed in watching a given program as it is telecast. For instance, on a Fred Waring program,
"live" dancers were seen dancing on the wings of an airplane as it
flew high above New York. Since this effect was achieved once,
it is safe to assume that similar effects can be done by the network
telecasting the Fred Waring program (Columbia Broadcasting
System). The Fred Waring special effect was achieved by the
Electronic Matting Amplifier which, in a manner of speaking, "cuts
holes" in a motion picture rear projection of a scene showing an
airplane flying above New York, with a second camera photographing the dancers "live" and superimposing them in the

"holes" cut into the motion picture film. The electronic details of how this effect is achieved are not important to playwrights; it is enough to know that such an effect can be achieved, although, as we said, not necessarily by all networks and not in all studios of a network.

By the use of rear projection of both slides and motion picture film, however, gratifying progress is being made in "live" production, as far as settings go, particularly exterior settings, toward the goal expressed in the words of Mr. E. Carlton Winckler, director of production operations, Columbia Broadcasting System, TV: "to give live shows the flexibility of film production." For instance, on the Fred Waring Thanksgiving 1952 show, telecast Sunday, November 23, 1952, a group of actors got into a sleigh and traveled some distance down a country road, following its several twists and turns, while completely realistic snow fell. It must be pointed out that the horse presumably pulling the sleigh was not seen; the television camera photographing the scene was in the position the horse normally would occupy. And the twisting, turning road with its woodsy background was, of course, motion picture film rear-projected. With suitable film available, a ship tossing on stormy ocean water has been simulated — the stormy ocean was on rear-projected film and the "ship" or "life raft" was a "live" set moved on rockers by an unseen stage crew.

The use of these new production techniques rapidly becomes widespread, so that it is possible to assume that by the time this book is published all the big networks will have them. As a matter of practicality, therefore, let it be repeated: if you have seen on an actual television program some effect you want in your script, it is logical to assume that the effect can be duplicated. Since production techniques are changing and improving every day, it is not possible in this book to state final, definitive limits. Use your common sense; even with marvelously expert rear-projections, your action in a "live" show still takes place within the four walls of that warehouse-like studio, so that a sporting car race, a track meet, a football game still are not — and probably never will be — practical as elements in a play to be done "live."

We will hazard the stating of a principle for "live" story settings: *Any* background can be provided by rear-projection of slides and/or motion picture film, but the "live" action played against that background must be of such nature that it can be contained within the four walls of a studio.

We are indebted to Mr. E. Carlton Winckler for the following summary of his remarks before the radio and television production group meeting of the American Association of Advertising Agencies 1952 Eastern Annual Conference:

"The production departments of the major Television Networks are spending a great deal of time these days trying to add scope to television production and to give live shows the flexibility of film production. Here at CBS-TV we have set up a special department called Effects Development to work out new methods of adding scope and believability to programs and of doing this with ease and sureness.

"As well as adding scope, these new production techniques accomplish two other things: (1) Through removing production limitations, they enable the program department to have a wider choice of story material; (2) They reduce costs of production.

"Some of the recent developments in this field are:

"A new scenic technique where, by developing standard hard-surfaced flats, scenic elements may be used in a building-block manner, producing more believable sets which can be put together without costly trucking charges. The development of special paint for use on these new type flats results in cleaner pictures and better Video output.

"A new combination of make-up ingredients and colored filters on the camera permits the gradual aging of characters required by the story's content, or even the changing of whole scenes before the eyes of the viewer.

"The effect of reflection in rippling water can now be added to any scene electronically without any water being present in the studio.

"Another headache of television has been scenes requiring rain. Because of the extended rehearsal periods, what appears to be a small shower on the air performance often resulted in a first class, dangerous flood in the studio. Electronic means have been developed by CBS-TV whereby a convincing shower or even a cloudburst can be accomplished with no water at all.

"Another important production instrument developed by CBS-TV which makes the scope of a program practically unlimited is the Matting Amplifier. This device can duplicate on a live television program practically anything that motion pictures can do with traveling mattes. With this handy gadget, people may travel on flying carpets; tiny live salesmen may wander through refrigerators pointing out the salable features; or whole ballets may be performed on the piano top. Even the famous 'invisible man' technique becomes entirely practical for live television with the Matting Amplifier. Live actors may appear in tiny model sets or walk up the stairs in a photograph. These examples are only a small fraction of the new production techniques available at CBS-TV, but there is plenty of unconquered territory still available for television production. We feel that we have only scratched the surface so far, and we have great hopes for the future of live television production."

Television playwrights dedicated to writing for the incredible new medium must watch, and keep watching, and learn, and keep learning as new techniques are developed.

The following listing of special effects will be of interest and value to television playwrights: some which seem highly technical have been included in the hope that somewhere, sometime, they will stimulate some playwright's imagination!

AUDIO EFFECTS

Audio Filters: For use in the audio circuits to produce sound as heard over phones, speakers, radios; from a distance, or muffled, for whatever reason.

Echo Chambers: Used with suitable audio circuits to add reverberations to voice, music or gun shots.

BREAKAWAYS

Breakaway Glass: Glasses, windows or mirrors can be cracked or shattered on cue by hidden mechanical force.

Breakaway Furniture: For fights or comedy effects, the furniture is broken, without injury to the actors.

ELECTRONIC EFFECTS

Wipes and Split Screens: Accomplished with a Wipe Amplifier, which produces Horizontal Wipes, Vertical Wipes, and in combination, Wedge Shaped Wipes.

Wipes may be stopped at any point, pre-set, and put on the air as a Split Screen. For example: the screen may be split in the middle with left coming from one camera and right from another. Likewise, screen may be split with top coming from one camera and bottom from another. In combination, upper left or lower right portion of picture may come from one camera with remaining portion from another. Wipes have been useful for Transitions, and Split Screen for combining material which ordinarily can't be picked up on one camera. For example: a live narrator and the film he's talking about can be shown as one composite picture.

Electronic Iris: Picture area is reduced by diminishing circle closing towards center. Process may be reversed. Picture makes slight rotation near midpoint. Effect is controlled by cameraman. May be used to emphasize face or object at end of scene.

Electronic Matting Amplifier: Has been used to produce a variety of effects, such as: flying carpets, disappearing people, full-size salesman with a miniature car, and miniature-size salesman walking around inside a full-size refrigerator. It has also been used to provide backgrounds for flip cards (title cards flipped into view), small articles sitting on black cloth, and movie film.

Camera Monitor Amplifier: This is required to feed a monitor (a TV receiving set offering to a viewer inside a studio the action actually being photographed in that studio) directly from a camera. Has been used in taking pictures of monitors and TV receivers. For example: TV receiver commercials have been picked up on one camera, fed by way of a Camera Monitor Receiver to the TV set being demonstrated and the

TV set then picked up for air by another camera. (Like a show-within-a-show!)

Double Friction Head: Permits taking a very high Angle Shot, beyond the Panning range of a single head. Also permits camera to be tilted on side, a very effective way to make flat surfaces, such as a dance floor, appear to slope, and dancers to defy gravity.

FANS

Wind: A breeze or a hurricane from silent fans.

FIRE EFFECTS

Flicker effect for Fireplaces: Produces a convincing effect of firelight on faces and objects close to the fireplace.

Flames for Fireplaces and Camp Fires: A realistic technique to permit the use of real flames in these effects.

Fires in Miniature: Some very convincing effects can be achieved with Sterno, talcum powder and smoke candles.

Lacapodium Torch: Very spectacular. For great sheets of flame. Uses compressed air tank as force to project flame.

LENS

Filters: Colored filters can be employed in fantasies to age people rapidly, cause them suddenly to become grotesque or transform clothing and settings from "rags to riches."

MIRRORS AND GLASS

Periscope Mirror: Gives a very low camera angle, or high angle, without the use of costly cranes. A "must" for dancers or fashion shows.

Guillotine Mirrors: For giving the effect of very high or very low angle shots with a pedestal camera.

Transparent Mirrors: Look like ordinary mirrors, but when light is brought up from behind, they are transparent. Faces or scenes may be seen and photographed through them, or a camera may be placed unseen behind a mirror and yet be able to photograph through it although picture will *not* be absolutely crystal-clear.

PRISMS

360-degree Rotation: Produces complete rotation of picture. The practical method for rocking motion of planes, space ships, rotation of people in Ferris wheels, falling in space, and spinning into and out of transitions.

Multi-Image (Six facets): Five images rotate around center image, all remaining upright. Useful for dream, subconscious and transition of type effects.

Prism Kit: Consists of prisms that produce the following: (1) Two images that rotate around each other, images remaining upright; (2) Three images in straight line, line rotates and images turn, to remain upright; (3) Three images which rotate around center point, images remain upright; (4) Five images rotating around center image, images remain upright. This kit offers a wide variety for dreams, subconscious and transition effects.

PROJECTIONS

Disc Effect Projections: Front or rear projection effects for small areas: Produce water ripples, clouds, waterfalls, fire, moving background back of single windows of trains or autos.

Lobsterscope: This motor-driven variable speed device gives the illusion of a passing train.

Animatic Projector: A film-strip projector using 16-mm film and projecting each film frame as a slide. Film frames are changed by pressing a button and changes occur faster than the eye can see. Art work is done on the film, and the sequence cannot be changed.

Rear Projection Screens: One of the best methods of adding scope to your scenes and of providing quick changes or introducing authentic locales. Not a substitute for scenery;

and the effect is always more convincing with added foreground and middle ground pieces. The translucent screens used in rear projection may also be used most effectively as silhouette screens, for the projecting of interesting shadow patterns, or for other uses suggested by your imagination.

Slides: Special slides can be made if the network slide library doesn't have the one your script calls for. Special Panoramic slides are available for moving backgrounds. Sometimes these are equally as effective as motion picture projections.

SMOKE AND FOG

Fog: Available are Chemical Fog, and Oil and Steam. A Fog-Box is a glass-fronted box with self-contained lighting units. Chemical Fog is produced inside the box, and swirl of fog may be controlled and even worked on cue. Box is photographed on one camera and superimposed over scenes as desired. The most practical method to make fog.

Smoke: Full-scale or miniature may be produced in several ways.

Flash Boxes: A puff of rapidly-rising smoke, on cue. Useful for trick entrances, exits, or magic tricks.

Cobwebs: Spun rubber cement makes perfect webs to create undisturbed age and spooky atmosphere.

SNOW

You can have fallen snow on the ground, or anything up to a blizzard in progress.

TRICK EFFECTS

Squirting Telephone and other Comedy Effects: Water squirts out with bull's-eye aim, right on cue. Many "gag" effects are available.

Disappearing Sword, Daggers and Knives: The blade telescopes into the handle and a trigger releases the blade (already attached to the actor's costume, the actor being stabbed, that is) on the other side. No neater way to run a man through!

WATER PANS

Water Reflections: A shallow pan of water, properly lighted and agitated, provides realistic reflections for boat and ship-board scenes.

Pools, Small Ponds, Fountains: Metal pans suitably masked by scenic material give just the right touch to some scenes. Fountain effects may be added, if desired.

MINIATURES

Since everything is relative on the TV camera, miniatures may be used with dramatic effect. An abandoned lifeboat tossing on a stormy sea may be only a foot long actually, and it will toss in a small tank of water agitated by stagehands. Similarly, a stately mansion may be only an architect's model three feet high, while a medieval castle can be built of a child's stone building blocks.

MOTION PICTURE FILM; FILM CLIPS

Most networks maintain a comprehensive library of motion picture film to provide almost any background desired. In your script these are called FILM CLIPS. However, rarely if ever will you ask in your script for motion picture film to be *made especially* for your play and which requires that the actors be seen in the film. The cost is prohibitive! One writer, not knowing, asked that his principal characters be seen running down the gangplank of a liner moored at a dock and disappearing in a large crowd. The cost of this one shot alone would have been *greater than all the other production costs combined.* Naturally, the script was rewritten to eliminate this special shot, although a "stock shot" of the liner easing into the dock was shown with little trouble and expense.

THEATRE-IN-THE-ROUND

In this type of production, sets are eliminated. The action is photographed against black drapes, with only "set pieces" (furniture, fragments of sets like a pedestal, counters, large rocks, etc., etc.) used to provide settings. The TV camera works in very close, using almost entirely CLOSE-UPS, MEDIUM CLOSE SHOTS, to concentrate on the actors, and to avoid revealing the fact that there are no backgrounds, no actual settings. It is a moot question as to whether or not this technique is effective on television. "The Cameo Theatre," produced by National Broadcasting Company for a time, is an example of this type of set-less production. Plays written for the Theatre-in-the-Round tend to be all talk and little action, since the actors' movement is greatly restricted. The obvious virtue of such production is that it is much less costly than realistic sets. The outstanding success of "The Cameo Theatre" was "The Lottery," adapted by Ellen Violett from the short story by Shirley Jackson. "The Lottery" was a parable, a near-fantasy, and its highly stylized production was undoubtedly helped by the use of the Theatre-in-the-Round technique. The stylization may be the answer: if your play is Expressionistic, Impressionistic, Stylized, you properly may ask for a Theatre-in-the-Round production.

Usual Television Studio Layout

The sketches and photographs tell better than words how sets are built adjoining each other as closely as possible, with the all-over design, the all-over floor plan, laid out not only to allow the actors to move quickly from one set to another, but also to permit the moving of the television cameras and the sound booms from one set to another.

The ideal layout is to have all the sets lined up against one wall, with all the front area kept clear for the movement of actors, cameras, sound booms and technicians. If there are several sets, those in which most of the action occurs will adjoin each other, even though in the actual sequence of the play they do not, so to speak, adjoin. For instance, a play may begin in a living room, and move to a park bench, and from there to a railroad platform (for one scene, say), and then on to a cocktail lounge, with most of the action taking place in the living room and the cocktail lounge. These two sets would be built adjoining, while the park bench and the railroad platform might even be "wild" — that is, set up in whatever space may be available, not joined to the other sets.

Time and Sequence of Producing a "Live" Television Play

This book is not intended to consider problems of actual production of a "live" television play. But one detail may be interesting to the playwright: the time required between the start of production and the actual telecast on the air. The following sequence was provided by the Columbia Broadcasting System:

PLANNING PHASE. Before production begins, the script has been approved and the actors cast. The fifteenth and fourteenth day before air time — Preliminary conferences are held, and rough sketches of the sets are considered.

BUDGET CONTROL PHASE. The thirteenth day before air time — Production conference and cost estimates. Props, graphic arts, wardrobe and special effects are integrated, as they all affect total cost. Question: Are we within the budget? The twelfth, eleventh, tenth, ninth and eighth day before air time — Final approval of all designs and costs given. Work strongly underway.

PRODUCTION PHASE. The seventh and sixth day before air time — Selection of stock (from scenery inventories on hand), and construction assembly. The fifth, fourth and third day before air time — Building, painting and drying the sets. Second day before air time — Sets, lights are trucked to the studio, installed, to be ready for Last Day — Air Time. . . . All sets in place; actors, directors, technicians rehearse play in actual sets.

Of course, during this period of preparing the physical production of the play, the actors and the director have been rehearsing the play, in a rehearsal hall, away from the studio. With almost no exceptions, in producing a half-hour play, the actors and the director and the cameramen *do not see the sets until the final day,* perhaps some twelve hours before they go on the air. For the hour play, two days rehearsal in the sets is given; perhaps thirty-six hours before air time.

The point is, for playwrights, and a point which your author cannot pound home too much or too often: *Make your intention clear at all times to the technicians who must produce your play!*

One final word, cancelling out, apparently, all the limitations given in this chapter:

Many effects have been listed in an effort to show television playwrights that there are *fewer* limitations in live television than might appear to be the case, at first glance. It is the playwright's imagination which sparks the creation of *new* effects and which opens new horizons.

Therefore, you television playwrights must not abandon a valuable plot treatment because of doubt that live television can handle it. Rather, you should confer, if possible, with a good production man who can very probably help to solve your production problem.

A television playwright should never be limited by the mechanics of production; live television just can't afford that!

4

Camera Directions

Don't be afraid of the television camera! Its use is not a mystery, but only the understanding and application of a few technical terms, common sense and the imagination which makes you a writer.

This chapter is written in the first person. I, the author of this book, am talking to you as if we were facing each other across a desk. I have been so faced at least two thousand times in my capacity as editor of a half-hour dramatic television show. The question always is — and asked fearfully, if the writer is new to television: "But what about camera directions — aren't they terribly hard?"

They aren't hard. I tell potential writers of television plays that it's necessary to indicate only four kinds of camera directions in a script:

1. An "establishing" or "geography" shot.

2. A CLOSE-UP on the face of one of your characters if by his expression (interpreted by the actor) we, the viewers, are told that he has reached some decision or is experiencing some reaction that will influence the progress of your play toward its climax and denouement.

3. Shots which tell your story visually.

4. Shots which indicate passage of time, change of scene, or some special effect.

Let's explore the terminology of camera directions; then we'll discuss each of the above four categories, as they arise in defining the terms.

FADE-IN: an effect in which the scene literally "fades" into vision from total black (BLACK SCREEN).

FADE-OUT: The opposite of FADE-IN. The scene "fades" into total black. It has become universal usage that television plays FADE-IN when they start, and FADE-OUT when they end, a usage taken over from motion pictures. A FADE-IN also indicates the start of a new sequence of closely-related action *within* the play. A FADE-OUT ends such a sequence. Also, to indicate the passage of considerable time, a FADE-OUT, FADE-IN is indicated. The longer and slower the FADE-OUT, FADE-IN, the greater amount of time we assume to have elapsed. Audiences have been so trained by motion pictures that they accept this usage completely. If you want to indicate the passage of a short amount of time, indicate a DISSOLVE (to be discussed next). If days, weeks, months, years elapse between one sequence of action and the next, indicate FADE-OUT, FADE-IN.

Starting Your Play

OPENING SHOT:

FADE-IN: FULL SHOT OF THE SUNDECK OF A HOME
DESIGNED FOR MODERN LIVING. AN AWNING
PARTIALLY COVERS THE AREA. GAY FLOWERING
PLANTS ARE IN BOXES LINING THE WALLS OF THE
HOUSE AND ON AS MUCH OF THE BALUSTRADE AS WE
SEE. A PING-PONG TABLE IS CENTERED IN THE SHOT.
MARY, A LOVELY, VITAL YOUNG WOMAN IN SHORTS,
A SPORT SHIRT, AND WEARING A CAP WITH A VISOR,
IS LAUGHING AS SHE FURIOUSLY ENGAGES MIKE
IN A GAME OF PING-PONG. MIKE IS OLDER, PUFFING A
BIT WITH EXERTION, BUT MANAGING TO KEEP UP.
HE WEARS SLACKS, A SPORT SHIRT. SUNLIGHT
DRENCHES THE SCENE.

MARY (LAUGHING, PLAYING)

Whitewash me, will you?

MIKE (GASPING)

If only I get out alive —

CUT TO

CLOSE SHOT: THE TABLE, ETC.

Ending Your Play
MIKE IS HOLDING MARY TIGHTLY IN HIS ARMS,
AS THEY STAND BY THE PING-PONG TABLE. HEAVY
RAIN IS FALLING, BUT THEY PAY NO ATTENTION.
AS MIKE TRIES TO KISS HER, MARY PULLS AWAY A BIT.

MARY (HALF LAUGHING, HALF CRYING)
If you dare to say I'm all wet, I'll —
I'll — *strangle* you!

MIKE (GENTLY, DEEP FEELING)
No need. I'm already drowning — drowning in
your love — (HE KISSES HER. SHE RESPONDS
FERVENTLY)

FADE-OUT

THE END

*Indicating Passage of Time and/or End of one
Sequence, Start of Another*
MIKE IS EXITING INTO THE HOUSE. HE STOPS AT
THE DOORWAY, TURNS BACK, LOOKS AT MARY
SCORNFULLY.

MIKE (SARCASTICALLY)
Will you *ever* grow up?
MARY DOESN'T REPLY. SHE LOOKS AT HIM
DEFIANTLY. FOR AN INSTANT THEIR GLANCES LOCK.
THEN SHE LAUGHS MOCKINGLY.

MARY
I hope not!
SHE TWIRLS HER PING-PONG PADDLE GAILY.
ABRUPTLY, MIKE EXITS. AT ONCE MARY DROOPS.
LISTLESSLY, SHE TOSSES THE PADDLE ON THE
PING-PONG TABLE, PULLS OUT A HANDKERCHIEF,
MOPS HER FACE, THEN SUDDENLY STARTS TO CRY.
SHE RUNS TO A PLANT WITH ONE FLOWER ON IT,
VICIOUSLY PULLS THE FLOWER OFF, THROWS IT

DOWN, STAMPS ON IT. THEN SHE WEEPS AGAIN,
AS WE SLOWLY

FADE-OUT

FADE-IN

CLOSE SHOT: THE SAME PLANT, NOW COVERED
WITH BLOOMS. IT IS NIGHT, BRIGHT MOONLIGHT.
WE HEAR A DOOR OPEN AND CLOSE SOFTLY. FOOT-
STEPS APPROACH, GETTING LOUDER.
THE CAMERA PULLS BACK AS MIKE COMES INTO THE
SCENE, STANDS BY THE PLANT, LOOKS AT IT,
TOUCHES ONE OF THE BLOOMS. MIKE IS DRESSED
IN EVENING CLOTHES, WITH A WHITE TUXEDO.

MIKE (SOFTLY)

Well, at least *you* are growing up!

OUT OF SCENE, MARY SPEAKS

MARY (OFF CAMERA)

You wouldn't be talking to me, would you, Mike?

THE CAMERA PULLS BACK STILL FURTHER AS
MARY WALKS INTO THE SCENE. SHE IS WEARING
A LOVELY STRAPLESS EVENING DRESS. SHE STOPS,
SMILES, AS MIKE TURNS TO SPEAK TO HER.

I'll comment on the preceding scene to point out that in addition to the fairly long lapse of time indicated by the FADE-OUT,
FADE-IN, an additional time device was used: the flowering plant.
As the first sequence ended, Mary pulled off the only flower. After
the FADE-IN, at the start of the new sequence, the plant is covered
with flowers, showing *visually* the elapse of time. Also, the mood
was changed by light (sunlight into moonlight); and the costume
changes by both Mary and Mike create a different and later "feel"
in the scene. And (never missing a chance to drive home a point)
note that the *transition* between scenes was accomplished visually
by the use of the plant. (Two plants would be required in production: one with a single flower; a second, identical with the
first, covered with blooms. In "live" television, a property man
[stagehand] would quickly substitute the second plant for the
first, during the FADE-OUT, FADE-IN.) Finally, if this were "live"
television, note that Mike has time quickly to change from slacks

into evening clothes, since he leaves the scene early; and that Mary has time to change quickly during the FADE-OUT, FADE-IN, and also while Mike is shown contemplating the full-flowering plant, and is speaking his line of dialogue.

DISSOLVE: An effect in which one scene blends into another, with the first scene disappearing and the second remaining clear, and with the action continuing in the second scene. A DIS-SOLVE is used to indicate a short elapse of time in a given scene, or to move from one scene to another where the action is either simultaneous with the action in the first scene, or occuring very soon after the action in the first scene.

Example (from *Caprice*, by Frank P. De Felitta, produced in *Armstrong's Circle Theatre*.)

FADE-IN:

IT IS NIGHT. IT IS RAINING. WE ARE OUTDOORS. WE OPEN ON A LARGE POSTER ENCLOSED IN A GLASS CASE. THE RAIN BEATS AGAINST THE GLASS. THE POSTER READS: "TONIGHT — ALL-KREISLER RECITAL — THE LOHMAN SYMPHONY ORCHESTRA — (IN LARGE LETTERS:) — VICTOR KAROLL, SOLOIST." IN THE BACKGROUND, DIMLY, WE HEAR THE OPENING STRAINS OF KREISLER'S "VIENNESE CAPRICE".

DISSOLVE TO:

INSIDE. A CLOSE-UP OF VICTOR KAROLL PLAYING THE VIOLIN. A SPOTLIGHT IS DIRECTED UPON HIM. OTHERWISE HE IS SHROUDED IN DARKNESS. THE SHOT IS CLOSE ENOUGH SO THAT WE JUST MISS SEEING HIM ACTUALLY PLAYING THE VIOLIN. AFTER A FEW BARS WE:

DISSOLVE TO:

A CLOSE-UP OF SUSAN. WE PEEK OVER HER MUSIC STAND AS SHE SITS THERE, SCARCELY BREATHING, STARING RAPT AND IN WONDERMENT OFF SCREEN AT VICTOR. HER EYES ARE LARGE SAUCER-LIKE DISCS. HER VIOLIN IS POISED LIMPLY BENEATH HER CHIN: SHE CANNOT PLAY. SHE CAN ONLY STARE AND

WORSHIP. THE BOWING ARM OF A FELLOW VIOLINIST
WANDERS IN AND OUT OF SCREEN RIGHT. WE STAY
HERE A FEW BARS, THEN:
DISSOLVE TO:
HENRY HATTER, CYMBALS IN HAND, HE STANDS,
STARING THROUGH HIS HANGING TRIANGLE AT
SUSAN. TO HIS LEFT STANDS ANOTHER MUSICIAN
HOVERING OVER KETTLE DRUMS. HENRY'S EXPRESSION
BEARS A SLIGHT TRACE OF ANNOYANCE, BUT MOSTLY
HE SEEMS WORRIED. HIS EYES SHIFT TO VICTOR
AS WE MOVE IN THROUGH THE TRIANGLE, TO A
CLOSE-UP:

In this example, the DISSOLVE has been used not only to move from
one scene (The Poster) to another (The Concert in Progress) but
it has conveyed the sense of *time in progress,* from the moment
that we are told that there *is* a concert (The Poster), through the
progression of the concert, as the effect of Victor's playing is shown
first on Susan and then on Henry, in relation to Susan.

Another Example (Also from *Caprice*)

HENRY SIGHS AND SHAKES HIS HEAD, THEN
SUDDENLY READIES HIMSELF FOR A MUSIC CUE
COMING UP . . . HE STRIKES THE CYMBALS.
DISSOLVE TO:
VICTOR'S DRESSING ROOM. WE OPEN ON A
CLOSE-UP OF A GLASS OF WATER AND A SMALL
BOX OF TABLETS RESTING ON THE CIRCULAR
TABLE. WE PULL BACK AS PAUL APPROACHES
THE TABLETS. IN THE BACKGROUND WE HEAR THE
NOISE OF A THUNDEROUS OVATION. PAUL REMOVES
TABLET, THEN, PICKING UP THE GLASS OF WATER
WITH HIS FREE HAND, TURNS TO THE DOOR AND
STANDS EXPECTANTLY.

In addition to the unmistakable change of setting, we have a sense
of the elapse of a short period of time, both from Paul's action
in preparing the tablet and the glass of water, and from the sound

of the ovation, suggesting the end of the concert. (Note: Here's another situation where *sound effects* play a great part in expanding the *scope* of the scene.)

CUT: Abrupt change of scene and/or setting without any action or camera effect in between. A CUT is used to indicate action that is happening simultaneously in several places, or between several characters. It is also used to speed up action, as when the villain is chasing the hero, and we CUT from first one to the other, and back and forth, each CUT coming more rapidly, and so increasing the tension and the suspense. It is also used for variety, to keep one scene from appearing on the screen too long. Thus, for ten seconds or so, we may see the heroine's profile, as she speaks. Then, as we CUT, we see her full face, while she keeps on speaking *without* interruption. If the speech is long, a third CUT may be used, perhaps to a shot which will show the heroine in the environment where she is speaking — all done for visual variety. Importantly, a CUT is used to indicate a character's reaction to what another character has just said, or to some action that has just happened.

In the preceding example, a CUT has been used to show action going on simultaneously among several characters. Following is an example of a CUT used to indicate a reaction (REACTION SHOT).

JOE, PAT AND JOHN ARE SITTING AROUND A TABLE
LITTERED WITH PAPERS. JOE RISES, POUNDS THE
TABLE WITH HIS FIST. HE SPEAKS DIRECTLY TO PAT.

JOE (ANGRILY)

Pat, *you* made this stupid mistake! *You're fired!*

PAT

But, Joe, I didn't — I —

JOE

No backtalk! Get out!

CUT TO:

CLOSE-UP OF JOHN, AS PAT AND JOE KEEP TALKING,
OFF CAMERA. JOHN MOISTENS HIS LIPS, LOOKS
FEARFULLY FROM ONE TO THE OTHER, TRIES TO

SPEAK, FINALLY DECIDES NOT TO, HANGS HIS HEAD.
MEANWHILE —

PAT (OFF CAMERA)

You'd fire me without giving me a chance to —

JOE (ALSO OFF CAMERA)

You had your chance!

PAT (OFF CAMERA)

Maybe I'm not the only stupid one —

JOE (OFF CAMERA)

Don't try shifting the blame!

CUT TO:

THREE SHOT, JOE, PAT, AND JOHN.
JOHN RISES.

JOHN

I — I think I'll run along!

Note that in the scene of violent argument between Pat and Joe, *the camera is on John,* in a REACTION SHOT, in which John conveys through his visual reaction better than he could in words his fear, his sense of guilt, his decision not to do anything about the situation which might involve him.

You, as playwright, must indicate the CUTS which tell the story. You need not (and most television directors prefer that you do not) indicate CUTS for tempo or suspense, or for visual variety. (In this respect, a television play script differs from a motion picture script, in which every camera position, or SHOT, is numbered and described.)

PAN: Short for "Panorama." Television has taken over from motion pictures their accepted meaning of this word — "moves." "THE CAMERA PANS RIGHT" means that the camera, remaining stationary on its base, moves RIGHT, in a horizontal plane. "THE CAMERA PANS (OR TILTS) UP" means that the camera, remaining stationary on its base, is turned UP by the cameraman in a vertical plane. A PAN SHOT can be made UP, DOWN, RIGHT, or LEFT, to follow a moving object or person; or it can simply PAN the setting or the scene to describe it visually. The point is, in a PAN SHOT, the camera *remains stationary on its base or pedestal.* In contrast is the

MOVING SHOT: when *the whole camera moves* on its base or pedestal, which has wheels. In motion pictures, sometimes a track is laid for the camera wheels to move on, and so insure perfect smoothness. In television, on the smooth television studio floor, a track normally is not necessary. Thus, if you have two characters strolling along a corridor, and it is dramatically necessary to stay with them, the camera moves with them. There are variations in describing this movement, e.g.,

MOVE IN: The camera literally moves in, is physically moved on its wheels to, say, a closer shot or a CLOSE-UP, or a TIGHT SHOT, or whatever the intention of the playwright and/or the director may be.

Another variation:

PULL BACK: The camera literally is pulled back, away from the scene being photographed, to increase the field of vision, that is, the scope of the shot. Another:

DOLLY: A "dolly" is something with wheels on it, like a baggage truck. Used in connection with a camera, it means that the camera is moved on the wheels of its base or pedestal. So we can DOLLY IN, and less commonly, DOLLY BACK (in the backward movement, ordinarily MOVE BACK, or PULL BACK is used).

Before we go any further, let me point out that these terms, far from being mysterious or esoteric, are nothing but common sense. It's like learning to drive a car: you are told of the brake, the clutch, low gear, second, high, free wheeling, overdrive. Similarly, since a camera can be manipulated in two ways — physically, and by using a change in the lens — what you are learning are *only* the simple mechanics of this manipulation. Let's go on:

ANGLE SHOT: Just what it says. The camera is tilted UP or DOWN at an ANGLE, in order to secure a dramatic effect.

Example (from *Cappie's Candles,* by Edward Rogers Knowlton)

FADE-IN: MEDIUM CLOSE SHOT OF A MASS OF ROCKS, WHICH SEEM TO LEAD FROM A CRUDE LANDING

PLACE, SINCE WE HEAR THE SURF BEATING RIGHT
AT HAND.

A FISHERMAN IN OILSKINS COMES IN PAST THE
CAMERA (that is, he walks from *behind* the camera
into the scene being photographed). AS HE STARTS
TO CLIMB THE ROCKS, THE CAMERA PANS UP IN
AN ANGLE SHOT FOR A MOMENT, THEN PANS DOWN,
ALSO IN AN ANGLE SHOT, TO PICK UP DR. BARTON
STARTING TO CLIMB FROM THE BOTTOM OF THE
ROCK MASS.

As you see, a dramatic effect to heighten the steep rock mass is
secured by using an ANGLE SHOT UP and then an ANGLE SHOT DOWN.
Your playwright's imagination and the nature of your setting and
story determine when you want to indicate this effect. For instance: if you wanted to show an adult from a child's point of view,
and you wanted to create the child's feeling that the adult is a
giant, physically and perhaps in authority, you could indicate "AN
ANGLE SHOT, LOOKING UP AT THE ADULT FROM THE CHILD'S POINT OF
VIEW." Then the camera would shoot from a position close to the
floor, UP at the adult, and your effect would be achieved.

CLOSE SHOT: The "normal" shot in television, one in which the
     performers are seen from the knees or the waist up. Abbre-
     viation: CS

CLOSE-UP: A shot in which the face of a performer fills the screen;
     or in which an object or detail is seen, full-screen size, for
     emphasis. Used on an actor to allow his portrayal of emo-
     tional reactions or moments of decision indicated by his
     expression. Also used frequently in television to make transi-
     tions from one scene or sequence to another, i.e., we FADE-OUT
     on a CLOSE-UP of Margie, showing her struggling with tears;
     then we FADE-IN on a CLOSE-UP of Tom, laughing gaily. Abbre-
     viation: CU

FULL SHOT: Explains itself. Shows the entire scene or setting
     where the succeeding action is to take place. Also called a
     GEOGRAPHY SHOT, since it establishes locale of a scene.

FOLLOW SHOT: A variation of a MOVING SHOT in which the camera
     moves behind the actor as he moves, or behind an object, like

a speedboat, as it moves. Sometimes we say, also, THE CAMERA FOLLOWS a given character, or object, in indicating its use.

LONG SHOT: A "full shot" of a scene taken from a distance, as of a valley from a mountain peak, or the Lincoln Memorial in Washington from the opposite end of the reflecting pool. Abbreviation: LS

MEDIUM SHOT: A closer shot than either a LONG OR FULL SHOT, showing the actors, usually full-length, and much more detail of setting and background than in a FULL OR LONG SHOT. Can be used as an ESTABLISHING GEOGRAPHY SHOT. Abbreviation: MS

MEDIUM CLOSE SHOT: A shot halfway between a MEDIUM SHOT and a CLOSE SHOT. Abbreviation: MCS

SHOT: Generic term for any shot of any description. Describes the scene to be photographed and the method of photographing it, i.e., CLOSE SHOT, PAN SHOT, MOVING SHOT, etc., etc.

SPLIT SCREEN: Explains itself. The screen usually is split into two halves by a vertical division, so that action going on simultaneously in each half is seen. Usually used for both ends of a telephone conversation when it's desirable to show both people talking. However, can be used for any two scenes when you want the action to be seen simultaneously.

STOCK SHOT: In practice, scenes on motion picture film, already made, which can be rented or bought from film libraries. For instance, you may indicate, "STOCK SHOT OF TIMES SQUARE, NEW YORK;" and the producer of your play would go to a film library and buy 100 feet of stock shot, or whatever length might be needed. Literally: film shots which are "in stock", in the department store sense.

FILM CLIPS: Lengths of motion picture film which are inserted into the "live" action of a "live" television play. For instance, you might specify, "FILM CLIP, A WESTERN CATTLE RANCH WITH MOUNTAINS IN THE DISTANCE, AND WITH A ROUND-UP TAKING PLACE IN THE FOREGROUND." Usually FILM CLIPS are used for exteriors, out-of-doors shots, as ESTABLISHING GEOGRAPHY SHOTS. Often they can be rented or purchased as stock shots. Sometimes special film is taken with the principals of your television play appearing in filmed scenes. This procedure is very expensive, and it is earnestly recommended that you so write your "live" television play that no film clips requiring the appearance of your "live" principals will be required. In your script, FILM CLIPS are indicated as follows:

Example (from *Only This Night,* by Ira Avery, produced on *Armstrong's Circle Theatre.*)

MICHAEL AND JANE ARE SITTING AT A TABLE FOR
TWO IN AN ELEGANT CAFE.
                    MICHAEL
I've found the magic city —
                    JANE
New York? (MICHAEL NODS) And — the rest of it?
          MICHAEL (RISES, SMILES)
Would you be surprised to find a chariot waiting
for you?
  JANE (RISING, GATHERING HER WRAP AROUND HER)
Nothing would surprise me!
DISSOLVE: INTO
FILM CLIP: CARRIAGES ROLLING THROUGH CENTRAL
PARK AT NIGHT. CUT TO:
LIVE ACTION: MCS OF MICHAEL AND JANE IN THE
BACK OF A CENTRAL PARK CALÈCHE, WHICH ROCKS
GENTLY. A SUGGESTION OF SHADOWY TREES GLIDING
BY IN THE BACKGROUND.
SOUND: DISTANT TRAFFIC NOISES, THE CLOP-CLOP OF
HORSES' HOOFS AND THE CREAKING OF THE CARRIAGE.
                    JANE
It's a beautiful chariot, Michael.

TRUCKING SHOT: Same as a MOVING SHOT, in which both the camera and the characters or objects being photographed are moving.
TWO-SHOT: Shot in which two actors appear.
THREE-SHOT: Shot in which three actors appear.
TIGHT SHOT: Between a CLOSE SHOT and a CLOSE-UP. Used to concentrate dramatic action at climactic moments, or for great emphasis.

WIDE-ANGLE SHOT: A variation of the FULL SHOT in which the camera is nearer the actors or objects being photographed, with a wide field, and shallow depth. Used for groupings, or for action covering an extensive setting so that this action may be seen continuously, instead of in a series of CUTS.

SUPERIMPOSITION: Literally, the superimposing of one scene on top of another, for a special effect. You may want to recall visually, for the sake of the audience, a person whom the character in the main scene is thinking about. So, you SUPERIMPOSE the person being thought about on top of the main scene. This superimposed person can also talk, and carry on dialogue with the characters in the main scene. So the SUPERIMPOSITION is useful in fantasy, in limited flashbacks, in visualizing a "stream of consciousness" effect, in indicating "thoughts", or in indicating any similar imaginative, nonrealistic effect. A quick example: In the actual scene, a group of school children is singing "The Star Spangled Banner". As the song reaches the climax, the Stars and Stripes are SUPERIMPOSED, so that we see the flag waving over the children as they sing.

SUBJECTIVE CAMERA: A somewhat "highbrow" term to describe the use of the camera, in effect, as a living character, with the camera's lens being the "eye." Employed, for instance, when the CAMERA PANS around an empty room, or an outdoor scene, with no actors present, as if the Camera were making note of the scene, as if it were using its "eye" like a human eye.

LIMBO: Just that — nothing. "Nothing," in the sense that no backgrounds, no sets, no scenery are shown; characters are photographed against total black. This effect can be achieved by keeping all light off any possible background, and then concentrating it on the characters being photographed. Useful for transition scenes when two characters, say, meet in a hurry, or unexpectedly, or briefly, or at a climactic moment, when the scenery, the sets, count for nothing. Strongly identified with the "theatre-in-the-round" technique, where no sets are used — only drapes, or a cyclorama.

WILD SOUND: Sound — dialogue, music, special effects — recorded without any attendant photography. "Wild sound" can then be projected with whatever picture track may be desired.

VOICE-OVER: Narration or commentary, spoken "live" or previously recorded, by a person not necessarily appearing in the photographed scene, although the words so spoken must fit the action being described or commented on.

MATCHED-DISSOLVE: Technique used in transitions from one scene to another, when the object or scene *ending* one sequence matches or approximates the object or scene *beginning* the succeeding sequence. For instance, a scene ends on a CLOSE-UP of a rose held in your heroine's hands. In a MATCHED-DISSOLVE, the next scene *begins* with a CLOSE-UP of a faded rose held in your hero's hands, and with your hero revealed, when the CAMERA PULLS BACK, in a different setting.

BALOP (or TELOP): TIGHT SHOT or a CLOSE-UP of a still photograph or card, i.e., "still" in contrast to "moving". Used most frequently as an ESTABLISHING or GEOGRAPHY SHOT, showing a photograph (or still picture) of, say, the exterior of a Colonial mansion which it would be impossible or too expensive to build in a studio for a "live" telecast. More familiar, perhaps, to the casual reader, is the BALOP of the cards carrying commercial messages which are flipped, turned, or withdrawn, in television "commercials."

WIPE: A technique of transitions much faster than a DISSOLVE, but not as fast as a CUT, by which one scene is literally "wiped off", while another appears. Used usually for fast change of scene, or the start of a new sequence of action, although it does not have the connotation of the elapse of time that a DISSOLVE or a FADE-OUT has.

ZOOM: Movement of the camera, or of a special camera lens, accomplished very fast, to create the effect of coming in for intense concentration on a scene, character or object. Everyone is familiar with this technique, as used by newsreels, to concentrate attention on a play in a football game, so that the viewer seems to be hurtled from the grandstand into the thick of the scrimmage. Obviously used for high dramatic effect at climactic moments.

MULTIPLE IMAGE (or PRISM SHOT):

A special camera lens using a prism throws multiple images of the same subject on the screen, instead of just one image.

Well, there are your CAMERA DIRECTIONS AND TERMS. They add up to just one goal: *clarity.* You'll use them for only one purpose: to make your intent as the playwright *clear at all times.* Since you are writing for television, a visual medium, you will need to write visually at all times, seeing in your mind's eye the scene you are putting down on paper and which you want to see re-created in action on the television screen. So, the most important of all camera directions you'll want to indicate are those which *tell your story visually.* Here's a television play which does that: it's the opening of *Way of Courage,* by Roger Garis. The following passage is quoted from the as-broadcast script, using the full camera directions Mr. Garis used, and in their convenient abbreviated form:

OPENING SHOT:

CS OF TWO MEN SEATED ON OPPOSITE SIDES OF A
DESK. ONE IS DR. FULLBRIGHT. HE IS MIDDLE-AGED,
SYMPATHETIC, WEARS A BUSINESS SUIT. A STETHO-
SCOPE DANGLES FROM ABOUT HIS NECK. ON THE DESK
ARE BLOOD-PRESSURE APPARATUS, PRESCRIPTION
PAD, APPOINTMENT BOOK, ETC. ACROSS FROM HIM
SITS CHICK CONOVER. CHICK IS 30–35, STRONG,
LIKABLE, A FOREMAN IN AN AIRCRAFT FACTORY.
HE GOT A PURPLE HEART IN THE LAST WAR, AND IS
THE SORT OF FELLOW YOU'D CHOOSE FOR YOUR
BUDDY IF YOU WERE GOING INTO SOME FAST ACTION.
HE'S NOT ANY HERO — AT LEAST TO HIMSELF —
AND IS, IN FACT, JUST ABOUT AN AVERAGE GUY. BUT
RIGHT NOW HE ISN'T AVERAGE. RIGHT NOW HE'S
CARRYING A BURDEN ALMOST TOO HEAVY FOR AN
AVERAGE GUY. HE SITS IN HIS CHAIR WITH A STUNNED,
RATHER VACANT LOOK ON HIS FACE. FOR SEVERAL
SECONDS NEITHER HE NOR THE DOCTOR SAYS

ANYTHING. THE ONLY SOUND IS THE LOUD TICKING
OF A GRANDFATHER'S CLOCK IN THE CORNER OF THE
OFFICE. CHICK STARES STRAIGHT AHEAD. THEN
HE FUMBLES IN HIS POCKET, TAKES OUT A PACK
OF CIGARETTES, PUTS ONE IN HIS MOUTH.
CUT TO:
TIGHT SHOT OF CHICK. HE'S GOTTEN MATCHES
FROM ANOTHER POCKET, TRIES TO STRIKE ONE, FAILS,
DROPS THE MATCH, TAKES ANOTHER, FAILS TO
LIGHT THIS ONE ALSO.
CUT TO:
CS OF DOCTOR AND CHICK, AS BEFORE. THE DOC
TAKES OUT HIS MATCHES AND WITHOUT A WORD
STRIKES ONE, LIGHTS CHICK'S CIGARETTE FOR HIM.
CHICK TAKES ONE DRAG, THEN LEANS BACK IN HIS
CHAIR, STILL WITH THAT FIXED EXPRESSION. HE
PUTS THE CIGARETTE IN HIS MOUTH AGAIN,
FUMBLES WITH BOTH HANDS TO BUTTON HIS OPEN
SHIRT WHICH UNTIL NOW HAS BARED HIS BREAST.
THE SOUND OF THE TICKING IS GREATLY EXAGGERATED
NOW.
CUT TO:
CU OF CHICK. HE HEARS THE TICKING AS HE MIGHT
HEAR THE THUD OF HIS OWN HEART. IT INCREASES,
BECOMES ALMOST UNBEARABLE. PULL BACK
SLIGHTLY TO SHOW CHICK LEANING FORWARD, TENSED.
THE DOCTOR'S HAND REACHES OUT AND GRASPS
CHICK'S ARM. CHICK LOOKS DOWN AT THE HAND.
AS HE DOES SO, THE THUD STOPS, GOES BACK TO THE
NORMAL SOUND OF A TICKING CLOCK.
THE DOCTOR'S VOICE IS HEARD:

    DOCTOR (OFF CAMERA, MAINTAIN CU ON CHICK)
— feeling better now?
      CHICK (NOT COMPLETELY OUT OF IT YET)
Huh? Oh, yeah — sure —
CUT TO:
CS OF BOTH

DOCTOR

We don't often tell patients things like this. But
you said you had to know —

CHICK

Yeah. I had to know.

From this beginning, we are told visually that a likable man has
had an examination, probably of his heart (from the stethoscope);
that the result of the examination has been unnerving; that the
doctor is a sympathetic person; that the news comes as a sudden
blow to the patient, enough to upset normal habits (his inability
to light a cigarette, which he has reached for automatically). All
this before a word is spoken. SOUND has added to the dramatic
effect, however, through the analogy of the ticking clock with the
thudding of the patient's heart. This opening is truly visual; it
could not be understood or comprehended unless you *saw* it; in
fact, you could *only* see it, because, as pointed out, there is no
word spoken until a powerful dramatic situation has been set,
visually.

A literary agent once gave an author a large dictionary as a
Christmas present. On the gift card, she wrote: "Here are the
words! You re-arrange them, and I'll sell them!"

So it is with your CAMERA TERMS AND DIRECTIONS. They are the
elements of your craft of writing for television. All of them, without exception, are based on necessity and common sense, and they
are as ordinary as a carpenter's tools. But under the spur of your
imagination, they can turn your writing for television into work
that is something fine and memorable, passionate, moving, hilarious, high art.

Mr. Garry Simpson, a leading television director, was kind
enough to read this chapter, and to offer the following comment:

"It is not necessary to indicate any camera directions. The TV
director knows what to do, and he is limited by time and a few
cameras, so it is impossible sometimes to shoot a complicated
visual sequence. *Fast* montages are very difficult for this reason.
The author should indicate the *ideal*, however, and the TV director
will get the closest to that impression that he can with the money,
time and gear he has.

"I have a strong dislike for black screens [i.e., on TV receiving sets] for long periods of time. I don't approve personally of holding a FADE-OUT a *long* time to indicate the passing of months and years. It would be better to have a *visual* indication of this time passage — calendars (over-used), summer turning into winter, a house in the day and the same house (exterior) at night, etc.

"The ideal, of course, is to have a *visual* time lapse that *progresses* or *comments* on the story."

From Mr. Simpson's remarks, I want to pick out two things for your special consideration:

1. "The author should indicate the ideal" — to do so means that you as author must use what camera terms may be required to indicate this ideal;
2. "The ideal, of course, is to have a *visual* time lapse that *progresses* or *comments* on the story".

Concerning paragraph 2, a montage or a time-lapse device should function like any other cover scene: it should advance the story, as Mr. Simpson has declared.

The hardest thing in writing with a television camera in mind is *to begin.* Shall it be with a FULL SHOT of Grand Central Station? Or shall it be with a TIGHT SHOT of a kitten cringing from the thousand rushing feet of the crowds disgorged from the trains?

The answer is simple. Begin, always, at the moment of greatest impact, for the dramatic intention you have in mind, with clarity your guide at all times. Your television camera will obey your command: a FULL SHOT or a TIGHT SHOT — it's up to you, the playwright, to tell it what to do. These CAMERA TERMS AND DIRECTIONS are your signposts.

5

Problems of Time

THE PROBLEM OF TIME has crept up on us — no, has leaped out and tackled us! — in preceding chapters, and will do so in chapters to come, inescapably. We must in television playwriting first consider all-over Time, which is the length of our play. Having accepted the limits of all-over Time — the half-hour play (twenty-two minutes to twenty-four minutes actually), the hour play (fifty-two to fifty-four minutes actually), the fifteen-minute play (actually thirteen minutes), and whatever other variation there may be (such as a ten-minute "spot"), we can forget all-over Time and move on to talk about Time within the all over limit, especially as it governs technique in "live" television plays.

Time in "Live" Television Plays

Time dictates physical movements of the actor from one set to another.

Time dictates what costume and make-up changes can be made.

Time, therefore, dictates the *scope* of your story, makes mandatory that you attack your material (begin your play) as near as possible to the climax. Actually, before starting to write, the television playwright should think backwards from his climax, and start his play at the point where enough situation is piled up, in terms of his characters, to *create the climax* he is aiming for. When this point has been determined, the playwright knows where to begin.

George Pierce Baker once asked his first-year playwriting class what was the chief aim of the playwright, once the curtain had gone up on his play. Mr. Baker refused to accept several cautious answers, such as "to entertain the audience," "to get the story started", "to make the exposition clear", etc., etc. Finally, he said imperturbably, "Once the curtain has gone up, the chief aim is to get it down again." Which is another way of saying, "attack your material as close to the climax as possible, starting from the point where there is enough piled-up situation to *create* the climax". (And this rule applies to television plays, whether "live" or filmed, where the all-over Time limit reigns.)

Frankly, the author of this book does not see how any television playwright can begin to write until he knows the end he is aiming for, until he has determined the *scope* of his story, governed by all-over Time.

Transitions in "Live" Television

Transitions from one scene to the next following require Cover Scenes: "A Cover Scene keeps the action going, *and should advance the plot*, without the presence of one or more of the principal characters who must appear in an immediately following scene perhaps in a different costume and/or make-up; and, in the case of 'live' television, in a different set which may be as far away as fifty feet across the studio from the preceding set".

Following is an example of a simple Cover Scene, from *Way of Courage*, by Roger Garis. The immediately preceding scene is given to establish the *need* for a Cover Scene allowing Chick and Ellen to move from the hallway set to their living room set.

Chick has been told that he has only a short while to live. He and his wife, Ellen, have just visited their attorney, where Chick made a will, without telling the attorney about Chick's imminent death.

CUT TO SHOT OF ELLEN AND CHICK IN HALLWAY. THEY HAVE BOTTLED UP THEIR LAUGHTER, BUT AS THE DOOR CLOSES BEHIND THEM, THEY LET LOOSE.

                              ELLEN
(LAUGHING, CLINGING TO CHICK'S ARM) Chick, you were wonderful —

CHICK
(MIMICKING THE ATTORNEY) Happy landings!
ELLEN
— that lawyer was so *serious!* And when he asked
where you were going —
CHICK
— I thought of three or four good cracks — poor
Cliff —
THEY ARE WALKING TOWARD THE ELEVATOR NOW,
CAMERA FOLLOWING.
ELLEN
— he would have fainted . . . .
CHICK
— probably passed out cold on a volume of Black-
stone . . . . . (HE PUSHES ELEVATOR BUTTON)
ELLEN STOPS, LOOKS AT CHICK, SUDDENLY GRAVE,
SPEAKS IN A WHISPER . . . . . .
DOLLY UP FOR CU OF CHICK AND ELLEN
ELLEN
— that was the right way, wasn't it, Chick?
CHICK
(LOOKING AT HER TENDERLY) That was just right —
ELLEN
We really — did pretty well —
CHICK
We did fine. (CHICK KISSES HER)

NOTE: Now, Ellen and Chick both must be in the next scene,
which follows in a few seconds of *elapsed time.* They must walk
(or run!) at least fifteen feet (in this case) to the next set. We could
FADE-OUT, FADE-IN, and have a long (seemingly, to the viewer)
period of blank screen. Instead, the author devised the following
cover scene, which *advances the plot,* since it shows the couple's
daughter, Linda, at a climactic moment when she is waiting for
news about her history examination which is tied-in closely with
the basic situation of Chick's imminent death.

Here starts the Cover Scene:

DISSOLVE TO CU OF LINDA IN LIVING ROOM. SHE IS
SITTING IN A STRAIGHT-BACK CHAIR IN FRONT OF THE
TELEPHONE. SHE IS STIFF, TENSE, STARING AT THE
INSTRUMENT AS THOUGH IT WERE ABOUT TO COME
ALIVE ANY MINUTE. PULL BACK FOR LONGER SHOT
OF ROOM. THE CRIB IS AGAINST THE WALL, THE
BABY ASLEEP. ELLEN APPEARS IN DOORWAY
FOLLOWED BY CHICK. THEY TAKE OFF THEIR COATS
AND HATS AS THEY COME FORWARD.

ELLEN

Linda! What on earth are you doing?

And so on, into the scene. The Cover Scene is the brief, interesting shot of Linda crouched by the telephone, and it served its
purpose of allowing Chick and Ellen to reach the living room set
from the hallway set.

In principle, this simple scene illustrates *all* cover scenes,
according to our definition.

One variation, used frequently, is to hold the camera in CLOSE-UP
on one character, while a second character, to whom the first
presumably is talking, slips away into position on another set for
the next scene. Meantime, the first character has kept on talking
as if the second character were there all the time. For example:

MED. CLOSE SHOT:
A LUXURIOUS LIVING ROOM. MAE, IN CLINGING
NEGLIGEE, IS WEEPING AS SHE BESEECHES FARLEY
NOT TO LEAVE HER.

MAE

Darling, you can't go! I've given you everything!

FARLEY

All but love. You've tried to buy me.

MAE

That's not true! All this — luxury — was meant
only as a proper setting for our romance —

FARLEY

It stifles me. I can't work.

MAE (WORKING UP A RAGE)
If you go, I'll destroy it — I'll destroy myself!
FARLEY
You're a vain, jealous woman unable to face the
truth!
CUT TO CLOSE-UP OF MAE.

(At this point, the actor playing Farley hurries over to the next
set for the next scene, while Mae keeps on talking. Of course, the
audience doesn't see Farley go, because the camera is CLOSE-UP on
Mae. The illusion is complete that Farley is still there listening.)

MAE (IN CLOSE-UP)
You ungrateful, thankless wretch! I've faced the
truth that you can't compose music, and I've
continued to provide you with a luxurious home
while you waste your time — and my money!
Why should I do this — why? Only because I
love you —
(SHE RETREATS A LITTLE) No — don't come near me
— keep away from me — go to that common
little girl who's taken you away from me!
DISSOLVE
MED. CLOSE SHOT: MABEL'S BEDROOM.
FARLEY SITS ON THE EDGE OF THE BED, HIS HEAD IN
HIS HANDS. MABEL STANDS OVER HIM PROTECTINGLY.
And so on, into the scene.

The Cover Scene here, the Transition, is Mae's long, climactic
speech which is so written (e.g., her warning: "Don't come near
me!") that as played, the illusion would be complete that Farley
is listening, when actually he has slipped away to the next set for
the next scene. And Mae's speech certainly advances the plot,
since she in effect sends Farley away to her rival.

It should be obvious that, by reversing the excluding process,
more time can be gained for Farley. Say, for instance, that he is
wearing a lounging robe in his scene with Mae, and has to put on
a suit, topcoat and hat for his scene with Mabel. The playwright

then would start the Mabel scene with a CLOSE-UP on Mabel, as follows:

DISSOLVE
CLOSE SHOT OF MABEL, IN HER BEDROOM. SHE SPEAKS
TO FARLEY

[He is not there, mind you, but is busy putting on his pants.]

MABEL (PASSIONATELY)
Oh, Farley! you've come to me, at last you've come! Darling, I've been waiting for you, it seems forever! Don't ever leave me — don't *ever* leave me again!

[Actually, she'll wait — and speak — only long enough for the actor playing Farley to change costume and get into position.]

SHE MOVES FORWARD AS THE CAMERA PULLS BACK,
REVEALING FARLEY ADVANCING TO MEET HER
WITH OPENED ARMS. THEY EMBRACE.

The actor playing Farley now has the time needed for Mae's climactic speech, *plus* the time required for Mabel's welcoming speech, to move from one set to another, and to make possible costume changes.

Still another way to allow more time for possible make-up or costume change on the part of Farley is to let Mabel speak her lines and play a scene with Farley, while Farley speaks into a microphone out of scene, as the wardrobe technician assists him in his costume change. For example:

DISSOLVE
CLOSE SHOT OF MABEL, IN HER BEDROOM. THERE
IS THE SOUND OF A DOOR SLAMMING. SHE TURNS
AROUND, STARTLED, LOOKS AT FARLEY, OUT OF
SCENE, SPEAKS.

MABEL

Darling!

FARLEY (OFF CAMERA, SPEAKING INTO A
MICROPHONE, WHILE HE CHANGES COSTUME)

Dearest, don't move! I want to remember you like
this — with the light in your hair!

MABEL

You've come — to stay?

FARLEY (OFF CAMERA)

Don't ask me questions for a while. Just let me rest,
looking at you, at the love in your eyes.

MABEL

It shines only for you.

FARLEY (OFF CAMERA)

I believe that now — I'll believe it even though
my wife keeps trying to poison my mind against
you.

MABEL

What mind *I* have is yours.

SHE ADVANCES TOWARD THE CAMERA, WHICH PULLS
BACK AHEAD OF HER TO A MEDIUM SHOT AS FARLEY
ADVANCES INTO THE SCENE . . . . . MEETS MABEL,
AND THEY EMBRACE.

Now the actor playing Farley has available for his movement
and costume change the time needed for Mae's climactic speech,
plus the time required by Mabel's welcoming speech, *plus* the
time required for the playing of the little scene when Farley is off-
camera, but *not* off-mike.

The technique of the camera excluding a character (in this case,
Farley) also is done regularly by PANNING to an object, frequently
a clock, and holding on it briefly, when we DISSOLVE into a MATCH-
ING SHOT of a second clock indicating the passing of time. This is
called a MATCHED DISSOLVE, and it is a device beloved by writers
and directors, who are apt to employ a fresh rose instead of a clock,
DISSOLVING from the fresh rose onto a faded one, to denote the
passing of time artistically. And — ho hum — we are familiar
with the fluttering leaves of the calendar which can flutter away a

day or ten years of time with no trouble at all. Oh, writers, find a
new time elapse device, if you can!

The point is: by *excluding* the actors through PANNING to a clock
or a rose, or whatever, the camera allows these actors to scurry
away into position for the next scene, if they are in it.

An effective MATCHED DISSOLVE used particularly for heavily
dramatic or "psychological" plays is DISTORT. In this technique,
the lens of the camera is so manipulated that the image seen by
the audience literally becomes distorted — blurred, twisted, out
of focus — until the next scene dissolves into view, through a
MATCHED DISSOLVE, and a similar distorting of the lens of the
camera photographing the *new* scene becomes clear as the new
scene opens and progresses.

Transitions in Filmed Television Plays

The only Time affecting television plays filmed for telecast is
all-over Time. Since each scene is made separately in a filmed
television play, movement from one set to another is not a consideration, nor are costume and make-up changes.

Transitions Through the Technique of a Photographic Montage

The dictionary defines "montage" as "a series of scenes, each of
extreme brevity, following in rapid succession, used to present a
stream of inter-connected ideas". This definition is specifically
given, as "montage" applies to motion pictures, and therefore, to
television.

In television, a "montage" not only indicates and covers a time
lapse both visually and aurally, but it also can and should advance
the plot. Usually, a montage shows action perhaps not too interesting and dramatic in itself but which is vitally necessary to
telling the story and so to advancing the plot. Following is a
montage from *The D. O. Basket*. Walt, Lavy's husband, has taken
to his bed with a bad cold. It's necessary to show Lavy's unceasing
care of him, together with the result of this arduous effort both on
her and on him. This double result is an important plot development.

LAVY LEANS OVER WALT, AS HE LIES IN BED. HE PULLS
HER DOWN AND KISSES HER. SHE CLINGS TO HIM.

WALT

Darling!

LAVY (WHISPERING)

I'm glad you did that. Now we'll die together.

WALT

Don't be silly. I'm getting good and warm. Believe
I can sleep. Why don't you trot along, and have
the house nice and straight when I get up, so that
we'll be *well* together?

SHE PULLS AWAY FROM HIM IN SUDDEN IRRITATION,
SINCE HE HAS TOUCHED HER SORE POINT . . . HER
HORRID UNTIDINESS. HE DOESN'T NOTICE, TURNS
AWAY, SAYS SLEEPILY . . . . .

WALT

Your fur coat did the trick. I'm very glad, dear,
that your fur coat has appeared only *twice* in the
D.O. Basket. Now, run along.

LAVY BACKS AWAY FROM HIM. SHE IS TORN BETWEEN
FURY AND PITY — FOR HERSELF. FURY WINS. SHE
STOOPS, PICKS UP A NAVAJO RUG FROM THE FLOOR,
STALKS TO THE CHAISE LONGUE, FLINGS THE RUG
ONTO IT, STRAIGHTENS IT OUT SAVAGELY, PLUMPS
HERSELF DOWN ON IT, SITS GLARING AT WALT,
WHO IS OUT OF SCENE. FROM HIS DIRECTION COME
GENTLE SNORES.

DISSOLVE INTO A MONTAGE . . . MUSIC UNDERNEATH

1. LAVY'S HANDS STIRRING MILK AS IT HEATS IN A
   PAN ON AN ELECTRIC BURNER

LAVY'S VOICE (OVER MUSIC)

Yes, dear! Coming, dear!

2. LAVY'S HANDS SQUEEZING A MOUNTAIN OF CUT
   ORANGES

LAVY'S VOICE (OVER MUSIC)

Yes, dear! In *just* a moment!

3. LAVY'S HANDS POURING OUT A CUP OF COFFEE

LAVY'S VOICE (OVER MUSIC)

Yes, dear! (A PRODIGIOUS YAWN) No, dear, I
didn't say anything — I'm just so *sleepy!*

(END OF MONTAGE . . . MUSIC OUT)

DISSOLVE INTO

THE BEDROOM. LAVY IS ASLEEP ON THE CHAISE
LONGUE, IN A PAIR OF WALT'S HEAVY PAJAMAS.
BRIGHT SUNLIGHT STREAMING IN. SHE AWAKES WITH
A START AS WALT COMES INTO THE SCENE, TYING
HIS TIE. SHE SITS UP, ATTEMPTS TO GET OFF THE
CHAISE LONGUE. HE GENTLY PUSHES HER BACK DOWN.

WALT

No, dear. I'm well. I'm going to the office.

LAVY

I'll fix your breakfast.

WALT

Already had it. Why don't you spend the day in
bed and get caught up?

HE KISSES HER ON THE NECK, BELOW AN EAR. SHE
CATCHES HIS HAND.

LAVY

Walt, *are* you — ?

WALT (CUTTING)

I said I was well. I'll be glad when *you* are.

LAVY

Why, Walt, it was nothing, looking after you. I
loved doing it.

WALT

Thank you, dear. I'll be glad when *you're* well.
Come down in the late afternoon and we'll
have dinner out. Now, hop into bed —

HE HELPS HER OFF THE CHAISE LONGUE AND THEY
MOVE TOWARD THE BED. SHE CLIMBS IN. HE
GRABS HER ARM.

WALT

You ought to change the linen!

LAVY

Walt, dear, I'm not afraid of *you!*

WALT (SOBERLY)

May you never be.

LAVY

What a strange remark —

WALT

Go to sleep, my beloved little Lavy.

HE STOOPS AND KISSES HER. SHE CLOSES HER EYES,
SNUGGLES UNDER THE COVERS. HE STRAIGHTENS UP.

WALT (WHISPERING)

My untidy little Lavy!

LAVY (HALF ASLEEP)

What did you say?

WALT

Never mind. (WHISPER) You'll find out — soon
enough, I'm afraid.

DISSOLVE

First, note, most importantly of all, that "Lavy's hands" are
specified in the Montage. Well, gentle reader, *these are not the
hands of the actress playing Lavy:* They are the hands of a
double. The actress playing Lavy is busy changing into the pair
of Walt's pajamas, during the Montage. This device of *doubling* —
hands, feet, backs of heads, etc., etc., is one of the most useful ever
devised for Time Lapses and Montages. And while the actress
playing Lavy *speaks* over the Montage, she speaks into a microphone set up at the spot where she is changing costume, out of
scene, obviously. So, as long as the actor's *face* does not have to
be seen ON CAMERA, a double can do whatever has to be done in
the MONTAGE.

We've carried the scene above on past the Montage for two
reasons: first, having seen Lavy's loving care of Walt (in the Montage), we are both incensed and interested by his implied threat
to her in the little scene right after the Montage; so, the Montage
served the purpose of advancing the story; second, Walt is in the
scene immediately following the one above, and the device of
DOUBLING permits the actor playing Walt to get from the bedroom
set to the set where Walt is selling Lavy's fur coat. The dialogue
you're about to read follows *immediately* after the DISSOLVE in
the bedroom.

DISSOLVE

CLOSE-UP . . . WALT'S HANDS . . . MUSIC UNDERNEATH

WALT IS UNWRAPPING LAVY'S FUR COAT FROM
HEAVY PAPER . . . CAMERA STAYS ON COAT.
> WOMAN'S VOICE

About two hundred, I'd say.
> WALT'S VOICE

It cost *five* hundred!
> WOMAN'S VOICE

But, sir, a second-hand fur coat —
> WALT'S VOICE

Is that the best you can do?
> WOMAN'S VOICE (SUDDENLY)

You're sure it isn't *stolen?*
> WALT'S VOICE

Certainly not! Of course, it isn't mine, but I *paid*
for it!

THE FUR COAT IS PICKED UP AND SHAKEN OUT
> WOMAN'S VOICE

Well, don't get your back up, mister!
> WALT'S VOICE

Lady, if you only knew — my back *is* up!

DISSOLVE

A final note: if there happened to be any problem in the studio
layout of the sets which might prevent the actor playing Walt
from moving from the bedroom set to the sale of the fur coat in
time, these voices in the sale scene could be recorded *in advance*,
completely eliminating any possible Time problem in the Transition.

Also, the sale scene could be (in fact, *was*, when *The D.O.
Basket* was produced) played in LIMBO (no set), with the fur coat
lying on a table which would be (and was) the only prop visible
ON CAMERA.

In the following is another Montage, using recorded voices, and
then going on into action in which *no voices* are heard. It isn't
necessary to use voices at the end of this Montage, because the
intent of the Montage is sufficiently established in the beginning
of the Montage. This Montage is from *Red Tape*, by Martha
Fulton, produced on Armstrong's Circle Theatre.

In *Red Tape,* Marge is the mother of a youngster who rides a
bus to school. The bus has a bad tire, and Marge has attempted
to get it changed. She is incensed by the red tape she encounters,
and finally decides to organize a boycott of the school bus, until
the bad tire is replaced. Hence, the Montage is *absolutely vital*
to the plot, to the advancing of the story, and its use *saves Time*
enormously, through conveying the idea of Marge's several telephone calls, but without going into the repetitious detail of showing each telephone call realistically.

During the following photo-Montage, the bad tire is superimposed in the background.

FILM — WHEELS AND FEET —
SUPER WOMAN ON PHONE — TAKE OUT FEET
FILM — LEAVE WHEELS.

> MARGE (ON FILTER, RECORDED)

Agnes . . . this is Marge Dudley. I'm getting up
a motor pool to take the kids to school. The bus
really isn't safe, because . . . . . .

DISSOLVE TO WOMAN IN LIMBO, PHONE TO EAR,
NODDING AND WRITING ON PAD. MARGE'S VOICE
CONTINUES OVER.
CUT TO MARGE.

> MARGE'S VOICE (ON FILTER, RECORDED)

In spite of everything I could do the school system
refuses to do anything about the tire. So it seems
like it's up to *us* . . . . . .

CUT TO ANOTHER SUBURBAN HOUSEWIFE REACHING
TO PICK UP HER PHONE WHICH IS RINGING.

> MARGE'S VOICE (ON FILTER, RECORDED)

Now let's see . . . . . I thought if you'd take your
two, and Bill Bronson and Mary Stanford . . .
and could you call . . .

CUT TO HAND DIALING A NUMBER.
CUT TO ANOTHER HAND REACHING TO PICK UP PHONE.
DISSOLVE TO FILM — WHIRLING TIRE.
FADE OUT.

From these two examples of MONTAGES, which constitute TRANSITIONS and TIME LAPSES both, we can deduce the following principle:

When it is necessary to show Action which is vital to the advancing of the story, and which usually involves a Time Lapse, and which very likely would be repetitious if shown in realistic detail, use a MONTAGE. A Montage can be done visually only (but with music underneath it) or it can be done with either "live" or recorded voices, and it can, if necessary, employ doubles for the principal actors as long as these principals' faces do not have to be seen. Finally, a MONTAGE *could* be done against LIMBO (Black Screen) with *only* voices, although this type of Montage probably would not hold attention for more than a few seconds; and unless the play is a stylized one, it should always be possible to find some visual action (even if it be only a newspaper headline) for the audience to see, while it hears the voices.

Montages, of course, are used as frequently in filmed television plays as they are in "live". The *development of the story* is what sets up the *need* for a Montage, not the *method* of producing that story ("live" or filmed). All of us have seen countless Montages in motion pictures, where the technique originated, and we have heard them on radio equally often.

An adroit use of Time, therefore, means that you have all the elements of your plot so arranged as to present the utmost in drama that your story provides. Difficulties with Time in your script may mean (1) that you are trying to tell *too much* in the all-over Time period; or (2) that you have *too little to tell*, that you have not yet found the heart of your material, its climactic peak; or (3) that you have not attacked your material (begun your play) at the right instant of piled-up situation which will create by its inner tensions the climax and resolution you are aiming for.

Category (1) is a common occurrence in inept television plays written to be filmed. Category (2) will bring you second-act trouble in the half-hour play, and third-act trouble in a three-act play, because you run out of story. Category (3) will bring you a diffuse, rambling structure likely to fall of its own faults into the "narrative" pitfall, meaning many little scenes which end before they get started, and resulting in frustration for the viewer who likes to settle in and watch a firm, tightly-knit unit of your play get underway and go places.

As in life, Time on television is inexorable; in life, Time waits for no man, and on television, no man will wait for Time, if you have bungled its supreme functions in the plays you write for telecasting.

6

Exposition

THE OVERLORD OF TELEVISION, Time, rules despotically in the realm of Exposition. Because of their need to get the facts of the play told to the viewers as rapidly and as directly as possible, television playwrights have resorted to every technique known to stage dramaturgy, and they have taken over from radio and motion pictures some additional ones.

In spoken exposition, the prologue, the aside, the monologue, the narrator have been added to the conventional stage play technique of the butler and the maid talking about the lady of the house, who then makes her entrance into the situation her servants (and the playwrights) have set up. From motion pictures, legitimately enough, visual exposition has been borrowed. From radio come sound effects, the "echo chamber", and the "filter", devices firmly established, and accepted by viewers as standard operating procedure by the television playwright in his briefing audiences on the situation, and often the characters, of the drama about to be unfolded.

But most important of all, Time has forced into use what may be the *best* method of exposition in the writing of plays for television. It's this: *The sooner the principal characters come on camera and carry the burden of their own exposition — in action, through illustrative incidents which set the situation, start the plot going, and characterize the people — the better the television play is.*

There isn't *time* for the butler and the maid, or the next door neighbors, to talk about the heroine of the play, setting up the situation she will walk into. Let the lady appear at the Fade-In and play a scene with the butler or the maid or the neighbors, if any one of them is legitimately a part of the story; let her give *her own* exposition! If the butler and/or the maid and/or the neighbors are *not* a legitimate part of the story, involved indispensably in the plot, let the lady talk to some one who is! This "some one" *should* be another of the principals of the story.

No doubt the technique of talking about principal characters before they appear has lingered on partly because stage stars love "entrances" and not infrequently they demand them. If a star is discovered on stage when the curtain rises, she is apt to be an unhappy star, or at least faintly miserable, although her total role may be fat to the point of obesity. She *still* hasn't had that "entrance", that build-up accomplished by old-fashioned exposition, when she sweeps onto the stage, while everything stops and the audience applauds its love and admiration. So stage playwrights write exposition which talks about the situation and the star; then she (or he) enters.

Let it be pointed out to stars of television plays that an entrance on television is not the same as an entrance on the stage, and that what is to be coveted is to be in front of the camera as *long* as possible. The best chance to achieve this aim is to be in front of the camera the instant the opening scene Fades-In; and a star, or the principal actor of a television play, can do that only if the television playwright has so constructed his play that it is *necessary* for the principals to be on hand, when the opening scene Fades-In.

This is not flippancy, this minor digression on the habits of stage stars. A serious point is to be made: *Time* is controlling your television play inexorably; the principal characters *should* be in front of the camera as long as possible, consistent with the telling of the story. Therefore the television playwright must justify their presence; and the way to do it is to let them carry the burden of the exposition. Of course, it may be a lot harder than the conventional butler-and-maid-and-neighbors technique, but the reward is that the television play will be a lot better, through immediate interest in the principal characters as they are seen in the dramatic situation they will play out to the end.

Example: Exposition in Action, with the Principals on Camera at Fade-in
       (from *The D.O. Basket,* by Edward Barry Roberts)

OPENING SHOT:

FADE IN: FULL SHOT: THE KINDERLING LIVING ROOM.
WALT SITS IN A COMFORTABLE CHAIR, HIDDEN
BEHIND THE SPORTS SECTION OF THE NEWSPAPER.
LAVINIA ENTERS, IN A FUR COAT AND HAT, CARRYING
HER BAG, BUT WITHOUT GLOVES. SHE IS YOUNG
AND ATTRACTIVE. SHE GOES TO THE BOOKCASE,
CONSULTS THE TITLES BRIEFLY, PULLS OUT A BOOK,
LOOKS BEHIND IT, FEELING IN THE SPACE . . . PUTS THE
BOOK ON TOP OF THE BOOKCASE.

LAVINIA

Walt, dear —

WALT

Um. . . .

LAVINIA

Walt, dear, I *was* reading "Human Sacrifice in
Ancient America" last night, wasn't I?

WALT

Ummmm. . . .

LAVINIA

I thought so, but it was put back in the bookcase,
and I was sure *I* had put it under the bed just
before I went to sleep. So I wasn't sure.

SHE PUTS HER BAG ON THE COUCH. WALT'S
NEWSPAPER QUIVERS. LAVINIA GOES TO THE SLANT-
TOP DESK, OPENS IT JUST A LITTLE AND FEELS INSIDE.

LAVINIA

Oh, dear.

SHE GIVES THE TOP A LITTLE PUSH, TO CLOSE IT.
IT FALLS OPEN AND A MASS OF THINGS BEGINS TO
OOZE OUT.

LAVINIA

Oh, my!

SHE STARTS TO MOVE ON, BUT HER EYE IS CAUGHT.

LAVINIA

Oh, *good!*

SHE TAKES A SCARF FROM THE HEAP.

LAVINIA

My red scarf. It's been lost for ages.

NO SIGN FROM WALT. LAVINIA TAKES THE SCARF
WITH HER TO THE MAGAZINE RACK, STUFFS IT
LIGHTLY INTO ONE SECTION, WHILE SHE PULLS OUT
THE MAGAZINES ONTO THE FLOOR. SHE PEERS IN.

LAVINIA

Oh, dear.

SHE RISES, LEAVING THE MAGAZINES ON THE FLOOR.
WALT LOWERS HIS PAPER. WE SEE HIM FOR THE
FIRST TIME . . . . A HANDSOME, GLOWERING YOUNG
HUSBAND.

WALT

The magazines.

LAVINIA

Dear, which one do you want? I'll bring it to you.

WALT

Don't want one — just put 'em back.

LAVINIA

I will, dear, soon as I find my gloves.

WALT

Which gloves?

LAVINIA

My black ones. *Do* you?

WALT

Do I what?

LAVINIA

I think you're a cruel husband, if you do know, and
won't tell me. I can't go to church without them.
Won't *you* come to church, Walt?

WALT

No church spirit in my heart. I can't stand the way
people leave the hymn books scattered on the
seats.

LAVINIA

What a *silly* excuse! But *do* you know?

WALT

Lavinia, where *should* your gloves be?

LAVINIA

Why — (SHE PAUSES, THINKS, BEAMS) Walt, you're a lamb!

SHE EXITS. WALT COMES TO THE MAGAZINE RACK, TOUCHES THE MAGAZINES ON THE FLOOR WITH THE TOE OF HIS SHOE. SUDDENLY HE STRAIGHTENS, LISTENS INTENTLY, LOOKING IN THE DIRECTION LAVY WENT. SHE COMES BACK, WITH THE GLOVES. HE WALKS AWAY FROM HER TO THE WINDOW. SHE STANDS DRAWING ON THE GLOVES.

LAVINIA (SERIOUSLY)

Walt, I'm worried about you.

WALT

The magazines — you didn't put 'em back.

LAVINIA

I *will*, dear. Right after church. Before I get dinner. And will you please see if the meat grinder walked into your tool chest? I'll need it, if we're to have tamale loaf. I forgot to ask the butcher to grind the meat. You *love* tamale loaf, but without the meat grinder —

WALT (CUTTING IN)

I didn't hear you close the dresser drawer. Did you?

LAVINIA

The dresser drawer?

WALT

The gloves.

LAVINIA

Well, what difference does it make? I'll close it when I put the gloves back.

WALT SLASHES SAVAGELY AT THE DRAPES WITH HIS PAPER. LAVY RUNS TO HIM.

LAVINIA

Walt, are you all right?

SHE TURNS HIM AROUND TO FACE HER.

LAVINIA

I *am* worried, dear. Lately, you've taken
unimportant things much too seriously. If I
didn't know how kind you are, I'd say you're
becoming a martinet. Dear, *do* read what the
psychiatrists say about people who are too exact.
Next thing you know, you'll be washing the
doorknobs before you touch them.

WALT

Good idea. I'll do it while you're at church.

SHE STEPS AWAY FROM HIM

LAVINIA

Walt Kinderling, we've been married eleven
months and that's the first time you've been rude.

WALT (BROKENLY)

Why not — why *not* — why *not* close a dresser
drawer?

LAVINIA

But I *will*, darling, when I put the gloves away.
I'd just have to open it again if I did it now.
Will it hurt anything if the drawer stays open till
I get back from church?

WALT WALKS AWAY, BACK TO THE MAGAZINE RACK,
STANDS LOOKING DOWN AT IT. LAVINIA FOLLOWS
HIM.

LAVINIA

Walt, either *things* run *you*, or *you* run *things*. I,
for one, do not propose to have my life dominated
by magazines, or dresser drawers, or — or —
(SILENCE) I *know* they're horribly orderly in the
Navy, but I'm not in the Navy and you're not
either, any more, and this is a home and life is to
be lived, not arranged in neat piles.

SHE GOES TO THE DOOR. HE DOESN'T MOVE OR
LOOK UP.

LAVINIA

Goodbye, dear.

SHE GOES OUT. HE STOOPS, STARTS PUTTING THE
MAGAZINES BACK IN THE RACK. SHE RETURNS.

LAVINIA

Dearest, I can't find my set of car keys. May I
borrow yours, just this once?

WITH A GHASTLY SMILE, WALT TAKES HIS KEY RING
OUT, DETACHES THE CAR KEYS, GIVES THEM TO HER.
SHE TAKES THEM, REACHES UP SWIFTLY, KISSES
HIM FULL ON THE MOUTH, TURNS, RUNS OUT.
HE TAKES A STEP TOWARD HER, STOPS, SAVAGELY
KICKS THE MAGAZINES, AS WE . . . . FADE OUT.

In this example from *The D. O. Basket,* both principal characters are on camera at the first FADE IN. In visual exposition the
FULL SHOT sets the locale, is the "geography shot," telling us where
the scene is. Action begins at once, rather peculiar action, with a
tantalizing aspect, to intrigue interest; almost at once the conflict
is set through Walt's reaction to Lavinia's untidiness, a reaction
which builds with the repetition of this characteristic, repetition
which at the same time is greatly varied, through the choice of
incident to illustrate the characteristic. The principals are being
characterized, through their diametrically opposed reaction to the
incidents, and the story is underway. We are told the background
facts; how long they've been married, their habits, their essentially
tender and idyllic relationship; but at the same time, the deep conflict between them is set up by the end of this one short opening
scene. We feel that the story will concern what Walt will do about
Lavinia's habits; and we know that she will fight him to the last
ditch, in a loving way, since she comes out clearly and states her
point of view (a logical statement, not dragged in by the heels).
Finally, this *has* to be a television script, because the indispensable
action is visual, not spoken dialogue. *To conclude:* each character in this excerpt is carrying his or her own exposition *given
in action.*

Example Two (from *High Steel* by Stewart Pierce Brown). Watch out for the exposition given visually, by sound effects, by lighting effects, by props, as well as spoken exposition given by the principals who are on camera from the opening fade-in of the live action.

OPENING SHOT:
A SIGN WHICH READS:

THE GIBSON-SMITH TOWER
A MODERN 85-STORY OFFICE BUILDING
BEING ERECTED BY THE KENT CONSTRUCTION CO.
NEW YORK, NEW YORK

DOLLY IN TIGHT CU, "THE KENT CONSTR. CO."
DOLLY BACK TO REVEAL SIGN ON FOREMAN'S SHACK
IN SHADOW OF BEAMS AND GIRDERS OF SKYSCRAPER.
SOUND: (FLUSH WITH OPENING) RIVET GUNS,
WHIRRING WINCHES, CLANG OF HEAVY METAL,
MEN'S SHOUTS, ETC.
THE END OF A GIANT I-BEAM PASSES ACROSS FRONT OF
SHACK AND BEGINS SLOW ASCENT. AS IT GOES UP
OUT OF FRAME AN ELDERLY, WHITE-HAIRED MAN
STEPS OUT OF SHACK AND WATCHES IT DISAPPEAR.
ALMOST IMMEDIATELY HE IS JOINED BY TWO
YOUNGER MEN, BEN AND TOM. BEN CARRIES A SHEAF
OF PLANS AND BLUEPRINTS.

TOM
Hey, Pop, your mouth's open.

POP
Yeah, I know — I opened it.

TOM
Somebody's going to drop a hot rivet in there if you're not careful.

BEN (INDICATING BEAM ABOVE)
Is that it?

POP
The last one . . . all the way up to the 85th floor. They'll be putting her in tomorrow.

TOM
A day ahead of schedule. Good for us, I think we're terrific.

POP (GOOD-NATUREDLY)

Huh! A fat lot of good you did!

TOM

What do you mean? Why, this modern 85-story office building would be a modern 3-story office building if it weren't for my boys and me.

POP

(TO BEN, WHO HAS BEEN WATCHING BEAM ASCEND)

You going on up there to put her in tomorrow, Ben?

BEN (FROWNING)

Well — ah, no — no, I'm not. I — I've got to be on the fourth level tomorrow, with the electricians. (POP AND TOM EXCHANGE A GLANCE)

TOM

I'll do that for you, Ben. I'll stay down there and you —

BEN (CUTS)

No, that's okay — I'll see the electricians — you go on up. (LOOKS AT WATCH) As a matter of fact, I better see them now, before quitting time. I'll see you later. (HE EXITS)

TOM (DISAPPOINTED)

Yeah, sure . . . I'll see you. (A METAL GATE CLANGS SHUT AND THE ELEVATOR WINCH WHIRS, OFF R.)

POP

The fourth level! He hasn't been any higher than that for a week. What's the matter with him? You're his friend — can't you talk to him or something?

TOM (SHRUGS)

What can you say?

POP

The men are saying plenty.

TOM

They think he's yellow?

POP

I don't know if they've gone that far yet, but they sure are losing respect for him. That ain't good,

Tom. (THEY ENTER SHACK AND POP BUSIES
HIMSELF SORTING BLUEPRINTS ON THE LONG DESK
TABLE) For a guy who wants to be top man on his
next assignment, that ain't good.

                    TOM (THOUGHTFULLY)
He really *does* want to head up that next job . . .

                    POP
So does Mac — and you don't see *him* sitting
around on the fourth level. (CROSSES TO WINDOW)
Come here — look at that guy.

CUT TO FILM CLIP:

BEAM SLOWLY ASCENDING SIDE OF BUILDING —
IMPRESSION OF GREAT HEIGHT.

CUT TO:

CU MAC, STANDING ON BEAM AS IT ASCENDS,
SIGNALLING WITH FREE HAND. HE LOOKS COCKY
AND COMPETENT.

CUT BACK TO INTERIOR OF SHACK:

POP AND TOM

                    POP
Now, Ben used to be that way, too. I've seen him
climbing up there like a human fly. Now . . .
(SHRUGS)

                    TOM
Pop, you know as well as I do, what's the matter.
He saw Pete fall.

To catalogue the exposition given in several ways in the preceding example: *Visually:* The sign sets the locale, the scene,
directly and completely. *Sound effects:* the rivet guns, the whirring winches, the clang of heavy metal, the men shouting, all
indicate that construction of the building announced by the sign
is in full swing. *Lighting effects:* the shadows of the skeleton
beams and girders across the set tell us the stage of construction
the building has reached. *Props:* the moving end of the giant
I-beam strikes a dramatic note, begins to set the tenseness of the
situation soon to be given in spoken exposition. Also, the props
carried by Ben (sheaf of blueprints and plans) help to set him as

an engineer. *Spoken exposition:* by two principal characters (Tom and Ben) and a principal supporting character (Pop) both characterizes the speakers and sets a suspenseful situation: the placing of the last heavy beam on the eighty-fifth floor. The story is strongly underway when Ben, by his reaction to the suggestion that he will be on the eighty-fifth floor, makes us suspect him of possible cowardice, for which we are inclined to pity him, since he is an attractive, strong character. So much, therefore, is accomplished in this beginning through so many different ways of giving exposition, that it is a model of its kind.

So far, and in some detail, we have seen the most usual methods of Exposition: exposition given by the principal characters in a play; and visual and aural exposition. These are perhaps the methods you will use most frequently. Following are samples of unique techniques of Exposition, usually identified with a particular program, such as Robert Montgomery Presents. These methods are, however, perfectly capable of adaptation for any program, within the choice of the playwright and/or the producer of a program for which he is writing.

Narrator
(From *Maquisard,* by Irving Gaynor Neiman, based on a novel by Albert J. Guerard, and presented by Robert Montgomery on "Your Lucky Strike Theatre.")

MR. MONTGOMERY (THE NARRATOR) STANDS BEFORE
A HEAVY OUTLINE DRAWING OF A MAP OF FRANCE
WITH BATTLE LINE INDICATIONS AS OF THE BATTLE
OF THE BULGE. NEAR BORDEAUX IS AN INDICATION
OF THE ORILLON POCKET. . . . AND THE LOCATION,
NEARBY, OF SOGNAC.
                    MONTGOMERY
We are in the little town of Sognac, France, and it
is three days before Christmas, 1944.
(INDICATES ON MAP)
The liberating armies have swept far to the East . . .
. . . and the only Germans remaining on French

soil are bottled up in small pockets along the
coast, for future disposal.
(INDICATES ON MAP)
Free French forces, made up of the Maquis,
weary fighters of the underground, have held
Orillon pocket for months. Now, fresh, mecha-
nized American troops have moved in for the final
operation. (BEAT . . . *meaning* A PAUSE)
DISSOLVE TO:
PHOTO OF FRENCH TOWN AND PAN ROOFTOPS.
        MONTGOMERY (CONT'D)
This is the little town of Sognac, France,
threatened by the Germans five miles to the west
. . . but Christmas is just three days away . . . .
and every one knows that Christmas can bring
happy miracles. . . .
DISSOLVE TO:
MADAME MARCEL'S CAFE IN SOGNAC. . . . THIS IS THE
MAJOR SET. . . . THE BAR HAS SEVERAL PEOPLE IN
IT, AND THE ATMOSPHERE IS GENERALLY GAY.

And so on, into the play itself. Sometimes, such a Narrator appears several times during the course of a single Act, to bridge
time lapses and scene changes with a summation of intervening
action. In *Maquisard*, Mr. Montgomery appears again at the start
of Act II and of Act III to set the scene and give the Exposition —
not only the events that have happened "between the Acts," but
also hints of events the audience may expect to happen. Radio
writers will recognize this familiar technique, which also has been
used on the legitimate stage, notably in Thornton Wilder's *Our
Town.* The Narrator is a "special" technique, and it is not generally
recommended for usual practice by a free lance writer unless he is
so requested by an editor or a producer.

Pre-recorded (Stream of Consciousness)
(From *Mr. Bemiss Takes a Trip,* by William
   Dudley, produced on Armstrong's Circle Theatre)
OPEN ON CLOSE-UP OF SMALL DOOR SIGN

READING "ROOMS AND BOARD".
CUT TO VESTIBULE OF BOARDING HOUSE,
SHOWING FOOT OF STAIRS AND ONE OF THOSE
MARBLE-TOPPED VICTORIAN MONSTROSITIES WHOSE
EXTRA-LARGE OVAL MIRROR IS SURROUNDED BY
VARNISHED COWS' HORNS, OSTENSIBLY FOR
HOLDING HATS.
ON THE MARBLE-TOP THE MORNING MAIL IS STREWN.
PERRY BEMISS COMES DOWN THE STAIRS, WEARING
A TOPCOAT AND CARRYING HIS HAT. PERRY IS A
NICE-LOOKING MAN IN HIS VAGUE THIRTIES WHO
BEARS THE MANTLE OF HUMILITY WITH UNOBTRU-
SIVE GRACE. WHEN THE MEEK INHERIT THE EARTH,
HE WILL UNDOUBTEDLY BE A PRIME MINISTER, BUT
UNTIL THEN HE IS THE CLASSIC EXAMPLE OF THE MAN
NO ONE WOULD NOTICE IN A CROWD.
HE APPROACHES THE MARBLE-TOP CURIOUSLY, AND
WITH AN EXPRESSION OF GENTLE HOPE FINGERS THE
STREWN LETTERS. THEN HE CATCHES SIGHT OF
HIMSELF IN THE MIRROR, REALIZES HE IS SLOUCHING,
SQUARES HIS SHOULDERS, FAVORS HIMSELF WITH A
BRAVE SMILE, THEN GOES BACK TO THE LETTERS.
HE PICKS ONE UP.
CUT TO:
ENVELOPE ADDRESSED:
    MR. CHARLES GIBBS
    547 WEST 49TH ST. CITY.
CUT TO:
PERRY, ESSAYING A SNEER
PERRY (VOICE OVER)

VOICE OVER means that Perry's voice is heard, while his lips do not move. This is the "pre-recorded, stream of consciousness" technique of exposition, and also of the "aside," as will be seen later. "Pre-recorded" means that the actor previously has spoken these lines into a recording machine, lines which are played back when required. So, actually, VOICE OVER here means Perry's thoughts.

Charlie Gibbs! Big oaf. (LOOKS DAUNTLESSLY AT
HIS REFLECTION IN THE MIRROR) That's what I
said — *oaf!* And I'll say it to your face, by golly!
(WIGGLES HIS HEAD DECISIVELY, AND ADDS) . . . . .
some day.
PUTS DOWN THE LETTER, THUMBS THROUGH A FEW
MORE, PICKS ONE UP.
CUT TO: ENVELOPE ADDRESSED:
    MISS FAY CARTWRIGHT
    547 WEST 49TH ST. CITY.
PERRY SIGHS A MOONCALF SIGH
          PERRY (SOFTLY, VOICE OVER)
Fay. What a beautiful name. (ADDRESSES HIS
REFLECTION) Miss Cartwright . . . Fay . . . I
realize I have no right to say this — but you're
beautiful. (OVER HER IMAGINED PROTEST) Oh, yes,
you are! I know I probably startled you, sweep-
ing you off your feet this way — but that's the
kind of person I am. I . . . .
HE DROPS THE LETTER IN A PANIC AS HE HEARS
FOOTSTEPS ON THE STAIRS. BACKS AWAY AS
FAY CARTWRIGHT COMES DOWN. SHE IS PRETTY
IN A ROUTINE SORT OF WAY, AND SMILES AGREEABLY
AT PERRY.
          FAY
Good morning, Mr. Bemiss.
          PERRY (GULPING)
Good morning . . . . . Miss Cartwright.
SHE LEANS OVER THE MAIL AND STARTS
LOOKING FOR LETTERS. PERRY STANDS
BEHIND HER, HIS MIND IN A WHIRL.
          PERRY (VOICE OVER, WITH A DETERMINED
             FROWN ON HIS FACE)
Fay . . . . do you know what I'm going to do!
I'm going to walk you to the streetcar
this morning!
HIS RESOLVE FORMED, HE SWALLOWS AND OPENS
HIS MOUTH, BUT ALL THAT COMES OUT IS A

PRELIMINARY GURGLE. FAY, HAVING FOUND HER
LETTERS, TURNS TOWARD HIM AND SMILES AGAIN.

FAY

Did you say something?

PERRY (IN MISERY)

It's a nice day.

FAY

Yes, isn't it.

PERRY

I'm looking forward to the walk . . . That is,
to the streetcar . . . That is, the walk to the
streetcar.

From Perry's "recorded thoughts," or exposition, we learn his
own concept of his character in contrast to the actual character
as people surmise it to be. We also learn that he is enamoured of
Fay, setting the beginning situation of the play. And we are
interested, because we *have* been given an insight into Perry's
character, that of a lovable, shy "little man." It would not have
been possible to present these particular factors of Exposition so
quickly and so well in any other form of Exposition than the "Pre-
Recorded, Stream of Consciousness." And this technique becomes
an Aside in the speech where Perry "thinks" out loud for us, while
standing behind Fay, and in her presence.

This technique of the Aside, which is a form of Exposition, becomes hilarious comedy later in "Mr. Bemiss Takes a Trip," when
Perry is confronting his arch-enemy, the sarcastic clerk in the
music store where Perry also works. Distinguish carefully in
the following excerpt between the "Voice Over- Pre-Recorded"
and Perry's actual speech, spoken aloud and heard by the other
character, Cornelius.

CORNELIUS (ELABORATE SATIRE)

Seems somebody had the idea you were going
to kick over the traces and get away from
it all! (HE LAUGHS LOUDLY) Fly to Havana!
Boy, I can see you doing the rhumba with
some señorita!

> PERRY (VOICE OVER)
> Oh, you think it's all very funny, do you?
> Well, I'll tell you something, you big —
> (THEN ALOUD, NERVOUSLY) It was — a mistake.
> CORNELIUS (GOOD-HUMOREDLY)
> Naturally! Do you think I'm a dope?
> PERRY (VOICE OVER)
> By golly, I'd like to answer that!

As in the previously cited examples, Perry's "voice over" speeches are, in effect, the traditional Aside of stage dramaturgy. This Aside technique also can be used for any sort of exposition desired, and to further the plot, as well. Suppose Perry said, in an Aside, while talking to Cornelius, "You stand there laughing, but some day I'm going to kill you!" in such a tone that the audience believed it — the Aside then would be both a strong Plot step and an Exposition of Perry's true intention, as compared with his bland, humble look.

The Monologue or Soliloquy

It is not necessary to cite examples of the Monologue. This is the baldest sort of exposition, when a character talks directly into the camera, or to a photograph of another character, or to a rose, or what have you, and tells the audience what it must know. One would not be so stuffy as to say it should never be used; but certainly the Monologue and/or Soliloquy should be avoided unless the playwright feels himself capable of matching Shakespeare and his *Hamlet,* or Goldsmith and his Prologue in *She Stoops to Conquer.*

Other Characters "Expose" the Plot and Principals

This is the exposition technique which television playwrights should resolutely abstain from. If the reader detects a note of scorn in these few words, he is right: *this* sort of exposition has no place in television playwriting. You know the kind:

THE SCENE IS A PARLOR. LIBBY, THE MAID, IS
DUSTING. JAMES, THE BUTLER, IS ARRANGING
FLOWERS.

LIBBY

James, the butler, you sure do arrange
flowers lovely.

JAMES

Libby, the maid, you sure do dust fine.

LIBBY

I'm dusting to please the Mistress. Today
is her birthday —

JAMES

Don't tell me! I know! She's eighty-four
today and is she spry!

LIBBY

She sure is spry. She asked for her roller
skates and any minute now I expect to hear
her skating downstairs.

JAMES

Is she having the birthday party we worked
on so hard all week?

LIBBY

That she is. Forty-five people are coming,
and everybody is supposed to bring skates.

JAMES

The Mistress is the best skater of the lot.

LIBBY

You don't have to tell me! All those skating
prizes in her bedroom —

JAMES

All over the house, you mean! Medals and prizes
everywhere.

LIBBY

You know, the Mistress's ambition is to live
to be a hundred and go skating on her hundredth
birthday.

JAMES

I know. She says that every birthday.

ENTER THE MISTRESS, ON ROLLER SKATES.
SHE SKATES TO LIBBY AND JAMES.

MISTRESS

Tallyho! I'm going to live to be a
hundred and go skating on my hundredth
birthday!

You think that's silly, perhaps? Well, it's no sillier than the playwright who uses such outmoded exposition. Let's recast this
morsel in exposition correct for television playwriting!

THE SCENE IS A PARLOR. LIBBY, THE MAID,
IS DUSTING. JAMES, THE BUTLER, IS
ARRANGING FLOWERS. AT ONCE A WOMAN'S
VOICE IS HEARD, OFF CAMERA.

MISTRESS (OUT OF SCENE)

Tallyho!

LIBBY AND JAMES FLATTEN THEMSELVES AGAINST
THE WALL, AS THE MISTRESS ENTERS, ON ROLLER
SKATES. SHE DOES A WIDE, EXPERT CURVE,
AND ZOOMS UP TO LIBBY AND JAMES.

MISTRESS

Eighty-four today, by gosh! And I'm going
to live to be a *hundred* — and skate on my
hundredth birthday! Every year I say it, and
every year I get closer to my life's ambition!

LIBBY

Oh, Ma'am, you skate the finest of all!

MISTRESS

Well, guess you *could* say I won those prizes
all over the house — fair and square!

JAMES

Of all the forty-five guests coming to the
birthday party, Madam is the fairest and
squarest!

MISTRESS

James, you're the most gallant butler a lady ever
had, and you, Libby, are the prettiest maid!

SHE EXECUTES A PIROUETTE

If any of those forty-five guests forgets to bring
their skates, they'll be sent right back home

after 'em. Nobody's going to mess up my party,
when you two have worked on it so hard, all week!

In *recasting* this bit, *every point* of exposition covered in the
first, old-fashioned way is covered. And it's done in Action, with
the Principal Character (Mistress) on Camera *at once,* setting the situation and characterizing herself through both action
and dialogue, with interest aroused immediately. Gentle reader,
go and do likewise!

It is perhaps apposite to re-state what this author believes to be
the fundamental rule of exposition in television playwriting:

The sooner the principal characters come on camera and carry
the burden of their own exposition, in action, through illustrative
incidents which set the situation, start the plot going, and characterize the people — the better the television play is!

7

Contrasts in Technique

THE CLASSIC NOVEL of modern American literature, *On Borrowed Time*,* by Lawrence Edward Watkin, achieved such recognition that it has been adapted in every major dramatic form: a stage play, a motion picture, a radio play, and a television play. In each form, *On Borrowed Time* has been enormously successful. It is interesting and instructive to compare the techniques required to tell the basic story in each of the media. The novel itself is constructed in leisurely fashion, with many delightful and moving chapters and passages of necessity omitted in all four dramatic media. The omissions illustrate the relentless condensation, the straight, forward-moving line of drama, in contrast with the novel: *with the greatest condensation demanded by the television play.*

Yet the values and characters of the television play are as complete and as fully realized as those of the novel; and the final impact of the basic story is as great.

The novel has been published, and is available in most public

---

* The novel: published by Alfred A. Knopf. Copyright, 1937, by Lawrence Edward Watkin. Used by permission. The play, copyright, 1937, by Paul Osborn. Used by permission. The screenplay, *On Borrowed Time*, copyright 1939, by Loew's, Incorporated. Screenplay written by Alice D. G. Miller, Frank O'Neill, and Claudine West. Used by permission. The radio play: written by Paul Peters; broadcast February 17, 1946, The Theatre Guild on the Air, presented by the United States Steel Corporation. Used by permission. The television play: written by Norman Lessing; produced by The Playwrights, June 25, 1952, for the Celanese Theatre. Used by permission.

libraries. The stage play has been published in two versions: one, the complete, original text; the second, a condensed acting version very close to the television play. You are referred to the libraries for these two play versions, also. The motion picture version and the radio play have not been published.

On Borrowed Time: The basic story

In the town of Chatfield lives Pud, a six-year-old boy whose real name is John Gifford Northrup. He is the only child of Dr. Jim and Susan Northrup. Dr. Jim is the son of Julian and Nellie Northrup, who live with Jim and Susan. Grandfather Julian is Gramp to Pud; and between the lovable and somewhat irascible old man and his grandson is an idyllic friendship and a perfect companionship. All that Gramp says and does Pud tries to say and do; and Pud fills Gramp's life completely. Since Gramp is outspoken, sometimes profane and a church-goer only under compulsion, Grandma Northrup is constantly perturbed about how Pud is going to turn out under such (to her) baleful influences.

In complete agreement with Grandma is Mrs. Demetria Riffle, astonishingly enough the elder sister of Pud's lovely mother, Susan. Demetria's husband disappeared after a brief time of married woe; and Demetria has turned herself into a self-righteous, gossipy, nosey keeper of other people's business.

One of Gramp's small comforts is a swallow of kummel. After such a swallow, following a mild quarrel with Grandma, a strange dark man, Mr. Brink, appears, and asks Gramp to go with him. He is insistent; but Gramp succeeds in driving him away.

Dr. Jim and Susan are killed in an automobile wreck, as they are returning from a hurry call in a neighboring town. A Boy Scout, thumbing a ride, had slipped from a rock and fallen in front of Dr. Jim's car. Dr. Jim swerved and crashed down a steep hill.

After the double funeral, Grandma tries to reason out the meaning of the tragic deaths. She believes she heard the voice of God, as the minister preached the funeral sermon; she convinces herself that she and Gramp are not fit — especially Gramp — to bring up the orphaned Pud. Demetria shares this agreement, especially after she learns that Pud has been left a substantial sum of money. She even wants to adopt Pud; but Grandma is unwilling to go this far, although she thinks Demetria should have a strong hand in

Pud's rearing. Gramp and Pud both are outraged at the idea; they despise Demetria.

Gramp writes Reverend Murdock, enclosing a generous check "for a copy of the funeral sermon." He remarks that he's done his "good deed." Pud picks up the remark and says that Gramp now may have any wish he makes come true, because of the good deed.

Shortly afterward, a neighbor's boy is caught stealing apples from Gramp's favorite tree. Gramp makes the wish that any one he catches up that tree might have to stay until Gramp gives him permission to come down. The wish works: the neighbor boy can't get down until Gramp permits him to. Pud points out the working of the wish; Gramp is sceptical, until Pud climbs the apple tree and cannot get down until Gramp gives him permission. (This situation is the premise on which the story is built.)

Soon after, Mr. Brink (Death), takes Grandma away with him. Gramp and Pud are left alone to fight the machinations of Demetria to get control of Pud and Pud's money.

One day when Gramp and Pud both are sitting under the apple tree, Mr. Brink appears again, asking Gramp to come with him. (It is notable that both Gramp and Pud can hear and see Mr. Brink, who remains invisible and inaudible to everyone else.) Mr. Brink refuses to leave without Gramp. Gramp therefore asks one last favor: an apple from his favorite tree which he asks Mr. Brink to secure for him. Mr. Brink agrees; climbs the apple tree; and then is told exultantly by Gramp that he can stay until Gramp decides to let him down.

With Mr. Brink (Death) stopped and so with all menace removed, Gramp and Pud embark on joyous living. Demetria is ordered off the place permanently. But she is not so easily stopped. Snooping around, she sees Gramp supervising the building of a high fence around the apple tree. She learns about Mr. Brink, and decides that Gramp is insane.

Demetria decides to have Gramp committed to an insane asylum, and arrives with a Mr. Grimes, head of the asylum. Grimes, a harsh, unfeeling man, is prepared to remove Gramp in a straightjacket. But Gramp, sure of his position, shoots Grimes through the stomach, knowing that Grimes cannot die with Mr. Brink held captive in the apple tree.

Grimes does not die, nor does a fly which the doctor attending Grimes tries to kill with poison. In fact, nobody has died — as Gramp points out to the doctor. Demetria is defeated.

Strong pressure is put on Gramp by several people, including Mr. Brink, to let Death come back into the world. But Gramp is holding out, to protect Pud. He would be willing to let Mr. Brink down and go with him, if someone kind and loving and responsible would get Pud. He discusses with Pud the possibility of his (Gramp's) going away. The boy, grief-stricken, disappears.

While everyone is away searching for Pud, the boy appears alone at the apple tree. Mr. Brink sees him, and teases him into trying to climb the apple tree. First Pud must climb the high fence; he does so, under Mr. Brink's goading, and falls, and is injured so that he can never walk again.

Gramp now is faced with the fact of Pud's being a cripple all his life. Carrying the boy in his arms, he arrives at the apple tree for a discussion with Mr. Brink. Mr. Brink promises to take both Pud and Gramp, if Gramp lets him down out of the apple tree. Gramp does so. Mr. Brink takes first Gramp, then Pud; and as the rejuvenated old man and the healed, frolicking boy go off into Eternity, they hear Grandma's voice calling them, and they hear the bark of Betty, the old dog who had touched the apple tree with her nose and died; and we know that all of them will be united happily forever after.

ON BORROWED TIME
Summary of Television Play
(Hour Length)
Playwright: Norman Lessing

Characters in the Television Play

PUD	BOY IN TREE
GRAMP	DR. EVANS
GRANNY	LAWYER PILBEAM
MARCIA	MR. GRIMES
DEMETRIA	NOTE: the cast is stripped down
MR. BRINK	to absolute essentials for telling the story.

Sets in the Television Play
>   The front yard with the apple tree
>   The living room of the Northrup home
>   The front porch
>   Dr. Evans' office
>   (The first three actually comprise a unit set)

ACT I

NIGHT. ESTABLISHING SHOT of the apple tree, in which we also see, through a window, Gramp at his desk, composing a letter. CUT TO INTERIOR: Pud is on the floor with a picture book. Granny wipes her eyes with a mourning handkerchief. Marcia brings her a drink, as Granny isn't feeling well. Pud asks, "Why do they put dead people in coffins?" This line of questioning brings the exposition of the recent death of Jim and Susan. Pud then remarks, "I must never forget that I'm an orphan," which is motivation for introducing the name of Demetria, with consequent explosions from Gramp. Granny asks, "Whom are you writing to?" Gramp's reply, "to Murdock," introduces essential plot element of the "good deed," and Pud's advice to Gramp to "make a wish." Pud goes off to bed. Granny and Gramp argue over Pud's upbringing. Pud returns hurriedly — he has seen the boy stealing apples. CUT TO THE APPLE TREE: The thieving boy escapes, and Gramp makes his wish that anyone caught in the tree would have to stay. CUT TO LIVING ROOM: Demetria arrives; the fight scene between her, Gramp and Pud is played. Gramp and Pud exit, leaving Granny and Demetria. Granny wonders if Demetria should rear Pud. Demetria inquires about Pud's inheritance. Demetria at once wants to adopt Pud, but Granny demurs. Marcia enters briefly, long enough for Demetria's antagonism to her to be shown. When she exits, Demetria announces she will go to Lawyer Pilbeam and get adoption papers fixed. Scene ends with Granny seized by a spell of weakness.

DISSOLVE OUTSIDE

Still moonlight. Action is continuous. Gramp is looking for Pud. Mr. Brink introduced for the first time, leaves when Gramp orders him off. Pud enters, revealing he also has seen Mr. Brink. Then he and Gramp go in the house.

FADE OUT. FIRST TIME LAPSE

FADE IN ON THE APPLE TREE. Morning. The thieving boy is in the tree again. Pud and Gramp dash on. The boy can't get out of the tree, until Gramp permits. Then the boy runs away. Pud climbs the tree, has to have Gramp's permission to get down. But *before* he's down from tree

DISSOLVE TO

Granny's room. Marcia brings Granny a cup of tea, receives admonition "always to let Gramp have his pipe." Marcia goes. Mr. Brink arrives, takes Granny.

DISSOLVE TO

Pud hanging from the tree branch, terrified. Finally Gramp lets him down. Then Marcia enters, crying that Granny is dead.

End of Act I. SECOND TIME LAPSE

COMMERCIAL

ACT II

FADE IN: FRONT PORCH AT TWILIGHT. Gramp is there, grieving. Marcia enters. Gramp says he is sorrowing because Granny didn't "forgive him." "Oh, but she did," cries Marcia, and leaves to get Gramp's pipe. Pud enters. Gramp and Pud must stick together, turn over a new leaf. Marcia returns with the pipe, leaves to fix supper. Mr. Brink arrives. Gramp defies him, but without success, until he thinks of the device of asking for one last apple. Mr. Brink climbs the tree and is captive. The basic situation of the play is now set.

FADE OUT. THIRD TIME LAPSE

FADE IN: DR. EVANS' OFFICE. Present: Dr. Evans, Lawyer Pilbeam, Demetria. Demetria tells of Mr. Brink, of having seen fence being built. Pud has told her why. Pilbeam observes that if Gramp were out of the way, Demetria would get Pud. She protests that Gramp is insane. Finally, Dr. Evans agrees to talk things over with Grimes, head of the asylum.

SLOW DISSOLVE TO

Partially completed fence around apple tree. Present are Pud, Gramp and Mr. Brink. Gramp rejoices that nothing can hurt him now. Demetria, Dr. Evans and Lawyer Pilbeam enter. Demetria induces Gramp to speak to Mr. Brink. He does so, apologizing for keeping Mr. Brink in the tree, says he did it just so that old hellion Demetria can't get Pud. He's going to keep Brink in the tree until it's time for Brink to take Demetria. Then, he turns to the others and says, "Well, that's it." He is amazed that none of them heard Brink speak, until Pud suddenly confirms that he had heard. Evans tries now to pick an apple, and is prevented by Gramp. Demetria, Dr. Evans and Pilbeam then leave. Gramp asks Brink why the others can't hear him (Brink) speak? But Mr. Brink won't go into that now. Gramp and Pud leave, with Mr. Brink still in the tree.

FADE OUT. FOURTH TIME LAPSE

FADE IN: THE LIVING ROOM. Present: Marcia, Pud, Gramp. Marcia sees Dr. Evans and a gentleman coming up the walk. She goes out to keep them from touching the tree. Pud sent off to bed. Enter Dr. Evans and Grimes. Grimes has come to haul Gramp off to the asylum. (Revealed that Demetria is waiting out in the car.) In this TV version, there is no fly-killing attempt. Gramp gets his pistol and shoots Grimes.

End of Act II. FIFTH TIME LAPSE

COMMERCIAL

ACT III

FADE IN: THE APPLE TREE, AT DAWN. Dr. Evans has just killed the mouse on the end of the fishing pole by touching the pole to the tree. He thus proves to his personal satisfaction the lethal quality of the tree. As Pilbeam arrives, Evans is calling softly to Mr. Brink, receiving no answer. Evans tells Pilbeam that Grimes isn't dead, although he should have been; declares Gramp is not crazy. Gramp enters; Evans offers to apologize for having said Gramp is crazy. Gramp brushes his remark off; talks to Brink, learns of "mouse in the face," thus proving to Dr. Evans that Gramp is talking to an actual Mr. Brink. Dr. Evans then reminds Gramp of suffering people who cannot die. Gramp is still stubborn; Dr. Evans warns him he'll do everything he can to compel Gramp to let Mr. Brink down. Then he and Pilbeam leave. Gramp and Brink talk; Brink confirms that Gramp will be the first to die, when Brink comes down. Gramp, discouraged, exits.

DISSOLVE

INTERIOR, LIVING ROOM. Pud alone, playing train. Gramp enters. There is a warm scene of how much they love each other. Then

Gramp tries to convince Pud of Demetria's essential goodness, and Pud runs off crying.

DISSOLVE TO

TREE. Demetria and Evans hurry to scene. Evans reveals that he has spoken to Gramp (in a scene which we neither see nor hear in the TV version) and says that Gramp has reached a decision: Gramp enters, and plays a scene of attempted reconciliation with Demetria, in which she says she will send Pud to a little girls' school. Gramp rebels against Pud's being made into a sissy; he changes his mind — he won't go with Mr. Brink, after all. Demetria says that Dr. Evans will commit Gramp to an asylum. Whereupon Gramp plays with Mr. Brink the scene of "double talk" about taking Demetria, frightening Demetria so that she leaves hurriedly after promising not to interfere again. Dr. Evans, however, remains, while Gramp talks again with Mr. Brink, who ends by saying, "You poor man!"

FADE OUT. SIXTH TIME LAPSE

FADE IN: THE LIVING ROOM. NIGHT. Pud has disappeared. Gramp and Marcia looking for him. Marcia leaves for "Jimmy's" house, hoping to find Pud.

DISSOLVE

OUTSIDE. Pud is there, his clothes tied in a bundle. He hides as Marcia hurries past. Pud starts to walk by the tree, when Mr. Brink stops him, and plays the scene of teasing the boy to climb the fence. Pud falls, and is injured.

FADE OUT. SEVENTH TIME LAPSE

FADE IN: BRINK IN THE TREE. CAMERA PULLS BACK, to show Gramp with Pud in his arms. Gramp makes his bargain with Mr. Brink, lets him down. Mr. Brink takes Gramp, then Pud. OFF CAMERA, Granny's voice is heard, "Jul-yen! Do you have to swear in front of the boy?" Gramp grins, and has the "curtain speech," spoken to Mr. Brink: "Shucks, I thought you said she'd changed!"

End of Television Play

The elapsed time is indeterminate; although it would seem to be about a week. The "time" that is important in the television play is the constructing of the scenes of "Live" action so that actors will be able to move from one set to another and to make any required costume changes, i.e., "cover scenes."

COMPARISON OF TECHNIQUES IN PRESENTING *On Borrowed Time*
DISCUSSION OF DIFFERENCES IN THE FIVE MEDIA:
THE NOVEL, STAGE PLAY, MOTION PICTURE, RADIO PLAY, TV PLAY

Characters

The novel names forty-two characters, major and minor; and literally hundreds are mentioned and inferred, so that the feeling pervades that a whole town and its citizens are parts of the story. And they *are* a part of the total effect of the novel, which requires an atmosphere of expansiveness to create verisimilitude.

The motion picture comes next in its lavish use of characters. Twenty-seven major and minor characters are named or identified; then there are crowds of townspeople, state police, church goers, stretcher bearers, internes, nurses, etc., etc. Once again, the illusion of an entire community participating in the story is successfully created.

The radio play comes next in number of characters; seventeen are named (including Trixie, the dog, certainly an integral part of the plot, as through the death of the dog, the lethal character of the apple tree is established). Among these seventeen is the Narrator, an indispensable radio device for setting the scene, the beginning action, and for recapitulating the story at the start of Act II and Act III. So far, the novel, the motion picture and the radio play all have used Susan and Jim, Pud's parents, as live characters participating in the action. However, they are expendable, in telling the basic story, and their tragic death is only talked about in the stage play and the television play. A detail: in the radio play the name of the dog is changed from Betty to Trixie, because "Betty" as a dog's name might be confusing to radio listeners.

The stage play reduces the number of characters still further toward the absolute minimum: fourteen are named, including three workmen, who are seen building the fence.

The television play presents only ten characters, all the workmen and the Sheriff being eliminated. The fence around the apple tree is shown as an accomplished fact, presumably being built between scenes; and technically, under the requirements of "live" television, it is set in place while the action is shown going on in Dr. Evans' office. It is worth while to name the characters essential to telling the basic story: Pud, Gramp, Granny, Mr. Brink, Marcia, Demetria, the boy in the apple tree, Dr. Evans, Lawyer Pilbeam, and Mr. Grimes, head of the asylum. *Not one* of these characters could be dispensed with; on the contrary, all characters *not* involved in the plot, like the workmen, are cut out. It would be difficult to find a better example of tight structure through use of characters absolutely indispensable to the plot.

Settings

The novel ranges at will over an entire town, into an adjoining town, and by inference all over the world, including the halls of the United States Congress, as the author extends the effect of the "cessation of Death".

The motion picture also goes where it must, to dramatize events in action in the setting where each event takes place (as, for instance, the accident which kills Jim and Susan; and the vital characterizing of Demetria as she haggles in the florist shop over the cost of the funeral flowers). It is a characteristic and a great virtue of motion pictures, in comparison with other dramatic forms, that they can *show* events instead of talking about them. Thus, in the screenplay, Mr. Brink is introduced in the most dramatic form out on the highway, accepting a lift in Jim's and Susan's car, after he has been characterized as an ominous figure.

Even the radio play approximates the motion picture in its extensive settings. Now Mr. Brink is seen (as he must be, to make him clear to the radio listeners) by Granny, out on the road with Demetria. After Mr. Brink is identified to Jim and Susan (and so to the radio audience), Granny sees him getting into Jim's and Susan's car, as he did in the motion picture. Only, we, the audience, have to be *told* this incident instead of seeing it for ourselves, as in the motion picture. Radio, of course, (except in the limitations which time inflicts, i.e., the unchangeable hour allowed on the radio network) also is free-ranging and can go anywhere it chooses for settings. A musical bridge, and lo! we are in another hemisphere, if desired.

The process of condensation becomes stringent. In the stage play, there are only three sets: the living room, Granny's bed room and the apple tree. And there is, in fact, a version of the stage play

performed successfully in a unit set like the set used by the television play: the living room, a front porch and the apple tree in
the yard, with the "front wall" of the living room removed, in
modern stagecraft technique, so that action in the interior can be
seen. Here, lighting plays the controlling part in directing the
attention of the audience to the desired acting area. That area
where the action occurs is lighted, the other areas (on the stage)
are kept in darkness. In television, the camera does this directing
of our attention.

Then, as mentioned, the television play concentrates action in
the living room, its front porch, and the yard with the apple tree;
but it adds Dr. Evans' office, where Demetria's plotting to secure
Pud is set.

In the television play, and in the condensed stage version, Mr.
Brink comes for Granny as she knits in the living room. In the
novel, the screenplay and the radio play, Granny dies in her bed.
Similarly, Pud's terrible fate after his fall is revealed in his bedroom, in the novel, the radio play and the screenplay. In both
stage versions and in the television play, Gramp comes on screen
carrying Pud in his arms, a condensation of action highly effective
pictorially in these two media. And it is good that it is effective,
because if Pud's bedroom had to be shown, not only would the
action be slowed down, but another set would be required. If it be
true, and this author thinks it is, that the technique of the motion
picture and thereby of all dramatic forms is the portraying of the
crest of a series of waves, each higher than the one before (rising
action), then the handling of the after-effects of Pud's injury in
stage and television versions is a fine example.

The Action

There are five major plot elements to be "set" in the basic plot
line:
1. The idyllic relationship between Gramp and Pud.
2. The endangering of this relationship by the death of Pud's
   parents.
3. The presence of Mr. Brink and his intentions toward Gramp.
4. The conflict between Demetria, and Gramp and Pud.
5. The power of the apple tree to hold people captive.

The entire story grows out of these five elements. They are juggled, in the different presentations, and do not always appear in the same sequence. The novel, the screenplay and the radio play tend more to be alike, since with their scope and freedom of setting they are less restricted in their manner of telling the story. *Of these three*, the radio play is the most restricted, because of the time limitation (one hour on the network).

The stage play and the television play are severely condensed, because of the nature of their presentation, with the television play being the more condensed.

The novel sets first the happy friendship of Pud and Gramp. Mr. Brink appears as a "dark stranger" in Chapter 2, on page 13 of a 269-page book. He is not identified by name, Mr. Brink, until Chapter 13, when he comes to "take" Granny.

In Chapter 5, Jim and Susan are killed; and in the following chapter, the basic conflict between Demetria, and Pud and Gramp is set.

By now, Gramp and Pud are in serious difficulty. Death has appeared, to menace Gramp personally; and Demetria is present, determined to get Pud. No solution of the difficulty is in sight, until at the end of Chapter 11, when Gramp realizes the power of the apple tree to hold people captive. One fourth of the novel (in pages) has been told, over presumably several weeks of time. The reader can anticipate what's going to happen, although as yet Gramp does not know that he will capture Mr. Brink in the tree. However, all five plot elements are established.

The novel has two sub-plots: the story of Jason Tate, Demetria's roomer; and the romance of Marcia Giles and Bill Murdock. Jason Tate is dropped completely in all other media. Marcia and Bill appear as a romatic team in the screenplay (although his name is changed to Bill Lowry and he is no longer the minister's son). Bill is dropped from the radio play, the screenplay and the television play. Marcia remains because she is an integral part of the plot. The dog, Betty, called Trixie in the radio play, is dropped entirely and not even mentioned in the television play. As a character, the dog is important because her death motivates Gramp's building the fence. But in the television play, the lethal character of the tree is assumed and the fence thereby built — further illustration of the condensation dictated by the limitations of "live" television.

The stage play establishes in the opening scene three of the five elements: Gramp's and Pud's friendship; Demetria's opposition to them; Mr. Brink's first "call" on Gramp. However, Jim and Susan have not yet died (but in the opening scene of the television play, they have died, and the time is soon after their funeral . . . a further condensation). Now, in the stage play, Granny dies *before* Gramp realizes the power of the apple tree, heightening the suspense dramatically; we, the audience, see her death, and tremble for Gramp, since we have seen Mr. Brink "call" for Gramp. It is not until the next scene that Gramp establishes the power of the apple tree (Scene Four); and in Scene Five Mr. Brink is captured. Act I ends here, logically: one-half of the play has been presented, for an elapsed time of about one hour, ten minutes.

The radio play adopts somewhat the narrative style of the novel and the screen play. After the Narrator has set the scene, Pud's and Gramp's relationship is established. Immediately following, Demetria's opposition is set. But before we learn anything about Mr. Brink, Jim and Susan are introduced, and their trip to Gainesville planned. While they are traveling in their car, Granny and Demetria (now out on the road) stop them to talk about a "strange, dark man", whom Granny sees get in Jim's car. So far, the basic element of Gramp's being threatened by Mr. Brink is not set; it has taken all this time to "kill off" Jim and Susan, a plot step which has already happened when the television play opens. Note, however, that the incident of Jim's and Susan's trip is necessary in order logically to *talk* about Mr. Brink, since on radio, he obviously cannot be seen. The space (or time), therefore, has not been wasted; the difference in techniques between visual and aural media sets the conditions of telling the story. Now, having established a mysterious "strange, dark man", we know his identity when he (Mr. Brink) comes to menace Gramp. This first appearance of Brink occurs immediately following his identification on the road, being played, that is, as soon as possible while the knowledge of him is fresh in listeners' minds. Note, too, that Mr. Brink is visible only to Granny out on the road, and that Demetria cannot see him.

There is an important time lapse at this point. In the interval,

Jim and Susan have been killed, vital exposition which is spoken to Gramp by Mr. Brink himself (and so to the listeners). That is, the radio play combines Mr. Brink's first appearance to Gramp with the news of Jim's and Susan's death, and so firmly establishes him as Death. This condensation helps greatly to shorten the all-over time of the story and also makes a great dramatic impact on the listeners. The end of the First Act of the radio play comes when Gramp realizes the strange power of the apple tree. Slightly more than one-third of the total available time has been consumed. The radio play, it is recalled, is in three acts.

Even more narrative and expansive is the screenplay. It dispenses with all the side-ventures of the novel, no matter how delightful; but it adds new scenes further to point up the tragi-fantasy of the story, and to characterize the principals more fully. For instance, Demetria is shown in a starkly revealing scene forever setting her character, as she haggles over the cost of flowers for Jim's and Susan's funeral. On the bright side, Gramp and Pud are shown in a richly humorous scene when their jalopy breaks down in front of the church as they're returning from a Sunday fishing expedition, the worst possible humiliation, from Granny's point of view.

The clue to the added scenes is that *all of them involve the principals* of the story. Jason Tate is dropped completely. Marcia's and Bill's romance is played down, portrayed just enough to meet the public liking for "young love" in a story. Mr. Brink himself is "built up"; he opens the screen play in a highly dramatic and pictorial scene to establish for all the rest of the picture a haunting quality of impending tragedy and doom which is at the same time tinged with such deep humanity and love that the death of Pud and Gramp comes as a happy rather than a sad ending. As long as Gramp and Pud are together, what matter whether they are alive or dead? And the ending of the screenplay is a scene of pure exaltation, both pictorially and dramatically — and humanly.

So — of the five major elements, that of Mr. Brink is set at once, in the screenplay. Immediately following, the death of Jim and Susan is portrayed, with Demetria introduced as the emissary to break the news to Pud, Gramp and Granny. So, even before we have met Pud and Gramp, the power of Mr. Brink and his peculiar part as a character in the story are established. Very soon, we meet Granny, Betty (the dog), Gramp and Pud. The idyllic relationship is set, and also their conflict with Demetria. Let's note again that *all* this vital action is *on the principals,* each *acting out* his or her responsibility — not talking about it.

Soon after Jim's and Susan's double funeral, Gramp does his "good deed", with its possibilities pointed out by Pud. There follows more incident to heighten Demetria's greed; then the boy is caught in the apple tree and Gramp's wish is spoken. But the demonstration of the carrying out of the wish is some distance ahead, because enough suspense has been established (1) by the initial introduction of Mr. Brink, (2) by the conflict over Pud, (3) by our hope that Pud and Gramp will be able to stay together, so that it is not necessary either for interest or from a limitation of time to take this important plot step.

Soon Mr. Brink appears to Gramp for the first time, and is driven away. Here a long time lapse occurs, with the next sequence devoted to further amusing details about Gramp and Pud (the disastrous return from the fishing trip), and to Demetria's denunciation of Marcia. Out of this last develops the scene ending with the demonstration of the power of the apple tree to hold a person captive. Mr. Brink then appears and "takes" Granny; and the five basic plot elements have been established. The motion picture is nearly over, about an hour of elapsed time. (Note: and the time of the *entire* television play is between fifty-two and fifty-four minutes!)

We have recognized elsewhere in this book that the condensation demanded by time limitations on a television play discards the narrative technique for the "Isben" technique — with everything possible having happened before the first Fade-In. To state this fact another way: What is the best point of attack on your material? *It is as near to the climax as possible, with all "first act" events having happened ahead of time.* The playwright must not, of course, rob himself of material for dramatizing (acting out) the forward movement of this piled-up situation toward the climax. The skill comes, then, in selecting just the point where the protagonist is sufficiently involved in a strong situation, with the main conflict quickly established *in action* which we watch.

So, at the very opening of the television play, Gramp is writing his letter to Rev. Murdock, his "good deed". It is *after* the funeral of Jim and Susan; Marcia is already a member of the household. Very soon, the thieving boy is caught in the apple tree; and Gramp makes his wish now (instead of the second time the boy is caught) that any one caught in the tree would have to stay there. Demetria appears, and her conflict is set in *one* scene, ending with her declaration that she'll go see Lawyer Pilbeam about adopting Pud. The row has induced a spell of weakness in Granny.

Cutting outside, Gramp is seen, looking for Pud. Mr. Brink appears for the first time, and is ordered off. Pud appears, saying he too has seen Mr. Brink.

Now comes the first time lapse. In *elapsed playing time*, about twelve minutes have been consumed (23½ pages out of a 100-page script).

It's the next morning. The thieving boy is in the tree again, and can't get down without Gramp's permission. Pud climbs the tree, and can't get down. *Before* he is let down, we cut to Granny's room, where Mr. Brink arrives and "takes" Granny. This scene is played concurrently (in time) with the scene of Pud held in the apple tree. Cutting back to this scene, Gramp lets Pud down; Marcia arrives to announce Granny's death. End of Act I. About 34½ pages of the script have been presented; seventeen or eighteen minutes of elapsed playing time. (In the stage play, nearest in technique to the television play, about one hour of playing time has elapsed at this point. Contrast one hour with eighteen minutes! Yet nothing essential has been left out; the values of the basic story are all there. This condensation was achieved by beginning the television play with all "first act" events having happened *before* the TV play starts.)

In the first scene of Act II of the TV play, Mr. Brink is captured in the apple tree. Next comes Demetria's scene in Dr. Evans' office in which she tells of having seen the newly built fence (actually being set in place by stage hands while this scene is played), declares her intention to consult Mr. Grimes, head of the asylum. We dissolve then to the apple tree, with the fence around it. Gramp saves Dr. Evans' life (Demetria also is present) when he attempts to pick an apple. Frightened, every one leaves, except

Gramp and Pud (and of course Mr. Brink). Suspense is maintained by Mr. Brink's refusing to answer Gramp's question about why Gramp and Pud are the only ones who can hear Mr. Brink. The climactic scene of Act II comes that night when Mr. Grimes appears to hustle Gramp off to the asylum, and is shot by Gramp. (The fly-killing attempt is dropped, as it is not needed to prove the point that no one can die while Mr. Brink is in the tree.) Now 68 pages of the 100-page script have been presented; about thirty-five minutes of elapsed playing time.

Act III opens with Dr. Evans having just killed the mouse on the fishing pole, as he explains to Lawyer Pilbeam when he arrives. (It is the next morning.) While he apologizes to Gramp, Dr. Evans declares he will do everything in his power to compel Gramp to free Mr. Brink. When the others have left, Mr. Brink confirms to Gramp that he will be the first to go. Follows a scene with Gramp and Pud, in which Gramp attempts to convince the boy that Demetria is not wholly bad. This scene is needed as motivation to make Pud run away, which he does, ending the scene.

There is an indeterminate time lapse, through a dissolve, and the next scene is played by the apple tree. Motivated by Dr. Evans' threat, Gramp attempts a reconciliation with Demetria, but is horrified by her intention to put Pud in a school for little girls. He then plays the "double talk" scene with Mr. Brink, frightening Demetria so that she runs away, promising never to interfere again. Suspense is maintained by Mr. Brink's ending the scene with his sad, "You poor, poor man", spoken to Gramp.

There is a considerable time lapse here, to night time. Pud has disappeared. Gramp and Marcia leave to find him. Pud comes out of hiding, is teased by Mr. Brink into climbing the fence, falls, and is injured. The play is then played out to the end; Mr. Brink comes down, takes Gramp, then Pud; we hear Granny's voice (out of the scene); and the play is over. Fifty-two to fifty-four minutes, total playing time. It was done by ruthlessly cutting out every element not necessary to telling the basic story. Yet persons who saw the television play and no other form of *On Borrowed Time* know the story as well as the person who read the novel or saw the motion picture.

If the author of this book were you, an earnest and determined student of television playwriting, he would read this chapter; then make a bee-line for the nearest library, there to read and study the novel and the two versions of the stage play. Having assimilated the technical points of our first six chapters, you will ponder with new understanding and profit the changes the novel and stage play went through to turn into the television play. Such contemplation can make this chapter one of the most valuable in this book; and it is humbly hoped that said chapter may prove an accurate map, guiding you to new knowledge.

8

History of a One-Act Play

THIS CHAPTER tells the success story of a new television playwright, Frederic Manley, who turned his own one-act play, *The Prison in Paradise*, running nearly an hour of playing time, into a half-hour television play, running about twenty-four minutes. Yet none of the values of the original one-acter were lost; indeed, all of the human and dramatic values are increased in the shorter, tighter, terser, more visual television play.

Since it is pointless to discuss these two versions — stage and television — until you are familiar with them, comment on the changes made to create the television play appears at the end of this chapter. The full text of the television play, with title changed to *Best Trip Ever*, follows. Then, a "line" synopsis of the stage one-acter appears; also, master scenes of the two versions are given.

BEST TRIP EVER
A Play for Television
by
Frederic Manley

CAST: Tilly Galvin
Alma Haggerty
Hawkins, middle-aged policeman
Jackson, brisk young executive

Crane, middle-aged doctor
Little girl, age seven
Radio announcer

SET: Described in the action, as it is seen.

TIME: The present. Two succeeding days in winter.

(FADE IN AERIAL LONG SHOT OF AN AMUSEMENT
PARK, BEYOND WHICH LIES THE SEA. SURF IS HEARD
IN THE DISTANCE.)

(DISSOLVE TO MCU OF WEATHER-BEATEN SIGN WHICH
IS DECORATED WITH DRAWINGS OF BATHING
BEAUTIES. THE SIGN BEARS THE WORDING, "PARADISE
PARK", UNDER WHICH HAS BEEN NAILED A BOARD
READING, "CLOSED FOR WINTER.")

(DISSOLVE TO SHOT OF TILLY GALVIN ON BOARDWALK.
SHE IS A TALL, HEAVY-SET WOMAN, WRAPPED
TIGHTLY IN A COAT.)

(FOGHORN BLOWS MOURNFULLY IN THE DISTANCE
AND CONTINUES AT INTERVALS THROUGHOUT THE
ACTION. A TORN NEWSPAPER IS BLOWN ALONG.)

(TILLY PASSES TWO SHUTTERED STALLS, "MIRTHLAND"
AND "PARADISE PIZZERIA", AND THEN COMES TO A
STALL THAT HAS A DOOR LEADING TO THE INTERIOR,
AND FURTHER TO STAGE RIGHT, A DISPLAY WINDOW
ABOVE WHICH IS A SIGN, "NEPTUNE CURIO SHOPPE —
MRS. ALMA HAGGERTY, PROP.")

(A LITTLE GIRL WANDERS IN FROM THE OPPOSITE
DIRECTION. SHE IS SHABBY BUT WARMLY WRAPPED
UP AND IS BOUNCING A BALL. SHE STARES CURIOUSLY
AT TILLY.)

LITTLE GIRL

Aren't you the frozen custard lady?

TILLY (PLEASED)

Why yes, I am. But my place is closed down for
the winter.

LITTLE GIRL

I don't see why. Frozen custard'd be just as good
now as it was then. I'd like one right this minute.

TILLY

It'd freeze you right into a lump of ice if you ate
one now. But tell you what — you look me up
next summer and I'll give you an extra big scoop.

LITTLE GIRL

What do you do all winter when there's no
custard to sell?

TILLY

Oh I just — put up my storm shutters and
try to keep warm.

LITTLE GIRL (LOSING INTEREST)

Oh. Well, goodbye.

TILLY

Goodbye.

(GIRL GOES OFF, BOUNCING HER BALL.)

(TILLY IS ABOUT TO KNOCK ON DOOR OF CURIO SHOP
WHEN HAWKINS, A STOCKY, MIDDLE-AGED COP,
STROLLS IN.)

HAWKINS

Nasty raw day, Miss Tilly!

TILLY

Aren't you right, Mr. Hawkins! Wind cuts
through this winter coat like it was made out of
cheesecloth!

HAWKINS

Seems a shame you and Mrs. Haggerty can't get
away for the cold months. Gets pretty nasty
down here so close to the ocean.

TILLY

Oh, I don't mind for myself but —

(GOES CLOSER TO HIM)

I do worry about Mrs. Haggerty with that awful
cough of hers. And — and did you know she
had a fainting spell yesterday?

HAWKINS

No! Is that a fact!

TILLY

Yes! 'Course she wouldn't tell you. *I* wouldn't

even know about it 'cept I happened to be there.
But — you will try and help me keep an eye
on her, won't you, Mr. Hawkins?

HAWKINS

Sure thing I will, Miss Tilly. I always make a
point of looking in — once a day anyway.

TILLY

Oh, thank you, Mr. Hawkins, that makes me
feel a lot better.

(HAWKINS STROLLS ON. TILLY RAPS ON DOOR OF
CURIO SHOP AND RECEIVING NO ANSWER, GOES TO
WINDOW AND LOOKS INSIDE. CAMERA DOLLIES IN PAST
HER HEAD AND PEERS THROUGH WINDOW.)

(WE SEE ALMA HAGGERTY SEATED INSIDE, LISTENING
TO AN OLD RADIO. SHE IS A FRAIL LITTLE WOMAN
WITH QUICK, BIRDLIKE MOVEMENTS. SHE WEARS A
NEAT HOUSEDRESS. SUDDENLY SHE BEGINS TO
COUGH. TILLY RAPS ON THE PANE, BUT ALMA DOES
NOT HEAR HER, SO SHE RAPS AGAIN, LOUDLY THIS
TIME.)

TILLY

Alma, let me in! It's freezing out here!

(ALMA LOOKS UP, STARTLED, THEN JUMPS UP, WAVES
TO TILLY, GOES TO DOOR AND OPENS IT.)

ALMA

Tilly, you're just in time! They're telling about
the contest now!

TILLY

Oh, Alma . . .

ALMA

Well, come *on!*

(CUT TO INTERIOR AS TILLY ENTERS SHOP. IT IS
FILLED WITH THE USUAL PARAPHERNALIA OF A
SEASIDE CURIO STALL, SUCH AS KEWPIE DOLLS, SHELLS,
POST CARDS, ETC. ALSO A TABLE, CHAIRS, STOVE,
ETC., AND SOME OF ALMA'S PERSONAL BELONGINGS.
ALMA RUSHES TO THE RADIO, FOLLOWED BY TILLY.)

ANNOUNCER

— so remember, ladies, tomorrow's the day you've
longed for; the day when Fireside Coffee
announces the lucky winners in its gigantic Miami
Vacation Contest! Be sure to tune in at four-
thirty tomorrow to hear the winner's name.
It could be you!

ALMA

It *will* be us!
(TILLY SHAKES HER HEAD, AMUSED. THERE IS A
PAUSE ON THE RADIO, FOLLOWED BY DANCE MUSIC.
ALMA TURNS THE RADIO'S VOLUME DOWN.)
It will, too, Tilly; you wait and see. I've been
praying for us to win. We've never won a contest
yet, outside of that ninth prize once, and it's
our turn now, it certainly is!

TILLY

I wish we could win, Alma, for your sake.

ALMA

Don't you want to go too?

TILLY

Of course I'd like to go. But mostly I'm thinking
how much good it'd do you — all that sunshine
and fresh air.

ALMA

Of course! That's what I'm planning on!

TILLY

But promise me you won't be too disappointed if
we *don't* win. You know how many contestants
there are and everybody's worked just as hard
as we have —

ALMA

I know all that, Tilly. But this time I'm extra sure
we'll win the prize. And do you know why?

TILLY

Why?

ALMA

Because — (WHISPERS TO TILLY AS THOUGH

DIVULGING A GREAT SECRET) — because my husband
says we're going to win!

TILLY

Your husband?
(ALMA GOES AND LOOKS AT PICTURE HANGING ABOVE
COUNTER — A MIDDLE-AGED MAN WITH
MUSTACHE.)

ALMA

Yes, can't you see it? Something about his eyes —
the way they're looking at me this morning.

TILLY

Oh, Alma, it's just a picture!

ALMA

Maybe so, but this morning there's something
different about it — like he was trying to tell me
something. Like he was saying, 'You're going
on a trip, Alma! This time you really are.
You're going to win that contest!'

TILLY

Now, Alma —

ALMA

All the time we were married, we were always
planning to take a trip but somehow we never did.
Something always happened, like the year we
even had to get a refund on tickets we'd already
bought and give the money to his sister.

TILLY

What a shame —

ALMA

But this time's different, and he knows it and is
trying to tell me. It's like he's saying, 'Alma,
we never did get to make that trip together but
the next best thing is for you to have a trip
now and you're going to!'

TILLY (TOUCHED)

Well — I hope you're right, Alma. I sure do
hope you're right.

(ALMA GOES INTO KITCHEN, PICKS UP COFFEE POT
FROM GAS PLATE, AND POURS TWO CUPS.)
ALMA (OVER ACTION)
I'm right as rain, Tilly. You'll see. Tomorrow
will be our lucky day!
(SHE RETURNS TO FRONT ROOM WITH COFFEE)
Have a cup of coffee.
TILLY
Alma, I thought you promised the doctor you'd
cut down on account of your cough.
ALMA
Oh, that! Doctor Crane's as bad as you are,
worrying about that cough! There's nothing wrong
with me that a little sunshine won't take care of.
Now, when we get to Miami —
TILLY
(PUTTING DOWN CUP, NOW SERIOUS) Oh, Alma,
listen! How many contests have we entered, you
and me?
ALMA
Why .... fifteen or twenty, I guess.
TILLY
And we haven't won any! So let's not get all
worked up about this trip until we're sure.
ALMA (IGNORES THIS)
Just think what a good time we'll have in Miami!
Accommodations in the very best hotel!
Flowers and pretty sailboats and palm trees and
nice warm water! Tilly, do you suppose we
ought to get bathing suits?
TILLY
My goodness, I haven't done any sea bathing in
years!
ALMA
Me neither. Not in this chilly water up here.
But down there it'll be all warm and lovely, and
then when we finish our swim, we'll walk back

nice and easy and have ourselves a fine seafood
special in the hotel dining room!

TILLY (LAUGHS)

You make it sound so wonderful, Alma, we almost
don't need to go.

ALMA

Oh, that's not the half of what we'll do, Tilly!
After lunch, maybe we'll feel like a nice ride out
to where they have those Indians and alligators
and things and then after dinner, we'll treat
ourselves to a movie and then maybe a moonlight
boat ride —

TILLY (PLAYING ALONG)

Goodness, Alma, don't we ever get any rest?

ALMA

Sure we do, Tilly! In the biggest, widest, softest
beds in the world!

TILLY (LAUGHING)

And I'm staying right in mine till noon!

ALMA (GROWING EXCITEMENT)

No such thing! We can't waste a minute of our
wonderful two weeks. We'll have a nice breakfast
sent up and eat it in bed, and then we'll be ready
to start out again! It's going to be the time of
our lives, Tilly! And we mustn't waste a minute
of it — not a single second!
(SUDDENLY SHE GOES INTO PAROXYSM OF COUGHING
AND COLLAPSES INTO A CHAIR. TILLY HURRIES
TO HER AND PATS HER ON THE BACK.)

TILLY

Alma! You mustn't get so worked up, Alma!
It always starts you coughing.

ALMA

Oh, I'll be all right, Tilly. All I need is a little
rest and sunshine. You'll see.
(THERE IS A KNOCK AT THE DOOR.)

ALMA

You stay put, Tilly. (SHE GOES TO DOOR AND

OPENS IT TO ADMIT DR. CRANE)
CRANE
Good morning, Mrs. Haggerty.
ALMA
It certainly is a good morning, Doctor! Tilly and
I have just been making plans for our trip to
Florida!
CRANE
Oh?
ALMA
Yes, and we're going to — Oh, wait, Doctor, this
is my friend — my very dear friend — Miss
Galvin. Miss Tilly Galvin. Tilly, this is Doctor
Crane.
TILLY
How do you —
CRANE
How do you do. Er — what's this about Florida?
TILLY (QUICKLY)
Oh, it isn't anything for sure, Doctor. It's only
that Alma and I've entered a contest —
ALMA
Which we're going to win! And I've got something
here to show you. (TO TILLY) You, too, Tilly.
(SHE GOES TO COUNTER AND SEARCHES UNDER IT,
THROWING THINGS ABOUT. WHILE SHE DOES SO,
CRANE LOOKS QUESTIONINGLY AT TILLY. SHE
SMILES, INDICATING THAT CRANE SHOULD TREAT
THE IDEA INDULGENTLY)
ALMA (RETURNING WITH A PLACARD)
Look!
(INSERT: CU OF PLACARD, WHICH READS, "GONE TO
MIAMI. BE BACK IN TWO WEEKS.")
TILLY (SOMEWHAT EMBARRASSED)
Oh, Alma!
ALMA
See, that's us. We're going to Miami! Down
south where the birds go!

CRANE

Well — er — when is this, Mrs. Haggerty?

ALMA

Why . . . I hadn't thought. When, Tilly?

TILLY

Well . . . . whoever wins the contest leaves first
of next week.

CRANE

What sort of contest?

ALMA

Look! I'll show you!
(SHE OPENS AN OLD LEDGER IN WHICH THERE ARE
PASTED A NUMBER OF NEWSPAPER PICTURES OF
CHILDREN)

CRANE (PUZZLED)

Pictures of children — ?

ALMA

Yes, but every last one of them grew up to be a
famous motion picture star! All fifty of them. You
have to identify them and send in the correct
names to the Fireside Coffee Company and
that's what Tilly and I did —

TILLY

We don't know that they're all correct, Alma —

ALMA

Yes, we do! (TO CRANE) Some of them were very,
very hard. (POINTS OUT PICTURE) See if you can
guess who that is.

TILLY

Now Alma, Dr. Crane doesn't care who it is.
Don't pester him.

ALMA

You'll have to excuse me, Doctor, but I'm so happy
and excited about Tilly and me winning this
trip to Miami. You just don't know how —

CRANE (INDULGENTLY)

Well, anyway, it isn't as if you were actually
sure of winning. I just dropped by to see how

you were getting along — if you are taking the
medicine I gave you and — (CAREFULLY, WITH
A GLANCE TOWARD TILLY) the general situation.

ALMA

Oh, I'm taking the medicine! And Miami's an
awful healthy place to visit, isn't it?

CRANE

I believe it is. Only, in this case, I'm not sure —

ALMA

Doctor, if you only knew how Tilly and I have
worked and worked and prayed to win that
contest! And how many hours we argued and
worried about Irene Dunne.

CRANE (PUZZLED)

Irene Dunne?

TILLY (HASTILY)

She was one of the pictures in the contest, Doctor.
At least we think so.

CRANE

Oh. Well, sit down, Mrs. Haggerty. I think we
should have a little talk.

ALMA

My goodness, I haven't offered you any coffee.
Let me heat some up — it won't take a minute.
(BRIGHTLY) Fireside Coffee, of course!

CRANE

No, please don't bother. I couldn't —
Yes, I could, come to think of it. I'd enjoy a cup.

ALMA

I'll only be a minute. (SHE EXITS, CLOSING
KITCHEN DOOR BEHIND HERSELF)
(FOR A MOMENT TILLY STANDS AWKWARDLY
WATCHING THE DOCTOR, WHO LOOKS AFTER ALMA,
THEN DOWN AT HIS BRIEFCASE AS THOUGH HE WERE
PREOCCUPIED)

TILLY

It would be a wonderful trip for Alma, Doctor.
Two weeks in Miami — all expenses —

CRANE

Miss — uh, Galvin? (TILLY NODS HELPFULLY)
Mrs. Haggerty says you're a friend of hers. . . .

TILLY

Why, yes. I guess she's really my best friend
and I — well, you might say I'm the only friend
she has in the world.

CRANE

I see. Do you happen to know if Mrs. Haggerty
has any relatives nearby?

TILLY

Not a one, Doctor. I don't think she has any
relatives at all except some cousins out in Nebraska
and she hasn't heard from them in years.

CRANE

Hmmm. Then I'm afraid you're the only one
who can help me.

TILLY (FRIGHTENED)

Doctor — what is it?

CRANE

(PAUSES, GLANCES AT KITCHEN DOOR, THE REST OF
THE SCENE IS PLAYED IN LOWERED VOICES)
I have some news for Mrs. Haggerty; news I don't
want to tell her unless I have to.

TILLY

What . . . kind of news?

CRANE

You realize that anything I tell you . . . (TILLY
NODS) I took some X-rays of Mrs. Haggerty's
chest the other day. They were unfavorable.

TILLY

Unfav — ? That means . . .

CRANE

I . . . I'm sorry, Miss Galvin . . . Your friend is
very seriously ill.

TILLY

Alma?

CRANE

I need your help before I decide whether or not
to tell her. She may not have very much longer
to live.

TILLY

But you're wrong, Doctor. I know you are! It's
just a cough, that's all. Just a —
(CRANE SHAKES HIS HEAD, TILLY STARTS TO RISE)
She needs to get away from here! If we could
only manage to win that trip and maybe stay a
little longer, somehow . . . !

CRANE (SHAKES HIS HEAD)

It's too late for anything to help, Miss Galvin.
It's just a matter of time now —

TILLY

You mean — you mean there's nothing we can do?
(HE NODS) (SHE RISES AND GOES QUICKLY TO HIM)
Oh, Doctor, don't tell her; don't let her know!

CRANE

(PAUSES, MAKING DECISION) Under the circumstances . . . . no, I'm not going to. There's no need
for it. I'm sure anything you can do for Mrs.
Haggerty —

TILLY

Yes, anything . . .

CRANE

The main thing is to keep her happy and as
comfortable as possible. Just let her do what she
wants as long as she doesn't get too excited.
Do you think you can manage it?

TILLY

I don't know, I . . . . Yes, I'll try.

CRANE

(PICKING UP COAT, PUTTING IT ON) Good. And,
naturally, I'll keep in touch with you.
(TILLY, CLOSE TO TEARS, NODS DUMBLY. CRANE
STANDS AWKWARDLY FOR A MINUTE) I . . . why, of
course, you know how sorry I — (TILLY NODS

AGAIN. SHE IS ALMOST CRYING NOW) Yes; well . . .
(GOES TO DOOR, TURNS TO SAY SOMETHING, THEN
CHANGES HIS MIND)
Goodbye. (TILLY MURMURS SOMETHING INAUDIBLE.
CRANE OPENS OUTER DOOR AND EXITS. FOR A
MOMENT TILLY STANDS STILL.)
(THE KITCHEN DOOR OPENS)

ALMA (OFF)

Tilly?
(TILLY STOPS SHORT, LOOKING ALMOST PANICKY.)
Tilly?

TILLY (STRAINED)

Y — yes?

ALMA

Come and help carry things in.

TILLY

You needn't bother, Alma. The Doctor's gone.

ALMA

He has?
(TILLY GOES TO MIRROR ON WALL, TRIES TO
COMPOSE FACE AND DRY EYES.)

TILLY

Yes, he . . . he had another case. An emergency.
(ALMA APPEARS IN KITCHEN DOOR WITH HEAVY
TRAY ON WHICH THERE IS A FANCY CHINA COFFEE
SERVICE AND PLATE OF COOKIES.)

ALMA

But — but why? He said he wanted coffee so I
fixed everything up nice.
(TILLY RUNS TO HELP HER — TRAY IS SET DOWN
ON TABLE.)
I think it was real mean of him to leave! I was
going to make it kind of a little party — (SHE
PICKS UP CUP AND SAUCER, IT CLATTERS. SHE PUTS
IT DOWN.)

ALMA

Listen to that, will you. All this to-do
about the contest and the trip has my hands

shaking so I can't do a thing! (HOLDS UP
HANDS) See? I don't know how I can manage
to wait until tomorrow. For the announcement!
(TILLY HAS BEGUN CRYING SILENTLY. ALMA TURNS
TO HER.)

ALMA

Why, Tilly, what's the matter?

TILLY

N-nothing. I . . . I'm just thinking about tomorrow too. Same as you are.

ALMA

Well, but that's nothing to cry over, is it?

TILLY (WORKING HARD TO CONTROL HERSELF)

No. I — I guess I just let myself go.
(RISES) I better be off now.

ALMA

No, stay! We've got so much to talk about!

TILLY (STRUGGLING INTO HER COAT)

I can't, Alma. I didn't even get my bed made
this morning.

ALMA

Well, you come back tonight and we'll cook
supper.

TILLY

All right.

ALMA

Maybe you could get a copy of one of those
fashion magazines so's we can look up and
find out what's the right thing to wear for
winter resorts this year.

TILLY (AT DOOR)

Yes, Alma. I'll buy one. Goodbye.

ALMA

Goodbye.
(TILLY GOES OUT DOOR. DISSOLVE TO BOARDWALK.
THE WIND IS HIGHER NOW, BLOWING ALONG SMALL
BOXES AND BITS OF PAPER. TILLY WALKS SLOWLY
AWAY, HUNCHED INTO HER COAT. HAWKINS, THE COP,

IS STANDING IN FRONT OF ONE OF THE OTHER SHOPS.)

> HAWKINS

What's the matter, Miss Tilly?

> TILLY

I'm so worried I can't see, Mr. Hawkins. The doctor's been there.

> HAWKINS

Yes, I saw him go in.

> TILLY

She's just as bad off as she can be, Mr. Hawkins. (STRIVING TO CONTROL HERSELF) He doesn't — know just how long it'll be —

> HAWKINS

Now isn't that a crying shame! Is — is there anything in the world I can do, Miss Tilly?

> TILLY

No, there's nothing to do. Except that she shouldn't get — shouldn't get excited and worked up about things. You'll let me know if anything — if anybody bothers her?

> HAWKINS

Sure I will — !

> TILLY

Like another visit from that young fellow who's always trying to buy Alma's place so's he can turn it into an orange drink stand.

> HAWKINS

I'll let you know right off if she has any visitors. 'Course if anybody made any real trouble for her, I'd break him in two.

> TILLY

I know you would, Mr. Hawkins. You're a real friend.

(UP ON WIND AND PULL BACK ON THIS COUPLE, THE ONLY SIGN OF LIFE ON THE BOARDWALK.)

(DISSOLVE TO CLOSE-UP OF ALMA, WRAPPED UP IN A FLANNEL BATHROBE AND STANDING JUST BELOW THE

PICTURE, LOOKING UP AT IT ALMOST AS IF IN A
TRANCE.)

ALMA

This is the day, Howard — the day they're going
to tell us. But I don't know why I'm telling you
when you've known all about it all along and all
that's going to happen, too. Oh, it's going to be
a fine, wonderful trip, Howard! If only I was
going to take it with you, it'd be the best — the
best trip ever!
(DISSOLVE TO CLOSE-UP OF OFFICER HAWKINS AT A
WALL PHONE.)

HAWKINS

Miss Tilly! There's a fellow just been asking
for Mrs. Haggerty. . . . Nope, never saw him
before but you said I was to let you know if she
had any strange visitors. I got no right to keep
him from going in to see her long as he behaves
himself. So you better come over right away.
(DISSOLVE TO ALMA'S SHOP. A WELL-DRESSED,
EFFICIENT YOUNG MAN IS WAITING. HE WEARS AN
OVERCOAT AND LOOKS OCCASIONALLY AT A NOTEBOOK
WHICH HE CARRIES.)
(ALMA COMES OUT OF INSIDE ROOM, BREATHLESS.)

ALMA

I'm sorry to keep you waiting, but I hadn't
quite finished dressing —

JACKSON

That's quite all right. You're Mrs. Alma Haggerty?

ALMA

Yes.

JACKSON

The Mrs. Haggerty who entered our Miami Vacation Contest?
(BEFORE ALMA CAN REPLY, TILLY BURSTS IN DOOR.)

ALMA

My goodness, Tilly, are you going to a fire
or something?

TILLY

Alma . . . !

ALMA (THE HOSTESS)

This is *my friend,* Miss Tilly Galvin. I — er
I don't believe I know your name.

JACKSON

I'm Jackson. District Manager for Fireside
Coffee.

ALMA

Ohhhhh!

TILLY

Mr. Jackson, it's real nice of you to come down
and tell us about it yourself, but — we didn't
really expect to win, did we, Alma?

JACKSON (SMILES)

You ladies *did* send in an entry under the name of
Alma Haggerty?

TILLY

Uh — yes! Didn't we, Alma?

ALMA

Wha — ?

TILLY

The contest!

ALMA

Uh . . . Yes!

JACKSON

(GOES TO HER, SMILING, AND EXTENDS HAND)
Then let me be the first to congratulate you!

ALMA

Con — (LOOKS DOWN, SEES HIS EXTENDED HAND, AND
TAKES IT LIMPLY IN HERS) For what?

JACKSON (SMILING)

Can't you guess?

TILLY

Y — you don't mean . . . . Alma and me, we . . .

JACKSON

(NOW OFFERING HIS HAND TO TILLY, WHO SHAKES IT
NUMBLY)

You certainly did! Yours was the very first
entry received to identify all fifty pictures
correctly.
(TILLY IS SPEECHLESS. ALMA LOOKS FROM
ONE TO THE OTHER IN CONFUSION.)

ALMA

What's he saying, Tilly?
(JACKSON LAUGHS, LOOKS UNDERSTANDINGLY
AT TILLY.)

TILLY

We . . . I t-think he's saying . . . (TO JACKSON,
ALMOST AFRAID TO SAY IT) We . . . won the
contest? We're going to . . . to Miami?

JACKSON

That's exactly it!

TILLY

(AFTER A PAUSE IN WHICH SHE DIGESTS THIS)
Alma! Alma, did you hear?
(ALMA IS STARING GLASSY-EYED AT JACKSON)
Alma, we won! We won the trip!

ALMA

But . . .

TILLY

(HUGGING HER) We're going to Miami!

JACKSON (LAUGHING)

Well! How do you feel, Mrs. Haggerty?

TILLY

She feels just wonderful! Don't you, Alma?

ALMA

(STILL CONFUSED)
Why . . . yes. Wonderful . . .

TILLY

(TO JACKSON) And you know what? She had an
idea we were going to win, right from the
start! Oh, Mr. Jackson, the hours we
spent looking through old movie magazines
and sitting through double features twice
just to help us guess the pictures! And

all the trouble we had with Irene Dunne —
I mean, with her picture! You remember,
Alma!

JACKSON

(TO ALMA) But you really felt you were going
to win, Mrs. Haggerty? Right from the first?

ALMA (CALMLY)

Oh, I knew we would win the contest. My hus-
band was sure of it. (JACKSON LOOKS MYSTIFIED.
ALMA SMILES UP AT HER HUSBAND'S PICTURE.
SUDDENLY SOMETHING SEEMS TO SHOCK HER INTO A
REALIZATION OF WHAT'S HAPPENED) Oh, Tilly, the
trip! We're going! *Really* going!
(TILLY AND JACKSON BOTH LAUGH AT HER)

TILLY

(GOES TO ALMA, HUGS HER AGAIN) 'Course we are!
Aren't you happy!

ALMA

Happy! I . . . why, I've been waiting for something like this to happen — waiting all my
life.

JACKSON (TO TILLY)

You'll hear the announcement on the air this
afternoon. And we'll have to make a few arrangements, of course. . . . Can you come
in town to our office sometime today?

TILLY

Oh, of course!

JACKSON

(GIVES TILLY A BUSINESS CARD) Then here's
our address. See you this afternoon.

TILLY

Yes, fine! I'll be there.

ALMA

What for?

JACKSON

Oh, just a few details about the trip,
Mrs. Haggerty.

ALMA (VAGUELY)

Details? Oh. . . .

JACKSON

Yes; well, congratulations again, ladies.
Good day.

TILLY

Goodbye.

ALMA

Goodbye and thanks so much. (HE SMILES AND
EXITS)

ALMA (AFTER PAUSE)

Well — it's really true, isn't it?

TILLY

I guess it must be, Alma.

ALMA

Just think! Just think — !

TILLY

(IMPULSIVELY, GOING TO HER) Oh, Alma,
we're going to have fun in Miami,
aren't we?

ALMA

'Course we are! The most fun ever!
(STARTS TO PACE ABOUT EXCITEDLY)
Seeing the sights . . . taking in all that
sunshine . . . getting treated like a couple
of queens, Tilly! (TILLY BEGINS TO SHOW
ALARM OVER ALMA'S EXCITEMENT.)

ALMA

Doing all the wonderful things we've
read about, too, like going to night clubs
and . . . and having breakfast in bed, and —

TILLY

(WORRIED, PUTTING A CAUTIONING ARM ON HER
SHOULDER) Alma. . . .

ALMA

And all for free, too! We don't have to
pay a cent, not a blessed, red — (SHE
BEGINS COUGHING)

TILLY

Alma, you mustn't! You're getting too . . .
too excited . . .
(ALMA REACHES FOR COFFEE CUP AND BEGINS
TO DRINK.)

TILLY

No, don't!
(BUT ALMA CONTINUES TO DRINK, THEN SETS
DOWN CUP.)

ALMA

Well, who wouldn't get excited, going on a
trip like this one just five days from now!
But don't you worry now. I'll be all
right. I'll be all right.
(DISSOLVE TO CLOSE-UP OF DR. CRANE,
SEATED AT DESK)

CRANE (CAREFULLY)

Well, now, Miss Galvin, you're asking me for
a positive yes or no about this trip and
I can't give it to you. With a case like
Mrs. Haggerty's, it's difficult to say just
what effect a trip would have. Of course,
there's bound to be a lot of extra moving
about and excitement and that's not the
best thing for her —
(PULL BACK TO SHOW CORNER OF DOCTOR'S OFFICE
WITH HIS DESK. TILLY IS SEATED AT ONE SIDE.)

TILLY (EAGERLY)

But it might do her some good, mightn't it?
I mean, all that sun and fresh air?

CRANE (SHAKING HEAD)

I'm sorry, no. No permanent good. It might
make her happy, Miss Galvin — that's all. And
of course, if a person is happy, they are
apt to feel better.

TILLY

Then you think —

CRANE

No, I'm not advising you to let her do it.
She would enjoy it, of course, but on the
other hand, the extra strain and effort can't
possibly be recommended for a woman in her
condition. The only things that can prolong
your friend's life, Miss Galvin,
are rest and quiet.

TILLY

But what am I going to do! I can't
tell her she mustn't make this trip.
I can't!

CRANE

And I can't very well *forbid* Mrs.
Haggerty to make this trip without
telling her the truth about her condition.
And even if I did forbid her, she'd
probably go ahead and do it anyway.

TILLY (DESPERATELY)

But I can't decide! It's not up to me.
Please — !

(CUT TO CLOSE-UP OF DOCTOR.)

CRANE

I don't know what else to say, Miss Galvin —
honestly I don't. It's too bad Mrs.
Haggerty should find out about winning the
trip — just at this time. I — I don't see
how you can possibly tell her the truth about
her condition now. But if the excitement and —
and all the preparations for the trip are too
much for her — (SIGHS) well, if there's
too much trouble, let me know. Perhaps we can
figure out something.

(DISSOLVE TO BOARDWALK. IT IS DESERTED.
THEN TILLY ENTERS, WALKING SLOWLY AND
RELUCTANTLY TOWARD ALMA'S SHOP. THE
WIND IS RISING. A NEWSPAPER BLOWS
DREARILY ACROSS THE WALK. TILLY HAS HER

HAND ON THE DOOR-KNOB OF THE SHOP, THEN
HESITATES, AS THOUGH SHE DARE NOT ENTER,
AND WALKS ALONG BOARDWALK TO WINDOW. SHE
LEANS AGAINST IT, TRYING NOT TO CRY BUT
WHEN SHE CATCHES SIGHT OF THE "MIAMI" SIGN,
SHE BEGINS TO SOB QUIETLY.)
(THE LITTLE GIRL WANDERS IN, STANDS WATCHING
HER.)

LITTLE GIRL

What's the matter?

TILLY (STARTLED)

Oh — oh, nothing.

LITTLE GIRL

Don't you have any place to go — so you can
get out of the cold?

TILLY

Yes, I do, honey. I'm going right in here
to — to see my friend. You better run home
and warm up, too.

LITTLE GIRL

Yes, ma'am. Will you remember me next summer
and when I come to buy a frozen custard, give
me an extra big one?

TILLY

Yes. Yes, I will, I promise. Goodbye, honey.
(LITTLE GIRL RUNS OUT, BOUNCING BALL. A
NEWSPAPER BLOWS ACROSS SCENE. TILLY TAKES
A DEEP BREATH, OPENS DOOR AND WALKS INTO
SHOP. FADE OUT.)

END OF ACT ONE

ACT II

(FADE IN INTERIOR OF SHOP. ALMA AND
TILLY ARE FINISHING A SPARSE LUNCH,
SERVED ON A FOLDING TABLE.)

ALMA

Goodness, that wasn't very much! Or
very good, either.

TILLY (WORRIED, PRE-OCCUPIED)
It was a plenty, Alma —

ALMA
I'm certainly tired of eating out of cans
but it's so far to walk before you get to
a store that has fresh things. I certainly
am going to enjoy two weeks of three good
meals a day and service, too!
(RISES ENERGETICALLY AND BEGINS PUTTING
THINGS AWAY.)

TILLY
Here, I'll do it —

ALMA
No, I'm going to do a real good cleaning
today. I've been meaning to get things
straightened out for the longest time, anyway,
but what with my cough and the bad weather
and everything — well, now's my chance to do
it up right.

TILLY
You mustn't do too much at once —

ALMA
Only five days till we start on our trip.
That doesn't leave me much time.

TILLY
Time? For what?

ALMA
Why, closing up the shop.

TILLY
All you have to do is just lock it up
and that's that.

ALMA
Oh, no, Tilly! My husband used to say
there'd be so many things to do before
we could go off on a trip. Like —
(GOES ABOUT ROOM, POINTING OUT FOLLOWING
JOBS) — putting up the shutters and

getting locks for the doors and turning off
the water . . . .
(HER VOICE SLOWS DOWN AND SHE MOVES MORE
SLOWLY, AS THOUGH THE SUDDEN REALIZATION OF
THE AMOUNT OF WORK TO BE DONE WERE TIRING
HER ALREADY) . . . and storing away the stock . . .
and putting covers on the counters. . . . and . . .
(SHE LAUGHS AND GOES TO PICTURE OF HUSBAND
WHILE TILLY WATCHES, WORRIED)
It'd be awful nice to have him here right now . . .
(SHE MOVES A FEW SOUVENIRS ABOUT IN AN ATTEMPT
TO PUT THEM IN ORDER)
TILLY
Well, you've got me, Alma. You know I'll do
anything —
ALMA
No, you don't know what goes where, Tilly.
TILLY
Well, if you'd just show me —
ALMA (FIRMLY)
No, you've got your own work.
(TILLY WATCHES HER, VERY WORRIED, AS
ALMA PICKS UP COFFEE CUP AND TAKES
ANOTHER SIP.)
TILLY
But, Alma —
ALMA
(ROUSING HERSELF: SMILING AND
MANEUVERING TILLY TO DOOR)
Now you go on home and worry about *your*
place!
TILLY
No, Alma, listen! You musn't —
ALMA
(SMILING AND OPENING DOOR) Go *on!*
TILLY
But you'll get all tired . . .

ALMA

No, I *won't*! (FORCED) 'N if I do, I . . .
I'll sit right down and perk up, thinking
about the trip . . . the trip . . . (HEEDLESS OF TILLY
SHE WANDERS AWAY FROM DOOR. TILLY HESITATES,
WATCHING ALMA CLOSELY, THEN EXITS.)
(CUT TO EXTERIOR AS TILLY CLOSES DOOR
BEHIND HERSELF. SHE PAUSES, LOOKING
EXTREMELY WORRIED, THEN GOES TO WINDOW
AND PEERS INSIDE, CAREFUL NOT TO LET ALMA
SEE HER. ALMA GOES AIMLESSLY TO ONE OF THE
CHAIRS AND PICKS UP PILLOW ON IT. SHE HOLDS
IT FOR A MOMENT, THEN LETS IT SLIDE TO
FLOOR. THEN SHE WANDERS TO WINDOW AND SCOOPS
A SMALL PILE OF SOUVENIRS TOGETHER. MEAN-
WHILE, TILLY HAS QUICKLY DRAWN AWAY FROM
WINDOW AND STANDS TO ONE SIDE. ALMA IS
SUDDENLY OVERCOME WITH WEARINESS AND DROPS
INTO A CHAIR. THE CAMERA PULLS IN FOR A ONE-
SHOT OF TILLY, WHO, LOOKING ALMOST PANICKY,
TAKES A COUPLE OF STEPS ALONG BOARDWALK, THEN
QUICKLY OPENS HER PURSE AND TAKES
OUT THE BUSINESS CARD GIVEN TO HER
BY JACKSON. AFTER LOOKING AT IT FOR
A MOMENT, SHE PUTS IT AWAY AND HURRIES
DOWN THE BOARDWALK, A DETERMINED LOOK
ON HER FACE.)
(DISSOLVE TO:FIRESIDE COFFEE BRANCH
OFFICE. MR. JACKSON STANDS BESIDE DESK
IN FRONT OF SPREAD, A LAY-OUT ADVERTISING
THE CONTEST AND SHOWING A MIAMI HOTEL,
ETC.)

JACKSON

I just don't understand it! (POINTING TO
ENVELOPE ON DESK) Here you've got train
tickets, hotel reservations . . . You've won
yourselves a trip that's the prize of a

lifetime, and now you want to give it all up!
(PULL BACK TO SHOW TILLY SEATED)

                    TILLY
I didn't say that! We just want more time
to . . . to get things settled. I *told* you
she's sick!

                    JACKSON
But then, the whole thing is really a
medical problem, isn't it, Miss Galvin?
I mean — it's up to the doctor to say whether
she should go or not. And we've got to know
because the winners must be announced this
afternoon.

                    TILLY
But the doctor won't say. That is — he's
worried about her going but he won't come
right out and tell her not to. It's all been
left up to me and I — I just don't know what
to do. So, if you could just give us
a little more time —

                    JACKSON
But I've already explained to you, Miss
Galvin, that's impossible. Our show is
broadcast from the West Coast, and by this
time they're all set to go.

                    TILLY
Can't you get 'em to put off announcing the
winners — just for a few days?

                    JACKSON
No, I can't, Miss Galvin. We've promised it
for this afternoon. We can't afford to disappoint all our listeners. Think of the
hundreds and hundreds of other contestants
who're waiting to hear. We can't disappoint
all these people, Miss Galvin.

                    TILLY
No, I guess not. (NEW IDEA) All right, then,

just go ahead and announce it but give us more
time before we go.

JACKSON

I can't do that either, Miss Galvin. We've
made all the reservations in advance — trains,
hotels, everything for the first of next week —

TILLY (DESPERATELY)

But can't it be changed — !

JACKSON (KINDLY BUT FIRMLY)

No, it can't, Miss Galvin. We've got all sorts
of publicity tied up with this and — and our
future broadcasts and lots of other
things, too. (PAUSE) So I'll have to
know definitely by three this afternoon.
Otherwise, they'll need to announce
another winner.

TILLY (RISES)

I know —

JACKSON (COMES TO HER)

You won't let us down, Miss Galvin? We
were all set to show you and your friend
the best time money can buy. So you must
play fair with us and make up your mind —

TILLY (TAKES A DEEP BREATH)

I *have* made up my mind, Mr. Jackson. If
Alma wants to go on this trip she can. I'm
not going to try and stop her. She's entitled
to have some fun while she still can.
So, if you'll just please let me have those
tickets — ?

(SHE HOLDS OUT HER HAND. DISSOLVE TO THE
SOUVENIR SHOP. ALMA HAS MANAGED TO GET IT
IN FAIR ORDER BUT IT HAS BEEN QUITE AN
EFFORT FOR HER AND SHE SITS IN HER CHAIR
DOZING. SHE HEARS A SOUND, JUMPS UP, SEES
TILLY OUTSIDE AND GOES TO ADMIT HER. TILLY
CARRIES ENVELOPE.)

TILLY (WITH FORCED GAIETY)

Well! Guess where I've been!

ALMA

Where?

(TILLY HESITATES, LOOKING AT HER.
THEN, EVEN MORE GAILY:)

TILLY

In town getting our tickets and things!
Here!

ALMA

(MOVING A FEW SOUVENIRS ABOUT) No, you
go ahead. I . . . I've been working . . .

TILLY

Oh, I can tell you have. The place looks
fine!

(HESITATES, THEN GOES TO TABLE AND TAKES
TICKETS, ETC., FROM ENVELOPE) Oh, look!
We get our train in Boston!

ALMA

We do?

TILLY

Yes! Won't that be something! Boston's
almost a trip in itself!

ALMA

I know . . . How are we going to get there?

TILLY

Why . . . I hadn't thought. (FORCES LAUGH)
But we will!

ALMA (AFTER A PAUSE)

It. . . . it's going to be an awful lot of
work, isn't it?

TILLY

W-work? 'Course not! (BIG SMILE) Just
think, Alma, we're famous, almost! I
wouldn't be a bit surprised if the papers
sent photographers!

ALMA

Photographers?

TILLY

Yes, and maybe some reporters, even.

ALMA

Oh . . . (TURNS AROUND, FACES TILLY)
Tilly . . .

TILLY

Yes?

ALMA

If they *do* come, the people from the
papers, I mean, I . . . well, I don't want
them here. Not with all this getting
ready to do . . .

TILLY

Why . . . all right. 'C-course you don't!
(PAUSE AS ALMA LOOKS GUILTILY AT FLOOR.)

ALMA

Besides, there's only three times you
should get in the papers, I always say:
when you're born and when you get married
and when . . . well, anyway, I'd rather they
didn't come here . . . (ANOTHER STRAINED
SILENCE) Tilly. . . .

TILLY

What?

ALMA

I just thought . . . (WITH A FEEBLE LAUGH)
It's foolish, but . . . well, wouldn't it be
awful if the doctor said I couldn't go to
Florida? I mean, if he wanted me to
stay here . . . ?

TILLY

What makes you think —

ALMA

Oh, I don't! I just said, wouldn't it
be awful if he thought I was too sick?

TILLY

But you're not! (CONFUSED) That is —

ALMA

After all this planning . . . then we couldn't
go. But we could put it off 'till I'm
feeling up to it. We could do that.

TILLY

No, we couldn't, Alma. They wouldn't let us.

ALMA

I just thought that . . . that . . . Well, someone's
got to make sure of things like that! I . . . I
can't just run off without planning anything!

TILLY

You're not planning things, you're just —
Alma! You *do* want to go . . . don't you?

ALMA

'Course I do! I'm just being practical, that's
all; thinking of my health, and everything
I've got to do, like closing up my shop and —
and getting clothes — I haven't got any
clothes, you know — and —

TILLY

(CROSSING TO KITCHEN) I'll help you, Alma. I'll
do everything!

ALMA

That's what you say now, but . . .
Well, would you pay the gas bill?
I've owed them for months, and if I
run out and buy a lot of clothes, how
am I going to pay the gas company?

TILLY

I'll pay them, Alma! I'll get the money
somehow!

ALMA

(SQUEEZING PAST TILLY INTO FRONT ROOM
AS THOUGH TRYING TO ESCAPE HER)
And . . . and the phone; what about that?
They've been after me for what I owe and
if I run off this way, they'll take it
right out of here!

TILLY

(FOLLOWING) We'll only be gone two weeks,
Alma! Once we're on the way, you won't
even think of these things!

ALMA

(ESCAPING AGAIN, PACING BACK AND FORTH TO
AVOID TILLY) Yes, I will; you don't know!
I'll be thinking of the shop every minute,
all the time. Like how thieves could break
in and the pipes might burst and . . . oh, everything! They say you leave a house like this
and it falls to pieces. Maybe you don't care
about your place, Tilly, but this is the only
home I've got. The only —

TILLY

Now, don't get excited, Alma! Talk sense!

ALMA

I *am* talking sense! You can run off to
Florida without even thinking if you
want, but I'm not going to!

TILLY

(SLOWLY RELEASING HER) Not going to what?

ALMA

(WITH ATTEMPTED BRAVADO) To . . . to go to
Florida. Not for a couple of months, anyway.

TILLY

(BEWILDERED) A couple of . . .

ALMA

I can't, Tilly! Not now, when there's so much to do!
(TILLY DROPS IN A CHAIR, UTTERLY BEWILDERED
BY THIS TURN OF EVENTS)

ALMA

But — that's no reason why *you* can't go, Tilly.
We sent it in under my name, but Mr. Jackson
knows that you worked on it, too. You could find
somebody else to go with you.

TILLY (BLANKLY)

I don't know anyone —

ALMA

But I'm sure you could find somebody, easy.
I — I wouldn't ruin the trip for you, Tilly.
I wouldn't ever do that. (PAUSE) Or — or maybe
they'll let us put the trip off for a few months.
I'll bet they would — if we asked —

TILLY

I tell you they won't, Alma. I've already asked.
Anyway, we couldn't wait, even if they'd let us.
You've got to go right now.

ALMA

Why now?

TILLY

(HESITATES, THEN SPEAKS SLOWLY AND QUIETLY)
Because you're sick, Alma.

ALMA

I know, and that's just the reason I can't go now!
The real reason, I mean. I feel too tired.

TILLY

I don't just mean you're tired. I mean sick,
really sick!

ALMA

I know. It's my cough, that's what it is.
I'm worn out with it, Tilly. You don't know.

TILLY

Yes, I do, Alma, only —

ALMA

Then wait for me. See things my way!

TILLY

But, Alma —

ALMA

(TURNING ABRUPTLY) Oh . . . let's not talk
about it any longer!

TILLY

(AFTER A PAUSE) Alma . . . before we knew we'd
won, you wanted the trip, didn't you?

ALMA

Yes. You know I did.

TILLY

You liked talking about it; I mean, pretending
we were going. Now we've won . . .
(CAREFULLY) Alma, you never really cared about
going at all, did you? (TRIES TO FORCE ALMA
TO LOOK AT HER) *Did you?* (ALMA LOOKS
UNCOMFORTABLY AT FLOOR) It's just the talk that
makes you happy . . . (REALIZING THE
SIGNIFICANCE OF HER WORDS, TO HERSELF) Happy . . .

ALMA

Did you ever stop to think they have the same
Atlantic Ocean down there that we do up here?
The very same, only you can't swim in ours till
a little later. That's what my husband always
used to say when we thought of taking a trip to
Virginia Beach.

TILLY

That's true —

ALMA

He said — well, we're already in one seaside
resort — why go to all that trouble to get to
another one? And that's just as true of Miami, too.

TILLY

Yes —

ALMA

But that needn't stop you, Tilly. You really
ought to go ahead and take the trip by
yourself, if you can't think of anyone to invite
with you.

TILLY

I don't know whether I would or not. I don't
make friends as easy as I did once.

ALMA (WORKING AT IT)

Sure you would, Tilly. And — and even if you
didn't get to know many people, why — there'd be
all those things to see and do and — and —
(TRAILS OFF)

TILLY

Nothing's much fun if you're by yourself.

ALMA (HOPEFULLY)

Of course — of course, maybe you would have a
better time if you waited until later — when
I'm feeling stronger and we could go somewhere
together.

TILLY

I — I think you're right, Alma. I'd have a lot
better time if I waited and went on a trip with you.

ALMA

After all, there'll be other contests. Why, just
the other day it was I heard about one.
(TURNS TO TILLY, HER EXCITEMENT RETURNING)
And guess where to!

TILLY

(ENCOURAGINGLY) Where?

ALMA

(RISING, STARTING TO PACE AS SHE BECOMES
WRAPPED UP IN HER DESCRIPTION)
Mexico City! That's twice as good as just to
Miami. Why, it's another country, even.
And twice as far, too. Think what we'd see,
Tilly! Bullfights and fiestas and Mexicans
and pottery and — oh, hundreds of things.
We can win, too. It took us fifteen contests
to do it the first time, but now our luck's
changed. We'll win again.
(IMPLORINGLY) Won't we, Tilly?

TILLY

(SOOTHINGLY, AS TO A CHILD) Yes, we'll win again.

ALMA

And we'll have fun, too! I'm always saying
'It's time you had some fun, Alma!' I haven't,
though, not for the longest time.
(SHE POURS HERSELF ANOTHER CUP OF COFFEE)

TILLY

No, Alma, don't —

ALMA

(UP FROM CUP) Mmm?

TILLY

Nothing . . . go ahead.

(TILLY RISES AND STARTS TOWARD PHONE)

ALMA

Where are you going, Tilly? I want to tell
you about the new contest —

TILLY

I've got to call Mr. Jackson, Alma, and
tell him we've changed our minds.

(SHOT TO INCLUDE THEM BOTH, TILLY AT PHONE
DIALING AND WAITING FOR ANSWER. ALMA IN
CHAIR, EXCITED AND PLEASED AT THOUGHT OF THE
NEW ENTERPRISE. MOVE IN TO CU OF ALMA
AS HER SPEECH PROGRESSES)

ALMA

Yes, just thank him kindly but say we're
saving ourselves for Mexico.

(SHE GOES AND STANDS AGAIN UNDER HER
HUSBAND'S PICTURE)

ALMA

I just know we'll win, Tilly. You can laugh at
me if you like but I can tell — just from looking
at Howard's picture. He told me we were going
to win the other contest and he's right about
this one, too. I can tell! He's saying — 'Alma,
you're going on a long, long trip — just the
kind of a trip we always wanted to take together.
You're going on a long, long trip . . . . . the
best trip ever!'

(FADE OUT)

END OF ACT II

THE PRISON IN PARADISE
"LINE" SYNOPSIS OF ONE-ACT STAGE VERSION
*(Not to be confused with the Master Scene Breakdown
farther along)*

SCENE: The Neptune Curio Shoppe in Paradise Park, an amusement center in a seaside resort somewhere south of Boston, Mass.

TIME: Ten A.M. in the present. Winter.

CHARACTERS: ALMA HAGGERTY   *On the radio*
            TILLY GALVIN   FIRST ANNOUNCER
            DOCTOR TALBOT   SECOND ANNOUNCER
                                ACTRESS, AS VENITA HEATHERLY
                                ACTOR, AS ROMNEY
                                THIRD ANNOUNCER
                                ACTRESS, AS MERCEDES BRENT

AT RISE: Stage is empty. Radio playing, full volume. Light glows in kitchen (out of scene) and the shadow of a slowly moving figure is cast upon the screen shielding kitchen door.

1. First Announcer says winners in Swirlafoam Soap Flakes jingle writing contest will be announced. Prize: trip to Miami.
2. Alma hurries in from kitchen to listen.
3. Second Announcer announces today's installment of "Divorcee's Diary". Gives commercial for soap. Alma turns radio down, takes jingles she has written and reads them aloud, in several versions.
4. Tilly enters. They talk about contest, reveal longing to win.
5. Alma takes cup of coffee; Tilly disapproves. Alma's illness revealed, as coffee is forbidden by doctor.
6. Alma talks of her dead husband, and of the trips they used to go on.
7. Alma turns up radio: "Divorcee's Diary" is on; a scene from it is heard on the radio. Alma and Tilly discuss plight of radio heroine.
8. Alma turns radio down. More discussion about longing for trip to Miami. They make detailed plans about their clothes, how they'll spend time in Miami.

9. Dr. Talbot arrives unexpectedly. Alma tells him about contest, and her hopes of winning.
10. Alma leaves to change into a dress from her kimono.
11. Dr. Talbot reveals fatal nature of Alma's illness to Tilly, leaves before Alma returns from changing into dress.
12. Alma enters, is disappointed that doctor is gone. Turns up radio to hear announcement of winners.
13. Third Announcer announces "Celluloid Love", gives soap commercial. Actress playing Mercedes Brent on radio is heard . . . building up to announcement of winners.
14. Radio announces that Alma has won contest, will go to Miami. Concludes with another commercial about Swirlafoam Soap. Tilly turns radio off.
15. At first overjoyed by her winning, Alma makes more plans for trip; then begins to "talk herself out of" the trip, inventing reasons why she should not go. Scene runs quite long.
16. Tilly takes position that she will go alone, if Alma refuses to go. Alma then begins to talk Tilly out of going.
17. Tilly realizes that the planning of the trip was what Alma enjoyed. Alma begins to talk about trip "next year" to Mexico City, when they win some possible future contest.
18. Tilly, realizing with tragic understanding Alma's plight, falls in with the "trip to Mexico City next year", knowing well that before "next year" Alma will be dead. The play ends on Alma's happy planning for the "best trip ever" — the "trip to Mexico City — next year".

COMMENT ON TRANSFORMING AN HOUR-LENGTH STAGE ONE-ACT PLAY INTO A TWENTY-FOUR MINUTE TELEVISION PLAY

Title

The Prison in Paradise, while a provocative title, was changed to "Best Trip Ever," which it was felt better described the poignant theme of the play.

Time

As a stage one-act play, THE PRISON IN PARADISE was up against the problem of an awkward "time curtain" (the lowering of the curtain to denote a lapse of time); the author solved the problem by having the action of the stage play continuous, thus making Alma's decision not to go to Miami come very fast. However, in order to give scope and fluidity to the powerful story; and, technically, in order to meet the requirements of Armstrong's Circle Theatre that the television play have a two-act structure, with a climax at the end of Act One, the television play was designed to occur on two succeeding days. Thus, suspense was heightened, and the structure was made "tighter" at the same time that it was made "looser", i.e., greater in scope.

Sets

This one-act play necessarily had to occur in one set. The television play, however, also used the boardwalk outside the boarded-up shops, thus giving the CAMERA a chance to paint pictorially the loneliness and desolation of the shut-down amusement park. Again, since the television play tells the story *from the point of view of Tilly*, the boardwalk set gives us, the viewers, a chance to see Tilly away from Alma, to learn her feeling about Alma; and through the device of the Little Girl character, to set the desolation and the time of the play very quickly, with a minimum of dialogue. Also, the two additional sets in the television play, the doctor's office and the executive's office, create opportunity for increasing the suspense, as we see Tilly struggling with the tragic problem of what to do about Alma and her fatal illness. Since more *time* elapses, Alma's decision, finally, not to go, is more dramatic. The Policeman presents the added concern of Alma's friends about her; and he justifies his presence in the plot by being the one to telephone Tilly when the executive appears. To sum up: the additional scenes, both pictorially and dramatically, illustrate the desirability of visual variety in a television play; and they demonstrate the ability of a television play to move freely anywhere in order to dramatize (show in action) the events, rather than talk about them.

Characters

All but one of the radio characters in the stage play were eliminated. One announcer is kept, necessarily, in the television play.

On the stage, dialogue spoken over a radio will hold effectively; but nothing is less effective in a television play than a *radio character:* It usually means that the CAMERA is photographing a radio with a disembodied voice coming out of it, creating a static and tiresome scene, difficult even to listen to for any length of time. Therefore, only the *minimum essential* radio dialogue is kept in this television play. The presence in the television play of the Little Girl, the Policeman and the Executive have just been commented on.

Dialogue

The dialogue in the stage play, while very fine indeed, is "talky" and too full for television. The television play's dialogue is shorter, terser, moves faster, with no long speeches (long compared to the stage play); yet no essential points are lost and characterization is just as full, perhaps even fuller and richer through reason of the fact that the CAMERA shows CLOSE-UPS in which by skillful acting the actor's reactions convey more than words could.

Matching speeches and scenes from the stage play and the television play are offered for your comparison, to show the condensation of dialogue in the TV play:

STAGE PLAY	TELEVISION PLAY
ALMA: But we'll win the trip, Tilly, I know we will. I prayed for us to win. Last night I said to Our Maker, I said, 'Tilly and I want to go to Miami. We *deserve* to go to Miami. We've never won a contest yet, outside of ninth prize once, and it's our turn now. It sure is. So let us get the two weeks' trip, with all expenses paid'! That's what I said. And I'm a firm believer in the power of prayer.	ALMA: It *will* be us! It will, too, Tilly. You wait and see. I've been praying for us to win. We've never won a contest yet, outside of that ninth prize once, and it's our turn now, it certainly is!
———————	———————
ALMA: Well, they'll pay our way	ALMA: Just think what a good

to Florida. Like I said, it's part of the prize.

TILLY: Oh, listen to us going on this way! Remember last year, Alma, when we were going to get that weekend in New York? I even bought a new dress for the trip, you were that sure we'd win.

ALMA: It was criminal, our not winning that trip, Tilly, it really was. You know we had the best entry. The judges must of —

TILLY: I never even got to wear the dress, not once.

ALMA: — they must of been bribed.

TILLY: Hmph! That's what you always say.

ALMA: The trouble with you is you have no faith, Tilly. I think faith is an awful important thing, myself. Like my husband always said — he was an awful smart man, you know — he'd always say, 'Alma, people should have faith. They should look for the silver lining.' That's what he'd always be telling me. 'Look for the silver lining'. And he'd say, 'You should let hope spring eternal', too.
TILLY: Not me. Not any more. Every time we've got our hopes up before, we've lost. You've been on lots of trips — you said so your-

time we'll have in Miami! Accommodations in the best hotel! Flowers and pretty sailboats and palm trees and nice warm water! Tilly, do you suppose we ought to get bathing suits?

TILLY: My goodness, I haven't done any sea bathing in years!

ALMA: Me neither. Not in this chilly water up here. But down there it'll be all warm and lovely, and then when we finish our swim, we'll walk back nice and easy and have ourselves a fine seafood special in the hotel dining room!

TILLY: You make it sound so wonderful, Alma, we almost don't need to go.

ALMA: Oh, that's not the half of what we'll do, Tilly! After lunch, maybe we'll feel like a nice ride out to where they have those Indians and alligators and things and then after dinner we'll treat ourselves to a movie and then maybe a moonlight boat ride —

TILLY: Goodness, Alma, don't we ever get any rest?

ALMA: Sure we do, Tilly! In the biggest, widest, softest beds in the world!

self — so winning doesn't mean as much to you. But me — I've never gone anywhere, really, and this is my big chance. But there's no use hoping . . . we won't win.

ALMA: We've got as much chance as anybody else, Tilly.

TILLY: No. Not us.

ALMA: Well, *I* think we're going to win. We're going to win and go to Florida and stay in a wonderful hotel — the best room in it, the radio said — for two whole weeks, all expenses paid. Wait and see, Tilly!

TILLY: If only we *could* win . . . if I could get away from this place in winter the same as every one else. Sometimes when I'm walking down the boardwalk this time of year I feel almost like everybody's died and I'm the last person alive, Alma . . . and when that wind comes in off the water I get so I vow I'll close up my shop and leave for good, no matter what. Alma, if I could just get away from here for a little while . . . if we could only win . . .

ALMA: Think of it, Tilly — two whole weeks! You and me living like queens in the best hotel in Miami, Florida! We'd have people to wait on us hand and foot!

TILLY: I . . . I'd get to wear the

TILLY: And I'm staying right in mine till noon!

ALMA: No such thing! We can't waste a minute of our wonderful two weeks. We'll have a nice breakfast sent up and eat it in bed, and then we'll be ready to start out again! It's going to be the time of our lives, Tilly! And we mustn't waste a minute of it — not a single second!
(SHE COUGHS HARD)

TILLY: Alma! You mustn't get so worked up, Alma! It always starts you coughing.

ALMA: Oh, I'll be all right, Tilly. All I need is a little rest and sunshine. You'll see.

(A KNOCK ON THE DOOR. THE DOCTOR IS ARRIVING.)

dress I bought for New York, wouldn't I? Remember the dress, Alma? It was pink, with a lot of shiny beads . . .

ALMA: Of course you'll get to wear it, Tilly!

TILLY: There's no point in buying a dress you never have a chance to wear . . .

ALMA: I tell you what — I'll get a new dress, too! We'll both get dresses, lots and lots of them.

TILLY: We'd need a couple for riding on the train . . . .

ALMA: Train? We'll fly down there! In a plane, all the way. That's part of the prize.

TILLY: No, not in a plane. Not with that cough of yours.

ALMA: Then we'll go on a train, one of those big fast ones, with a little room with a bathroom and everything all to ourselves, and a colored boy to wait on us whenever we want anything, anything at all. Like ice water and magazines and —

TILLY: And we'll buy all the most expensive meals in the diner, too.

ALMA: But wait till we get to Miami! You know, I can close my eyes and see our room right now, clear as anything. There'll be a chandelier, a big, tinkly one, and — and a rug half a foot thick —

TILLY: And beds as wide as they are long! You know what, Alma. All this month I've had to light my stove and go back to bed till it's warm enough to make my breakfast.

(Author's note: no need to pound this point any further. The scene continues for a length as great as that already given you, concluding with the arrival of the doctor. In other words, the Stage Play scene is about three times the length of the corresponding scene in the Television Play.)

STRUCTURE

Master Scenes of the Stage Play

1. Alma and the Radio Announcer. We learn that Alma has entered a radio contest which she expects to win. She also seems to have a bad cough.

2. Alma and Tilly. This scene is repetitious of the first, since Alma has to convey to Tilly the information we've just gotten in (1). We learn of Dr. Talbot's X-raying of Alma. There is quite a lot of talk about Alma's hopes of winning the contest, with much reference to her trips with her husband in the past, before he died. More radio scenes, entirely irrelevant to the plot, are heard. In this long scene, as Alma and Tilly discuss their hopes and plans, the play has been on for approximately twenty minutes with no advancing of the actual plot beyond the women's hope of winning. True, there has been some wonderful characterizing of Alma and Tilly, and our attention holds; but *the plot has not advanced,* after those twenty minutes of playing. Then the Doctor arrives.

3. Alma, Tilly, Doctor Talbot (changed to Dr. Crane, for better aural impact, in the TV play). The X-rays are touched on briefly; then the doctor must be told about the radio contest, dialogue which tends to be further repetitious as far as the audience is con-

cerned. Alma exits on a fairly trivial motivation in order to leave Tilly and the Doctor alone for a moment.

4. Tilly and the Doctor. Now the plot advances in a big step, as the Doctor reveals the facts of Alma's fatal illness to Tilly. He leaves before Alma returns. The play has been on for about thirty-three minutes (nine minutes *more* than the *total* playing time of the TV play).

5. Alma and Tilly, and then the Radio Announcer. After some irrelevant dialogue about Swirlafoam Soap Flakes, and the repeating of details of the contest which we already know, Alma and Tilly are announced as winners. Following this announcement, there is more irrelevant (although accurate and authentic and atmospheric) radio dialogue.

6. Alma and Tilly. After the radio is turned off, and with the knowledge that they have won the trip, Alma and Tilly talk until the end of the play (about twelve minutes), until Alma has talked herself out of the idea of going to Miami, and into looking ahead to a possible trip to Mexico City. In short, the point of the play is made in this scene, which closes the play on a note of deep pathos and high drama, since we know what Alma perhaps does not know, that she is soon to die.

Master Scenes of the Television Play

1. In a quick, full visual opening, the locale is set by the CAMERA, as Tilly struggles against the wind, along the deserted boardwalk. At once the Little Girl appears, and her brief scene characterizes Tilly as a kind, loving woman. Then the Policeman appears, and suspense about Alma's physical condition is strongly established. Alma is, in effect, characterized although she is not present, through the concern these friends have for her. So, we are already involved emotionally in whatever is going to happen to Alma, and we are anxious to see her — from Tilly's point of view, as Tilly sees her.

2. Tilly, Alma and the Radio Announcer. At once, the basic plot step is taken: Alma expects to win a radio contest awarding the Miami trip. We hear only *one* radio speech, and we know the winners will not be announced until the next day. Follows a discussion of their hopes; and Alma's husband (a vital factor in her

characterization) is introduced pictorially, which could not be done as effectively on stage. Alma's illness is further pointed up; but the total scene runs only about six minutes, as compared with twenty minutes for the stage play. Then the Doctor arrives.

3. Alma, Tilly and the Doctor. The details of the contest are told to the Doctor, *more interestingly and pictorially,* through the fact that the contest was changed from jingle writing to the identification of baby pictures. From the Doctor's reactions we sense his concern for Alma, should she win. When Alma leaves, her motivation is excellent, since she goes to prepare coffee for the Doctor.

4. Tilly and the Doctor. In a brief scene, hardly three minutes long, the Doctor's verdict is told to Tilly, and he leaves. The plot has advanced strongly and quickly; total playing time so far about eleven minutes.

5. Alma and Tilly. In a brief scene, Tilly's evasiveness builds suspense, particularly as we know from Master Scene 2 that the winner of the contest will be announced the next day. We, the audience, have our hopes and fears played on by the suspense of Alma's illness set up against the chance that she might win: if she does, what will happen? Whereas, in the stage play, this suspense is not held very long (in elapsed time), through the necessity for the stage play to be a continuous action.

6. Tilly and the Policeman. The suspense is further heightened by Tilly's being torn as to what to do — the *best* to do — for Alma, should she win.

7. Alma alone, talking to the picture of her husband. Here, greater poignancy is extracted from the situation, as we learn Alma's innermost thoughts about the trip, and also her horrible loneliness. Colloquially, we can say that the situation and the suspense are being "milked dry". Importantly, this one brief scene accomplished what the stage play needed several pages to do: to paint completely Alma's relations, past and present, with her husband. Technically, it is a Cover Scene to let the Policeman move to the wall telephone set from the boardwalk where we saw him with Tilly.

8. There has been a day's time lapse. The Policeman at a wall

telephone. His concern for Alma is revealed in his news to Tilly that a "fellow" is asking for Alma.

9.　Alma and the Executive, then Tilly, almost at once. Here, we see played out the news that Alma has won the contest, instead of hearing it, rather inadequately, as far as television goes, over the radio. Now, the "boom has been lowered"; what is Alma to do? Suspense about her illness has been built up until the news that she has won becomes almost tragic in its implications, and certainly full of suspense as to what will happen to Alma.

10.　Alma and Tilly. Alma's apparently reckless disregard of her physical condition, in her determination to go on the trip, further builds suspense, and motivates the next scene. (NOTE: to give Tilly time to move from the shop set to the doctor's office, Alma's *last* speech, and the doctor's *first* speech in the next scene, are played in CLOSE-UP, *excluding* Tilly, who quickly hurries to the doctor's office set.)

11.　The Doctor and Tilly. We learn that the trip probably will kill Alma, if she goes on it, and Tilly's problem is increased to climactic pitch.

12.　Tilly and the Little Girl, on the boardwalk. In a short, but intensely emotional scene, Tilly is shown as having arrived at some decision, but what it is we don't know. Act One ends at this high point of suspense and drama. *All* elements of the conflict have been introduced and worked up to the greatest possible tension, for suspense, to carry over, through the Commercial Announcement, into the second act.

13.　Opening of second act. Alma and Tilly. They are finishing lunch, and from their conversation, we learn that Alma has decided she will go on the trip. From the extension of the total elapsed time of the TV play, in contrast to the stage play, there is *time* to put Alma on an "up" peak, and hold her there, before the "down" curve begins — more time, again, than in the stage play, which had to be performed in continuous action. Alma's reactions and decisions, therefore, become more dramatic because they are more thoughtful, more "long drawn out."

14.　Tilly alone on the boardwalk. We have seen her leave Alma in a greatly disturbed frame of mind (Tilly, that is). When she pulls out the Executive's card, we know that she will attempt *something* — to try and work things out for Alma.

15. The Executive and Tilly. Tilly has come to ask for a postponement of the trip, until Alma is better. But this cannot be done — the announcement over the radio, nationally, will be made that afternoon. Here is a further "milking dry" of the situation. The scene ends with Tilly's taking the railroad tickets, in desperation, although suspense is still strong and the problem of Alma still very much undecided.

16. Alma and Tilly, played out to the end. As in the stage play, although in a much shorter time period, and with very much shorter dialogue, Alma talks herself out of going to Miami, and into looking forward to the "best trip ever" in her mind, the possible future trip to Mexico City, after another contest has been won, while Tilly knows, and we know, that she will die.

There were *five* Master Scenes, then, in the stage play, and *sixteen* in the television play, reflecting the fluid characteristic of television as compared with the static nature of a stage play. The result surely is greater richness of emotional impact from the television play, as through a diversity of scenes the tragedy of Alma slowly builds to its logical climax. Eliminated from the television play are all *extraneous elements*, even to the paring of words from individual speeches.

The trick, the "secret", the technique, is *Condensation* to vital, indispensable plot elements, with all human and dramatic values *milked dry*.

A detail in passing: The contest was changed from "Swirlafoam Soap" to "Fireside Coffee" in order to remove any satirical note of "radio soap operas" the original contest might imply. The snatches of "radio play" also in the stage play were satirical; and it was felt that this note of satire was distracting in a powerful and tragic human story, particularly as it was told under the intense, "concentrating" microscope of television.

Condensation — Condensation — Condensation! Action dramatized — played out for us to see — rather than talked about!

Best Trip Ever, by Frederic Manley, starring Enid Markey as

Tilly and Elizabeth Patterson as Alma, was produced on Armstrong's Circle Theatre. According to its producers, it remains one of the outstanding successes of this successful program.

Mr. Manley's adaptation of his one-act play into a television play was the first television play he had ever written, and the first literary work he ever sold.

9

The Half-Hour
Television Play: "Live"

Of course, there's no such thing as a half-hour television play. A half hour is the amount of time (less seconds-long "station break" commercial announcements and station identification signals) which a sponsor buys from the network or single telecasting station. Deduct the time for the cost-bearing commercials of the sponsor himself, and there is left the time for the so-called half-hour play, which runs sometimes a maximum of twenty-four minutes, more often twenty-two minutes.

In these twenty-two minutes, a play with a beginning, a middle and an end must be presented. Almost without exception, it will be a two-act play, ideally so written that there will be enough suspense, enough carry-over value, at the end of the first act to hold its audience through the long and most important middle commercial of the sponsor, who knows that his tag-end message may be lost because viewers turn off their television sets when the play is over.

It may be that the half-hour play of the future, filmed for television use, may run a maximum of twenty-seven minutes, leaving "both ends open" for local sponsorship. "Both ends open", or "open at both ends", means that time has been allowed at the beginning and at the end for a local sponsor's announcement. It is possible, although at present writing it seems inconceivable, that such a play may run without interruption from the beginning to the end, with no middle commercial. It seems inconceivable because so far no altruistic sponsor has appeared who is willing to forego that middle commercial, when his most important message is spotted in the most favorable position. There is at this time intense activity in film production centers both in the United States and abroad, where filmed television shows are being prepared against the day when there will be as many telecasting stations as radio stations at their maximum number. Since all these future stations may not be connected to the coaxial cable, i.e., they will not receive the programs of the coast-to-coast networks, they will have to be serviced individually. This service will come in the form of filmed television plays, just as motion picture theatres are serviced by plays on film. To repeat: these local television stations will telecast plays "open at both ends", sponsored locally. However, it seems safe to say that these filmed plays will provide for a middle commercial; hence their structure must be two-act.

So, the "half-hour" television play is a two-part, one-act play. Or, it is the second and third acts of the conventional three-act play.

What happens to the first act, if the half-hour television play is the second and third acts of the conventional three-act play?

The first act should have happened in the playwright's mind, and should be reflected in the skill of his exposition as he introduces his characters and gets the plot started.

Another way to say it is that before the first fade-in on a half-hour television play, everything has already happened, so that the play the audience sees is a resolution of this piled-up situation, with one forward development to show the final fate of the characters, resulting logically and inevitably from the situation where we first met them.

We have seen from the sections on Time and Exposition that it is imperative to start the story *at once*, ideally with the principal character or characters giving their own exposition. To illustrate from a successful half-hour television play produced "live": on the first fade-in, the heroine, a young woman, is seen unpacking books from a carton marked "Acme Moving Company". She has on a smock; she is putting the books onto a shelf. We can assume she is moving into the room where she is working. At once, the door bell rings. The heroine opens it, and a small girl throws herself

into the heroine's arms, saying, "Are you my Mummy? . . . .
Don't you know me, Mummy?"

Well, there we have an emotional situation within seconds of
the start of the play. In the next minute, we learn that the heroine
is *not* the child's mother, although she doesn't tell the child she is
not; that the child's real mother divorced her father when the
child was four; that the child is now eight years old; that she and
her father long for "Mummy" to come back home. All this is "first-
act material"; it is the piled-up pre-camera situation we've talked
about. Yet the story is well started, because the young woman,
our protagonist, is so characterized that we feel she is going to *do*
something about the lonely child, and what she does, we know,
will be the story. With these points in mind, read the opening of
the following play:

THE RUNAWAY HEART *

by Doris Halman
(Produced on *Armstrong's Circle Theatre*)
ACT I

FADE IN: OPENING SHOT:
A FURNISHED ONE-AND-A-HALF ROOM APARTMENT
IN A BIG NEW YORK CITY APARTMENT HOUSE.
THE FURNISHINGS ARE NOT NEW, AND THEY SHOW
SIGNS OF USE BY A LONG SERIES OF TENANTS,
SOME CARELESS; BUT ORIGINALLY THEY WERE VERY
GOOD. THE APARTMENT FACES AN OPEN COURT,
AND LOOKS OUT THROUGH A HUGE CASEMENT
WINDOW ON A SKYLINE OF MIDTOWN TOWERS AND
A DISTANT HIGH-FLUNG BRIDGE: BUT THIS VIEW
IS AT FIRST CUT OFF BY A LOWERED VENETIAN BLIND.
OPPOSITE THE WINDOW, A BOOKCASE AND AN
ARCH LEADING TO A TINY FOYER IN WHICH IS THE
ENTRANCE DOOR. GLASS-PANED DOOR TO A
NARROW KITCHENETTE IN ONE WALL, SIMILAR
DOOR IN THE OTHER LEADS TO THE DRESSING ROOM
AND BATH. TWIN STUDIO COUCHES, WING CHAIR

* Reproduced by permission of the author.

BESIDE SMALL TABLE WITH READING LAMP IN
WINDOW, DINETTE TABLE WITH TWO STRAIGHT
CHAIRS. HOUSE PHONE IN FOYER, OUTSIDE PHONE
BESIDE WING CHAIR. ON THE FLOOR NEAR THE
BOOKCASE, A HEAVY CARTON MARKED "ACME
MOVING COMPANY", CONTAINING BOOKS.
HARRIET CRANDALL KNEELS BY THE CARTON,
PUTTING BOOKS ON THE SHELVES. SHE IS A TALL
GIRL IN HER LATE TWENTIES, VERY ATTRACTIVE, WITH
A FIRM SWEET MOUTH AND LAUGHING EYES.
SHE HAS BEEN WORKING HARD, AND IS FLUSHED
AND WEARY, AND HER SIMPLE KNEE-LENGTH SMOCK
IS RUMPLED. AS SHE PAUSES TO BRUSH BACK A STRAND
OF HAIR . . . . THE DOORBELL EMITS A SMALL
"PING," AS IF SOMEONE TRIED TO RING IT — AND
DIDN'T. HARRIET LOOKS UP TOWARD THE FOYER,
DECIDES IT WAS A MISTAKE, TURNS BACK TO WORK.
THE DOORBELL REALLY RINGS. HARRIET GETS UP,
SMOOTHS HER SMOCK, GOES QUICKLY INTO THE FOYER
AND OPENS THE ENTRANCE DOOR.
A LITTLE GIRL EIGHT YEARS OLD, WEARING COAT
AND HAT, AND CLUTCHING A CHILD'S PURSE, STANDS
THERE ALONE, LOOKING UP AT HARRIET WITH ROUND
PLEADING FRIGHTENED EYES. THE LITTLE GIRL IS
SO TENSE THAT SHE CAN'T MOVE A MUSCLE, AND IT
TAKES HER A SECOND BEFORE SHE CAN SPEAK. . . . .
HER NAME IS LINDA, AS WE LEARN . . .

LINDA

Are you my Mummy?

HARRIET (BLANKLY ASTONISHED)

What . . . . . .

LINDA (SHE PAUSES)

Don't you know me, Mummy? I'm *Linda!*
(AS HARRIET STARES AT HER) You're just like your
picture, Mummy — (SHE IS CRYING NOW) —
Please, don't send me away!

HARRIET

Why, no, dear, I shan't send you away —

Come in, and don't cry, and we'll talk about
this, and then we'll find out everything's all right.
(PUTS HER HAND OUT TO THE CHILD)
Come on!

                    LINDA
(REACHES FOR THE HAND, CLUTCHES IT)
I was *so* afraid . . . . (ENTERS AND SUDDENLY
CLINGS TO HARRIET, SOBBING)
Ohhh . . . Mummy . . . . Mummy . . . .

                    HARRIET
(CARESSING HER) Don't cry, Linda — ssssh!

                    LINDA
(HICCUPING)
I thought — you didn't want me.

                    HARRIET
Why should you think your mother doesn't
want you, dear?

                    LINDA
The children at home — they say (SINGS IT AS
KIDS WOULD MAKE A TAUNT OF IT) Yah . . . Yah . . .
Linda Moore's mother didn't want her . . .
Linda's mother ran a-way! . . . (STOPS ON LONG
SOBBING BREATH)

               HARRIET (GENTLY)
Oh, I see.

               LINDA (PLEADINGLY)
I wouldn't be a bother . . . if you came back . . .
I promise, Mummy. I was only four then, but
I'm eight now . . . and I can take care of myself . . .

                    HARRIET
Linda, dear . . . . There are things you don't
understand . . . .

                    LINDA
Our housekeeper says you — walked out, but
Daddy says you were beautiful — and we just
weren't good enough for you. And you *are*
beautiful — you *are!*

HARRIET (LOW)
(SHE HAS A THOUGHT) Linda, is your Daddy here
with you? Is he waiting downstairs?

LINDA
No! He doesn't know where I am!
(SHE SMILES) It's a secret, Mummy.

HARRIET
Do you mean you ran away to find your mother?

LINDA
(NODS VIOLENTLY THROUGH HER TEARS)
Yes — from the others. They don't know I've
gone . . .

HARRIET
What others? Where are the others, dear?

LINDA
The second grade — our teacher brought us to
the zoo — all the way from Dirkstown — that's
where I live — Dirkstown.

HARRIET
And you just slipped way — and you didn't tell
any one?

LINDA
Nobody was looking — and then I asked a
policeman —

HARRIET
But your teacher will be worried about you, when
she finds you gone, and your Daddy will worry,
too. You don't want to worry your Daddy —

LINDA
He won't know till dinner time, and sometimes
he's late for dinner. (AS AN AFTERTHOUGHT)
Sometimes he doesn't come home for dinner
at all —

HARRIET
Oh . . . . .

LINDA
When somebody's really, really sick, and he has
to stay with them and make them well . . . .

HARRIET

But who stays with you, dear?

LINDA

Oh, the housekeeper gives me supper —
(RAISES PLEADING EYES) We'd have plenty of
time to get home — if we started now!
Mummy, let's start home now!

HARRIET

But, Linda . . . .

LINDA

Don't make me go back by myself.

HARRIET (SOOTHINGLY)

I think the best thing to do is to talk a little more,
until you're rested, and had something to eat —
(HARRIET IS REMOVING LINDA'S HAT AND COAT
AND HELPS HER INTO THE WING CHAIR)
You could drink a glass of milk, couldn't you?

LINDA (NODS)

(SHE SITS IN WING CHAIR, AT FIRST STIFFLY, THEN
PRESENTLY CURLING UP IN IT AND LOOKING WITH
INTEREST AROUND THE ROOM)

HARRIET

I'll be right back, dear.
(MEANWHILE ENTERS KITCHEN, TAKES GLASS FROM
CUPBOARD AND MILK BOTTLE FROM REFRIGERATOR,
POURS MILK INTO GLASS, RETURNS BOTTLE)
But when you left your little friends at the zoo —
how did you find this apartment?

LINDA

Oooh — I knew your address, Mummy — it's on
the envelope when Daddy writes you the check
every month.
(OUT OF LINDA'S SIGHT, HARRIET'S FACE IS SHOCKED)

HARRIET

You're a very observant little girl, Linda.

LINDA

. . . Mummy, why does it say "Mrs. Pennergas

Moore" instead of "Mrs. William Moore"?
Daddy's name is *William!*

HARRIET
(HARRIET BRINGS THE MILK INTO THE LIVING ROOM.
SHE SMILES, SPEAKS CASUALLY)
That's when there's been a divorce. Now, how
about drinking this milk, hmmm?

LINDA (TAKES MILK)
All right. (DRINKS) I guess I was hungry,
after all.

HARRIET
Didn't the policeman ask you questions when he
saw you were alone?

LINDA
He was nice. I just told him I was — was
turned around. He put me in a beautiful
checkered car — and told the driver where to go.

HARRIET
(TAKES EMPTY GLASS FROM LINDA, SETS IT ON
TABLE, FACE AVERTED)
But when you reached the apartment house,
Linda — what did you tell the doorman?

LINDA
I just asked him how to find apartment 17 T,
and he showed me the elevator . . .
(ANXIOUSLY) Wasn't that right?

HARRIET
(SMILES AT HER) Yes, of course! Linda . . .

LINDA
What, Mummy?

HARRIET
You know I didn't expect you this afternoon . . .

LINDA (LAUGHS)
You were surprised, weren't you, Mummy?

HARRIET
Very surprised. But you see, honey, I had other
plans, all made. (GENTLY) Would you mind very
much if I left you — for a little while?

LINDA (ANXIOUSLY)

You'll come back?

HARRIET

I'll come back as soon as I can. And when I do —
I may bring you a lovely surprise!

DISSOLVE

To ease your perhaps natural curiosity about what happens in
the rest of *The Runaway Heart*: Linda's father comes to the apartment (Harriet telephones him when she exits, above). He is of
course grateful to Harriet, who likes him, too. Harriet insists on
telephoning Linda's mother: we see her, a selfish, self-centered
woman who is about to leave on a long tour, and who wants no
part of Linda. The problem therefore is dumped right in Harriet's
lap: a wonderful little girl who thinks Harriet is her mother, and
an attractive doctor who without saying anything conveys his
need and Linda's for Harriet to come and live with them. Harriet
is torn; in the end, there is an indication that some day Harriet
will come and be Linda's mother — but before the ending, with
this inference, Harriet delicately and gently convinces Linda that
she is not her mother. The news makes no difference to Linda:
she has accepted Harriet as her mother, under any circumstances;
and we know that in the not too distant future, there will be a
happy family of Harriet, the doctor and Linda, in a real home.

Let's pound home the fact that this whole story develops out of
one situation quickly and strongly established: Linda's jolting
arrival at Harriet's apartment.

What, then, ideally and practically, constitutes a good half-hour
television play?

Firstly, a single situation is all that's needed, and all there's time
for. On this single situation, a story is built to a logical first-act
climax, with strong suspense. The second act picks up at this
climax, and moves through rising action to a high climax and on to
the denouement. There can be no subplot; as we have said and
will say again, if there is a subplot, the characterization will be so
superficial (through lack of time to develop it) that the characters
will never come to life, and your play will fail because it is not
believable.

Secondly, the characters must give their own exposition, in the single situation; and their dialogue must be so written that it characterizes, gives exposition and simultaneously *advances the story*. There is *no time* for minor characters who talk about the plight the protagonist is in, setting the scene for his entrance. To repeat: the sooner a television protagonist comes on camera and undertakes the responsibilities of his own exposition, the better the television play is. This circumstance makes it possible to state a rule from which your author believes there can be *no deviation:* exposition must be given *in action.* The playwright must devise dramatic illustrative incidents *at once* to show his protagonist *in* the situation of the play, *exposing* what's happened before the fade-in (i.e., the "first act"), and *advancing* the story . . . all three. *"Exposition in action."*

And . . . *the action must be kept on the principal characters.* There is no better example known to this author of "action on the principal characters" than *Romeo and Juliet,* in a long play. The entire cast of *The Runaway Heart* numbers only four persons: Linda, Harriet, the doctor, and the doctor's divorced wife (who is seen in split-screen effect, talking on the telephone to Harriet). It would be impossible *not* to keep the action on the principals of *The Runaway Heart.* However, to show you how "action is on the principal characters" in a half-hour play with a large cast, there is printed in full further along in this chapter the successful half-hour television play, *Billy Adams, American,* by Theodore W. Case, produced on Armstrong's Circle Theatre. *Billy Adams, American* will be commented on later.

Motivation in all playwriting is, of course, basic. It must be sound, clear, believable and understandable. But motivation in the half-hour television play is of the greatest possible importance: the brief playing time prohibits any long-drawn out presentation of *involved* motivation. You have your choice: strong, clear, simple motivation which can be presented "in action," as in *The Runaway Heart;* or intricate and involved motivation which consumes half of your first act playing time in the explaining of it. Once again: the *medium dictates its own rules!* Simplicity of concept, of motivation, is the solution; the *single* situation quickly established.

For example: to give a perhaps grotesque illustration, exaggerated to make the point:

Dad Jones is a widower with four children. His dead wife willed each child a sum of money to be paid on the child's wedding day. Now, Widow Smith has four children also. Her dead husband left each child a sum of money to be paid each child when married, but only if the child didn't marry until he (or she) was twenty-five years old, and only if the eldest child married first, the second child next, the third child third, and the fourth child last. And if one of the Smith children marries out of turn, his money goes to the others who agree to marry *in* turn. While if the Widow Smith herself marries again, she will lose all but her dower right in the estate her husband left her.

When the story opens, Dad Jones' oldest child (a boy) is in love with Widow Smith's third child (a girl, naturally). And the Widow Smith is in love with Dad Jones, whose children don't want him to marry again under any circumstances. However, he *could* love the Widow Smith; but if he married her against his children's desires, would he break up the happiness of his oldest child and the Widow Smith's third child, who also will lose her money?

The play's solution — its story development — is the matching of the Jones children with the Smith children (fortunately the sexes are right), although the oldest Smith child, out of spite and cupidity, tries to hold out in order to get the other Smith children's money, when they show signs of marrying out of turn. There is also the twenty-five year age detail, which has to be set aside as unreasonable by a properly empowered court of law.

Sounds contrived as the devil, doesn't it? Believe it or not, in one editor's experience, literally hundreds of half-hour television plays are written (but not produced) which are almost as involved in motive and concept. Naturally (or unnaturally) they turn out to be just so many thousands of words filling the necessary number of pages: they are confused, infuriating, without reality, without interest, and our poor brains are befuddled in the effort just to get the relationships and the facts straight. The entire play in the Dad Jones-Widow Smith story easily could be devoted to exposition alone. Of course, this illustration is exaggerated, but not very much, not very much, when your author thinks of the hundreds of contrived and complicated (as to motivation) half-hour television plays he has read. The word "contrived" is the final verdict: such intricately-motivated plays *always* are contrived.

Contrast the Jones-Smith saga's motivation with the simplicity of the premise in *The Runaway Heart* and (later) *Billy Adams, American*. In the first, the motive is Linda's need for a mother; in the second, it is the German father's burning desire to have his son Billy brought up as an American.

Another abyss to be avoided is the "god in the machine" solution, the solution "out of left field." Audiences have been known to rise and depart in a body from plays solved by a last-minute, extraneous, illogical force. Millions of irate television viewers turn to another channel in fury when they see such a television play. Yet, this deformed solution to a knotty dramatic problem is a great temptation to beginning television playwrights: it is so *easy* to solve Dick and Sally's quarrel over money (they are about to get a divorce because she is tired of cooking and washing and scrimping so that Dick can stay home and write his great American novel) — the solution is, Sally's Uncle Ed suddenly dies and leaves her a fortune, and now she can have everything she wants and also subsidize Dick while he finishes the aforesaid novel. *This is cheating!* The solution was not innately in the dramatic situation as set up. The author of such a play would not dare to reveal, in the first act, the fact that Sally had a rich uncle, because we, the audience, would know at once that at the proper moment, said uncle would turn up with his money bags and solve the dramatic problem. Suspense would be non-existent.

Of course, the Sally-Dick-rich uncle story *could* be told with the uncle in at the start of the play, provided, say, that he set up the condition to Sally: "You leave Dick, and I'll make you my heiress." The conflict, then, would be: "Shall Sally stick to Dick and poverty, or leave him for wealth?" Such a play could be dramatically sound, even though grey with mediocrity and triteness.

It may be unnecessary to explain the phrase, "god in the machine," but your author will risk insulting your intelligence and assuming a lack of experience in the history of drama: the Greek dramatists of antiquity frequently constructed their plays so that the action rose to an insoluble (by mortal standards) climax. At this climax, a mechanical device (the machine of the phrase) was lowered from the Greek version of the proscenium arch, carrying an actor impersonating a god. The god spoke to the humans involved in the insoluble situation, arbitrarily saying what was to happen, that is, resolving the climax by "divine" power. The god's solution may have had nothing whatsoever to *do* with the forces bringing on the climax; but his solution, being "divine," had to be accepted. In short, the "god in the machine," the *deus ex machina* (which of course is Latin and not Greek), was the rich Uncle Ed of his time, appearing at just the right moment to settle Dick's and Sally's problem. *This was cheating*, by our modern dramatic standards.

It may be argued that many novels and motion pictures, and some long plays, successfully have used the "god in the machine" solution in the form of outside melodramatic action (a flood, the Chicago fire, an air raid, etc., etc.). This argument would not be disputed by your author. He would, however, point out the adjective "long," meaning that with more time, such melodrama can be made believable; and he would remark that usually such melodramatic events show the characters in the play, the novel or the motion picture caught up and trapped and torn and twisted and changing spiritually (for either better or worse) during the action of the "left field" melodramatic device. For instance, a few years ago, a thunderingly successful motion picture, *San Francisco*, had as its climax the historical earthquake-fire which smote the city of San Francisco. While the earthquake-fire was shaking-raging, the principal characters in the story were going through a hell which made them much better people. Their progress was shown pictorially at the end of the picture when, hand in hand, quite a number of the principal characters were shown coming up over the brow of a hill, singing in unison. This scene was heavy symbolism, signifying the characters' triumph over their problems and over the catastrophe. And, of course, it was the end of the picture, inevitably; it might be said that the picture was made only to show the earthquake-fire in all its horror. Another motion picture, *Chicago*, used the historical Chicago fire for a like purpose; still another, *Hurricane*, was about a hurricane in the Pacific islands.

Nevertheless, all such solutions *are* "gods in the machine," "out of left field," and their success, in one man's opinion, was derived from the time and detail in which they could be shown, and from the scope of the stark physical catastrophes represented.

In a half-hour television play, this time and detail are not available. Please so construct your half-hour television plays that their "end is in their beginning," so that the resolution of the conflict is a *logical* result of the premise, the situation, first established. Have the strength of character to *refuse* Uncle Ed's "easy" money!

Flashbacks (dramatized incidents which have happened in the past, before the play begins) can be used successfully in the half-hour television play. Their use ordinarily means less story, a more static play. The contemporary situation which we are first told about usually has been created by the circumstances shown in the flashback; and almost without exception, the resolution of this contemporary situation comes out of the forces revealed in the flashbacks. One flashback may be used, or several. If several are used, the play then becomes the presentation of a contemporary situation, with the *story* (i.e., the developing action) happening in the past, at whatever times the playwright chooses as relevant. Then, after the final flashback has revealed *all* the story, all the facts we need to know, the final solution is given as a contemporary result.

It is extremely difficult, if not impossible, to present flashbacks in any "live" television play which require more than a superficial costume or make-up change by the actor. Common practice, then, is to have other actors resembling as closely as possible the actors of the contemporary situation appear in the flashbacks (in a "live" television play using flashbacks).

Sometimes only one flashback is used, to explain in dramatized form (rather than in exposition spoken in the contemporary situation) the facts we need to know, to understand and be interested in the contemporary situation and the story which develops out of it.

The following Act One from *Pilgrimage*, by Anne Howard

Bailey (presented on Armstrong's Circle Theatre and used by permission of the author), shows a contemporary situation created entirely by the events dramatized in the two flashbacks. In fact, the male love interest, Anthony, appears only in the flashbacks. In *Pilgrimage*, one actress played the elderly Lillian Marble, and a much younger actress, Lillian Marble as a girl of twenty.

In Act Two of *Pilgrimage*, two additional and fairly long flashbacks carry forward the story, in order to explain the climax and denouement of the contemporary situation, which is that the character, Julia Smith, having married Anthony abroad, has returned to Springford in order to give to the elderly Lillian Marble the second, matching half of a ring the young Lillian Marble had accepted from Anthony when, as a successful young novelist, he had left Springford forever. For at his death, as a mature and famous man, Anthony had asked his wife, Julia, to take the ring back to Lillian Marble, proof to Lillian that she was the woman Anthony had really loved all the years, although she and Anthony never consummated their love, nor even saw each other after she had sent him away to the fame and fortune she felt herself inadequate to share with him.

Please read this Act One, then re-read the capsule story of Act Two given above. You will see at once that *Pilgrimage* is a play impossible to write except with flashbacks telling the major part of the story, and explaining the basic motivations of the characters. (Act Two is not reproduced because it is felt not to be necessary to make the point of a half-hour play told chiefly through flashbacks.)

PILGRIMAGE
by
Anne Howard Bailey

CAST

LILLIAN MARBLE	The custodian of the Anthony Baxter Ford Museum. A sweet-faced, wispy woman just turning sixty. Her face is set in the patient lines common to those who have deserved, but barely

missed, the deep loves and high experiences of life.

(As a girl, of about 20. Slight, frail-looking with a sort of ethereal expression)

JULIA SMITH

The visitor. A tall, striking woman in her early 50's. More than casually Continental in her manner and speech. She is exquisitely dressed, and her manner fluctuates between a reserved charm, and sudden spurts of true warmth.

ANTHONY FORD

(As a boy of 21. Tall, almost dazzlingly handsome, with a personality so genuinely and unconsciously winning that he captivates everyone)

MR. TREXLER

A rather pompous, but withal good-hearted man in his mid-fifties. Obviously well-to-do, and well-thought-of.

HENRY PEELER

A mouse of a man — one of those fussy, dry-as-dust scholars.

MRS. ARTHUR DAWSON

A loud, bosomy, over-dressed woman in mid-thirties, whose quest for "culture" reaches horrifying proportions.

ARTIE DAWSON

Her brat of a son. About ten.

KAY STEVENSON

(A friend of young Anthony and Lillian. She is all that Lillian is not — at 20 — witty, alluring, provocative.)

EXTRAS, MEN & WOMEN
AT ANTHONY'S PARTY   (Act Two only)

Main Set

INTERIOR

The Museum — which was Anthony Ford's home in the early Twentieth Century. It includes the entrance hall, and parlor, and conservatory, which opens off the parlor.

The hall has a large desk with a small sign, with the word "Custodian." The parlor is roped off with a heavy velvet cord. It is decorated in typical turn-of-the-century style, with certain strange additions, such as cases of classified rocks, mounted butterflies, and other paraphernalia which have been turned over to the Museum Society by loyal adherents of the Anthony Ford cult. Prominent on the book shelves are collected copies of the Ford novels. In its static repose, jarringly broken by pathetic little reminders of a once vital personality — the room is like all museum rooms.

An open archway, with folded-back French doors, leads to the conservatory. Once cosy — with its stuffed couch, and potted plants — it is now only dank.

Frag/
Exterior
Wild door, with huge brass knocker, and museum plaque.

Exterior set/
Springford Pond. (Both in winter and summer) This need not be elaborate, and can consist of a bit of sloping shore, with a crude rustic bench, and a bit of the water.

(For the summer scene, there should be grass, of course, and perhaps a drooping willow.)

(For the winter scene, if possible, the water should be frozen, and the ground white with snow.)

Act I

OPENING SHOT:

frag/ Wild Door

OPEN ON CLOSE-UP OF THE BRONZE PLAQUE AFFIXED TO THE DOOR. IT READS:

Early Home of
ANTHONY BAXTER FORD
Novelist, Journalist, Man of Letters
Born on these Premises
July 10, 1892
Died in Capri, Italy
Sept. 20, 1949

DISSOLVE THROUGH TO:

INT: THE MUSEUM PARLOR

OPEN ON A MEDIUM SHOT OF LILLIAN MARBLE,
WHO STANDS BY AN OLD MAHOGANY DESK JAMMED
IN ONE CORNER OF THE CLUTTERED PARLOR. SHE
RUNS A CAREFUL DUSTCLOTH OVER THE TOP, PAUSES
TO REPLACE TENDERLY A DIP PEN WHICH HAS JARRED
LOOSE FROM ITS HOLDER. HER MOVEMENTS ARE
LOVING, REVERENT — AS IF SHE DRAWS A SORT OF
STRENGTH FROM THE HOMELY DUTIES. SHE LIFTS
HER EYES TO THE OLD-FASHIONED FRAMED PICTURE
WHICH HANGS ABOVE THE DESK. IT IS OF A
HANDSOME, SMILING YOUNG MAN.

CUT TO: CLOSE-UP OF LILLIAN'S FACE. AS SHE
STUDIES THE PICTURE, HER EYES NARROW IN A
LOOK OF LOVE AND DEVOTION. THEN ABRUPTLY,
SHE SHAKES HERSELF FREE FROM HER REVERIE,
AND BRISKLY POLISHES THE PICTURE.

SOUND: A BELL TINKLE IS HEARD AS A DOOR,
OFF, OPENS AND CLOSES. LILLIAN TURNS,
PURSES HER LIPS AND STARTS TOWARD THE DOOR
LEADING TO THE ENTRANCE HALL. SHE BRUSHES
PAST THE WORN WINGBACK, AND A KNITTED SCARF,
CARELESSLY DRAPED OVER THE BACK, AS IF THROWN
THERE BY SOME YOUTHFUL, HURRIED HAND, FALLS
TO THE FLOOR. LILLIAN BENDS, AND PICKS UP THE
SCARF. SHE HOLDS IT FOR A SECOND, LACING HER
FINGERS IN THE SOFT WOOL. SHE HALF LIFTS IT TO
HER CHEEK, AS IF THE TOUCH WOULD EVOKE A
MEMORY. THERE IS A HEAVY STEP IN THE DOOR.

MR. TREXLER (ENTERING)

Ah . . . Miss Marble. So here you are.

LILLIAN

Just — tidying up, Mr. Trexler.

TREXLER (HEARTILY)

Splendid. Ha ha. Last finishing touch — on your
last day, eh?

LILLIAN (HOLLOWLY)

My — last day. Yes.

TREXLER

I want you to know — it's the Anthony Baxter
Ford Memorial Society's loss — ah — your
retirement, Miss Marble. We've been very
fortunate in having you for our custodian these
thirty years.

LILLIAN (QUICKLY)

I'd gladly stay on, Mr. Trexler.

TREXLER

Now — now! Anyone as faithful as you have
been, Miss Marble — deserves a rest. Yes,
indeed. Although — it's the Society's loss, as I
said. (HE STARTS OUT, THEN HALF TURNS BACK)
After all — you knew Anthony Ford, didn't you?

LILLIAN

Yes. I knew him.

SOUND: BELL TINKLE OFF

TREXLER

Ah ha — a "customer!" (CHUCKLES AT HIS JOKE)
Well, I don't suppose you'll mind one more
tour through the old house, will you? (HE TURNS ON
HIS HEEL AND EXITS, WITHOUT WAITING FOR AN
ANSWER.)

LILLIAN (TO THE EMPTY AIR)

One — more — tour . . . (SUDDENLY SHE CLASPS HER
HANDS AS IF THE PAIN OF PARTING FROM THE
HOUSE IS TOO MUCH TO BEAR. HER BODY BENDS,
AND SHE TOUCHES THE WINGBACK FOR SUPPORT)
Ohhh. . . . . .

SOUND: THE BELL TINKLE: OFF.

LILLIAN PULLS HERSELF ERECT, AND THE CAMERA
FOLLOWS HER AS SHE GOES INTO THE ENTRANCE HALL.
THERE ARE TWO "CUSTOMERS" WAITING ON THE
LONG BENCH IN FRONT OF HER CUSTODIAN'S DESK.
ONE IS JULIA SMITH; THE OTHER IS HENRY PEELER.
JULIA SITS QUIETLY, HANDS FOLDED. PEELER HAS AN

OLD-FASHIONED PINCE-NEZ CLAPPED TO HIS NOSE —
HE STUDIES A SHEAF OF OLD PAPERS, WHICH HE
STUFFS INTO HIS POCKET AS LILLIAN ENTERS.

LILLIAN (QUIETLY)

Good afternoon. Welcome to Ford House.

PEELER (ANXIOUSLY)

I do hope I'm not too late. I just drove over
from the University. Tedious journey. Very
tedious. But there were some — ah —
discrepancies in these later notes I have here of
Anthony Ford's — (HE PATS HIS BULGING POCKET)

LILLIAN

Discrepancies — ?

(THE OTHER GUEST, JULIA SMITH, SITS FORWARD.
HER ATTITUDE IS INSTANTLY ALERT.)

PEELER (WASPISHLY)

These are original letters — written by the
hand of Anthony Ford. To the president of our —
ah — University. In them he describes this —
ah — homestead. But — there are — ah —
inaccuracies . . . (HE PURSES HIS LIPS AND TCHS)
Such as — ah — the grandfather's clock.
Ford mentions it as standing by the — ah —
(HE PLUNGES INTO HIS POCKET TO CONSULT HIS
NOTES)

JULIA (CUTS — QUIETLY)

Between the hat rack, and the staircase.

BOTH PEELER AND LILLIAN STARE AT JULIA.
LILLIAN'S EYES FLICKER A TRIFLE, SHE LEANS
FORWARD TO STUDY THE QUIET, ELEGANT STRANGER.

LILLIAN (AFTER A MOMENT)

The clock was moved into the parlor, when
the house was opened as a museum. (BEAT)
Shall we begin with the tour?

JULIA AND PEELER MOVE OBEDIENTLY IN THE
DIRECTION OF THE PARLOR. LILLIAN DELIBERATELY
MATCHES HER STEP WITH JULIA'S.

LILLIAN

You must have — known Mr. Ford quite well?

JULIA

Over the years. Yes.

LILLIAN

But — you're not from Springford.

JULIA

No. I knew him abroad. In Europe.

THE TWO WOMEN STAND A MOMENT, EACH
MEASURING THE OTHER.

SOUND: THE BELL TINKLES, AND INSTANTLY THE
DOOR OPENS WITH A JAR. MRS. ARTHUR DAWSON,
AND HER YOUNG SON, ARTIE, BURST INTO THE
QUIET ELEGANCE OF THE ENTRANCE HALL. THEIR
PRESENCE IS SHOCKING, ALMOST AN AFFRONT TO
THE ATMOSPHERE OF THE OLD HOUSE.

MRS. DAWSON IS BE-SPANGLED. SHE JINGLES AS
SHE WALKS. HER SON IS A FIDGETY, BOISTEROUS
CHILD, WHO IMMEDIATELY BREAKS FROM HIS
MOTHER'S RESTRAINING HAND AND RUNS AND SWINGS
ON THE VELVET CORD, ROPING OFF THE PARLOR.

MRS. DAWSON (LOUDLY)

Artie! — Artie — come back here! (SHE STOMPS
HER FOOT.) Come back to mummy, dear. Now
we're going through the museum like a little
gentleman, aren't we, dear? (ARTIE WRITHES
IN HER CLUTCH. SHE SMILES HOLLOWLY AT THE
OTHERS.) He's just — all boy.

LILLIAN (GENTLY)

We're beginning the tour.

MRS. DAWSON

My husband and I were just driving
when I saw the plaque, and I said,
"Arthur, stop the car. We might as well start
Artie out right — bein' interested in culture and
that sort of thing." (THEN) Artie! Put *that down!*

ARTIE HAS SEIZED A GOLD-TOPPED CANE FROM THE
UMBRELLA STAND IN THE CORNER AND IS MAKING

LIKE AN ACK-ACK GUN. LILLIAN MURMURS A
POLITE ASSENT TO MRS. DAWSON.

LILLIAN

Shall we all start with the parlor?
(SHE REMOVES THE VELVET CORD AND THEY MOVE
THROUGH THE ARCHWAY INTO THE PARLOR. JULIA
PEERS AROUND AS IF SHE RECOGNIZES EACH CORNER
AND CREVICE. PEELER BUSILY BEGINS SCRIBBLING
NOTES ON DOG-EARRED PAPER)

PEELER

Mmm. Perfect . . . for its period. Perfect.

LILLIAN (BEGINS SPEAKING IN A FACILE,
RATHER EXPRESSIONLESS WAY)

Anthony Baxter Ford was born in this house
on July 10, 1892. He was the only child of
Evelyn and William Ford, both of whom died
in the sinking of the *Titanic* in 1912. (YOUNG
ARTIE MAKES A HIDEOUS SOUND LIKE A DEPTH BOMB,
AND GLUGS TO INDICATE THE SINKING SHIP. HIS
MOTHER SMILES FONDLY, THEN FROWNS AT HIM,
WHEN SHE SEES THE OTHERS' STARE OF DISAPPROVAL.
AFTER A MOMENT, LILLIAN CONTINUES)

LILLIAN (CONT.)

. . . . From childhood, young Anthony showed
marked literary tendencies, which first began to
flower during his youth here in Springford — and
later reached a ripe maturity during his later
years, which were spent travelling abroad to the
four corners of the world. (SHE MOVES TO THE
GLOBE, AND FONDLY RUNS HER HAND OVER THE
SPHERE. SHE GOES ON) It was at that desk —
(SHE INDICATES THE OLD DESK PUSHED INTO THE
CORNER, AND HENRY PEELER IMMEDIATELY SCURRIES
OVER TO PEER AT IT CLOSELY) — that the first
short stories, and the beginnings of the novel,
Wayfarer, which was to catapult Anthony Ford
to fame, were written. Over here is —

PEELER (CUTS — WASPISHLY)
There are stains on this desk. Ink stains.
(HE SHAKES HIS HEAD AND CLUCKS) It's a shame . . .
a shame! On such mahogany —
              LILLIAN
I'm afraid — genius takes liberties. (SHE SMILES)
He had a way of shaking the ink off his dip
pen while he was concentrating. It didn't make
any difference if there was a priceless Persian rug
underfoot. . . .
              JULIA (SOTTO)
No. It didn't matter.
(LILLIAN AND THE OTHER WOMAN EXCHANGE
GLANCES. SOMETHING UNSPOKEN FLICKERS BETWEEN
THEM. THEN LILLIAN MOVES ON TO INDICATE A
BUTTERFLY COLLECTION AND ROCK COLLECTION IN
CASES ON THE WALL)
              LILLIAN
The young Anthony loved everything that lived.
He was interested in everything. The world
to him was a box of surprises . . . gathered for his
own special delight. (HER EYES NARROW WITH
MEMORY) I remember we used to spend —
(QUICKLY SHE BITES OFF HER WORDS)
              JULIA (INTERPOSING QUICKLY)
Many of his writings mention a place called
Springford Pond . . .
              LILLIAN (SOFTLY)
Springford Pond. Yes. It's a beautiful spot —
sheltered by great slim birches, the water like
fine blown glass — the air as rich as new wine . . .
I remember . . .
(ANTICIPATE BACKGROUND MUSIC TO SET THE
SCENE FOR A FLASHBACK, POIGNANT WITH MEMORY,
AND THE RE-LIVED JOY OF A CERTAIN MOMENT.)
(BEGIN SLOW FADE OF LILLIAN AS SHE IS SPEAKING,
AND ON CUE "I remember — ")
FADE TO:

EXT: SPRINGFORD POND (SUMMER)
OPEN ON A REFLECTION OF LILLIAN, LYING
STOMACH DOWNWARDS ON THE EDGE OF THE
POND, LOOKING INTO THE CALM WATER. SUDDENLY,
A SHADOW FALLS ACROSS HER, A PEBBLE IS
THROWN, AND THE WATER'S SURFACE IS DISTURBED
INTO A THOUSAND RIPPLES. LILLIAN TURNS,
STARTLED, AND LOOKS UP TO SEE ANTHONY FORD,
TALL, AND HANDSOME AND SMILING, LOOKING
DOWN AT HER.

LILLIAN (A LITTLE SCARED)

Ohhh!

ANTHONY

I couldn't resist. Anything as pretty as you
shouldn't be wasting your reflection in a lake.

LILLIAN

It's not a lake. It's a pond. And I'm not pretty.

ANTHONY

You are, though. Maybe not pretty, but inwardly
beautiful — as if you're lit from inside by a
million suns.

LILLIAN JUST STARES AT HIM. ANTHONY LAUGHS
AT HER SHY WONDERING LOOK, AND FLOPS DOWN,
CROSS-LEGGED BESIDE HER.

ANTHONY (GOES ON)

You don't mind if I try out some dialogue on you,
do you? Just for the feel of it . . . and the
sound of it?

LILLIAN (BEWILDERED)

I — I don't — know.

ANTHONY (CHUCKLES)

Don't look so upset. This is the way it's supposed
to happen. In books, two people meet and start
talking, and instantly they have everything in
common. And then — your story's begun . . .

LILLIAN

But — in real life, people never seem to be at

the right place at the right time. So they miss
each other — all the way around.

ANTHONY

You were *here* — looking in the pond, weren't
you? And I came along. What could be
righter than this? (LILLIAN TRIES TO SPEAK
BUT HE STOPS HER) And before you can say
"I don't know you" — you will. I'm Anthony Ford.

LILLIAN (REACTS. AT HIS NAME SHE
BECOMES EVEN SHYER)

Ohh. (PAUSE) Well, I'm Lillian Marble.

ANTHONY

Lillian. Lillian Marble. (HE LEANS FORWARD)
I remember you, Lillian Marble. When I was
eight years old, I sat behind you in the third
grade, and one day I stole an all-day sucker off
your desk.

LILLIAN

I remember. (THEN) I would have given it to
you if you had asked me. It was cinnamon.
(SHE SMILES, SUDDENLY AND SHYLY) I hate
cinnamon.

ANTHONY

Where have you been all these years, Lillian
Marble?

LILLIAN

Here. Right here in Springford.

ANTHONY

Well, I've been here, too. On vacations, that is.
And I guess we've followed different paths to
Springford Pond. But — I'm glad we finally
got together.

LILLIAN

You mean — *here?*

ANTHONY

Here. And — everywhere. (HE STANDS, GIVES
HER HIS HANDS AND PULLS HER TO HER FEET.
HE PUTS A LIGHT HAND ON HER WAIST.) And let me

tell you now. It wasn't just — dialogue. You
are lit from inside by a million suns.

FADE OUT:

FADE IN ON:

INT: MUSEUM PARLOR

OPEN ON CLOSE-UP OF LILLIAN WHO STANDS,
LIPS PARTED, EYES DREAMY, AS IF LOST IN A
MEMORY TOO DEAR TO LET GO OF.

CUT TO: THE OTHERS WHO LOOK AT HER
EXPECTANTLY. THEN JULIA LEANS FORWARD
SLIGHTLY.

JULIA

You were saying that — you remember?

LILLIAN

Wh-at? Oh! (SHE PULLS HERSELF INTO THE
PRESENT WITH A JERK) Ah . . . no matter. Shall we
go on? (SHE MOVES TOWARD AN OLD FIDDLE CASE
ON THE WALL AND SHIFTS INTO HER CRISP
CUSTODIAN'S VOICE) Over here is Anthony Ford's
old fiddle case. As a boy, he was very musical,
and possibly — if he had not been strongly
inclined toward writing — he would have
attained recognition in —

JULIA (CUTS)

Could you tell us — his favorite tune?

LILLIAN

What?

THERE IS A SNORT FROM HENRY PEELER, AT THE
FRIVOLITY OF THE QUESTION.

JULIA

I simply thought that — well, it's the personal
things that give a true picture of a man.
(SHE LAUGHS SLIGHTLY) After all, there *are*
biographies.

LILLIAN (REASSURED)

Yes, of course. (SHE TAKES A FEW STEPS AND STOPS
BESIDE AN OLD CRANK-TYPE PHONOGRAPH) You
asked what was Anthony Ford's favorite tune?

He used to play the "Kerry Dances" on this
phonograph — and fiddle to it by the hour.
JULIA
Really. A rather — unusual choice.
LILLIAN
No. Anthony Ford, as a boy was full of — lights
and sudden shadows. Like the Irish. Like —
sunlight, filtered through trees . . . .
JULIA (STARING AT LILLIAN CLOSELY)
Anthony used those very words once. To describe
a girl he once knew here.
THERE IS A SECOND'S SILENCE, AND LILLIAN
CATCHES HER BREATH. SHE AND JULIA EXCHANGE
GLANCES. SUDDENLY THERE IS A RESOUNDING
CRASH FROM ANOTHER PART OF THE ROOM. ARTIE,
WHO HAS ESCAPED FROM HIS MOTHER'S CLUTCH,
HAS LURCHED INTO A CLAW-LEGGED SMOKING
STAND. IT TOPPLES, AND RAINS A PIPE RACK, BRONZE
ASHTRAY, AND A HOB-NAILED MATCH HOLDER WITH
BLUE-TIPPED MATCHES, ONTO THE FLOOR. LILLIAN
SPRINGS TO RETRIEVE THE FALLEN MEMENTOS.
MRS. DAWSON SNATCHES ARTIE BACK FROM THE
DEBRIS.
MRS. DAWSON (SHARPLY)
Artie! Artie! Don't meddle!
LILLIAN IS STANDING OVER THE FALLEN SMOKING
STAND LIKE AN AVENGING ANGEL. HER SOFT EYES
BLAZE.
LILLIAN
How dare you? How dare you? (HER BREATH
COMES SHORTLY)
MRS. DAWSON (SMOTHERING ARTIE WITH
MOTHERLY PROTECTIVENESS)
Well — *really!*
PEELER (LIFTING HIS PINCE-NEZ — AMAZED
AT LILLIAN'S OUTBURST)
I say!
LILLIAN (HER VOICE SHAKES)
Please, let me remind you that this is a museum.

A place set aside to honor the memory of a great man
of literature. A — a man — (WITH DIFFICULTY
SHE PRONOUNCES THE NEXT WORD) *beloved* — for
his moving concept of people, and their emotions
— and honored for the brilliance and clarity of
his thinking.

> MRS. DAWSON (HOTLY)

There's no call to yell at the child. He's only
a boy. He's just high-spirited.

> LILLIAN (DISTRAUGHT)

But you don't understand! This house is all I —
(SHE CATCHES HERSELF) It's just as Anthony
Ford left it. (SHE IS AWARE THAT PEELER AND
JULIA ARE STARING AT HER STRANGELY. WITH
DIFFICULTY SHE MASTERS HER EMOTION.) I'm sorry.
But please try to cooperate with the mood and
spirit of the house. (SHE DRAWS A RAGGED
BREATH) . . . The winter after Anthony's parents
died, he did not return to college. Instead he
stayed here, alone in the big house, except for his
guardian, John Trexler, father of one of our
present trustees. It was a growing time for
Anthony. Already the seeds of his genius were
beginning to germinate. Already he had started a
draft of his novel, *Wayfarer*.

> PEELER (INTERRUPTS)

Are you sure of this fact, madam? There are no
records to substantiate your statement . . .

> LILLIAN (QUIETLY)

Yes. I am sure. (THEN, SHE CONTINUES) For
recreation during the winter, Anthony would go
skating on Springford Pond, and the people
of Springford became used to seeing him every
day, with his skates hanging off his shoulder —
and his coat thrown open on freezing days.
(AS SHE TALKS SHE HAS MOVED NERVOUSLY AROUND
THE ROOM.

FINALLY SHE STOPS BY THE WING-BACK. HER HAND

RESTS ON THE SCARF — CARESSING IT. JULIA
NOTICES THIS)

JULIA

That was . . . his scarf?

LILLIAN (FINGERS IT, THEN PUTS IT DOWN
AND MOVES OVER TOWARD THE BOOK
CASES AS SHE TALKS)

It was — a Christmas present. Of course, it was
bright yellow then . . . (HER VOICE TRAILS,
AND HER EYES MIST OVER) . . . yes . . . a bright
yellow . . .

FADE OUT ON CLOSE-UP OF LILLIAN'S FACE.

SOUND: MUSIC UP TO WASH OUT SCENE

FADE UP ON:

EXT: SPRINGFORD POND (WINTER)

OPEN ON CLOSE-UP OF A PAIR OF HANDS FASTENING
SOMEONE ELSE'S ICE SKATES. PULL BACK SLOWLY
TO SHOW ANTHONY, KNEELING BESIDE LILLIAN WHO
IS SEATED ON A LOG. HE SECURES THE BUCKLE,
AND LEANS BACK ON HIS LEGS, AND SMILES UP AT
LILLIAN.

ANTHONY (GAILY)

Belted, buckled — and ready to go!

LILLIAN

I'll fall. I know I will.

ANTHONY

Don't you trust my two strong arms?

LILLIAN (SHAKILY)

I don't trust my two weak ankles. Please —
not today, Anthony!

ANTHONY

You've been saying that ever since the freeze set
in. What am I going to do with you? You won't
ice skate with me — you won't bob-sled with me —

LILLIAN

I'm not very — adventurous, Anthony.

ANTHONY (HUMOROUSLY)

Tell me this. Will you *dance* with me? Will you
dance *only* with me — at the Cotillion tonight?

LILLIAN (EVASIVELY)

I — I can't promise.

ANTHONY

Why? Why not?

LILLIAN

I — wasn't planning to go.

ANTHONY

But — it's Christmas Eve — and it's the biggest dance of the year. Everybody in Springford will be there — and I want *you* there. With me.

LILLIAN

I'm not a very good dancer, Anthony. And I don't know many of your friends.

ANTHONY

You know *me*. That's all that's important. (PLEADING) Say you'll go.

LILLIAN (WISTFULLY)

Ohh — I wish things could be like this — right now — for always and always!

ANTHONY (BIG LAUGH)

You mean — ice bound, and winter sky, and cold as Christmas?

LILLIAN

I'm not cold, Anthony. I'm warm — so warm, inside.

ANTHONY

Are you — ? (HE LOOKS AT HER. HIS EYES KINDLE, AND HE LEANS FORWARD AND KISSES HER LIPS) Yes — you are at that. LILLIAN CLINGS TO HIM.

LILLIAN

Ohh — Anthony . . .

ANTHONY

Darling. My darling. (HE STANDS AND PULLS HER WAVERINGLY TO HER FEET. SHE SMILES AT HIM, AND WITH A SHY LITTLE GESTURE, SUDDENLY DRAPES A YELLOW WOOL SCARF AROUND HIS NECK)

LILLIAN (TIMIDLY)

Merry Christmas, Anthony.

ANTHONY LOOKS DOWN AT THE SCARF. HE FINGERS
IT, THEN DECISIVELY WRAPS IT AROUND HIS
THROAT. HE TILTS HER CHIN.

ANTHONY

Merry Christmas, darling — may we never be less
happy than this moment.

HE BENDS TO KISS HER AS THE SCENE
DISSOLVES:

FADE UP ON:

INT: MUSEUM PARLOR

AS THE SCENE TAKES FOCUS, THERE IS THE SHARP
CRACKLE OF FLAMES. OPEN ON A TIGHT SHOT OF
ARTIE, WHO DROPS A PIECE OF FLAMING MATERIAL
AND RUNS ACROSS THE ROOM TO HIS MOTHER WITH
A HOWL.

CUT TO: THE GROUP COMPRISING LILLIAN, PEELER,
JULIA AND MRS. DAWSON. ARRESTED BY ARTIE'S
SHRIEK, THEY LOOK QUICKLY IN THE DIRECTION OF
THE SOUND.

ARTIE (SCREAMING)

Mamma . . . mamma . . . it's burning . . . .

MRS. DAWSON SCREAMS. LILLIAN STANDS AS IF
TURNED TO STONE. HENRY PEELER LURCHES
FORWARD.

PEELER

Be calm, ladies!

HE BEGINS TO FLAIL AWAY, AND STOMP AT THE
FLAMING MATERIAL. MRS. DAWSON STOPS
SCREAMING AND GIVES ARTIE A JERK.

MRS. DAWSON

You bad boy! I told you never to play with
matches!

ARTIE SETS UP A NEW WAIL. PEELER STRAIGHTENS,
THE HERO TRIUMPHANT. WHERE THERE WAS A
BLAZE, THERE IS NOW ONLY A BLACK PATCH
OF ASHES.

PEELER

Not too much damage. Nothing important. Only
a scarf.

CAMERA CUT FAST FOR CLOSE SHOT OF LILLIAN'S
FACE. SOMETHING IN IT SEEMS TO CRUMBLE. HER
CHIN TREMBLES, SHE CLENCHES HER HANDS AND
BOWS HER HEAD.

CUT BACK TO A CLOSE-UP OF THE PITIFUL LITTLE
PILE OF ASH, LAST REMAINS OF WHAT WAS ONCE
A BRIGHT YELLOW SCARF. HENRY PEELER POKES IN
IT DISDAINFULLY WITH HIS TOE, AS THE SCENE
DISSOLVES.

THE END OF ACT ONE

TRANSITIONS IN THE "LIVE" HALF-HOUR TELEVISION PLAY

We have saved until last the question of transitions from scene
to scene in the "live" half-hour television play. Because usually
there are fewer characters, both major and minor, in a half-hour
play, devices and techniques to accomplish the desired transitions
and time lapses are harder to find. *It is axiomatic that the fewer
the characters, the more difficult the transitions,* transitions to
allow the actor or actors to move from one set to another, and to
make necessary costume and make-up changes, if any.

A secondary yet very important reason for reproducing in
following and in full the play, *Billy Adams, American,* is to show
the considerable amount of story, and incident within the story,
it is possible to get into a half-hour television play. As produced
on Armstrong's Circle Theatre, *Billy Adams, American,* gave the
effect of a very much longer play, because so much happens. Yet
this production was no longer than twenty-three minutes in
playing.

There is a discussion of the transitions at the end of the play,
which is reproduced by the kind permission of the author.

BILLY ADAMS, AMERICAN
by
Theodore W. Case

CAST

Doctor Braun	G. I.
Herr Krueger	Guard
Willi Krueger	Ship's Doctor
American Corporal	Ship's Nurse
Frau Schneider	First Immigration Officer
WAC	Second Immigration Officer
Reporter	

SETS

1. Park scene in postwar Hamburg
2. Living room in Krueger's flat
3. Pier where large liner is docked
4. Sickbay on ship
5. Section on ship's deck
6. Immigration office interior

FILM CLIPS

Ship at sea at night
New York harbor from incoming ship

Act I

FADE IN ON:
(LETTERING ON SCREEN, HEAVY GERMAN SCRIPT.
HAMBURG, 1952.)
DISSOLVE TO:
(PARK SCENE. THERE IS A BENCH, SOME GRASS IN
THE B.G. A SCENE OF POSTWAR HAMBURG, SOME
SHATTERED BUILDINGS, ETC. OPTIONAL BUT
DESIRABLE IF SOME INDICATION COULD BE GIVEN
THAT HAMBURG IS A PORT CITY.)
SOUND: SOME TRAFFIC NOISES IN B.G.; OCCASIONAL
WHISTLES OF TUGS AND NOW AND THEN THE
WHISTLE OF A LARGER SHIP.

(AS WE FADE IN, KRUEGER, WILLI AND DR. BRAUN
WALK UP TO THE BENCH)
            KRUEGER (INDICATING BENCH)
Come, Doctor, I know you have other patients.
You cannot waste so much time on me.
                BRAUN
What kind of a doctor would I be if I have not
a few minutes for an old friend? (ALL SIT, WILLI,
CLAMBERING UP LAST. HE LOOKS EXPECTANTLY
AT THE TWO MEN)
                KRUEGER
No, Willi. You go for a minute. We must talk.
(WILLI LOOKS HURT BUT DOESN'T MOVE IMMEDIATELY.
KRUEGER SPEAKS FIRMLY BUT NOT UNKINDLY)
            KRUEGER (Cont'd)
Go. (WILLI MOVES SLOWLY AWAY, KICKING A STICK
IN THE PATH) DOLLY IN FOR TWO SHOT EXCLUDING
WILLI.
All right, Franz . . . Tell me what you have to say.
Don't keep it from me — I am prepared.
                BRAUN
Nobody is prepared for what I have to say . . .
You are not an old man — but you have an old
heart — a very old heart . . . (KRUEGER
STIFFENS) If you are quiet and get plenty of
rest, if you never get over-excited . . . you may
have . . . . three months.
                KRUEGER
Three months . . . . but Willi! If there was
anything that could help . . . you would have
told me . .
        BRAUN (TOUCHES HIM ON SHOULDER)
Come to my office tomorrow. I will give you
something, in case there is any pain.
                KRUEGER
Thank you.
(EXIT BRAUN) (WE SEE THE EMOTIONAL PAIN ON
KRUEGER'S FACE AS HE TAKES A STEP BRINGING

WILLI INTO THE BG., AND TURNS TO LOOK AT THE BOY.
AS WILLI APPROACHES, HE SITS DOWN HEAVILY
ON THE BENCH. WILLI CLIMBS UP BESIDE HIM)

WILLI

Are you tired, Father?

KRUEGER

Yes, I am tired.

WILLI

(SEARCHING IN HIS POCKETS, HE BRINGS OUT TWO
MARBLES . . . LOOKS AT THEM AND THEN STARTS
TO THROW ONE UP AND CATCH IT)

KRUEGER

(WATCHES HIM INTENTLY FOR A MOMENT, THEN
AN EXPRESSION OF INTENSE PAIN CROSSES HIS FACE)
Ach, what's the use!
(BURIES HIS HEAD IN HIS HANDS)

WILLI

(LOOKS AT HIS FATHER AND IS VERY EMBARRASSED.
HE GETS DOWN OFF THE BENCH AND STARTS TO
PLAY CLUMSILY WITH THE MARBLES IN THE DIRT. AS
HE PLAYS, HE SUDDENLY SEES THE SHOES AND LEGS
OF AN AMERICAN CORPORAL WHO HAS WALKED
UP AND IS WATCHING HIM. HE LOOKS SLOWLY UP
TO THE FACE)

CORPORAL

What'ye tryin' to do, squeeze it to death?
(WILLI LOOKS MYSTIFIED) Here, lemme show ye
how it's done. (HE SQUATS DOWN BY WILLI, WHO
LETS HIM HAVE THE MARBLES) D'ye talk English?

KRUEGER

Excuse me, my son understands what you say,
but speaking he is not so good.

CORPORAL (IN A FRIENDLY MANNER)

Oh, yours, eh. Nice-looking kid.

KRUEGER (BEAMING)

Thank you. What he knows I have taught him
myself. His mother died in an air raid.

CORPORAL (SYMPATHETIC)

Oh. (RETURNS HIS ATTENTION TO WILLI) Ye hold
it like this . . . wrap this finger around it . . .
then ease your thumb down behind . . . What's
your name?

WILLI (SHYLY)

Willi.

CORPORAL (IMITATING)

Villi?

KRUEGER

That is the short name for Wilhelm.

CORPORAL (BREEZY)

Oh, William. Okay, Bill. Now you're holdin' it
right . . . ye just sight down that finger there . . .
(DOES SO) . . . and let 'er go.

(BOTH DO SO AND WILLI LAUGHS EXCITEDLY)

WE PAN UP FOR ONE SHOT OF KRUEGER.

(AFTER THE SOUND AND DURING THE NEXT FEW
LINES, HE BEGINS TO LOOK EXCITED AS THOUGH A
GREAT THOUGHT HAD OCCURRED TO HIM)

SOUND: THE DEEP HORN OF A LARGE TRANS-
ATLANTIC LINER BLOWS TWICE.

(KRUEGER HEARS IT AND WITH THE SECOND BLAST
HE TURNS AND LOOKS OFF)

CORPORAL (HEARD BUT NOT SEEN)

That's the ticket! You got the idea. Now, try
it again, Bill.

WILLI (ALSO HEARD BUT NOT SEEN)

Okay!

SOUND: ONE MORE DEEP BLAST FROM HORN.

CORPORAL (STILL HEARD BUT NOT SEEN)

That's the stuff.

(DOLLY BACK TO INCLUDE ALL AGAIN)

KRUEGER

(REACHES OVER TO TOUCH CORPORAL ON THE
SHOULDER)

Could you give me a minute of your time?

CORPORAL

(GETS UP ON BENCH. WILLI KEEPS ON PRACTICING.)
(DOLLY IN EXCLUDING WILLI)
Sure, Pop . . . what's on your mind?

KRUEGER (VERY SERIOUS)

Does Willi look anything like an American boy?

CORPORAL

Sure, they're all about the same . . . maybe a little
more meat on his bones, different clothes, sort
of . . . Why, thinkin' of takin' him to America?

KRUEGER (PRE-OCCUPIED)

I have tried. The consul said there was no
possibility. He says it is quite impossible at this
time.

CORPORAL

Too bad.

KRUEGER

Just think, here in Hamburg we live only seven
days from a new world.

CORPORAL

Pretty tough bringin' a kid up here, I guess.

KRUEGER

From the first, I decided Willi is going to be an
American. I do not want him to go through
what I have seen, what my father went through.

CORPORAL (SYMPATHETIC)

Yeah.

KRUEGER (HURRIES ON)

I had plenty of time, I thought. (PAUSE) Today
I receive bad news.

CORPORAL

(AFRAID HE'S GETTING INVOLVED IN SOMETHING.
HE STARTS TO RISE) Yeah, well, that's too bad.
I wish I could do something for you.

KRUEGER (TOUCHING HIS ARM)

Before you go, tell me if a little boy is lost in
the streets in America, what happens to him?

                    CORPORAL (VERY PUZZLED)
Why, the police'd probably pick him up.
                         KRUEGER
Police?
                         CORPORAL
Sure. Take him down to the station . . . find out
where he lived and get him home.
                         KRUEGER
What if he had no home?
                         CORPORAL
They'd turn him over to an orphanage, or some
society for adoption.
                         KRUEGER
Adoption!
                         CORPORAL
Sure. Lots of people want to adopt kids in the
States. If they can't have any they adopt 'em.
There's more demand than there is kids.
                         KRUEGER
Imagine! (HE STANDS WITH CORPORAL) Thank
you very much! Thank you very much!
          CORPORAL (LOOKING AT HIM STRANGELY)
Sure. It's all right. (HE STARTS TO LEAVE) Take
it easy, Bill. (EXIT CORPORAL)
                         KRUEGER
Get up, Willi. We are going.
                          WILLI
Where, father?
                         KRUEGER
Come. We have little time.
(AS HE TAKES WILLI'S HAND WE:)
FADE OUT:
FADE IN:
ON LIVING ROOM IN KRUEGER'S FLAT. IT IS SHABBY
WITH FURNISHINGS THAT ONCE WERE FAIRLY GOOD.
(WILLI SITS, LOOKING A LITTLE LOST, IN A LARGE
WING CHAIR. KRUEGER PACES UP AND DOWN IN
FRONT OF HIM, ALTERNATELY THREATENING AND

PLEADING WITH HIM AS HE TRIES TO CRAM AN
ELEMENTARY KNOWLEDGE OF ENGLISH INTO THE
EXHAUSTED BOY.)

WILLI

(HIS GERMAN ACCENT IS A LITTLE LESS PRONOUNCED
IN THIS SCENE. HOWEVER HE IS EXHAUSTED AND
NEAR HYSTERIA) My name is Billy Shervood . . . . .

KRUEGER

No. No. Not Shervood, Sherwood . . . . . wood.
You must not say "v", it is Sherwood.

WILLI

Shervood.

KRUEGER

No, no, no. Willi, you must get it right.

WILLI

(NEAR HYSTERIA AND ALMOST CRYING) My father,
I am so tired. I can't do it.

KRUEGER

(WITH GREAT PATIENCE AND KINDNESS) Not "my
father," Willi. In America boys say "Dad". You
must call me "Dad".

WILLI

I am trying, Dad, but I am so tired.

KRUEGER

All right, my boy, all right. If I only had more
time. Maybe we can find a name easier to say.
(PICKS UP A BATTERED COPY OF "LIFE", AS HE LEAFS
THROUGH IT) Thompson, Ferris, no . . . Adams.
Say Adams, Willi.

WILLI

Adams.

KRUEGER

Good! Now, what is your name?

WILLI

My name is Billy Adams.

KRUEGER (ENTHUSIASTICALLY)

Good!

WILLI

Why must I have a new name?

KRUEGER

In America you must have an American name.

WILLI

But why must I tell lies about where I live?

KRUEGER

Not lies, Willi. You will live there. It will be
true. You will be lost, and you will be found.
And when you are adopted, you will have a new
life, Willi. And so will I. Now get your coat,
Willi. We go to see the American motion picture
again.

(FRAU SCHNEIDER ENTERS)

FRAU SCHNEIDER

Never mind your coat, Willi.

KRUEGER (TURNS, FURIOUS)

What do you say?

FRAU SCHNEIDER

I say the boy is going to bed! You cannot drive
him like this, you will make him sick!

KRUEGER

You will not interfere, please.

FRAU SCHNEIDER

Five hours today, he has been sitting in the
Kinema . . . six hours yesterday; and when he
is home . . . you drive him, drive him, like a
horse! He is just a little boy.

KRUEGER

But, Frau Schneider! He must learn to speak
English like an American.

FRAU SCHNEIDER (INTENSELY)

He will speak nothing, he will go no place, if you
drive him too far. He must have rest; and so
must you, Herr Krueger. Let the boy go to bed.

KRUEGER (REFLECTS)

Maybe you are right. Everything could be spoiled.
Come, Willi. You will go with Frau Schneider.

WILLI

(CROSSES TO EMBRACE FATHER. HE LOOKS UP INTO HIS FACE) Good night, Dad.

KRUEGER (HOLDING HIM BY THE SHOULDERS) That's the boy. You learn well. (KISSES HIM ON BOTH CHEEKS) Good night, Willi.

WILLI (SHYLY)

No. Not Willi. My name is Billy Adams.

KRUEGER

(STARES AT HIM A MOMENT AS THOUGH SEEING A VISION OF WHAT IS TO COME) Goodnight, Billy Adams, American. (AS FRAU SCHNEIDER LEADS WILLI AWAY, CAMERA STAYS ON KRUEGER'S FACE, FULL OF VISIONS AND HOPES FOR THE FUTURE) FADE OUT.

FADE IN:

SCENE IS PART OF INTERIOR OF A PIER WHERE A LARGE LINER IS DOCKED. THERE ARE PILES OF PACKING CASES, AND THE BACKGROUND CONSISTS OF A HIGH WOODEN WALL, IN WHICH THERE IS A NARROW OPENING RUNNING TO THE FULL HEIGHT OF THE WALL. THROUGH THE OPENING CAN BE SEEN A SMALL PORTION OF THE GIGANTIC HULL OF THE LINER, JUST A TREMENDOUS BLACK SURFACE WITH ONE OR TWO PORTHOLES VISIBLE. FARTHER DOWN TO THE LEFT CAN BE SEEN THE SHORE END OF THE GANGPLANK COMING THROUGH ANOTHER OPENING IN THE WALL. A GUARD STANDS AT THE BOTTOM OF IT.

SOUND: THROUGHOUT THIS SCENE ARE HEARD THE SOUNDS OF A BUSY HARBOR, THE TOOTING OF TUGS, AN OCCASIONAL DEEPER WHISTLE OF A LARGE BOAT, AND NEARER, THE SOUND OF A CRANE AT WORK LOADING THE LINER.

(AN AMERICAN GI AND A WAC ENTER FROM RIGHT. BOTH CARRY HAVERSACKS AND HE HOLDS HER HAND, RUSHING HER ALONG A LITTLE. THEY STOP IN FRONT OF THE ENTRANCE TO LOOK AT THE SHIP)

GI (INDICATES SHIP)

Well, there she is! U.S.A., here I come!

WAC (INDICATES)

Is that where we go on?

GI

(PUTS DOWN HIS HAVERSACK AND REACHES IN POCKET FOR ENVELOPE) No — that's the baggage gangway. Just a minute, I'll give you your boat card.

(ENTER KRUEGER AND WILLI EITHER AROUND CORNER OF PACKING CASES OR DOWN AISLE BETWEEN THEM. KRUEGER IS TAKEN ABACK AT SEEING THE GI AND WAC, BUT WILLI WALKS RIGHT UP TO THEM.)

KRUEGER

Willi, wait!

WILLI

(WALKING RIGHT UP TO GI & WAC) Hello.

WAC

Hello, there.

GI

Here's the card. (SHE TAKES IT)

WILLI

Are you going to America, too?

KRUEGER (FINALLY HAS TO APPROACH)

Willi!

WILLI (TOO EXCITED TO HEED)

I go with my Dad. We are going to live there.

WAC

With your Dad, eh? You almost sound like an American.

(GI SHOULDERS HIS HAVERSACK, LOOKING IMPATIENT)

WILLI

My Dad has taught me everything. I am going to grow up like an American boy!

WAC

Well, that's swell. What's your name?

GI

Come on, we gotta get moving.

KRUEGER

(ALMOST ANGRILY HE RESTRAINS WILLI AS WAC
AND GI MOVE OFF)
Willi!

WAC (RESIGNED)

Okay, General. (FLASHES A BIG SMILE AT WILLI)
So long. (EXIT WAC & GI. DON'T SHOW THEM
GETTING ON BOAT)

KRUEGER

(PULLS WILLI BACK A LITTLE AMONG THE PACKING
CASES. WILLI SITS ON ONE) I told you not to talk
to people! You must do as I say! (HE TAKES A
STEP FORWARD AND LOOKS IN THE DIRECTION OF
THE GANGPLANK. CAMERA INCLUDES UNIFORMED
GUARD AT THE END OF IT. HE LEANS ON THE RAIL,
SMOKING. AFTER LOOKING AT HIM A MOMENT,
KRUEGER STEPS BACK AND SPEAKS) No. That is
not the one. We wait here, Willi, until my man
comes.

WILLI (CLIMBING UP ON A CASE)

Why can't we get on now?

KRUEGER

When that man goes, and another man comes,
then we go on the ship. (HE SITS NEAR WILLI AND
BOTH LOOK THROUGH THE OPENING AT THE SIDE
OF THE SHIP, POINTING)

KRUEGER

See. There is the ship that will take you to
America.

WILLI

(LOOKS SLOWLY UP TOWARD THE TOP AND HIS EYES
ARE TREMENDOUS) Dad — it's like a mountain!

KRUEGER

Just think, Willi, in six days we will be in New
York harbor.

WILLI (SEES SOMETHING OFF LEFT)

Look, they're changing.

KRUEGER (GETTING UP)

Fine. We go now.

(HE LOOKS DOWN TO THE GANGPLANK TOO AND SUDDENLY A LOOK OF HORROR COMES OVER HIS FACE)

Stop! Billy! It is not the one! It cannot be!

WILLI (TUGGING AT HIS ARM)

Come on, Dad. Let's go.

KRUEGER

But what can have happened?

(HE PAUSES IN INDECISION FOR A MOMENT. THEN HE MAKES UP HIS MIND. A LOOK OF FIERCE RESOLUTION REPLACES THE INDECISION)

We must. We must get on the ship! (TAKES WILLI BY THE ARM) Remember, not a word!

(THEY WALK TOWARD THE GANGPLANK. KRUEGER BOBS A HINT OF A BOW TO THE GUARD) Good morning. Frank not here today?

GUARD

Got a cold. At least that's what he says. So I get stuck for extra duty.

KRUEGER

Oh, I see. Then he must have told you about me.

GUARD

Not a word. What about you?

KRUEGER

(TAKES A DEEP BREATH AND PLUNGES IN) I work on the ship, loading baggage, you know. I was to be late today, and he was to let me on.

GUARD (QUITE MATTER OF FACT)

Got your boat card?

KRUEGER

Boat card? Oh yes. That was it. You see it has become lost. That was why I arranged with him to let me on.

GUARD

(HIS SUSPICIONS BEGIN TO BE AROUSED) Nobody arranges to get on this ship without a boat card. You'll have to get another.

KRUEGER

(BECOMING FRANTIC, HE TRIES TO SLIP BY) But my
job! I must get to my work!

GUARD (BARRING HIM)

Not a chance. What's the kid doing with you
anyway? He got a job on the boat, too?

KRUEGER

No. He comes with me because he has no mother.
He does not disturb anyone, but he must stay
with me.

GUARD

Yeah? Well, you still gotta get a boat card.
When you get the card, I'll let you on. (STANDS
DIRECTLY IN MIDDLE OF GANGPLANK)

KRUEGER

(HOPELESSLY DETERMINED, HE MAKES A LAST TRY
TO PUSH HIS WAY BY. PULLING WILLI BY THE
ARM, HE TRIES TO PUSH PAST) Can't you see, I
must get to my job. (HE STRUGGLES VIOLENTLY
WITH THE GUARD, WHO FINALLY SHOVES HIM BACK
OFF THE PLANK)

GUARD

You can't get on, I said, and I mean it!

KRUEGER

(STAGGERS BACK WITH THE VIOLENCE OF THE PUSH.
SUDDENLY A LOOK OF SURPRISED HORROR CROSSES
HIS FACE AND HE CLUTCHES AT HIS HEART. HE
STUMBLES BACK TO SIT ON A PACKING CASE) No! It
cannot be! Oh, no, not yet, not yet! (HE BEGINS
TO FALL SLOWLY OFF THE PACKING CASE AS WE
FADE OUT TO INTERMISSION)

END OF ACT ONE

ACT II

(THIS SCENE IS PLAYED IN LARGE CLOSE-UPS AROUND
WHAT LOOKS LIKE AN OPERATING TABLE ALTHOUGH
IT ACTUALLY TAKES PLACE IN AN OUT-PATIENT

DISPENSARY. IN IT ARE KRUEGER, DOCTOR AND
NURSE. DRESSED AS BEFORE, KRUEGER LIES
UNCONSCIOUS ON THE TABLE)

FADE IN:

CU KRUEGER'S FACE, THEN DOLLY BACK ENOUGH TO
INCLUDE DOCTOR AND NURSE BENDING OVER HIM.

DOCTOR

(HANDS HYPODERMIC NEEDLE HE HAS OBVIOUSLY
JUST USED TO NURSE) There. If anything'll
bring him around that'll do it. (KRUEGER'S
BREATHING GETS A LITTLE STRONGER. BOTH WATCH
HIM INTENTLY) I'm afraid he hasn't got much
longer to go, anyway, though.

(TAKES KRUEGER'S WRIST AND FEELS PULSE.
KRUEGER STIRS AND HIS EYES FLUTTER)

KRUEGER

(HIS EYES OPEN. HE LOOKS AROUND AND
IMMEDIATELY TRIES TO SIT UP) Where . . .
where am I?

DOCTOR (HE AND NURSE RESTRAIN HIM
GENTLY) Just lie still for a minute.

KRUEGER (STILL STRUGGLING)
But where am I? Where is Billy?

NURSE

Your little boy's all right. He's just outside.
(HOLDS UP THE GLASS OF WATER) Now, just sit
up slowly and sip this. (SHE AND DOCTOR SUPPORT
HIM AS HE SITS UP AND DRINKS. HE SWINGS HIS
FEET AROUND OFF BED)

KRUEGER

(BEGINNING TO LOOK A LITTLE BETTER. HE SHAKES
HIS HEAD TRYING TO REMEMBER) I can't remember,
I don't. . . . . (THEN AS HE DOES REMEMBER, HIS
FACE FALLS) Oh, I remember now. (THEN) It is
hopeless. I was a fool to think. . . . (SHAKES HIS
HEAD AND STARTS TO GET DOWN OFF BED)

DOCTOR

You can rest here a while if you want.

The ship doesn't sail for several hours.

KRUEGER (FREEZES)

Ship!

NURSE

This is the sick bay of the ship. You collapsed
at the bottom of the gangplank. It was the
nearest place they could bring you!

KRUEGER

God be thanked!

DOCTOR

Take it easy, now. You can go if you wish.
You know your way off the ship, don't you?

KRUEGER

(LOOKS DOCTOR IN THE EYE AS HE MENTALLY
APOLOGIZES FOR THE DECEPTION HE IS ABOUT TO
PRACTICE) Yes, I do, thank you, Doctor.

DOCTOR (PUTTING HAND ON KRUEGER'S
SHOULDER) You know, you got to take it easy
with that heart of yours. It won't last forever.

KRUEGER

Thank you, Doctor. I think it will last long
enough . . . now.

FADE OUT.

FADE IN:

FILM CLIP — SHIP AT SEA AT NIGHT. THEN DISSOLVE
TO DECK SCENE. IN THE FOREGROUND IS A SECTION
OF THE SHIP'S RAILING. BEHIND IT IS A SECLUDED
CORNER FORMED BY AN ANGLE OF THE SHIP'S
SUPERSTRUCTURE. THERE IS ONE PORTHOLE WHICH
CASTS A DIM LIGHT OVER THE SCENE. IT IS NIGHT.
SOUND: THROUGHOUT THIS SCENE IS HEARD THE
SLOWLY RISING AND FALLING SWISH OF WATER
AS THE LINER MOVES EASILY THROUGH A GENTLE
SWELL. AS WE FADE IN:

(THE SILHOUETTE OF A WOMAN LEANING ON THE
RAIL IS VISIBLE. SHE FACES THE CAMERA AND
IS SEEN IN THE EXTREME RIGHT OF THE PICTURE
ONLY. FOR A MOMENT THERE IS NO ACTION AND

THEN KRUEGER AND WILLI ENTER THE BG
KRUEGER MOTIONS WILLI INTO THE CORNER. HE
FOLDS A COAT AND PLACES IT ON THE DECK.
WHEN WILLI SITS HE IS BEHIND KRUEGER'S BODY SO WE
CANNOT SEE HIM. BOTH SIT ON THE COAT AND WE
JUST CATCH A WORD OR TWO FROM KRUEGER. THE
FIGURE AT THE RAIL TURNS AND WE SEE IT IS THE
NURSE FROM THE LAST SCENE)

KRUEGER

Now, Billy, say, "I live near the corner here."

BILLY

I live near the corner here —

NURSE

(TURNS AND LOOKS INTO THE CORNER. AS SHE SEES
KRUEGER, SURPRISE AND RECOGNITION APPEAR ON
HER FACE) Oh! Why..... (STARTING TO SPEAK,
SHE QUICKLY PUTS HER HAND ACROSS HER MOUTH.
SHE TURNS PURPOSEFULLY AND HURRIES OFF
RIGHT. WE DOLLY INTO THE CORNER)

KRUEGER

You sure you can do all I have told you, Billy?

WILLI

Yes, I can do it, Dad. But why must I say
those things?

KRUEGER (A BIT SADLY)

Yes. Billy, I think the time has come to tell you
why. Tomorrow the ship comes to New York.
Tomorrow you will be in America. (HE HEAVES
A SIGH) It has been good on the ship, Billy,
has it not?

WILLI

Yes, Dad, it has been the best time of my life.

KRUEGER

Even with the hiding, and being hungry,
sometimes?

WILLI

Yes, Dad.

KRUEGER

Well, now I will try to tell you why it is we have
had to hide like thieves, and say things that were
not always true, and do things that you knew
were wrong and will never do again. Life was very
hard in Germany . . . for me and for my father. It
is not wrong that life should be hard; but I think
it is wrong that a man can work so hard all his
life . . . and have nothing at the end. In America
if you work hard you will have something when
you are finished. And I want you to have
something, Billy. (THE BOY LOOKS STILL
EXPECTANTLY AT KRUEGER. HE HEAVES A SIGH)
Soon I am going to leave you, Billy.

WILLI

But why? Do you have to?

KRUEGER

Yes, I have to. (WILLI LOOKS AT HIS FATHER
WITH WIDE, SCARED EYES) You remember the
day we walked with Dr. Braun in the park?
He told me. Soon, Billy, I am going where your
mother is. (WILLI TRIES TO PUT HIS ARMS AROUND
HIS FATHER AND BURIES HIS HEAD ON HIS CHEST.
KRUEGER PUTS AN ARM AROUND THE BOY AND PATS
HIS SHOULDER SOOTHINGLY AS HE LOOKS STRAIGHT
AHEAD) Many things we have done were wrong;
but maybe this once it will be understood.
(HE HUGS THE BOY TIGHT A MOMENT)
I want you to remember me, Willi. I want to be
remembered. (SHAKES HIMSELF OUT OF THE
MOOD. HE GETS TO HIS FEET, HELPING WILLI)
We must sleep well tonight; and be strong
tomorrow. (THEY GO OFF RIGHT)
FADE OUT.
FADE IN:
FILM SHOT: SCENE OF NEW YORK HARBOR FROM AN
INCOMING SHIP. SUNNY AND CHEERFUL.
SOUND: HARBOR NOISES.

WE LAP TO LIVE CU (KRUEGER AND WILLI AGAINST
OUTSIDE OF CABIN WALL. SAME AS OTHER DECK
SCENE. PART OF A PORT HOLE SHOWS. THEY ARE
LOOKING UP)

KRUEGER

Who could believe it! Look at those buildings.
See the sun shining on all the windows!

WILLI

Is all America as beautiful as that, Dad?

KRUEGER (AWED)

I don't know!

WILLI

Look! That one is so high it touches the sky.

KRUEGER

Imagine what kind of people they must be, to
build like that! Think how free! What imagination!
What hope! (LOOKS DOWN AT WILLI) I am glad
for you. I am so happy. This is where you must
grow up.

DISSOLVE TO:

INTERIOR. CU DOCTOR, NURSE AND FIRST
IMMIGRATION OFFICER. OFFICER WEARS CAP WITH
IMMIGRATION DEPARTMENT INSIGNIA ON IT.
CU OFFICER.

FIRST OFFICER

You say you saw this man last night?

DOCTOR

I didn't see him. Miss Williams thought she did.

NURSE

I'm quite certain I did, Doctor. I remember
especially, because he seemed to be talking to
himself.

FIRST OFFICER

What'd he look like?

DOCTOR

Just a man who had a heart attack on the dock in
Hamburg. They brought him to sickbay for

treatment. I can't imagine why he'd want to
stow away.

(LAP CU REPORTER COMING INTO GROUP)

> REPORTER (WEARS NEWSPAPER PASS IN HAT)

Did I hear somebody say stowaway?

> FIRST OFFICER

You again!

> REPORTER

I seem to sense a story for my paper.

> FIRST OFFICER

Okay. Stick around.

> DOCTOR

As I said, I don't know what he'd be doing on
the ship. He can't live more than a few weeks at
the outside!

> FIRST OFFICER (SEEMS TO LOSE INTEREST)

Oh, I see. Well, you leave a description with my
man at the purser's office and we'll keep an eye
out for him.

> REPORTER

What about me?

> FIRST OFFICER

We'll be docking in a few minutes. Come to my
office on the pier.

> REPORTER

Okay.

(EXIT REPORTER AND FIRST OFFICER)

> NURSE

Wasn't there a little boy with him in Hamburg?

> DOCTOR (LAP CU DOCTOR'S FACE)

That's right — there was a little boy.

(BECOMES THOUGHTFUL) Maybe that's why . . .

(FADE ON THIS LINE)

FADE OUT.

FADE IN:

DECK SCENE. SAME CORNER AS BEFORE.

(KRUEGER AND WILLI COME FURTIVELY INTO THE
CORNER. KRUEGER CARRIES A BATTERED SUITCASE)

KRUEGER

Now is the time, Willi. All the passengers are off
and I don't think they watch so close. (WILLI
LOOKS UP EXPECTANTLY. KRUEGER INDICATES THE
CASE) You will wait until I drop this over the
rail. Then you must walk, but remember, walk
quietly, over the gangplank and onto the dock. I
will keep their attention away from you. And
when you are off safe, then I come too.
(LOOKS WILLI IN THE EYE) All right?

WILLI

(DOESN'T SPEAK BUT BOBS HIS HEAD IN THE
AFFIRMATIVE)

KRUEGER

Good. If you don't see me; if I don't get off . . .
you know what to do? (WILLI BOBS HIS HEAD
AGAIN. KRUEGER PUTS A HAND ON WILLI'S SHOULDER,
KISSES HIM ON THE CHEEK AND THEN STANDS AND
WALKS AWAY. AS WILLI WATCHES WITH WIDE
EYES. . . .)

FADE OUT.

FADE IN:

INTERIOR IMMIGRATION OFFICE ON PIER. THERE
ARE TWO PLAIN WOODEN DESKS WITH SWIVEL CHAIRS
AND A COUPLE OF STRAIGHT-BACKED HARD CHAIRS.
(THE FIRST IMMIGRATION OFFICER SITS BEHIND
ONE DESK AND THE REPORTER SITS ON A CORNER
OF IT)

REPORTER (FADE IN AS HE SPEAKS)

. . . well, I guess it's the same no matter what you
do. Anything on this stowaway deal?

FIRST OFFICER

Not yet. I think the nurse — (HE IS INTERRUPTED
BY THE DOOR OPENING AND SECOND IMMIGRATION
OFFICER ENTERING WITH KRUEGER)

SECOND OFFICER

All right, in there, Pop. (FOLLOWS KRUEGER IN)
Joker throws a suitcase in the water; and while

I'm tryin' to fish it out he sneaks down the
gangplank.

FIRST OFFICER

All right, Slater, good work. You'd better get
back to the ship.

SECOND OFFICER

Right. (EXIT)

FIRST OFFICER (TO REPORTER)

Could be the one. (PULLS UP A CHAIR FOR
KRUEGER) Sit down here. (AS KRUEGER SITS THE
OFFICER TAKES UP TELEPHONE FROM HIS DESK AND
LISTENS) Do you speak English?

KRUEGER

I do.

FIRST OFFICER (INTO TELEPHONE)

Jones? Get hold of the ship's doctor and tell
him I'd like to see him down here right away.
(TO KRUEGER) What's your name?

KRUEGER

My name is Krueger, but I have nothing to say.

FIRST OFFICER (FIRM, BUT NOT UNKIND)

Look here, now, you're in no position to take
that kind of an attitude. You've broken the law;
you can't just walk into this country without a
passport or anything.

KRUEGER

I am sorry. You must do your duty.

FIRST OFFICER

Of course, I'll do my duty, but I'd like to know
something about you.

KRUEGER

(HIS ONLY HOPE IS THAT WILLI HAS GOT OFF THE
DOCK) As you say, I have broken the law. I go
where you send me.

FIRST OFFICER (PUZZLED)

I don't get it.

REPORTER

Let me talk to him, Inspector; maybe I can get

something . . . (THEY ARE INTERRUPTED BY THE
SECOND OFFICER, WHO ENTERS PULLING WILLI BY THE
ARM)

SECOND OFFICER

Look what I just found trying to get off the pier.
We catch kids playing on the dock sometimes but
this one just don't look right. (KRUEGER FLASHES A
SLIGHT SCOWL AT WILLI. WILLI SHOWS NO SIGN
OF RECOGNIZING HIS FATHER)

FIRST OFFICER

Come over here, sonny. (WILLI CROSSES) What
are you doing on this pier? What's your name?

WILLI

My name is Billy Adams.

FIRST OFFICER

Billy Adams, eh? Where do you live?

WILLI (INDICATING)

I live near the corner here.

SECOND OFFICER

Yeah? What street? What number?

FIRST OFFICER

I'll handle it, Slater. You'd better get back to
the ship.

SECOND OFFICER (AS HE EXITS ANNOYED)

Yes, sir.

FIRST OFFICER

Look, Billy, we're your friends. I want you to tell
me the truth . . . You don't really live here,
do you?

WILLI (GETTING SCARED NOW)

Yes.

FIRST OFFICER (INDICATES KRUEGER)

Do you know this man, Billy?

WILLI (LOOKS DOWN AT FLOOR)

No.

FIRST OFFICER

Take a good look. Are you *sure* you don't
know him?

WILLI (LOWER LIP BEGINS TO QUIVER)
I don't know him.

FIRST OFFICER (SEEING HE HAS WILLI
ON THE RUN) Oh, come on now, Billy. Your name
isn't really Adams, is it?

WILLI (BRAVELY FIGHTING BACK TEARS)
My name is Billy Adams. I don't. . . . I live
near the corner.

FIRST OFFICER
What does your father do?

WILLI
My father. . . . my Dad. . . . he is (HERE WILLI
BREAKS DOWN AND RUSHES TO KRUEGER, BURYING
HIS HEAD ON HIS FATHER'S CHEST) My father,
I cannot.

(KRUEGER PUTS HIS ARMS AROUND THE BOY AND
PATS HIM ON THE BACK. THEY ARE INTERRUPTED
AS THE DOOR OPENS AND ENTER SHIP'S DOCTOR)

FIRST OFFICER
I guess we've got your man.

DOCTOR (LOOKING AT KRUEGER)
That's him, all right. And that's the boy he had
with him in Hamburg. I forgot all about the kid.

FIRST OFFICER
I don't get it. Why pretend the boy wasn't his?
And why'd the boy play along with it? He must
have been coached.

REPORTER
I think maybe there's a real story in this some
place.

DOCTOR
And I think I have an idea what it is. You see,
Herr Krueger has only a short time to live.
I think what he was trying to do was get the
boy over here.

KRUEGER
That is right. I wanted Willi to grow up in
America.

FIRST OFFICER (SYMPATHETIC)
You have relatives here . . . somebody?
KRUEGER
We have no one.
DOCTOR (AMAZED)
You mean if you got caught, you were just going
to abandon him . . . let him go in New York?
KRUEGER
American soldier in Hamburg has told me . . .
he said in America no children can be lost . . .
no children are without home. If little boy is
lost, he said, police will take him to be adopted,
he will have new family.
(ALL LOOK WIDE-EYED AT THE MAN'S FAITH)
DOCTOR
You mean you have so much faith in this country
you were willing to smuggle him in, and *abandon*
him if necessary, in the belief that no child
could be neglected in America?
REPORTER
Some faith!
DOCTOR
I wonder if you and I have as much!
(THERE IS A MOMENT'S SILENCE AS ALL THINK
ABOUT IT)
FIRST OFFICER (THOUGHTFULLY)
You know, I sort of half wish he'd got away with it.
REPORTER
Sonny, if you've got half the stuff your old man
has, you're the kind of fella we want here.
DOCTOR
Herr Krueger, if you have that kind of faith in
America, I'd like to see it justified.
FIRST OFFICER (HOLDS PALMS UP IN GESTURE
OF HOPELESSNESS) It'd take an act of Congress . . .
REPORTER (GETTING EXCITED)
It's been done before! I think my editor'd go

for the story! Once we get it in the paper —
with pictures. . . . !

KRUEGER (EXCITEDLY)

Thank you — thank you.
(HE TRIES TO RISE — SUDDENLY CLUTCHES HIS
CHEST AND SLUMPS BACK) Ohh . . .

WILLI (RUNNING TO HIM)

My father . . .
(KRUEGER MAKES AN EFFORT TO CONTROL HIS PAIN.
HE SMILES AT WILLI AND WAVES HIM AWAY)

KRUEGER

Now, Willi — do not make a fuss. Perhaps — a
glass of water — (HE SMILES AT THE BOY)

WILLI

Yes . . . my father. . . .
(THE DOCTOR NODS AT THE REPORTER)

REPORTER

I'll show you, son. . . .
(HE HOLDS THE DOOR OPEN FOR WILLI AND EXITS
WITH HIM)
(AS SOON AS THE BOY IS GONE, KRUEGER SLUMPS
OVER EVEN FARTHER. THE DOCTOR GOES TO HIM,
TAKES HIS PULSE, LOOKS MEANINGFULLY AT THE
FIRST OFFICER, SHAKES HEAD)

DOCTOR

Can you hear me, Herr Krueger? (KRUEGER NODS)
You know, of course, about your condition?

KRUEGER (NODS)

I do not want Billy to see. . . .

DOCTOR (TO FIRST OFFICER)

Isn't there something you can do about him?

FIRST OFFICER

Under normal conditions, Herr Krueger, you
would be returned to Germany. But in this
case . . . I will arrange for you to be transferred to
one of our Marine Hospitals . . . (PICKS UP
PHONE) Jones, get me the Chief in Washington . . .

KRUEGER

Willi . . . . what about Willi?

DOCTOR

There are some words on the base of that statue
out there in the bay . . . that I think apply to
these people. (THE DOCTOR PUTS AN ARM AROUND
KRUEGER AND HALF SUPPORTS HIM. DOLLY SLOWLY
IN ON KRUEGER'S FACE AS DOCTOR SPEAKS)

FIRST OFFICER

You got yourself and the boy over here . . . you've
come a long way on pure faith . . . faith in people
like us . . . ordinary Americans. Well, we're
going to do everything we can to see that faith
justified . . . I think I can promise you that Willi
will grow up an American boy!
(KRUEGER'S FACE LOOKS ALMOST UNBELIEVING)

DOCTOR

Do you understand, Herr Krueger?
(DOLLY IN FOR EXTREME CU OF KRUEGER. A SMILE
OF RADIANT HAPPINESS BREAKS OVER HIS PAIN-
TWISTED FACE)

KRUEGER

Ja . . . I — understand. . . . . .
FADE OUT.

THE END

❊   ❊   ❊   ❊

TRANSITIONS IN *Billy Adams, American*

ACT ONE

1. Between FADE OUT on Park Scene and FADE IN on Living Room
Scene: Here is an example of the difficulty of needing both
characters, Willi and Krueger, in the beginning of a new scene,
after the ending of the immediately preceding one. There was
only one way to accomplish the transition: SUBJECTIVE CAMERA
was used to "paint" for the viewer the drab living room, showing the conditions Willi and Krueger were living under. This
"painting" went on only long enough for the actors playing

Willi and Krueger to race from the Park Scene to their places in the Living Room.

2. Between FADE OUT on the living room and FADE IN on the Pier Interior. Two minor characters, the GI and the WAC, were used to give the time necessary for Willi and Krueger to move from the Living Room to the Pier. Yet, this was not a "padding" cover scene; the GI and the WAC served to establish the fact that a boat card was needed to get aboard the ship.

ACT TWO

1. Between FADE OUT in Operating Room and Film Clip of ship at sea: no problem, of course. Film was rolled on cue, and ended on cue, going into Section of Railing showing a Secluded Corner of the Deck.
2. Between FADE OUT on Secluded Corner of Deck and Film Clip of New York harbor, no problem, of course. After FILM CLIP, on into Outside Cabin Wall.
3. Between DISSOLVE from Outside Cabin Wall and Interior, Cabin, no problem, because neither Willi nor Krueger is needed at opening of scene in Interior, Cabin.
4. Between FADE OUT on Interior, Cabin and FADE IN, on Deck Corner, no problem, because Willi and Krueger have remained there while scene in Interior, Cabin was played without them.
5. Between FADE OUT on Deck Corner and FADE IN on Immigration Office, no problem, because neither Willi nor Krueger is needed at opening of this scene. Krueger arrives almost immediately, but the Reporter and First Officer have enough dialogue to speak to cover Krueger's movements from Deck Corner to Immigration Office. Play continues to END in this set.

You see now that there was only one difficult transition in *Billy Adams, American*. It came when both Willi and Krueger ended one scene (the Park Bench), and then had to open the next scene (Living Room). This difficulty points up the Axiom mentioned: *the fewer the characters, the harder the transitions*. This is not to say that you must not write half-hour plays with few characters, in order to dodge difficult transitions; it is merely to point out the hazards that must be surmounted in accomplishing such transitions. If you are aware of your problem, you can lick it!

And, of course, such problems in transitions do not exist in television plays written for filming.

In review, this chapter seems to have a lot of negative advice and warnings. What are the positive qualities of writing the half-hour television play based on the one situation quickly and strongly established? It is your author's opinion that the playwright writing with this technique must dig deeper for fuller realization of the values in his material; when he has found these values, he must handle them with far greater adroitness than if he had a plot and one or more subplots to play around with. He must develop his characterizations richly, think up unique, fresh, provocative, imaginative incidents through which to tell his story.

The result should be, *can* be, an important contribution toward the growth of a brand-new artistic form of dramatic writing: the half-hour television play, "live" or filmed, a form of television entertainment which is immensely popular, difficult to write, but surely here to stay.

10

The Half-Hour
Filmed Television Play

ANY TELEVISION PLAY written for "live" production can be produced as a motion picture for telecasting, even without additional
rewriting to put it into "motion picture" form. We'll discuss this
situation in a moment.

Not all television plays written for motion picture filming can
be produced "live". The controlling factors of Time (Transitions),
Make-up and Costume Changes, and Scene Changes determine
whether or not a "motion picture" play can be produced "live".

However, in this chapter we are not concerned with writing
"motion picture plays" to be produced "live". It is only to point
out these controlling factors that we have mentioned "live" production. We can say positively that any television play written
solely in terms of motion picture filming cannot be produced "live".

These terms are those already mentioned: Time (Transitions);
Make-up and Costume Changes; Scene Changes. In motion
picture filming, none of these controlling factors inhibits the telling
of the story. A heroine can be seen in a negligee with her hair in
curlers in one scene; then, three seconds later in elapsed time —
through a DISSOLVE — she can be seen dancing in a ballroom in
evening dress with an elaborate hair-do. No problem of Transitions (Time) arises in filming plays, because each scene is photographed as an entity unto itself. Since no problems of Transitions
can arise, no problems of Make-up and Costume and Scene
Changes can arise.

Therefore the scope of your story — your play — can be far

greater in television plays written for filming than in television plays written for "live" production.

In Chapter Two, the matter of Filmed Television Plays is discussed at some length, with the advantages and the disadvantages pointed out. Suppose now we pose some definite questions, and answer them.

1. Does a television playwright have to decide before he begins to write a television play whether it is going to be done "live" or on film? Is this, indeed, his judgment to make?

The answer is split several ways. If the playwright is aiming at a specific program already on the air, his decision has already been made for him by the producers of the program. If it is a "live" program, the playwright must write a "live" play. If the program is filmed, he preferably writes a television play for filming.

However, if a television playwright says, "I'm going to write a television play — just *any* television play," — he *must* decide if it is to be for "live" or film production. Probably, it is better to write such a play "live", because then this "live" play can be offered in *both* "live" and film markets. One qualification must be made: if the playwright will lose indispensable values in his story by writing it "live," better to abandon the "live" markets and aim for the film markets. Here we are covering ground we have already covered: can your story be told in settings contained within the four walls of a warehouse-like studio, plus the possibilities of film clips? Will the scope of your story mean that Time (Transitions), Make-up, Costume and Scene Changes render the telling impossible as a "live" play?

As an example of a television play which *could not be done "live"*, we cite the complete script of *What Hath God Wrought*, printed in full later on in this chapter. The reasons why *What Hath God Wrought* had to be filmed are discussed in great detail, and in their sum total supply the best answer for Question 1.

2. Can a television playwright write *any* play in "live" technique and then sell it for filming? Yes. The motion picture studio may or may not engage an "adaptor" to put the original playwright's play into "motion picture" form. All depends on the individual working procedures of the several motion picture studios and

directors. A good movie director can take a "live" script and shoot it (i.e., photograph it) without any further adaptation. However, the best professional procedure is to shoot from a "motion picture" script; therefore, it is suggested as a preference (but not a requirement) that a television playwright put his "live" play into "motion picture" form, if he is capable of so doing. *But it is not necessary to do so in order to sell a "live" script for filming.* And it is highly desirable that *all* television playwrights learn the simple technique of adapting their own plays into "motion picture" form. Your author sincerely believes that a close and faithful study of the script of *What Hath God Wrought* will enable any competent writer of "live" television plays to learn "motion picture" technique, because this script presents *all* the problems your author knows about which can arise in writing television plays in "motion picture" form.

Let's recapitulate:

1. *Any* "live" television play can be filmed, as it is written, in "live" form. Such a play may be embellished in the filming; and the original playwright preferably should be able to add this embellishment.

2. Not *all* television plays written in "motion picture" form can be produced "live", *as written.* Time (Transitions), Make-up, Costume and Scene Changes *may* prevent.

3. Therefore, the television playwright writing a TV play for the *general* market, and not for a *specific* program, should write his play "live", unless in so doing he loses indispensable story values. If he does face this loss, better to abandon the "live" market and concentrate on the film markets.

4. The procedures for selling a television play written for filming are exactly the same as for a "live" play, and are described in the chapter on Selling.

Following is the complete script of a half-hour television play written in motion picture technique for production and telecast on film. It is used by permission of E. I. du Pont de Nemours & Company, sponsors of the television program, "Cavalcade of America", for which this play was written by Richard Blake. Jules Bricken produced and directed this play for Screen Gems Productions (a subsidiary of Columbia Pictures, Inc.).

Comment on this filmed television play appears at the end of the script.

WHAT HATH GOD WROUGHT
by
Richard Blake

FADE IN:

1   FULL SHOT

— of an old print — or drawing — of Washington Square circa 1837. AS CAMERA MOVES IN TO CENTER on one of a row of houses, Voice comes over:

> VOICE (VAIL's)
> The year was 1837 — the place, a room on Washington Square in the City of New York.

DISSOLVE TO:

INT. STUDIO   NIGHT

2   SHOOTING ACROSS HALLWAY — TOWARD ENTRANCE

In f.g. a dramatic-looking man in the prime of life — SAMUEL MORSE — is greeting a newly arrived guest as he enters hall from o.s. . . . Morse starts to lead him into the candle-lit studio.

> VOICE (VAIL's)
> Our host was Samuel Morse — head of the American Academy of Design and one of the country's leading painters.

AS CAMERA DOLLIES IN after them, we see a large combination living room and artist's workshop, crowded with canvasses and pieces of sculpture. At a center table set with tea things a young man in his early twenties — ALFRED VAIL — is lighting a spirit lamp. Before a large bay window open to the summer night is a richly covered dais on which stands an elaborate chair draped with a velvet hanging. Five other guests are moving about, drinking tea and admiring an unfinished canvas on an easel. It is a painting of a woman seated on the dais. Morse and the new arrival join the group at the easel. As they greet the newcomer:

> VOICE (VAIL's)
> We were gathered to await the arrival of

important news — the names of four artists
selected to paint a set of murals in the rotunda
of the Capitol building in Washington.

3   CLOSE SHOT   MORSE
as he steals a furtive glance at his watch.

> VOICE (VAIL's)
> That Morse would be among them was a fore-
> gone conclusion. Official word was due at
> any moment by special messenger.

4   CLOSE SHOT   VAIL
at tea table. He picks up the tray of cakes.

> VAIL's VOICE (O.S.)
> Since there was no servant, I passed the cakes.

As he starts to pass the cakes, CAMERA PANS to INCLUDE an
intelligent-looking man in his middle forties staring down at
a crude telegraph on a small table. This is JAMES FENIMORE
COOPER.

5   CLOSE SHOT   COOPER
as Vail comes up and offers him tray of cakes.

> COOPER
> Ah, Vail, thank you.
>   (Takes cake, pleasantly)
> Samuel tells me you were a student of his.

> VAIL
> Not exactly, Mr. Cooper. I *was* a student at
> the University, but not an art student. We met
> through a mutual interest in — mechanics.

> COOPER
> Mechanics, eh? Then perhaps you can tell me
> what this is?
>   (Indicates telegraph)
> I assume it's another of Samuel's —
>   (Condescendingly)
> — inventions. But for what?

> VAIL
> It's a device for transmitting messages over
> large distances — instantaneously.

COOPER
(Amused)
Well, I needn't ask if it works.
(Conspiratorially)
You know, if I were as plagued by creditors as
our friend Morse is, I think I'd apply myself
to something more practical — like turning
lead into gold.

A guest has come up behind Cooper. He slaps him on the
back.

FIRST GUEST (VANDERLYN)
(Smiling)
Well, James — you've finally arrived as a
novelist. My ten-year-old son has just finished
'The Last of the Mohicans' — for the third
time!

Sound of doorbell ringing. They look off quickly toward:

6   GROUP SHOT AT EASEL (SHOOTING FROM ENTRANCE)
Silence — as Morse goes swiftly past camera and out of scene.
HOLD on others looking after him. In b.g. Vail mechanically
puts down tray. Sound of door closing. In a moment Morse
comes back, a sealed envelope in his hand. He strides to the
dais and mounts it, facing his guests, his face alive with
excitement as he tears open the envelope. The others wait
expectantly.

7   CLOSE SHOT   MORSE
as he quickly scans the note. His face falls.

MORSE
(Slowly)
The names, gentlemen, of the four artists
selected are John Trumbull —

8   CLOSE SHOT   A GUEST
This is the artist JOHN CHAPMAN. He is listening anxiously.

MORSE'S VOICE
John Chapman —
Chapman relaxes, smiling.

9   CLOSE SHOT   MORSE
as he continues.

MORSE

Robert Weir — and —

He musters a smile — looks off at:

10   CLOSE SHOT   FIRST GUEST

with Cooper and Vail at telegraph.

MORSE'S VOICE

— and John Vanderlyn.

FIRST GUEST

(Astonished)

Me?

11   GROUP SHOT

Morse has stepped down from the dais and comes forward slowly. The others crowd around him — all but Cooper, who remains rooted.

FIRST GUEST

It's a mistake! They *couldn't!*

MORSE

(Handing him note)

No. No mistake.

(Gamely)

Congratulations, John.

FIRST GUEST

I'll withdraw; you'll have my place!

MORSE

You'll do nothing of the kind!

FIRST GUEST

But three of us are serving under you in the Academy! How could they ignore *you?* It's an outrage! *Why . . . . ?*

12   CLOSE SHOT   COOPER

at telegraph.

COOPER

(Grimly)

Because the former President of the United States has been offended!

13   GROUP SHOT

as Cooper comes up and confronts the others. There is a drawn strained look on his face. They stare at him uncom-

prehendingly. Morse turns suddenly and moves out of scene.
Cooper looks after him, then:

COOPER

Yes, Mr. John Quincy Adams — a member of
the selecting committee. You may remember
that it was Mr. Adams who insisted that
foreign artists be included in the competition.
>(Bitingly)
Claimed there weren't four artists in America
good enough.

VAIL

>(Coming forward)
That letter in the Evening Post — !

FIRST GUEST

Letter — ?

COOPER

A letter was published in the Evening Post
attacking Adams for artistic snobbery. An
anonymous letter.

The others look off significantly toward Morse. CAMERA PANS
to show him in b.g. at dais, staring off through window.

COOPER'S VOICE

You're wrong, gentlemen. *I* wrote that letter.

Morse stiffens — but does not turn.

14   GROUP SHOT   FAVORING COOPER
as he faces the others.

COOPER

I — I'd hoped to be helpful, but —
>(Breaks off with a gesture — then:)
I will go to Washington and tell Mr. Adams
the truth myself. Meanwhile — perhaps we'd
better call it an evening.

The others nod and tactfully begin to leave. All but Vail and
Cooper. The latter starts toward Morse.

15   MEDIUM SHOT   TOWARD DIAS
as Cooper comes into scene. Morse's back is to him. Cooper
stops in f.g. There is a moment — then:

COOPER
(Wretchedly)
Well, Samuel, turn around and say it.

MORSE
(Turns, comes forward —)
(Leads Cooper to door)
You know what I said, James, when I read that
letter of yours? I said, 'I wish I had written
that myself.'

16 ANOTHER ANGLE

as they reach entrance. Morse holds out his hand. Cooper
takes it, moved.

MORSE
So you will not go to Mr. Adams, James. You
will not retract, for me, one word of something
I believe and wish I had written myself.

Cooper bows his head, leaves. Morse looks after him for a
moment, then goes slowly to the unfinished canvas. Vail still
watching in b.g.

MORSE
(Dully)
Well, Alfred, you have just witnessed the end
of a career.

17 ANOTHER ANGLE

as Vail comes forward.

VAIL
But Professor Morse! Just because Mr. Adams'
pride —

MORSE
Mr. Adams' pride!
(Bitterly)
There you have to tread lightly! But with
artists it's different. There you can use a heavy
tread!
(With mounting rage)
Let them starve in garrets! Let them slave for
twenty years! And then when recognition
finally approaches — cut it off! Tell them it

        was a delusion! Tell them they wasted their
        time.

Enraged, he snatches the palette knife from the easel and
slashes the canvas in two. Then he turns and stumbles
blindly toward fireplace, CAMERA PANNING. Vail watches
helplessly.

18 CLOSER ANGLE

as Vail comes into scene, stops. Morse is leaning his head
against the mantel. As he raises it, he sees the portrait of a
lovely, dark young woman framed above the mantel. He
stares at it.

                        MORSE
              (Heavily)
        May you never know what it is, Alfred —
        to lose a wife.
              (Turns submissively)
        That was God's will.
              (Then seething again)
        But this — this insult! This public repudiation!
              (Casts eyes aloft)
        I will never paint again! Never!

Vail watches him for a moment, then bows his head and starts
off. CAMERA PULLS BACK and PANS AWAY to HOLD ON FULL SHOT
of empty room as we

                                  DISSOLVE TO:

INT. STUDIO   DAY

19 FULL SHOT (SAME ANGLE AS SCENE PRECEDING)

The room is completely barren. The curtains are down — the
paintings stacked against the wall. Only the portrait of
Morse's dead wife still hangs over the mantel. In place of the
tea table stands a small stove, not nearly large enough to heat
the room. The dais is stripped of its rich covering, only the
bare boards showing. On the little table — on top of a pile
of old papers and other discarded miscellany — lies the telegraph, forgotten. Morse enters from o.s. carrying a tray on
which is half a loaf of bread and a single egg. He wears a long
overcoat to keep out chill — and looks tired, worn. Sound of

doorbell ringing. He puts tray down and crosses to entrance
. . . During above:

> VAIL'S VOICE
>
> Morse was true to his word. For six months
> he shunned his friends, avoided his old haunts.
> He gave up his chair at the university.
> Pride and poverty shut him off from the world.

20 MEDIUM CLOSE SHOT   ENTRANCE HALL

as Morse comes into camera. Vail in overcoat and hat enters
from o.s.

> MORSE
> (Shaking his hand)
> Well — Alfred! It's been a long time. Come
> in, come in!
>
> Leads him into studio

21 SHOOTING TOWARD ENTRANCE

as Morse leads Vail in. Vail stares about in dismay.

> MORSE
> Had lunch?
>
> VAIL
> (Quickly — noting the tray)
> Yes, yes — just finished.
>
> MORSE
> (Picking up egg)
> That's lucky. One egg would be a little hard
> to divide.
> (Drops egg in boiling pot on stove)
> Well — what brings you to town?
>
> VAIL
> (Hesitantly — going to telegraph)
> Well, sir — I — as a matter of fact, I came to
> see *you.*

22 ANOTHER ANGLE

Vail in f.g. at telegraph, his back to Morse at stove.

> VAIL
> (Improvising)
> I've got a problem. Work.

MORSE
(Eyeing him)
Work? From your letters I got the impression
your father's iron foundry out in Morristown
was just the place for a young mechanic.

VAIL
I thought so, too. But — well, my father and I
differed about some technical improvements.
We had words. I — I quit.
(Faces Morse)
I didn't know where to turn — except to you.

MORSE
I'm sorry, Alfred. I'm as embarrassed as you
must be.

23   MEDIUM CLOSE SHOT   AT STOVE
as Vail comes up to Morse.

VAIL
But you *can* help me, Professor. I've been
thinking about your telegraph. Have you done
any more work on it?

MORSE
I'm not interested in *more* ridicule. But if you
want to work on it — take it. You have my
blessing.

VAIL
I have only technical ability. It's not enough.
But with your imagination — your inven-
tiveness . . .

MORSE
(Ironically)
My flair for success — ?

VAIL
(Earnestly)
If a man believes in something, he should work
at it, shouldn't he?

MORSE
(Taking pot from stove)
Are you lecturing me, Alfred?

VAIL

No, sir. But I believe in —
          (Indicating telegraph)
— that. I'd hoped you might let me work on it
with you.

MORSE

          (Smiling)
And that is how *I* can help *you?*

VAIL

I thought you might need a technical assistant.

Pause. Morse crosses slowly to telegraph, CAMERA PANNING.

24   ANOTHER ANGLE

as Morse comes up to telegraph and looks down at it. In b.g.
Vail watches.

MORSE

It's imperfect. It has defects.

VAIL

It has possibilities!

MORSE

Who'd recognize them? Who'd put up the
money to develop them?

He starts back to stove

25   MEDIUM CLOSE SHOT   AT STOVE

Morse takes egg from pot as Vail comes forward.

VAIL

          (Eagerly)
I have money — not much, but enough for a
beginning. We'll raise more!

MORSE

          (Shakes head)
But all your money — none of mine —

VAIL

We can form a partnership. I'll be repaid!

MORSE

          (Dubiously)
But where would we work?

VAIL

          (Eagerly)

There's space in my father's foundry. It would
be just the place.

Morse paces for a moment, eyeing Vail. Then:

MORSE

(Quietly)

Did you and your father have a quarrel, Alfred?

VAIL

(Squirming)

Well — I — we —

MORSE

Never mind, Alfred. Don't answer that. I
wouldn't want to go into a partnership with —

(Smiles)

— a liar . . . . to Morristown!

Holds out hand. As Vail grasps it:

MORSE

(Excitedly)

To work! To create! Art is not the only way!

DISSOLVE TO:

INT. WORKSHOP   DAY

26   SLOW PAN SHOT

To show room lined with work benches and littered with
electrical equipment. Wires stretch across it shoulder high,
leading from a telegraph to another o.s.

VAIL'S VOICE

Within three months we were able to transmit
impulses of varying lengths by electricity.

CAMERA HAS PANNED to Vail and HOLDS. He is seated at the
other telegraph, tapping out a word on the key. On his lap
a thick batch of papers loosely stapled together — the dictionary. He stops tapping, consults dictionary, finds a word,
taps again.

VAIL'S VOICE

And with the aid of an elaborate dictionary
which Morse had devised, we were able to
transmit messages. But it was a slow process,
and practice didn't seem to speed it up.

MORSE'S VOICE (O.S.)

Alfred!

27 WIDER ANGLE

as Morse enters, a single sheet of paper in his hand. His eyes are shining with excitement.

MORSE

I've been an idiot — an idiot!

(Takes dictionary from Vail's lap; tosses
it aside)

That crazy dictionary!

VAIL

(Baffled)

But it works, sir.

MORSE

So does the U.S. Mail — if you're not in a hurry! But if you're in a hurry, you don't send *numbers* by code. You don't pore through a —

(Disgustedly)

— dictionary to find the words the numbers stand for! You send letters! You use the alphabet!

Hands Vail the single sheet of paper. Vail scans it silently.

INSERT: THE SHEET

It is a facsimile of Morse's original code.

VAIL'S VOICE

(Over insert)

Even a child could memorize this!

28 TWO SHOT   MORSE AND VAIL

as Vail looks up, awed.

MORSE

(Jubilant)

Precisely! One sheet of paper instead of five pounds of dictionary!

Sound of knock at door.

MORSE

(Jovially)

Come in — come in!

29   WIDER ANGLE

as door opens and Cooper enters, wearing overcoat and hat.
Morse and Vail go to him. As he stares about at the weird
interior:

>   MORSE
>
>   James — !
>
>   VAIL
>
>   Mr. Cooper — !

Morse pumps Cooper's hand. He is still staring about, duck-
ing under wires.

>   MORSE
>
> You can be the first to congratulate us!
> We're a success!
>
>   COOPER
>
> Success, eh? Then I take it the rumors are true.
>
>   MORSE
>
>   (Eyeing him)
> Rumors?
>
>   COOPER
>
>   (Smiling)
> I heard rumors you'd been planning to talk to
> the man in the moon. Thought I'd come down
> and investigate.
>
>   MORSE
>
> To see whether I'd gone mad?
>
>   COOPER
>
> Now, Samuel, can't I be interested in your —
>
>   MORSE
>
>   (Angrily)
> Delusions? I know what people are saying.
> And I think I know why you're here. You want
> me to return to New York, to go back to
> painting. You want me to give up this crackpot
> tinkering. Isn't that why you're here?
>
>   COOPER
>
>   (Mildly)
> Well — you *are* a painter.

MORSE

All right, and I'll go quietly. But only if you
insist. First I'm going to show you something.
(Sarcastically)
If I may.

Cooper assents with a gesture, uncomfortably. Morse goes to
bench and jots down something on a piece of paper. Then he
nods to Vail, who goes to the telegraph at the other side of the
room. Morse goes to the nearer instrument with the piece of
paper.

MORSE

(To Cooper)
You can get a better view at Vail's end.

30   MEDIUM CLOSE SHOT

As Vail sits at receiver and Cooper joins him, curiously eyeing
the set and the code in Vail's hand. Vail takes up a pad and
pencil.

VAIL

Ready, Professor.

31   CLOSE SHOT   MORSE

at other telegraph as he begins to tap out the message which
he holds in his free hand.

32   MEDIUM CLOSE SHOT   VAIL AND COOPER

Vail, consulting the code, takes down the message from
Morse on the pad of paper. We do not see what it says, but
Cooper does. As Vail writes down the last word and message
stops coming in over tape, CAMERA PULLS BACK AND PANS to
include Morse coming toward them. His own message is still
in his hand.

MORSE

Well, what does it say?

COOPER

(Reading from pad)
It says, 'Do you insist, James?'

33   ANOTHER ANGLE

as Morse hands the message he wrote to Cooper. Cooper
reads it. Vail watches in b.g. Cooper is still staring at the
message in his hand.

                           MORSE
Well, James, do you?
                          COOPER
                        (Soberly)
No, Samuel, I don't.
                           MORSE
Of course, to transmit over any appreciable
distance, we'd have to string the wires on poles,
have them properly insulated.
                          COOPER
                       (Cutting in)
How far is 'any appreciable distance'?
                           MORSE
                      (Still pacing)
There's the rub. Unfortunately after about
twenty miles an electric current on wire loses
its strength — dies out.
                     (Ruefully)
Twenty miles seems to be our limit. Just about
the distance it takes to tucker a horse.
                          COOPER
                         (Sighs)
Well, thank heaven I'm just a novelist. When a
horse gives out on one of my characters and
his message has to go on, I just give him a
fresh horse.
He says the words lightly, but the effect on Morse is galvanic.
He stops in his tracks, whirling about.
                           MORSE
That's it, James! A fresh horse!
                        (To Vail)
A fresh horse every twenty miles! Like the
pony express — riding in relays!
Comes forward excitedly.

34   ANOTHER ANGLE
as Morse comes up to a table in f.g. littered with batteries
and coils. Cooper and Vail come up beside him, caught up
in his excitement.

MORSE
(Pointing to coil)

Don't you see, Alfred? A booster on the coil!
Every twenty miles. It would send the
current on as strong as when it started.
Revitalize it! Relay it!

VAIL
(Slowly)

I think you're right; I think it'll work —

MORSE

I *know* it will! At last! Now we're ready!
Now we can show them!
(Paces)

But we need funds! Funds!
(Suddenly)

What about Congress? This invention's for
the people — to bring them closer together —
closer in trade, closer in understanding.
Shouldn't that interest Congress? Our next
step is Washington!

During above, CAMERA HAS MOVED IN FOR CLOSE SHOT OF
MORSE. IT HOLDS on him as we

DISSOLVE TO:

INT. COMMITTEE ROOM   DAY
35   MEDIUM FULL SHOT

This is a small room used by the congressional appropriations
committee. At a U-shaped table, five committeemen are
seated, listening without much attention to Morse, who stands
before them, speaking at a small table littered with charts
and drawings of his telegraph. . . . CAMERA IS SHOOTING past
MORSE toward committee members.

MORSE

. . . . and at each of these relay stations a
mechanical device applied to a wire . . . .

During above, CAMERA HAS MOVED IN TO CLOSE SHOT of a dry,
old, but somehow distinguished man who is the only one
really listening. This is JOHN QUINCY ADAMS. His expression
is impassive. Morse's voice fades and Vail's comes over:

VAIL'S VOICE (o.s.)
Yes, one member of the appropriations
committee was John Quincy Adams.

36   ANOTHER ANGLE FAVORING MORSE
as he continues speaking.

MORSE
. . . . and if a message can be sent through
one such relay — revitalized — it can be sent
around the world!

37   ANOTHER ANGLE   FAVORING ADAMS

ADAMS
Your intention then, Mr. Morse, is to set up
for demonstration a system of instantaneous
communication between this city and the city
of Baltimore — including these — ah —
relay stations?

MORSE
That is correct, sir.

ADAMS
(Tentatively)
Thirty thousand dollars is a considerable sum.

MORSE
(Quickly)
To spend for the public good? To increase the
speed of trade? To promote its growth? Will
it not be for the public good. . . .

38   CLOSE SHOT   ADAMS
as he listens impassively.

MORSE'S VOICE (o.s.)
. . . . to have the whole surface of the nation
channeled for those nerves that will send
out . . .

39   FULL SHOT   TOWARD MORSE

MORSE
(Continuing)
. . . . with the speed of thought, a knowledge of
all that is happening in the land, making
one neighborhood of the whole country?

He pauses. The committee men look at each other inquiringly.

ADAMS

If it works.

MORSE
(Somewhat heatedly)
I am asking for funds to demonstrate that
it *will!*

40   CLOSE SHOT   ADAMS

ADAMS

We are aware of what you are asking, Mr.
Morse. And why. You will hear from us in
due time.

41   FULL SHOT   FAVORING MORSE

He stares angrily at Adams — then swiftly begins to gather
up his papers as we

DISSOLVE TO:

INT. ELLSWORTH LIVING ROOM   NIGHT

42   CLOSE SHOT

of a friendly-looking man in his early fifties stooping over a
small table as he takes up a match and lights a cigar. He is
looking off, listening. This is HENRY ELLSWORTH.

VAIL'S VOICE

In the Washington home of Morse's old friend,
Henry Ellsworth, the Commissioner of
Patents. . .

CAMERA PANS with Ellsworth as he joins group at fireplace —
Morse, Vail and another young man, EZRA CORNELL. Morse
is seated, studying a technical drawing. Cornell is leaning
over his shoulder, explaining and pointing on drawing.

VAIL'S VOICE
(Continuing)
. . . . we waited for word from the committee.
We hadn't much hope, but we kept on planning, just in case.

Morse rises.

43   ANOTHER ANGLE GROUP SHOT FAVORING MORSE

As Cornell sits on the arm of the chair, watching him anxiously.

MORSE
(Pacing — thoughtfully)
I appreciate, Alfred, that your friend Mr. Cornell is an authority on this business of insulation — and I appreciate your bringing him to see me. And there is, of course, something to be said for laying the wire in pipes underground.
(Smiles)
You've both been saying it very persuasively for the past hour. But —
(Diplomatically)
Well, since Mr. Adams will block the appropriation anyway, isn't the whole argument academic?

VAIL
(Pressing him)
But in case Mr. Adams doesn't — ?

ELLSWORTH
(Chiming in)
You know, Adams may be proud. But he's also proud of America. The nation's interest has always been his, too.

MORSE
I don't want to be stubborn, but wire on poles seems simpler. And I can't help feeling that —

GIRL'S VOICE (ANN'S)
Father! Mr. Morse! Where are you?
All look off excitedly.

ELLSWORTH
In here, Ann!

44   ANOTHER ANGLE
as a young girl in her early twenties, wearing street clothes, rushes up breathless. This is Ellsworth's daughter, ANN.

ANN

It's granted! The committee met again after
dinner. The appropriation's granted! I knew it!
I knew it!

As the others react jubilantly, Morse goes quietly to Ann,
taking both her hands in his.

MORSE

Ann, you're going to have a reward. The
first message to be sent over my telegraph will
be yours. That's a promise.

ELLSWORTH

(Laughing)
And she'll hold you to it!

EZRA

(Extending hand to Morse)
Congratulations, sir. I still think you're
wrong about the piping, but I *hope* not.

Morse holds Ezra's hand, looking thoughtfully from him to
Vail.

MORSE

I was wrong about Mr. Adams, I could be
wrong about this piping.
(Smiles)
Let's put it to a vote. The three of us.

As Vail and Ezra grin delightedly —

DISSOLVE TO:

EXT. RELAY STATION   DAY

45   FULL SHOT

Against an old barn, under a shed, lie registers, correspondence and their magnets, batteries, reels of wire, acid baths,
etc., etc. At a telegraph, further refined than the last one we
saw, EZRA CORNELL is tapping out a message. . . . We are
SHOOTING FROM INSIDE barn and the telegraph setup is in f.g.
. . . . A worker passes with a reel of wire. . . . then a team of
horses dragging a plow enters scene and crosses slowly.
Vail is at the handles. The share is raised — the ground is
not being furrowed. The two men wave at each other, and
then Vail and his team are out of scene. . . . During above:

VAIL'S VOICE

In due time we were plowing ground and
laying pipe five miles beyond our first relay
station twenty miles out of Baltimore. That
afternoon, Morse and a group from Washington
were arriving to see the station in operation.

Ezra has finished sending his message. There is no answer;
the instrument is silent. He leans over it in quick concern —
then suddenly calls off.

EZRA

Vail — ! *Vail* — !

Vail comes running back into scene.

EZRA

The line — it's dead! The signal from
Baltimore — it's not coming in!

Excitedly Vail examines the instrument, tests it.

VAIL

It's not the mechanism. It must be the line.

EZRA

It can't be!

VAIL

All we can do is try to find out. Dig down
and test the couplings —
(Grimly)
Starting right from here.

He takes up a small crowbar.

46   ANOTHER ANGLE

as the two walk along a filled-in furrow that leads o.s. from
the telegraph set-up. They drop to their knees.

47   MEDIUM CLOSE SHOT

as they dig frantically with their hands at the filled-in furrow.

VAIL

I've got it!

48   CLOSE SHOT   VAIL

As Ezra joins him Vail has unearthed the coupling. He gives
it a smack with the crowbar and the pipe comes apart, the
enclosed wire severed. He picks up one end of piping and
stares at it.

INSERT: CLOSE-UP PIPE

The insulation is rotted around the wire it encloses.

49   TWO SHOT

as VAIL looks up slowly.

>   VAIL
>
> Rotted. Burned off.

Ezra takes the pipe from him, examines it, then drops it dully. Vail rises, mechanically kicking the dirt back over the pipe.

>   EZRA
>
> (Ruefully)
> The great authority on insulation! This
> *would* be the day!

>   VAIL
>
> Probably that 'hot process' we used to enclose
> the wire the last few miles. I'm afraid
> there's nothing we can do — in time.

>   VAIL
>
> (Gloomily)
> Yes — there goes the balance of our
> appropriation. Poor Morse! Another public
> repudiation.
> (Suddenly)
> Listen, Ezra! I've got an idea! When Morse
> and his party arrive, we'll act as though
> everything were in order.

>   EZRA
>
> What — ?

>   VAIL
>
> I'll tell you why. Come — we'll tell the men
> in the field.

As he starts off excitedly, Ezra following with a puzzled expression.

                                        DISSOLVE TO:

EXT. RELAY STATION   DAY

50   MEDIUM CLOSE SHOT

of Morse finishing a speech. He is standing beside the telegraph, at which Ezra Cornell sits. In b.g., Vail may be seen hovering by the team of horses still attached to the plow near the end of the shed.

CAMERA PULLS BACK to SHOW his listeners grouped about— John Quincy Adams and one or two other committee members . . . Ellsworth and his daughter Ann. . . . two newsmen taking notes . . . . three or four workers.

MORSE

(Smiling, confident)

Everything clear? To the gentlemen of the press?

(Newsmen nod)

All right, Ezra. Ask Baltimore to tell us how the weather is there.

As Ezra confidently begins to tap out the message and the others wait expectantly:

51 CLOSE SHOT VAIL

as he yanks — furtively but deliberately — at the bridle of one of the horses. It rears, neighing.

52 FULL SHOT GROUP

with Vail to one side. He quiets horse. All are looking toward him, the proceedings momentarily halted.

VAIL

I'll get them away.

53 MEDIUM SHOT VAIL

He seizes the plow and urges the horses off, bearing down on the handle. CAMERA PANS with him.

54 CLOSE PANNING SHOT PLOWSHARE

as it rips into the earth, catching the buried pipe leading into the terminus, dragging it up, snapping it. . . .

55 CLOSE SHOT TELEGRAPH

as the whole table set-up topples over, dragged down by the yanking wire and piping that leads to it.

56 CLOSE SHOT MORSE

He stands frozen, staring off, then rushes forward.

57 MEDIUM CLOSE SHOT RUPTURED PIPE

Horses and Vail are out of scene. We hear him shouting "Whoa!" Morse rushes up to the ruptured pipe — sees the damage — then turns and cries to the workers, who have come up slightly.

> MORSE
> (Stricken)
> Come on! Get more pipe! Mend it!

> VAIL
> (Eyes averted)
> The last pipe was laid this morning — five miles beyond.

58   CLOSE SHOT   EZRA

at telegraph, righting it guiltily.

59   FULL SHOT MORSE AND VAIL IN F.G.

Morse stares at Vail for a second, then turns toward the visitors.

60   ANOTHER ANGLE GROUP SHOT

as Morse comes up to visitors.

> MORSE
> (Dazed)
> I — I'm afraid the demonstration will have to be postponed. I'm sorry — I —

Adams' colleagues turn and walk off.

> MORSE
> (Desperately)
> But it can be repaired by to-morrow! There'll be more pipe by morning. You could stay the night at Baltimore —

Adams turns and follows his colleagues. . . . Then the newsmen go. Ellsworth and his daughter come up to Morse sympathetically, one on either side. In b.g. Vail stares at the ground.

> MORSE
> (Continuing dully)
> But it was an accident — !
> (to Ellsworth)
> An accident —

> ELLSWORTH
> (Gripping his arm)

We know that. I'll speak to Adams.
He starts off.

> MORSE
>> (Checking him)
>
> No!
>
>> (Wearily)
>
> I'll see you to your coach.

Leads Ann and her father off. CAMERA PANS, then HOLDS as they pass, on Ezra Cornell, seated at the telegraph. Vail enters scene.

> EZRA
>
> Well, at least an accident will sound better in the newspapers than faulty insulation.

Vail nods gloomily and sits on a packing case.

61   CLOSE SHOT   VAIL
staring into space.

> VAIL
>
> All I can see is a man muffled in an overcoat, boiling a solitary egg, in a barren room. A man giving up because his work has been publicly repudiated.

As he stares into the past:

> MORSE'S VOICE (O.S.)
>
> Vail — !

62   ANOTHER ANGLE
Vail rises in f.g., as Morse rounds the corner of the barn and comes toward him ominously. There is a moment as they face each other — then:

> MORSE
>> (Coldly)
>
> My compliments — partner.
>
> VAIL
>> (Staring at ground)
>
> I'm sorry, sir. I thought it would look better like — an accident.

looks off toward ruptured pipe. Morse's gaze follows him. Quickly he strides off toward pipe.

63   ANOTHER ANGLE AT RUPTURED PIPE

Vail and Ezra watch in b.g., as Morse comes forward and stoops down to examine pipe. He sees at once that the insulation is rotted.

MORSE
(Rising slowly)
Alfred —

Vail comes up behind him — Morse turns and faces him.

MORSE
(Smiling gently)
My compliments.

Puts a fatherly arm around Vail's shoulders and leads him back to shed as we

DISSOLVE TO:

NEWSPAPER HEADLINE
64   READING SHOT
One-column — old fashioned type. It reads: DEMONSTRATION OF MORSE TELEGRAPH A FIASCO.

VAIL'S VOICE
But Adams, strictly upright, insisted that an accident was not a defect — and voted to continue the appropriation.

WIPE TO:

EXT. COUNTRYSIDE   DAY
65   CLOSE SHOT
of Vail, atop a small telegraph pole to which he is fastening a wire. He smiles down as CAMERA PULLS BACK and TILTS DOWN to INCLUDE Morse at the foot of the pole, paying up wire to Vail. He, too, is smiling happily.

VAIL'S VOICE
But burying that wire *had* been a defect. So we strung it on poles. If the next demonstration was to fail, at least it would not be through faulty piping!

WIPE TO:

INT. LIVING ROOM   DAY
66   CLOSE TWO SHOT
Ellsworth and his daughter Ann. She is seated on the arm of his chair as he reads a headline from a newspaper.

ELLSWORTH
(Reading)
'Telegraph line from Baltimore to Washington
complete. Demonstration to be held in
chambers of Supreme Court.'
As they smile at each other.

DISSOLVE TO:

INT. SUPREME COURT CHAMBERS   DAY

67   MEDIUM CLOSE SHOT   MORSE
He is standing behind the court bench, the flag behind him,
speaking. On the bench before him is the telegraph, a model
still further refined. As he speaks, CAMERA PULLS BACK for
FULL SHOT. Grouped about are members of the press, pads
and pencils in hand — Adams, other members of the Committee, Senators and their wives, Cooper, Ellsworth and his
daughter Ann.

MORSE
And so I wish on this occasion that my friend
and partner, Alfred Vail, were standing here
beside me. It was he who renewed my faith
in the future of this invention. It was he who
kept that faith alive in many dark and
disappointing hours.

68   CLOSE SHOT   ADAMS
listening impassively.

MORSE'S VOICE
But Vail is in Baltimore, at the other
terminus of this line, waiting to return the
message.

69   CLOSE SHOT   MORSE
MORSE
However, there is on this occasion a happy
compensation. To Miss Ann Ellsworth —

70   CLOSE SHOT   ANN
listening, happy. She has a piece of paper folded in her hand.
Cooper in b.g.

MORSE'S VOICE
— the daughter of my old friend, the

Commissioner of Patents, I made a promise
that the first message to be sent over this
circuit would be hers.

71 FULL SHOT   TOWARD MORSE
looking off at Ann.

MORSE

I would like to ask Miss Ellsworth to come
forward.

Ann starts toward bench.

72 MEDIUM CLOSE SHOT AT BENCH
as Ann comes up behind it to Morse.

MORSE

What will the message be, Ann?

She hands him the folded slip of paper. He opens it.

73 CLOSE SHOT   MORSE
His eyes light with pleasure as he reads the message — to
himself.

74 CLOSE TWO SHOT   ANN AND MORSE
He leans toward her and whispers.

MORSE

From the 23rd Verse of the 23rd Chapter of
Numbers. Am I right?

Ann nods.

MORSE

(Faces others)

You will hear the message, ladies and gentlemen, when it comes back from Baltimore.

Starts to sit down at telegraph.

75 through 78   SERIES OF QUICK FLASHES
of Ellsworth, Cooper, Adams — all watching, tense, expec-
tant. Sound of telegraph key tapping begins to come over.

79 CLOSE SHOT   MORSE
seated, tapping out the message. CAMERA MOVES IN for
CLOSE-UP of instrument, with Morse's hand tapping on the
key.

80 CLOSE-UP   A SIMILAR INSTRUMENT
As CAMERA PULLS BACK, we see where we are — in the corner

of a small room. Hunched over the instrument is Vail. Ezra
Cornell and two other official persons are leaning over him
as Morse's message comes in. There is no sound other than
the clicking of the keys. Vail is writing down the message.
It is an audible transmission. Presently it stops. There is a
moment — then Vail begins to tap out the message himself.

INT. COURT CHAMBER   DAY

81   MEDIUM SHOT TOWARD MORSE

He is standing as the message comes in on tape. Others are
grouped about closely. The transmission stops — the message is ended. Morse rips off the tape, reading it swiftly.

82   MEDIUM CLOSE SHOT   MORSE

deeply moved.

> MORSE
>
> The message — ladies and gentlemen —

83   MEDIUM GROUP SHOT   TOWARD MORSE

> MORSE
>
> 'What hath God wrought!'

There is a moment of silence, almost reverent. Then Morse
picks up Ann's slip of paper and slowly hands it to Adams.

84   CLOSE SHOT   ADAMS

as he reads it. He nods slowly — also moved.

85   CLOSE SHOT   MORSE

as he turns away from Adams, his eyes finding some distant
point of their own o.s.

> MORSE
>
> I was wrong in saying Alfred Vail is not beside
> me. He is not an instant away.

CAMERA PULLS BACK and PANS, FOLLOWING MORSE'S gaze to the
open window — the open sky. The others follow his gaze,
too.

> MORSE
> (Continuing)
> In due time, he could be across the world, and
> still not an instant away.

86   MEDIUM SHOT   TOWARD MORSE

still looking off raptly.

MORSE

We are only the instruments employed by the
Almighty to discover His wonders.

There is a moment of silence — then Adams steps forward.

ADAMS

(Smiling)

In addition to the Almighty — perhaps we
may also thank . . .

He looks off toward:

87 CLOSE SHOT   COOPER

smiling.

ADAMS' VOICE

. . . the author of a certain anonymous letter
and . . . .

88 TWO SHOT   MORSE AND ADAMS

as Adams holds out his hand. Morse takes it.

ADAMS

. . . the mistake of a certain old man.
Without that mistake, you might still be
painting. It was a mistake of no little conse-
quence to the world.

FADE OUT:

THE END

WHAT HATH GOD WROUGHT
by
Richard Blake

Characters

SAMUEL MORSE	JOHN QUINCY ADAMS
ALFRED VAIL	SEVERAL COMMITTEEMEN
JAMES FENIMORE COOPER	HENRY ELLSWORTH
JOHN CHAPMAN	EZRA CORNELL
JOHN VANDERLYN	ANN ELLSWORTH
A GUEST	SEVERAL WORKMEN
SENATORS AND THEIR WIVES	SEVERAL NEWSMEN
	A HORSE PULLING A PLOW

SETS: (INCLUDING INSERTS)
1. Old Print of Washington Square, New York, circa 1837 (insert)
2. Morse's studio (full set)
3. Entrance hall into studio
4. Morse's and Vail's workshop (full set)
5. Sheet of paper showing Morse's code (insert)
6. Committee Room (full set)
7. Ellsworth living room (full set)
8. Relay station (exterior, full set)
9. Pipe with rotted insulation (insert)
10. Newspaper headline (insert)
11. Countryside (exterior, full set)
12. Supreme Court Chamber (full set)
13. Small room (full set)

       Recap: Eight full sets. One "fragment" (Entrance hall to studio).

       Four Inserts (Extreme close-ups of inanimate objects which visually establish a dramatic point).

TIME: Elapsed time: from sometime in the year 1837 to May 24, 1844, actual date of the sending of the words, "What hath God wrought."

The scope of the filmed television play in comparison with a "live" telecast is perfectly illustrated by the expert script, *What Hath God Wrought.*

It is not impossible, but it is extremely improbable, that any "live" half-hour play would present so many characters: nine speaking parts identified by name, and extras (senators and their wives, guests, committeemen, workmen, newsmen) numbering perhaps twenty or thirty. One character *would* be impossible in "live" television: the horse pulling a plow. Since the action in which the horse participates is climactic, absolutely essential to the plot, and required to be done at the exact moment it occurs in the story, it would be foolhardy to attempt this action in a "live" show, even if the detail of the plow tearing into the pipe could be done in a "trick" special effect shot. The alternative in a "live" show would be to talk about this action instead of show it — an unsatisfactory idea, dramatically.

Furthermore, eight full sets in a "live" telecast would demand a studio and a budget both so large as to rule out the doing of a play with so many full sets. You see, in motion picture production, a set is built, and then *all the action in that set* is photographed, regardless of where in the story the action takes place. If a motion picture begins and ends in a ballroom set, the beginning and the end will be photographed, and then that set is removed to make way for the next set. In "live" television, this procedure is impossible: *all sets* must be built and kept standing *at the same time,* to be used as the action of the play requires. Also, there are two exterior sets in *What Hath God Wrought* that would be extremely difficult to do "live": the Relay Station, which requires that an actual ditch be dug, with the earth showing; and the countryside, which shows a man at the top of a telegraph pole. To photograph this scene properly in "live" television, a large "sky backing" or cyclorama would be needed that would occupy a frightening amount of space in the average studio. It *could* be done; but the difficulties would be immense.

It is specified that the action begins in the year 1837; it is a matter of history that the words "What Hath God Wrought" were telegraphed May 24, 1844. In the play, the second date is not specified, probably because the actual elapsed time is not important, while *events* are. Costume and make-up changes hint at the passage of time, however; both are difficult to do, especially make-up changes, in a "live" telecast.

From a time standpoint, therefore, *What Hath God Wrought* is constructed in narrative fashion rather than in "tight" dramatic fashion. And we have seen that the narrative technique is eminently more suited to motion pictures. Note that automatically it demands a greater number of sets, not only to avoid visual monotony, but to meet the requirements of the episodic character of the narrative. Very skilfully, however, the scenarist has concentrated his individual episodes (or sequences) into tight segments of the total story, so that the all-over effect is of sustained drama. Major time lapses occur between

1. SHOTS 18 and 19. Elapse of time indicated by set, costume and make-up changes.

2. SHOTS 25 and 26. Elapse indicated: new set, voice of narrator telling us that three months have gone by.
3. SHOTS 34 and 35. Elapse indicated: new set; Morse explaining working of relay stations from sketches and models which were just conceived at the closing of the previous scene. Costume, make-up changes, also.
4. SHOTS 41 and 42. Elapse indicated: last dialogue in previous scene was "you will hear from us in due time"; new set, new characters, voice of narrator telling of waiting for the expected word.
5. SHOTS 44 and 45. Elapse indicated: new set, obvious developments in plans announced in previous scene, new characters; make-up and costume changes. Also, narrator's voice describing progress of events.
6. SHOTS 49 and 50. Elapse indicated: obvious progress in plans announced in preceding scene.
7. SHOTS 63 and 64. Elapse indicated: Insert of newspaper headlines reports failure of attempt in preceding scene. But narrator's voice carries forward action by describing decision of Adams to continue the appropriation.
8. SHOTS 65 and 66. Elapse indicated: Ellsworth (acting as narrator) reads newspaper headlines announcing completion of telegraph line. . . . a considerable elapse of time from preceding scene.
9. SHOTS 66 and 67. Elapse indicated; new set, many new characters (extras), grouped for climactic action described in newspaper headlines of preceding scene; costume and make-up changes.

SPECIAL NOTE: It has been said elsewhere in this book that a FADE-OUT, FADE-IN is used to denote a lapse of time. In this script, please observe that DISSOLVES indicate time lapses. DISSOLVES are much faster than FADES, and do not leave the television receiving screen blank (or black). There are two possible reasons for this script's using DISSOLVES: one, the story is very full, very long for the half-hour play, and the seconds of time gained by using DISSOLVES mount up, and help in the over-all count; two, there is a school of thought among television directors, either for filmed TV or for "live," which believes emphatically that the TV receiving screen should *never* be left blank (or black). Such directors never use FADES except at the beginning and the end of a play; and that is the case with *What Hath God Wrought*.

SOME EXAMPLES OF THE TRANSITIONS IN THIS SCRIPT REQUIRING FILMING. . . . . THAT IS, THEY COULD NOT BE DONE "LIVE."

BETWEEN SHOTS 18 AND 19: At the end of SHOT 18, Morse's studio is seen elaborately furnished. Seconds later (in elapsed time) SHOT 19, it is seen "completely barren." Unless duplicate sets were built, one furnished, one "barren," this transition could not be done in "live" television. Morse also has costume and make-up changes impossible to do "live."

BETWEEN SHOTS 34 AND 35: At the end of SHOT 34, the CAMERA is CLOSE-UP on Morse. In SHOT 35, perhaps four seconds later in elapsed time, he is seen addressing the committeemen. As written, this transition could not be made "live." It could be done, with a little "doctoring," such as using Vail as a Narrator (voice over), while the CAMERA shows us the committeemen, long enough to allow the actor playing Morse to make a lightning costume change, and to move physically from the preceding set to the new set.

BETWEEN SHOTS 49 AND 50: In two or three seconds of elapsed time, the stage properties would have to be changed, if the scene is done "live"; and the several actors of the committee would have to move into correct position. Practically impossible to do "live" as written.

BETWEEN SHOTS 63, 64 AND 65: SHOT 64, strictly speaking, doesn't count, as it is an INSERT. But at the end of SHOT 63, Vail is seen with Morse's arm around his shoulder, at the Relay Station. At SHOT 65, he is seen on top of a small telegraph pole, and with a costume and perhaps make-up change. Impossible to do "live."

SOME INTERESTING TECHNICAL POINTS

Describing Shots

Motion pictures have developed a writing technique which aims first of all (as *you* should) for clarity, for conveying the scenarist's exact intention to the technicians who will produce his script. Let's examine SHOT 2. It's INT. (INTERIOR) STUDIO — NIGHT. The place of the SHOT is told, for the scene designer. The lighting is told, for the lighting expert. The director and cameraman are told where the camera is to be set up: SHOOTING ACROSS HALLWAY — TOWARD ENTRANCE. (WHAT ARE YOU READING NOW? ALL CAPITAL LETTERS, OF COURSE. The point is, whenever THE CAMERA IS INVOLVED, THE WORDS OR PHRASES ARE INDICATED IN CAPITAL LETTERS, for the benefit of the director and the cameraman, studying the part the CAMERA plays in each shot). More about the lighting: NIGHT is specified by the scenarist. None of the SHOTS following in this scene (through SHOT 17) specifies lighting requirements, because the scene does not change. However, whenever a change *does* come, the lighting is specified: SHOT 19, INT. STUDIO: DAY. Since this lighting effect does not change throughout the scene, no more SHOTS in this scene carry lighting specifications. However, on SHOT 26: INT. WORKSHOP: DAY. . . . lighting is specified. And so on. You, as scenarist, the "master mind," the *first* mind concerned with creating the play, must always tell the technicians, for their easy reference, what lighting you want in the scene. [SHOTS are numbered, of course, so that they can be cemented (literally glued) together in sequence in the cutting room, by the film cutter and the film editor. This number is written on a blackboard in chalk, and photographed at the beginning of *each* scene, so that assembling the finished motion picture in the first "rough cut" becomes an arithmetical matter of putting numbers into sequence.]

Kinds of Shots

We have remarked before that the motion picture CAMERA WORKS IN CLOSER in filming a play for telecast, because of the small size of the TV receiving screen. LONG SHOTS are impractical in filmed television because the details and the human figures become almost unrecognizable. Such SHOTS are used chiefly for ESTABLISHING or GEOGRAPHY SHOTS.

With this thought in mind, examine the SHOTS in *What Hath God Wrought*. By far, the greater majority are CLOSE SHOTS. GROUP

SHOTS are used when the action demands the presence of several characters. There is one SLOW PAN SHOT (SHOT 26) carefully specified SLOW, because more than on the large motion picture screen, a PAN SHOT on the television receiving screen must be slow; else a meaningless blur is the result. GEOGRAPHY SHOTS, ESTABLISHING SHOTS are used sparingly, only to set the scene visually, in *What Hath God Wrought*.

You'll see ANOTHER ANGLE specified (as in SHOTS 16 and 17). This means literally ANOTHER ANGLE, a variation, on SHOT 15, MEDIUM SHOT TOWARD DAIS. ANOTHER ANGLE is frequently specified for visual variety, to break up a "talky" sequence, or to place emphasis on a different speaker in a continuing dialogue sequence. For instance, in SHOT 17, the character Vail comes into the scene to speak to Morse, and the CAMERA must record his entrance without losing Morse. So, ANOTHER ANGLE of the *same kind of shot* (MEDIUM SHOT, SHOT 15) is called for.

The SHOTS most useful, and most frequently used, in filming plays for telecast, are, then: CLOSE SHOT, MEDIUM CLOSE SHOT, MEDIUM SHOT, and, to set the scene, ESTABLISHING SHOT or GEOGRAPHY SHOT (FULL SHOT).

The play, *What Hath God Wrought*, is a model of its kind for filmed television. The principles it demonstrates apply to any length television play written for filming. And the underlying principle of all dramatic writing applies, as ever: *complete visualization* by the playwright of the scene he is setting down on paper, *with his intention made clear* at all times to the technicians who must produce his script.

11

The Fifteen-Minute
Television Play

THE FIFTEEN-MINUTE television play (actually twelve and a half or thirteen minutes of playing time) is now mainly restricted to the day-time serials. It costs less to produce, obviously, whether production be on film or "live." Correspondingly, the air time costs the sponsor less. The sponsor of a fifteen-minute program (like Modern Romances) still can get representation of his wares through his commercial message, much less expensively.

The fifteen-minute television play must get into its beginning situation "like a whirlwind," *and there is no exception to this principle.*

Sometimes it is written straight through, with no middle break. In this case, its structure is "open at both ends," for a beginning and ending commercial message from the sponsor, the one preceding, the other following the play itself. But there are variations of this commercial break, depending on the wish of the sponsor. The time available for the dramatic story may be broken up into two, three or four segments, with a commercial between each one.

The best plan is to watch the program for which you want to write, and then to devise your dramatic structure accordingly. It can be added that writing for fifteen-minute, day-time programs usually is done on assignment only. Send a Query Letter to any program which interests you to find out if its producers will read unsolicited material (see Chapter 15, Selling).

The fifteen-minute television play *should* have a "gimmick" ending, a fast, quick, basic, meaningful switch at the end, like a "blackout," an ending identifiable to most writers as "the O. Henry ending," where there is a sudden reversal of values and situation for a "between the eyes" surprise pay-off.

The fifteen-minute play is a form where story, plot twists and turns that develop rapidly, one out of the other, may count more than characterization. If you can also achieve characterization, so much the better! The strong premise or opening situation, costuming, make-up, novelty of setting, action, violence — these things take the place of carefully written characterization — unless you can write characterization as well as these other perhaps more important fundamental ingredients into your fifteen-minute play.

It is likely that the fifteen-minute television play will have a larger number of incidents than a half-hour television play, although each incident will not be as long. *More* incidents, developing out of the instantaneously established basic situation, comprise the structure of the fifteen-minute play. You should not let your viewing audience stop once, as it follows your twisting, turning, developing story toward the "reverse" surprise ending.

Following is the complete script of a successful fifteen-minute television play produced on film for the Short-Short Drama Program, and written by Anne Howard Bailey.

Comment on this script follows at the end of the chapter.

IMPERSONATION
by
Anne Howard Bailey
CHARACTERS

PETE	the boy. About 19, shabby, wiry, thin, with a hostile, haunted expression.
KAY GERARD	the woman. About 30, beautiful, svelte, exquisitely dressed, with a rather unusual understanding.
STACY	the dick. Heavy set, open face, about 40. Neat blue suit.
BARTENDER	bulky, saturnine. About 38.
CONDUCTOR	typical tired, harassed Pullman conductor in 50's.
PASSENGERS	MEN, WOMEN of varying ages. One small child.

SETS

FRAG. Wild wall made to look like side of brick warehouse.

Rear platform of streamline train.

Club car of train, with bar, cocktail table, and smoking section.

Roomette car, with corridor, with several doors, one practical roomette, typical with large window, seats opposing each other on either side of window.

1. EXT. FRAG. WILD WALL. CLOSE-UP OF PETE'S HEAD. IT IS OUTLINED AGAINST A WILD WALL OF BRICK. HIS FACE IS TERROR-STRICKEN, BEADED WITH SWEAT, HAUNTED WITH THE WILD, RESTLESS FEAR OF THE PURSUED. HE LOOKS FRANTICALLY FROM LEFT TO RIGHT. SOUND: IN THE DISTANCE A POLICE WHISTLE SHRILLS, AND A SHOUT IS HEARD. PETE GULPS A BREATH OF AIR INTO HIS STRAINING LUNGS, AND PLUNGES OUT OF THE FRAME.

2. CUT TO: CLOSE-UP OF THE RAILROAD DICK, AGAINST A REAR PROJECTION SHOT (IF POSSIBLE) OF RAILROAD YARDS. (OTHERWISE USE WILD WALL) THE DICK SQUINTS INTO THE CAMERA, SHADES HIS EYES WITH HIS HAND, THEN BRINGS UP A WHISTLE AND BLOWS A BLAST.

DICK

There's the kid! Head him off!

3. CUT TO: CLOSE SHOT OF RUNNING FEET IN RAGGED, FRAYED TROUSER LEGS.

4. CUT TO: FILM CLIP OF A STREAMLINE TRAIN PULLING OUT OF RAILROAD YARD.

5. CUT BACK TO: RUNNING FEET WHICH PICK UP TEMPO.

6. SUPERIMPOSE: TURNING RAILCAR WHEELS, PICKING UP TEMPO.

7. DISSOLVE TO: CLOSE-UP OF PETE, OUTLINED AGAINST THE DOORWAY TO THE VESTIBULE OF THE STREAMLINER. HE HAS JUST PULLED HIMSELF ABOARD — THE SPRING HAS TAKEN HIS LAST OUNCE OF ENERGY. HE SWAYS IN THE OPEN DOORWAY, MOVING IN TIME TO THE MOTION OF THE TRAIN. HIS YOUNG FACE IS SICK WITH RELIEF AND FATIGUE. SWEAT BEADS HIS FOREHEAD, ALTHOUGH HE SHIVERS AS THE COLD AIR KNIFES THROUGH HIM. HE GASPS A COUPLE OF TIMES AND FEELS IN HIS SHIRT POCKET FOR A CIGARETTE. HE PULLS OUT A PACK.

IT IS EMPTY. SUDDENLY HE IS ALERTED. THE
DOOR TO THE CLUB CAR IS PUSHED OPEN. PETE
STIFFENS, THEN FORCES HIMSELF TO RELAX.

8.   CUT TO: MEDIUM SHOT OF A YOUNG COUPLE WHO
STEP OUT ONTO THE PLATFORM. SHE IS YOUNG,
BLONDE, BAREHEADED, AND FUR WRAPPED. HE
IS TALL, IMMACULATE IN A TWEED OVERCOAT. A
FEW GRAINS OF RICE SILT OUT OF HIS HAIR,
THEY BOTH LOOK SHINY WITH LOVE. A WED-
DING RING, VERY NEW, GLITTERS ON HER
FINGER. THEY ARE LAUGHING AS THEY
EMERGE, AND DO NOT IMMEDIATELY SEE PETE.
AS THE CAR DOOR CLICKS SHUT BEHIND THEM,
THE MAN TAKES THE GIRL IN HIS ARMS, FOR
A LONG AND FERVENT KISS.

9.   CUT TO: PETE. HE IS EMBARRASSED. HE LOOKS
AROUND FRANTICALLY FOR A WAY TO ESCAPE.
THERE IS NO WAY EXCEPT THROUGH THE CLUB
CAR. PETE MAKES AN ABORTIVE MOVE FOR
THE DOOR.

10.   PULL BACK FOR MEDIUM SHOT AS THE GROOM
LOOKS UP, SEES THE SHABBY BOY, STARING. HE
GLARES.

PETE (HOARSELY)

Uh . . . excuse me . . .

FRANTICALLY, HE BRUSHES PAST THE COUPLE,
LEANS HIS WEIGHT AGAINST THE DOOR, AND
ERUPTS INTO THE CLUB CAR.

11.   PAN DOWN THE CLUB CAR, FROM PETE'S EYE
VIEW. THE VISTA IS APPALLING. IT IS ONE OF
THOSE DIVIDED CARS, WITH A BAR, A SECTION
WITH SMALL COCKTAIL TABLES, AND A THIRD
SECTION WITH ROWS OF CHAIRS, AND SMOKING
STANDS. PETE IS AT THE BAR END.
IT IS CRAMMED WITH TYPICAL CROSS COUNTRY,
STREAMLINER PASSENGERS, BUSINESS EXECU-
TIVES, A FEW ARMED FORCES OFFICERS,
BEFURRED MATRONS, A BEVY OF MODELS, A

FEW CONVENTIONEERS, ETC. THE AIR IS BLUE
WITH SMOKE AND LAUGHTER. WAITERS RUN UP
AND DOWN THE AISLE WITH DRINK TRAYS.

12.   CUT TO: CLOSE SHOT OF PETE. HE LOOKS DOWN
AT HIS SHAPELESS PANTS, HIS THIN, CRUMPLED
SHIRT, HIS FRAYED LEATHER JACKET. HE
STICKS OUT LIKE A SORE THUMB. THE BAR IS
CLOSEST. GRATEFULLY, PETE FALLS AGAINST IT,
HUGGING THE CURVE. THERE IS A SORT OF
ANONYMITY IN STANDING AT A BAR.

13.   CUT TO: THE BARTENDER AS HE MOVES DOWN IT.
HE SPEAKS TO THE MAN AT PETE'S RIGHT.

> BARTENDER

What's yours?

> MAN

Scotch and . . .

THE BARTENDER NODS. HE FIXES PETE WITH A
PENETRATING EYE.

> BARTENDER

Yes . . . ?

PETE GULPS. HIS MOUTH OPENS, BUT THERE IS
NO SOUND. THEN —

> PETE (OFFHAND)

Scotch — and —

THE BARTENDER PEERS AT HIM.

> BARTENDER

How old are you, bud?

PETE DRAWS BACK IMPERCEPTIBLY. HIS EYES
SHIFT NERVOUSLY.

> BARTENDER

What are you tryin' to pull, son . . . ? You
ain't drinking age . . . (HE LEANS FORWARD)
Lemme see your —

> PETE (CUTS HOARSELY)

Skip it. Just skip it . . .

HE JERKS AWAY FROM THE BAR. THE BARTENDER
AND THE MAN EXCHANGE GLANCES AND LAUGH.

14.   CUT TO: PETE LOOKS BACK OVER HIS SHOULDER

AND SEES THEM WATCHING HIM. HE NEARLY
CRASHES INTO A WAITER WHO IS COMING DOWN
THE SWAYING AISLE, FULL TILT.

15. CUT TO: A COUPLE OF MODELS AT A COCKTAIL
TABLE. THEY TITTER AT PETE'S CLUMSINESS.
HE LOOKS DOWN AND SEES THEM WATCHING
HIM. HIS NERVOUSNESS IS MOUNTING. HE GNAWS
ON HIS LOWER LIP. HE STUMBLES INTO THE
THIRD COMPARTMENT, SINKS GRATEFULLY INTO
A LEATHER CHAIR, BESIDE A SMOKING STAND.
THE CHAIR ON HIS RIGHT IS EMPTY. A MAGA-
ZINE IS ON IT. PETE SNATCHES IT UP AND
OPENS IT AT RANDOM. HE HOLDS IT, LOOSELY.
HIS EYES ROVE.

16. PAN OVER TO: MAN ON PETE'S LEFT. HE IS
OVERSTUFFED AND SLEEPY. HE PUTS DOWN A
FRESHLY LIT CIGARETTE ON THE TROUGH, LEANS
BACK, SIGHS DEEPLY AND CLOSES HIS EYES. PETE
IS WATCHING HIM. PETE'S GAZE GOES TO THE
CIGARETTE. IT BURNS STEADILY.

17. CUT TO: CLOSE SHOT OF PETE. HE LICKS HIS
LIPS. HIS EYES HUNGRILY DEVOUR THE
CIGARETTE. HE GLANCES AROUND. NO ONE IS
LOOKING. FURTIVELY PETE INCHES OUT HIS
LEFT HAND. HIS FINGERS GROPE FOR THE
CIGARETTE. SUDDENLY THERE IS A PIERCING
BLAST ON A WHISTLE. WITH A GASP OF HORROR,
PETE STARTS TO HIS FEET. THE MAN ON HIS
LEFT WAKES WITH A SNORT.

18. FAST PAN TO: THE CORNER OF THE SMOKING
SECTION WHERE A SMALL BOY, HELD FIRMLY
BETWEEN HIS FATHER'S KNEES, SHRILLS ON A
TOY POLICE WHISTLE.

19. CUT FAST BACK TO: PETE WHO REALIZES THAT
ALL EYES ARE DIRECTED AT HIM. HE PLUNGES
FOR THE DOOR, AND BURSTS THROUGH IT TO THE
PLATFORM CONNECTING TWO CARS.

20. CAMERA FOLLOWS HIM AS HE CROSSES TO THE

ROOMETTE CAR, WITH A CURVE TO THE AISLE AT
EITHER END FOR THE GENTLEMAN'S AND
LADIES' PARLORS. PETE BOLTS UP THE NARROW
CORRIDOR, SWAYING CRAZILY FROM SIDE TO
SIDE. HE PASSES 6A, 6B and 6C . . . SUDDENLY,
THERE IS A CLICK BEHIND HIM. HE FREEZES
AGAINST THE COMPARTMENT WALL. THE
DOOR TO 6B BEHIND HIM OPENS.

21.　CUT TO MEDIUM SHOT OF STACY, EMERGING
FROM THE ROOMETTE. HE IS IN A DARK BLUE
DOUBLE BREASTED SUIT, THE COAT IS UNBUT-
TONED AND A DETECTIVE'S BADGE IS CLEARLY
VISIBLE, CLAMPED TO HIS BELT. HE HUNCHES
HIS SHOULDER TO SETTLE HIS SHOULDER
HOLSTER.

22.　CUT TO: PETE: HIS EYES WIDEN WITH TERROR.

23.　CUT BACK TO STACY. HE DOES NOT LOOK AHEAD
OF HIM IN THE AISLE, INSTEAD HE SETS OFF
THE OTHER WAY, TOWARD THE CLUB CAR,
BUTTONING HIS COAT. HE STOPS AT THE END OF
THE AISLE TO LIGHT A CIGARETTE.

24.　CUT TO PETE: HE TAKES A STEP OR TWO IN THE
OTHER DIRECTION, JUST AS THE PULLMAN
CONDUCTOR ROUNDS THE CURVE OF THE AISLE.
THE CONDUCTOR IS STUDYING HIS PASSENGER
LIST. HE DOES NOT SEE PETE.

25.　CLOSE-UP OF PETE: HE IS SUSPENDED FOR A
SECOND IN A PIT OF HORROR, BOTH AVENUES
OF ESCAPE CUT OFF. THE TRAIN GIVES A
MIGHTY LURCH. PETE STAGGERS BACK A STEP
OR TWO, AND REACHES TO STEADY HIMSELF
AGAINST THE DOOR TO 6B. IT OPENS UNDER HIS
WEIGHT. PETE IS CATAPULTED INTO THE
ROOMETTE.
INT: ROOMETTE

26.　CUT TO: MEDIUM SHOT OF KAY GERARD, WHO
SITS QUIETLY IN THE VERY CORNER OF THE
ROOMETTE, BESIDE THE WINDOW. HER LEFT SIDE

IS TO THE WINDOW, AND A FUR SCARF IS
DRAPED CASUALLY AROUND HER SHOULDERS
AND LEFT ARM TO PROTECT THEM FROM THE
DRAUGHT. A FOLDED NEWSPAPER IS ACROSS HER
LAP. AS SHE TURNS, STARTLED BY PETE'S
UNEXPECTED VIOLENT ENTRY — THE PAPER
FALLS TO THE FLOOR. SHE GASPS WITH
SURPRISE.

27. CUT FAST TO: PETE. HE IS SHOCKED TO SEE AN
OCCUPANT OF THE ROOMETTE. HIS REACTION IS
QUICK. HIS HANDS GO TO HIS JACKET POCKET
— IT BULGES WITH SOMETHING OF THE SHAPE
OF A GUN.

PETE (DEADLY)

Don't scream, lady. Or I'll — (HE MENACES
WITH THE SHROUDED GUN)

28. CUT BACK TO: KAY. HER INITIALLY SHOCKED
EXPRESSION RELAXES. SHE ELEVATES AN
EYEBROW SLIGHTLY, AS SHE APPRAISES THE
TERRIFIED BUT BELLIGERENT BOY.

KAY (AFTER A PAUSE)

I'm not going to scream.

PETE

Money. All you got.

SHE NODS TOWARD HER PURSE WHICH IS ON THE
OPPOSITE SEAT.

KAY

Help yourself.

PETE GIVES HER A LOOK. HE CAN'T FIGURE HER
CALM. HE MAKES A MOVE TOWARD THE PURSE.

PETE (PUZZLED)

Hey . . . ?

KAY

I haven't any choice, have I? (BEAT) If that
really *is* a gun you're carrying in there.

PETE (TOUGH)

Listen . . . (HE MENACES AGAIN)

KAY (AMUSED)

I'm not calling you.

HE GIVES HER A WARY LOOK AND SCRAMBLES
THROUGH THE PURSE. HE RIFFLES HER WALLET
AND COMES UP WITH ELEVEN DOLLARS AND
THIRTY CENTS

PETE

You travel light, don't you?

KAY

The gentleman is paying my expenses.

PETE (STARTING UP)

The dick . . . ? (HE PATS HIS WAIST TO
INDICATE THE BADGE)

KAY

You're very observant.

PETE

Listen, lady — when you're runnin' —
you — ! (HE BITES OFF THE WORDS) *You*
wouldn't know about runnin'.

KAY

No? (SHE LOOKS AT HIM) I used to foxhunt
once. And sooner or later, foxes go to earth.
(BEAT) I'm afraid they'll catch you —
sometime.

PETE (SNORTS)

You're a funny dame. (SHE SMILES AT HIM)
I never talked to a dame that looked like
you — and dressed like you, before. I thought
you'd be different.

KAY

How — different . . . ?

PETE

Oh . . . like them classy dolls in the movies.
They sound like ice in a glass, when they
talk, y'know. Like they ain't human. (THEN)
I'm sorry to take your money, lady. But I
gotta.

HE MOVES IN THE DIRECTION OF THE DOOR.

KAY

Where are you running *to?*

PETE (INSTANTLY SUSPICIOUS)

Now you sound dumb. Think I'd tell you?

KAY

What are you running *from?*

PETE (VERY TOUGH NOW)

Listen . . . .

KAY

Don't be so proud of yourself. We're all
running . . . one way or another.

PETE GIVES HER A PUZZLED LOOK. HE DOESN'T
KNOW WHETHER SHE'S PLAYING HIM, OR WHAT.
HE SHRUGS AND MOVES TO THE DOOR.

29.   CUT TO: TIGHT SHOT OF DOOR. THERE IS A
CLICK, AND THE KNOB TURNS.

30.   CUT TO: PETE. HIS FACE IS FROZEN IN TERROR.
WITH A SILENT, PANTHER-LIKE LEAP HE
THROWS HIMSELF IN THE CORNER OF THE
ROOMETTE, BEHIND THE OPENING DOOR. HE
GESTURES MEANINGFULLY WITH HIS FIST IN
HIS POCKET.

31.   CUT TO: KAY. HER EYES ARE STEADY,
UNREADABLE.

32.   CUT TO: DOOR. STACY OPENS THE DOOR AND
LEANS IN. HIS EYES TRAVEL UP AND DOWN KAY.

STACY

You all right?

KAY (CASUALLY)

I'm fine.

STACY

Want anything . . . coke . . . cigarettes . . . ?

KAY

I'm fine.

STACY (HUMOROUSLY)

Don't go 'way.

KAY (WRY GRIN)

I'll wait for you.

STACY NODS, PULLS HIS HEAD OUT OF THE
DOOR AND SHUTS IT FIRMLY.

33.   CUT TO: PETE. RELIEF FLOWS OVER HIM IN A
SICKENING WAVE. HIS SHOULDERS DROOP.
WEAKLY HE SINKS DOWN.

34.   CUT TO: KAY. SHE STUDIES HIM. ALTHOUGH
HER FACE IS INSCRUTABLE, HER EYES FLICKER
WITH WARMTH. PETE LOOKS UP, CATCHES HER
EXPRESSION. HE STANDS, HUNCHES HIS
SHOULDERS.

PETE

One squeak outta you, and I'd a blasted you.

KAY (GRAVELY)

I know.

PETE

I'm gettin' outta here . . .

KAY (ALARMED)

Wait . . . . !

BUT PETE YANKS THE DOOR OPEN. CAUTIOUSLY
HE STICKS HIS HEAD OUT. THE CORRIDOR IS
EMPTY.

35.   CAMERA GOES WITH HIM AS HE SLIDES OUT INTO
IT, LOOKS WILDLY TO THE LEFT AND THE RIGHT.
HE STARTS IN THE DIRECTION OF THE CLUB
CAR, THEN CATCHES HIMSELF. HE TURNS UP
THE AISLE. HE SLOWS AT THE CURVE OF THE
CORRIDOR. HE HEARS VOICES.

36.   MEDIUM SHOT OF STACY AND THE CONDUCTOR
AT THE DOOR OF THE CAR.

STACY

Okay, Cap, if you're going to be here for a
while, I think I'll hop back to the club car for
a quick one . . .

37.   CLOSE-UP OF: PETE. NOW HE IS REALLY
TRAPPED. HIS EYES BULGE. LIKE A FLEEING
RABBIT, HE STUMBLES BACKWARDS TO 6B,
FUMBLES WITH THE DOOR, AND FALLS INTO IT.

38.   PAN TO: KAY. SHE REGISTERS NO EMOTION AT

HIS SECOND ENTRANCE, MERELY SHIFTS
SLIGHTLY IN HER CORNER. PETE LEANS AGAINST
THE DOOR, CHEST HEAVING. HIS HANDS DANGLE
LOOSELY.

KAY (FINALLY)

Lose your gun?

PETE'S HANDS JERK UP TO HIS POCKET, THEN,
STUCK WITH THE FUTILITY AND HOPELESSNESS
OF HIS POSITION, HE SINKS DOWN, MISERABLY.

PETE

Okay, lady. Yell your head off. I'm beat.

KAY (AFTER A MOMENT)

You'll find cigarettes in my purse, if you
want one.

PETE GIVES HER A PENETRATING LOOK, REACHES
FOR THE PURSE AGAIN, AND SHAKINGLY
EXTRACTS THE PACK. WITH TREMBLING
HANDS HE FITS ONE TO HIS LIPS, LIGHTS IT,
DRAWS A LONG SHUDDERING BREATH.

KAY

Light me one, will you?

HE HANDS HER THE FIRST, THEN LIGHTS
ANOTHER. TAKES A DRAG OR TWO.

PETE (DULLY)

Why didn't you scream?

KAY

Because — I know — what it feels like. To
be the fox.

PETE (STARES)

You? (HE LAUGHS)

KAY

Ever hear of the Sunland State Farm for
Girls? (PETE GAPES) I've got a diploma.

PETE (DISBELIEVING)

Don't gimme that . . .

KAY

Where did you break out from? Rockwell
Reformatory — or — Brinton State Farm?

(PETE MUTTERS SOMETHING IN HIS THROAT)
I don't care, you understand. It doesn't
matter. But it's one of them. You've got the
look. And you're running too fast.

PETE (FINALLY)

You think you're pretty smart, don't you?
What are you — one of them dressed-up
society dames that travel around, givin'
"How To Make Good" lectures? Baloney.

KAY

What have you got against good clothes?
You could stand a grey flannel very nicely.

PETE (DISGUSTEDLY)

Ahhhhh . . . (HE HUDDLES DEEPER IN HIS JACKET)

KAY

I know. It makes it easier, doesn't it? To
despise what you know you can't have. (SHE
LEANS FORWARD.) But don't you see — you
can have what you want! If you're willing
to work for it.

PETE

Work? Don't gimme that stuff! Who'd hire
me — with a record!

KAY

Someone hired *me*.

PETE'S EYES TRAVEL OVER HER, FROM THE
EXPENSIVE SHOES, TO THE BEAUTIFULLY CUT
SUIT, TO THE FURS. SOMETHING VERY NEAR TO
AWE KINDLES IN HIS EYES.

KAY

Ever live on a farm? (PETE SHAKES HIS HEAD)
Well, you can about go crazy — wanting
things. When I was your age, I wanted them
so much I ran away. But I didn't find what
I wanted in the city. All I found was trouble,
because I got a job in a place that fenced
stolen goods.

PETE (BITTERLY)

So how was you to know? That's the way it
was with me. I'm caught in a car my buddy
stole, so I get time. They don't give you a
chance.

KAY

Maybe you're supposed to — make your
own chances.

39. CLOSE-UP OF: PETE. HE TAKES A LONG DRAG
ON HIS CIGARETTE AS HE THINKS THIS THROUGH.

KAY

When I got out, I had it tough for a while.
Missed a few meals even. Then I got a job as
a receptionist in a model agency. Then I
started modelling —

PETE (CUTS)

Then some rich guy sees ya — and — (HE
SNAPS HIS FINGERS) so it's the end of the
rainbow.

KAY

No. Not quite. I went abroad — and
modelled in France. Worked with designers
there. (BEAT) I pay for my own clothes.

PETE (FINALLY — AWED)

I guess you done all right.

KAY

It isn't easy. But, everybody gets one free
throw.

PETE (URGENTLY)

Lady, you really believe that?

KAY (AFTER A PAUSE)

I know it.

PETE LOOKS DOWN. HE KNEADS HIS HANDS.

PETE

I used to like cars. You know, taking 'em
apart, 'n stuff. Sometimes I used to think
maybe I could even design one . . . a sort of
low job . . . fast . . . a racer . . . maybe — (HE

HESITATES) If I'm lucky — and they don't
catch up with me . . .

KAY

Why don't you go back?

PETE (STARTS UP)

Hey!

KAY

It's your business. It's your life.

PETE

Yeah! *My* life!

KAY

How long have you got to serve? A year —
six months? (PETE'S FACE FLICKERS) You
can learn a lot in six months . . . Start out
clean.

PETE

You think I'm crazy . . . ?

SOUND: THE TRAIN WHISTLES.

40. CUT TO: PETE. HE JUMPS AT THE SOUND, A-
TREMBLE WITH FEAR.

KAY (PRESSING HER CHANCE)

Look at you! Afraid of a train whistle. Do
you want it to be like that — the rest of
your life? Afraid of a sound, a step? Afraid
to turn a corner?

PETE LOOKS DOWN AND TRIES TO STEADY HIS
HANDS.

PETE

I — I don't know. (HE LOOKS AT HER) But
you got the breaks . . . If I could be *sure.* . . .

KAY

Make your own breaks. Begin now. I
promise you it will turn out all right.

SHE CATCHES HIS EYES. HE LOOKS AT HER.
RESPECT AND A SORT OF WORSHIP IS DAWNING
IN HIS EYES.

PETE

You — promise . . . ?

KAY

I promise.

PETE

If I thought that . . . ? But . . . it turned out okay for you . . . didn't it?

KAY (TIGHTLY)

It turned out *swell* for me.

SOUND: THE TRAIN WHISTLES AGAIN. THERE IS A CHANGE IN THE SOUND OF ITS SPEED.

PETE (HESITANTLY)

I know this stop. It's Mintonville. I could be back at the farm by morning.

KAY

Then go! (URGENTLY) Go *on* . . .

PETE

Look, lady . . . if anything happens . . . good, I mean . . . It's because of you. Can I — write you somewhere?

THERE IS THE BAREST FLICKER IN KAY'S FACE. SHE SEEMS TO WITHDRAW SLIGHTLY.

KAY

I — I don't know. But maybe — we'll meet again . . .

THE TRAIN IS SLOWING TO A STOP. KAY PUTS OUT HER HAND TO HIM.

KAY

Don't wait . . . Go now!

PETE

Okay. And — the best to you, ma'am. (SLIGHT LAUGH) But then, you got it, don't you?

KAY

Yes. The best. Good luck.

HE SQUEEZES HER HAND, AND IS GONE. THE DOOR CLICKS BEHIND HIM.

41. CLOSE SHOT OF KAY. HER RIGHT HAND SUDDENLY CLENCHES IN AN AGONY OF REPRESSED EMOTION. AWKWARDLY SHE BENDS, PICKS UP

THE FALLEN NEWSPAPER. SHE OPENS IT OUT
FLAT ON HER LAP.

42. CAMERA CRANE AND PAN DOWN FOR: BLOWUP
SHOT OF HEADLINES. THEY READ: "International
Woman Smuggler Sentenced". BELOW
THERE IS A TABLOID PICTURE COVERING THE
WHOLE FRONT OF THE DAILY.

43. CAMERA ZOOMS IN FOR TIGHT SHOT OF THE
PHOTO. THE PICTURE IS OF KAY, BEING LED
THROUGH THE STATION BY THE DETECTIVE,
STACY

44. CUT TO: TRAIN WINDOW. THERE IS A RAP ON
THE WINDOW. KAY PEERS OUT. FRAMED IN THE
DARKNESS IS PETE'S WHITE FACE. HE MANAGES
A SMILE AND HOLDS UP A CLENCHED FIST OF
VICTORY.

45. CUT TO: KAY. SHE SMILES AND GIVES HIM THE
GOOD LUCK SIGN.
THE TRAIN STARTS WITH A JERK. THE JAR
THROWS KAY BACK, AND HER FUR SCARF SLIPS.

46. CAMERA GOES IN FOR TIGHT SHOT OF HER LEFT
WRIST WHICH IS HANDCUFFED TO THE ARM OF
THE SEAT.
THE TRAIN GATHERS MOMENTUM, AND KAY
LEANS BACK IN HER SEAT AS:
THE SCENE DISSOLVES:

THE END

Miss Bailey advises that *Impersonation* was written for "live"
production. "But then," she continues, "the chances are so great
that most fifteen-minute television plays will be produced on film
that I broke it down into 'numbered shots' for filming. However,
some short-short plays are done 'live,' so that it is good sense to
bear in mind transitions, possible costume and make-up changes,
and the time element as these technical considerations apply in
any television play done 'live.' "

A study of the script of *Impersonation* will reveal that, while it
was filmed, it could have been done "live" just as easily, from a
technical standpoint.

The current day-time serials, fifteen minutes long, almost invariably are done "live," so that Miss Bailey's admonitions to watch transitions, costume and make-up changes are very much to the point.

In view of the tight, tense, single-episode nature of the fifteen-minute television drama, it is unlikely that costume and make-up changes involving any great alteration in the appearance of the actor will occur. Similarly, since, by the nature of the fifteen-minute play, the action *must* be kept on the principal or principal characters, transitions are apt to be simple, because the television camera — in a "live" production — simply will follow the principal or principal actors from one set to another, scarcely ever losing him (or them) for any appreciable length of time.

Note that there are 46 CAMERA SHOTS specified in the script of *Impersonation*. Now, check in Chapter Ten, which reproduces the script of a *half-hour* filmed television play: there are 88 CAMERA SHOTS specified. Each author was, of course, writing independently; but it was not by chance that the fifteen-minute play uses approximately half the number of CAMERA SHOTS used by the half-hour play. The inevitability of the Time element operated in each case, dictating the number of CAMERA SHOTS the Available Time would permit. There might have been some slight variation in the number — 42 or 43 or 45 or 47 SHOTS in the fifteen-minute play — or 87 or 89 or 90 SHOTS in the half-hour play — depending on the length and variety of individual scenes. But in general these two scripts show you the maximum length in terms of CAMERA SHOTS of the fifteen-minute and the half-hour filmed television play.

Remember the wise man's remark to his friend? "Forgive me for having written you a long letter — I did not have time to write a short one."

He was saying, of course, that the shorter the writing, the more difficult — the more selective, the more concentrated, the more condensed it must be, with all attention centered on *only* the indispensable ideas to be conveyed.

12

The Hour-Length
Television Play

FOLLOWING IS THE complete text of an hour-length television play produced "live" on the Kraft Theatre NBC television hour. Physically, the play is set up here as the author wrote it. If all the "rules" are not slavishly followed, the author's meaning is made clear at all times. As you are reading, note the "narrative" style of the play as contrasted with the highly-compressed, "Ibsen technique" of the half-hour television play. In *The Inn,* the author "begins at the beginning"; the first act has not happened before the first FADE-IN. Actual playing time of *The Inn* is about fifty-two or fifty-three minutes, almost two and a half times the playing time of the average "half-hour" television play.

THE INN
by
Roger Garis

Characters

BILL GUERNSEY, 30–35	CHESTER HARPER, 40
TWO MEN IN LOBBY — MIDDLE-AGED	DAN, *the jailer,* 40
(BENNIE & HAL)	EARL KENT, *Sheriff,* 50
MARCIA, 25–28	MRS. BUTTERWORTH, 50
FRED LENNON, 55	PETE HASKINS, 60
A MECHANIC, 35–40	HORACE HASKINS, 33
A WOMAN (BUS PASSENGER)	MALE EXTRAS FOR MOB
TAXI DISPATCHER, MIDDLE-AGED	JOE GAINES, 30
SODA CLERK, 15	BOB JONES, 30

SETS (Including visual devices like the OPENING SHOT)
1. Highway sign
2. Exterior, front door of the Hormuth Inn, with sign
3. Lobby of Inn (full set)
4. Small bedroom (fragment)
5. Garage (fragment)
6. Taxi office (fragment)
7. Drugstore soda fountain (full set)
8. Hormuth jail with small outer room, inner room with three cells (full set)
9. Exterior jail (full set)

SOUND EFFECTS WITH SPECIFIC PLOT SIGNIFICANCE
1. Rock hurled through glass window
2. Voices of mob members (male)
3. Bus arriving and departing OFF CAMERA

THE INN

ACT I

FADE IN ON CU OF SMALL SIGN, SUCH AS IS USED
ON HIGHWAYS AT APPROACHES TO TOWNS. LEAFLESS
TREE-BRANCH MOVES ACROSS FACE OF SIGN, AS IF
SIGN WERE UNDER A TREE AND THE BRANCH MOVED
BY WIND. THE SIGN READS:
    "TOWN OF HORMUTH . . .
      WELDON 14 M."
DISSOLVE TO CU OF LARGER WOODEN SIGN, SWINGING
IN WIND. THIS SIGN READS "HORMUTH INN." PAN
DOWN TO INN DOOR. BILL GUERNSEY COMES INTO
PICTURE. ABOUT 30–35, PLEASANT LOOKING, NOT TOO
SOPHISTICATED BUT WITH AN EASY MANNER. HE
WEARS COAT AND CARRIES SUITCASE. HE GLANCES
UP AT SIGN, THEN OPENS DOOR AND ENTERS. CUT TO
SHOT OF INN LOBBY AS BILL IS ENTERING. IT IS A
RATHER DOWN-AT-THE-HEELS HOTEL IN A SMALL
TOWN ANYWHERE. THERE IS A COUNTER, BEHIND
WHICH THERE ARE PIGEON HOLES FOR MAIL AND

KEYS, AND ON COUNTER A "SLAP-BELL" FOR CALLING
CLERK. SEVERAL SPITTOONS AROUND. A PAY
TELEPHONE ON THE WALL, AS WELL AS LARGE CLOCK.
UPSTAGE A STAIRCASE. A SMALL TABLE WITH
MAGAZINES CENTERED. DULL WALLPAPER, A FEW
DULL PICTURES ON WALLS. THE WHOLE ATMOSPHERE
IS ONE OF DRABNESS. THERE ARE THREE OR FOUR
CHAIRS IN THE LOBBY. TWO OF THE CHAIRS ARE
OCCUPIED BY MEN, ONE OF WHOM IS READING A
NEWSPAPER, THE OTHER DIGGING AT HIS NAILS WITH
A PEN-KNIFE. THE MEN ARE OF NO PARTICULAR
TYPE BUT ARE ROUGHLY DRESSED AND NOT ESPECIALLY
IMPRESSIVE. BEHIND THE COUNTER, OR RECEPTION
DESK, IS A GIRL. YOUNG, PLAINLY DRESSED, SHE IS
NOT EXACTLY PRETTY BUT VERY ATTRACTIVE. THERE
IS A DEFINITE SHYNESS ABOUT HER, A WITHDRAWAL.
HER NAME IS MARCIA LENNON. AS BILL WALKS
TO DESK CAMERA DOLLIES UP FOR CU OF BILL AND
MARCIA. BILL PUTS DOWN SUITCASE.

                    BILL
CHEERFULLY
Hi.

                    MARCIA
Hello.

                    BILL
You open for business?

                    MARCIA
Yes, of course —

                    BILL
LEANING ON COUNTER, LOOKING AT MARCIA WITH
THAT SPECIAL FRIENDLINESS A GUY HAS FOR A
PRETTY GIRL.
Thought I might get a room for tonight. Tried
a short-cut off Route Forty-One and got lost,
and ended up here.
HE SHARPENS HIS APPROACH ANGLE — THIS GIRL
IS REALLY ATTRACTIVE

You know how it is — whenever you try to make
time —

MARCIA

PUSHING REGISTER TOWARD HIM, CUTTING OFF HIS
SPEECH BUT NOT TOO ABRUPTLY

Sign this, please.

BILL

SOMEWHAT CHASTENED

Oh. Sure.

HE SIGNS REGISTER

MARCIA

READING

William . . . . is that Guernsey?

BILL

Yeah. Guernsey. Like the cow. Used to get
kidded about it at school. They had some pretty
potent nicknames for me.

HE SMILES ENGAGINGLY

What's *your* name?

MARCIA

STARTLED A BIT AT THE SUDDENNESS OF THE
QUESTION

My name? Marcia. Marcia Lennon.

BILL

Glad to know you. This town's —
What is it again?

MARCIA

Hormuth.

BILL

Hormuth. Funny, I didn't see it on the road-map.
First I knew it was here was when I drove down
the main street. At least I guess it's the main
street. Got a garage, stores, a barber-shop and a
bank.

MARCIA

I'm afraid you'll have to carry your bag yourself,
Mr. —

BILL

Guernsey. Like the cow.

MARCIA

Mr. Guernsey. We don't have bellboys.

CUT TO MEDIUM CU OF TWO MEN IN LOBBY CHAIRS.
THE ONE READING PAPER HAS LOWERED IT AND IS
STARING HARD AT BILL

BILL

VOICE — MAINTAIN CU OF MEN

That's all right. It's not heavy. I travel light.
Even on long trips. I'm with Holly Smith Company.
Air conditioning. I make surveys —

MARCIA

VOICE — MAINTAIN CU OF MEN

Here's the key.

SHE HAS CUT HIM OFF AGAIN, BUT NOT UNKINDLY

Your room is number eight — top of the stairs,
turn left.

MAN STARING AT BILL NUDGES COMPANION SHARPLY.
OTHER MAN HALTS NAIL-DIGGING, LOOKS UP
QUESTIONINGLY, AND AT SIGNIFICANT NOD OF HIS
FRIEND'S HEAD HE TOO STARES AT BILL

BILL

VOICE — MAINTAIN CU OF MEN

I'll find it all right. Say — don't happen to have
a movie in this town, do you?

MARCIA

VOICE

We don't have much in the entertainment line.

THE TWO MEN ARE STILL STARING AT BILL. THE
ONE WITH THE PAPER GLANCES AT HIS COMPANION
IN A "WELL, WHAT DO YOU THINK?" FASHION

BILL

VOICE

What do you do for fun?

MARCIA

VOICE

Oh — go for walks; some of us read —

THE NAIL-DIGGER NODS ABRUPTLY, CONFIRMING HIS
FRIEND'S JUDGMENT. HE, TOO, HAS APPARENTLY
RECOGNIZED BILL. THE TWO ARISE QUICKLY AND
EXIT. CUT TO CU OF BILL AND MARCIA. BILL IS
LEANING ON COUNTER AGAIN, GAZING UP AT MARCIA
APPRECIATIVELY.

BILL

Don't suppose you'd go for a walk with me —
show me the town? You know, the Welcome
Stranger routine?

MARCIA

I'm afraid I can't — I — have things to do —

BILL

GRINNING

Okay. Thanks anyhow.

HE PICKS UP BAG.

Top of the stairs, turn left — number eight. Right?

MARCIA

Yes, that's right.

BILL WAVES A FRIENDLY HAND AND STARTS TOWARD
STAIRS. CUT TO CU OF MARCIA. SHE IS LOOKING
AFTER BILL, IN THE MANNER OF A GIRL WHO THINKS
SHE MIGHT LIKE THE GUY IF SHE KNEW HIM BETTER
— AND HALF WISHING SHE COULD. DISSOLVE TO
SHOT OF HOTEL ROOM — BED, WASH-STAND, BUREAU,
NOT MUCH ELSE. CERTAINLY NOT THE RITZ-
CARLTON. BILL ENTERS. HE LOOKS AROUND, DROPS
BAG, GOES TO BED, TESTS IT; IT'S NOT SO GOOD. HE
SHRUGS BECAUSE HE'S BEEN IN PLACES LIKE THIS
BEFORE. HE CLOSES DOOR, TOSSES HAT ON BED,
TAKES TOPCOAT OFF, OPENS BAG ON BED, HANGS EXTRA
SUIT UP IN CLOSET. TAKES A FEW THINGS OUT OF
BAG, PUTS THEM IN BUREAU DRAWER. TAKES OFF
JACKET, SHIRT AND WRIST-WATCH, GOES TO WASH-
STAND, HOISTS PITCHER TENTATIVELY, LETS STREAM
OF WATER POUR INTO BASIN. IT SPLASHES, HE
STEPS BACK, AND CONTINUES MORE CAREFULLY,
TAKES SOAP FROM STAND, SLOSHES WATER ON FACE,

WASHES, DRIES, PUTS SHIRT AND WRIST-WATCH
BACK ON. AS HE IS BUTTONING SHIRT HE GOES TO
SINGLE WINDOW, PEERS OUT. WHAT HE SEES DOESN'T
INTEREST HIM MUCH. HE TURNS, GOES TO BED,
TESTS AGAIN, LOWERS HIMSELF GINGERLY, STRETCHES
OUT. HE YAWNS, LIES STILL FOR A MOMENT, TURNS
ON ONE SIDE, THEN THE OTHER. HE IS RESTLESS.
HE GETS UP, GOES TO WINDOW AGAIN, LOOKS OUT,
SHAKES HEAD — NO IMPROVEMENT. HE GLANCES
AT WRIST-WATCH, AND COMING TO A DECISION HE
PUTS ON NECKTIE, JACKET AND TOPCOAT, GETS HAT
AND GOES OUT DOOR. CUT TO MEDIUM CU OF DESK
IN LOBBY. THERE IS A NEW DESK CLERK — A MAN,
ABOUT 55, GAUNT, UNSMILING. HE IS FRED LENNON,
MARCIA'S UNCLE. HE HAS BOTH HANDS ON THE
COUNTER AND IS STANDING STIFFLY, AS THOUGH
WAITING FOR SOMETHING TO HAPPEN. HE IS LOOKING
TOWARD STAIRS. HE HAS SEEN BILL. PULLS BACK
SLIGHTLY AS BILL ENTERS.

BILL

FROWNING. HE THOUGHT THE GIRL WOULD BE THERE.
Where's Miss Lennon?

FRED

DELIBERATELY
Miss Lennon?

BILL

Yeah, the girl who was here before. That's her
name, isn't it?

FRED

That's her name.

BILL

Where'd she go?

FRED

IN EXPRESSIONLESS VOICE
She had to go out.

BILL

Will she be gone long?

FRED

Can't say.

BILL

STARING AT HIM A MOMENT — HE DOESN'T LIKE
THE GUY

You the manager?

FRED

Owner.

BILL

What's your name?

FRED

Fred Lennon.

BILL

SUDDEN CHANGE OF MANNER — MAYBE HE'D BETTER
BE A BIT NICER.

Oh — Mr. Lennon! You Marcia's father?

FRED

Uncle.

BILL

CHANGE BACK AGAIN; AN UNCLE ISN'T SO MUCH

Oh. Uncle.

THEN MORE CHEERFULLY

Glad to know you. My name's Bill Guernsey.

FRED

NOT CRACKING A SMILE

So the register says.

BILL

SET BACK A BIT

Yeah. Well . . . you don't know when Miss Lennon
will be back?

FRED

Can't say.

BILL

Uh-huh. Can't say. How far's the next town?

FRED

Weldon. Fourteen miles.

BILL

They got a movie there?

FRED

Yep.

BILL

Think I'll drive over. I don't suppose you can tell
me whether Miss Lennon — nope. You can't.
Thanks a lot.

HE EXITS TOWARD FRONT DOOR. FRED GAZES AFTER
HIM A MOMENT. THEN, WHEN HE SEES THAT BILL
HAS GONE OUT, HE GOES TO WALL TELEPHONE,
CAMERA PANNING AND DOLLYING UP FOR CU.

FRED

INTO PHONE

Get me Earl Kent, Helen — yeah, eight-six . . .
Hello — Earl there? Put him on quick. . . . Earl?
I think it's him all right. Can't be absolutely
positive but . . . What? . . . Gone after his car.
Said he was goin' to drive to Weldon.
But don't worry. I fixed it. He won't get the car.
Chester will be back tonight, then we'll know for
sure. Okay, I'll call you later.

HANGS UP RECEIVER. CUT TO MECHANIC LEANING
OVER MOTOR OF CAR, HOOD UP. TELEPHONE ON WALL
BACK OF CAR. MECHANIC IS DOING SOMETHING
WITH WRENCH. BILL COMES INTO PICTURE.

BILL

TO BACK OF MECHANIC

Hey!

MECHANIC

STRAIGHTENING, FACING BILL SLOWLY. HE IS A
PRETTY TOUGH-LOOKING GUY

Yeah?

BILL

That's my car.

MECHANIC

That so?

BILL

A NOTE OF ANGER CREEPING IN

I didn't ask to have anything done to it.

MECHANIC

You didn't?

BILL

No, I didn't. What goes on here, anyhow?
HE LEANS OVER, PEERS UNDER HOOD
What are you taking apart?

MECHANIC

Carburetor, points, carbon removal.

BILL

BEGINNING SPEECH STILL WITH HEAD UNDER HOOD,
STRAIGHTENING AS HE TALKS
If I wanted something done, I'd have told you.
What do you do around here, start overhauling a
car whenever you feel like it?
SILENTLY MECHANIC REACHES TO WINDSHIELD, TAKES
ORDER SLIP FROM UNDER WIPER, HANDS IT TO BILL.
BILL LOOKS AT IT.

MECHANIC

There it is.

BILL

LOOKING UP
This is a mistake. I never left any such order.

MECHANIC

Mistake?

BILL

Yes, a mistake. You're working on the wrong car.

MECHANIC

That's your license number on the order slip,
ain't it?

BILL

I don't care whether it's my license number or not.
I tell you you're working on the wrong car.

MECHANIC

TAKING SLIP FROM BILL
Sorry, buddy.

BILL

How long will it take for you to put it together
again?

MECHANIC

Couple of hours. Only quittin' time is in fifteen
minutes.

BILL

You mean I won't have the car tonight at all?

MECHANIC

Looks that way, mister.

BILL

That's dandy. You're sure I'll have it by morning,
are you?

MECHANIC

Oh, morning, sure. Ten, eleven o'clock.

BILL

Make it as early as you can. I got a long ride
ahead of me.

MECHANIC DOESN'T REPLY. BILL LOOKS UNDER HOOD
AGAIN. SHAKES HEAD IN DISGUST. EXITS. MECHANIC
WATCHES HIM, THEN GOES TO TELEPHONE. MOVE
IN FOR CU

MECHANIC

Eight-six . . . hello. Earl? He was here. He didn't
get the car. I told him what Fred said. Huh?
Little mad, that's all . . . he won't be back tonight.
Huh? Sure I think it's him . . . Anyhow, Chester'll
know. Yeah. Right . . . .

CUT TO BILL ENTERING HOTEL LOBBY. FRED IS
BEHIND DESK, LOOKING AT NEWSPAPER. AS BILL
APPROACHES HE RAISES HIS HEAD. DOLLY UP FOR
MEDIUM CU.

BILL

PUSHING HAT BACK ON HIS HEAD — HE'S GOTTEN
OVER HIS MAD NOW.

Say, any way to get to Weldon besides driving?

FRED

There's a bus.

BILL

What time does it leave?

FRED

LOOKING AT CLOCK
'Bout five minutes.

BILL

Think I'll take it. They got my car all apart at the
garage. Where does the bus leave from?

FRED

Front of the hotel.

BILL

AS THOUGH ARGUING WITH HIMSELF
It's not that I'm bugs about movies, but I feel like
getting out of this town for a while. It gives me
the willies.
LOOKS AT FRED
You know how it is — some places are like that.
No particular reason . . .
HE SEES THAT FRED ISN'T PAYING ANY ATTENTION
TO HIM AND STOPS. THEN:
Yeah. Well . . . . .
HE TURNS AND STARTS TOWARD TABLE WITH
MAGAZINES ON IT. MAINTAIN SHOT OF FRED, WHO
WATCHES BILL FOR A MOMENT, THEN GOES TO
WALL TELEPHONE, CAMERA PANNING BUT NO CU.
FRED TAKES RECEIVER OFF HOOK. WE SEE HIS LIPS
MOVE CLOSE TO TRANSMITTER BUT WE DO NOT HEAR
WHAT HE SAYS. CUT TO BILL AT MAGAZINE TABLE.
HE SELECTS ONE AND DROPS IN A CHAIR TO READ.
HE TURNS PAGES RESTLESSLY. HE TAKES OUT A
CIGARETTE. HE FEELS IN HIS POCKET FOR MATCHES.
DISCOVERS HE HAS NONE. HE RISES, GOES TO
COUNTER, CAMERA PANNING. FRED IS JUST
RETURNING FROM PHONE.
Got any matches?

FRED

Yep.
FRED REACHES BENEATH COUNTER, HANDS BILL A
PACK OF MATCHES. BILL GIVES HIM MONEY, RECEIVES

CHANGE, LIGHTS A CIGARETTE. HE LOOKS UP AT
CLOCK.

BILL

Bus ought to be about due.

FRED

Should be.

BILL

Guess I'll wait outside.

HE GOES TOWARD DOOR. FRED WATCHES HIM. BILL
OUT OF PICTURE, MOVE IN FOR CU OF FRED, STARING
HARD AFTER BILL. CUT TO SHOT OF STANDING SIGN,
"BUS STOP." BILL WALKS INTO PICTURE. STANDS
NEAR SIGN, WAITING. WOMAN, NO PARTICULAR
TYPE, WALKS ON, IN COAT, CARRYING BUNDLE. .
MOMENT AND SOUND OF APPROACHING BUS IS HEARD.
IT GROWS NEARER AND BILL IS ABOUT TO STEP
FORWARD WHEN THE MECHANIC FROM THE GARAGE
RUSHES TOWARD HIM, GRABS HIS ARM. WOMAN
STEPS FORWARD OUT OF PICTURE.

MECHANIC

Hey!

BILL

What?

MECHANIC

That overhaul. You gonna pay for it?

BILL

What do you mean, am I going to pay for it? I
didn't order it.

SOUND OF BUS PULLING TO A STOP

MECHANIC

You're gettin' a carburetor adjustment and a points
job. Besides carbon removal.

BILL

Look, I didn't need it!

SOUND OF BUS DOOR WHOOSHING OPEN

MECHANIC

Somebody's got to pay.

HE STILL HAS HOLD OF BILL'S ARM.

BILL

So ask the guy who signed the order blank.

HE HAS A SUDDEN CHANGE OF MIND

All right, I'll pay for it. Let go of my arm, will you?

MECHANIC DOESN'T OBEY. HE LOOKS UP QUICKLY TO
SEE IF BUS IS STILL THERE. AT THAT MOMENT THE
SOUND OF THE BUS DOOR WHOOSHING SHUT, AND
BUS STARTING. MECHANIC DROPS HIS ARM.

MECHANIC

Okay. Long as you pay for it.

BILL MAKES A DASH TOWARD THE BUS. HE STOPS
ALMOST INSTANTLY, WHEN HE SEES HE'S TOO LATE.
HE CONFRONTS MECHANIC IN EXASPERATION.

BILL

You made me miss that bus.

MECHANIC

FLATLY

Sorry, buddy.

BILL

You're sorry. Like you're sorry you took the wrong
car apart.

HE CONQUERS HIS RESENTMENT

What time is there another bus?

MECHANIC

Ain't any more, tonight.

BILL

That's fine. That's just wonderful. What is this,
a conspiracy?

HE GETS TRUCULENT, SHOVES HIS CHIN AT MECHANIC.

You people in Hormuth got a feud with Weldon,
you don't want anybody to go there?

MECHANIC SHRUGS, TURNS AWAY. BILL STARES
AFTER HIM IN ANGER. PULLS HAT DOWN HARD ON
HEAD. HE'S GOING TO GET TO WELDON TONIGHT IF IT
KILLS HIM. HE SWINGS ABOUT. CUT TO LONG SHOT
OF HOTEL LOBBY, WITH FRED BEHIND DESK. FRED
IS IN ATTITUDE OF WATCHFUL WAITING. DOLLY UP

FOR MEDIUM CU. BILL STRIDES INTO PICTURE.
HE IS MAD.

BILL

LOUDLY
You got a taxi service in this town?

FRED
Yep.

BILL
Would it strain you too much to tell me where it is?

FRED
Next block, right. On the right hand side.

BILL
Thanks very much.

HE STRIDES OUT. FRED WATCHES HIM GO. CUT TO
SHOT OF MARCIA DESCENDING STAIRS. SHE WALKS
SLOWLY, GAZING AFTER BILL, HALTS AT FOOT OF
STAIRS AS HER EYES REMAIN FIXED ON BILL'S
DEPARTURE. AFTER A MOMENT SHE GOES TO COUNTER,
CAMERA PANNING AND MOVING IN FOR MEDIUM CU.
WE SEE FRED AT TELEPHONE IN DISTANCE. WE
HEAR HIS VOICE:

FRED
Yeah. Yeah. I don't care how you do it — just
make sure he don't get a cab. I tell you Chester
will be back tonight. We got to keep him here
till then. Tell him anything — so long as he don't
leave. Okay. You just be sure!

AS FRED IS TALKING, MARCIA, HEARING HIM, TURNS IN
HIS DIRECTION. MOVE IN FOR CU OF MARCIA. AS
FRED CONTINUES MARCIA FROWNS, TRYING TO
FIGURE OUT WHAT IS HAPPENING. THE FROWN IS
MORE PRONOUNCED AS MARCIA BECOMES DISTURBED
AT WHAT SHE HAS HEARD. CUT TO MEDIUM CU OF
TAXI DISPATCHER SITTING IN CHAIR WITH FEET
ON A DESK, CHEWING A CIGAR. TELEPHONE ON DESK.
HE LOOKS AS THOUGH HE HASN'T MOVED IN AT
LEAST SIX MONTHS. CIGAR ASHES ON VEST.
BILL ENTERS.

BILL

This the taxi office?

DISPATCHER

MOVING NOTHING EXCEPT HIS LIPS

Yeah.

BILL

Can I get a cab to take me to Weldon?

DISPATCHER

Cabs all out.

BILL

When will you have one?

DISPATCHER

Hard to say.

BILL

ANGER FLARING AGAIN.

What do you mean, hard to say? Don't you know
where your cabs are?

DISPATCHER

Only got two. They could be anywhere.

BILL

SITTING ON CORNER OF DESK. NOW THAT HE'S OPENLY
ANGRY, HE'S MORE RELAXED ABOUT IT.

Mister, let me tell you something. You got a real
smart crowd in Hormuth. Yes, sir, real smart.
The garage takes my car apart by mistake. The
mechanic argues with me about paying for it
until I miss the bus. Now *you* got no idea where
your cabs are.

DISPATCHER

That's right.

BILL

When a cab does come in, send it over to the inn,
will you? Name's Guernsey. Like the — Oh,
skip it. Just send the cab to the inn.

DISPATCHER

Wilco.

BILL

Wilco. Well, you must have heard about the war,
anyhow.

HE HUNCHES HIS SHOULDERS, STRIDES OUT.
DISPATCHER REMOVES CIGAR, GAZES SPECULATIVELY
AT END OF IT. THEN HE SITS UP ABRUPTLY, PULLS
PHONE TOWARD HIM, LIFTS IT TO EAR, JIGGLES FOR
OPERATOR. CUT TO MEDIUM CU OF MARCIA STANDING
IN FRONT OF INN. SHE WEARS A COAT. SHE LOOKS
BOTH WAYS, AS THOUGH HOPING TO SEE SOMEONE,
AND APPEARS DISTURBED. BILL COMES INTO PICTURE.
BILL'S FACE IS SET GRIMLY, BUT WHEN HE SEES
MARCIA HE IS IMMEDIATELY A GAY GUY.

BILL

Hello.

HE STOPS CLOSE TO HER.

MARCIA

Hello, Mr. Guernsey.

BILL

On your way somewhere?

MARCIA

I just stepped out for a breath of air.

BILL

That's one thing you got plenty of — air. Nobody
can take that away from you.

MARCIA

You don't care much for Hormuth, do you, Mr.
Guernsey?

BILL

On the whole, no.

HE LOOKS AT HER DIRECTLY.

But there are one or two things that aren't too
hard to take.

MARCIA

Such as?

BILL

A WIDE GESTURE

Oh — scenery — the mountains in the background —

MARCIA

I see.

BILL

And a small section of its population. Limited,
as a matter of fact, to one.

MARCIA

IMPULSIVELY

Mr. Guernsey —

BILL

Yes?

MARCIA

Are you sure you've never been in Hormuth before?

BILL

A SHORT LAUGH

You mean a fellow could *forget* a place like this?
HE ACHIEVES A NICE NOTE OF SARCASM
Where everybody is so obliging —so friendly —
they can't do enough for you! Take that old
buzzard who runs the hotel —
HE REALIZES SUDDENLY THAT HE'S OVERSTEPPED HIS
MARK.
Sorry. I forgot he's your uncle.

MARCIA

That's all right.

BILL

It's funny, you living in a place like this. Haven't
you ever —
STOPS, EDGES A FEW INCHES CLOSER, NOT JUST TRYING
TO FLIRT BUT BECAUSE HE SERIOUSLY LIKES THIS
GIRL. BILL IS, IN FACT, FAIRLY SERIOUS ABOUT
MOST THINGS.
Look, isn't there somewhere we can go and talk?
Somewhere besides that —
A GESTURE
That hotel?

MARCIA

I don't know — there is a drug store across the
street — they have sodas —

BILL

Fine. Let's go there.

HE STEPS TO MARCIA'S SIDE, TAKES HER ARM. MARCIA
PULLS BACK. BILL'S GESTURE HAS BREACHED HER
PROTECTIVE WALL. THEN, TO HER OWN SURPRISE,
SHE FINDS SHE DOESN'T MIND IT SO MUCH AS SHE
HAD ANTICIPATED, AND ALLOWS HIM TO HOLD HER
ARM, AS THEY WALK OFF. DISSOLVE TO MEDIUM CU OF
SODA CLERK, ABOUT FIFTEEN, BEHIND SODA COUNTER.
HE IS A STUDIOUS FELLOW, WEARS GLASSES, AND IS
LEANING ON THE COUNTER ABSORBED IN A BOOK.
HE TURNS A PAGE, FROWNS, TURNS BACK, READS
AGAIN, THEN NODS IN UNDERSTANDING, FLIPS OVER
PAGE. MARCIA AND BILL ENTER, TAKE STOOLS.

MARCIA

Hello, Irving.

IRVING

LOOKING UP, ADJUSTING GLASSES, THEN RECOGNIZING
MARCIA

Oh, hello, Marcia.

MARCIA

Still on fossils?

IRVING

LOFTILY

Oh, no. I finished fossils. I'm in the Pleistocene
period.

MARCIA

TO BILL

Irving is taking a correspondence course in
geology.

BILL

That's fine, Irving.

IRVING

They send us mineral deposits for study. Last week
I got a ten-pound rock through the mail. Mr.
Harvey, the postmaster, thought it was a bomb
and soaked it in water.

MARCIA

I hope it didn't spoil it.

IRVING

Nope. Not much you can do to a rock. What'll you have?

MARCIA

I think I'd like a chocolate soda, vanilla cream.

IRVING

One black-and-white. Check.

BILL

That's good here.

IRVING

Two black-and-whites.

STARTS TO MOVE OFF, REMEMBERS BOOK, RETURNS, LOOKS CAREFULLY AT PAGE, TAKES STRAW FROM CONTAINER FOR BOOKMARK, INSERTS IT IN BOOK, AND EXITS WITH BOOK.

BILL

Marcia — you mind if I call you Marcia?

MARCIA

No, I don't mind.

BILL

My first name's Bill.

MARCIA

All right — Bill.

BILL

Marcia — how come you stay in a town like this? I mean, you're pretty, you're intelligent, you've got everything it takes — now, wait —

AS MARCIA STARTS TO INTERRUPT HIM

I'm not handing you a line. I'm reciting obvious facts. How is it you stay buried in Hormuth?

MARCIA

It's my home.

BILL

You mean you were born here?

MARCIA

No. I was born in Brockton. That's about fifty miles from here. My father died three years ago. I've been staying here with my uncle ever since.

                              BILL
I had a hunch you weren't from Hormuth.
                            MARCIA
Why?
                              BILL
You haven't got that Hormuth look.
                            MARCIA
Is that supposed to be a compliment?
                              BILL
Could be. Depends on the viewpoint.
PAUSE
Where do the fellows take you for dates around
here?
                            MARCIA
Oh, I don't know . . . over to Weldon to the
movies.
                              BILL
Well, I'm having a little trouble getting to Weldon
to go to the movies tonight. Everything seems
to be. . . . .
HE TRAILS OFF AS HE LOOKS UP.
CUT TO MEDIUM CU OF FOUR MEN STANDING A SHORT
DISTANCE AWAY, STARING AT BILL. THEY ARE
FRED, THE HOTEL OWNER, THE TWO MEN WHO
WERE IN LOBBY CHAIRS AT OPENING, AND A FOURTH
MAN, CHESTER HARPER. THEIR ATTITUDES ARE
GLOWERING, THREATENING. WE HEAR BILL'S VOICE
TRAIL OFF AT CUT, AS HE BECOMES AWARE OF THE
FOUR MEN AND SWINGS ABOUT ON THE STOOL. THE
MEN ADVANCE, CAMERA PULLING BACK, PANNING,
MOVING IN, SHOWING TWO MEN ON ONE SIDE OF
BILL, TWO ON THE OTHER. CUT TO CU OF
IRVING MOVING ALONG COUNTER TOWARD GROUP.
                            IRVING
BRISKLY
Hello, Mr. Lennon. What'll it be? Got some fresh
pineapple syrup . . . .
HIS VOICE DIES, AS DOES HIS BRISKNESS. HE SEES THAT

THE FOUR MEN ARE IN NO MOOD FOR SODAS.
IRVING MOVES QUICKLY OUT OF PICTURE. CUT TO
SHOT OF FOUR MEN AND BILL AND MARCIA.

FRED

This him, Chester?

CUT TO CU OF CHESTER. HE IS ABOUT 40, MEAN-
LOOKING. ALL RIGHT IN A FIGHT IF THE ODDS ARE
ON HIS SIDE. HE STARES AT BILL, EYES NARROWED,
TAKING HIS TIME. THEN HE NODS SLOWLY.

CHESTER

That's him.

CUT TO LONGER SHOT. THE TWO MEN WHO WERE IN
LOBBY MOVE SWIFTLY TOWARD BILL. ONE OF THEM
GRABS AN ARM.

BILL

MORE SURPRISED THAN ANGRY

Hey! What goes on here?

FRED

You positive, Chester?

CHESTER

Positive.

MARCIA

URGENTLY

Uncle Fred —

FRED

HARSHLY

Stay out of this, Marcia.

BILL

FAIRLY CALM, BUT STEAMING UNDERNEATH

Call your shots, Uncle Fred. Maybe you got some
kind of a game you play on visitors. Okay, I'll
play along. I'll even try to pin the tail on the
donkey.

SUDDENLY HE PULLS HIS ARMS FREE, AND LASHES
OUT VIOLENTLY, THRUSTING BACK THE TWO MEN
WHO WERE HOLDING HIM

But keep your hands off me!

THE SCENE IS INSTANT CONFUSION. THE TWO MEN

RECOVER AND RUSH AT BILL. CHESTER STEPS
FORWARD TO GET IN HIS LICKS. BILL GOES INTO A
FIGHTING STANCE, WILLING TO TAKE ON ALL
COMERS. MARCIA, FRIGHTENED FOR BILL, CLUTCHES
AT HER UNCLE. IRVING COMES INTO PICTURE ON
THE OTHER SIDE OF THE COUNTER, WITH MOUTH OPEN,
HOLDING HIS BOOK, AND GOGGLE-EYED. IT IS
IMPORTANT THAT EACH CHARACTER BE INVOLVED
INTENSELY IN SCENE.

MARCIA

Uncle Fred — don't let them —

FIRST MAN

Get him! Get the —

SECOND MAN

Shove me, will you? I'll bash your head in!

CHESTER

Let me at him! It was my sister . . .

FRED

STEPPING INTO FRAY, IN FRONT OF BILL, FACING
THE OTHERS, HOLDING HIS ARMS OUT AND SPEAKING
LOUDLY

Wait! Stop it!
You want to wreck the drug store?
Chester, move back!
You, Bennie, hold it! Don't anybody hit him!

FRED'S VOICE HALTS THE FIGHT. ALL KEEP THEIR
PLACES, BREATHING HARD. SLOWLY THEIR ATTITUDES
RELAX A LITTLE BUT NOT ENTIRELY. THEY'RE STILL
READY TO GO AGAIN AT A MOMENT'S NOTICE.
BILL KEEPS HIS GUARD UP. MARCIA IS BACKED AGAINST
THE COUNTER, HANDS GRIPPING THE EDGE. CHESTER
REMAINS THE MOST TRUCULENT, AND MAKES
MOTIONS AS THOUGH HE WERE COMING AT BILL
AGAIN. FRED PUTS A HAND AGAINST HIM, HOLDING
HIM OFF.

CHESTER

GROWLING

The sneaking, dirty —

FRED

SHARPLY

Cut it, Chester! There'll be time enough for that!
CHESTER SUBSIDES, MUTTERING. FRED TURNS TO BILL.
You coming along, or will we have to make you?
CUT TO CU OF BILL. HE STARES FROM ONE TO THE
OTHER OF HIS ATTACKERS IN COMPLETE CONFUSION.
HE RUNS HIS HAND THROUGH HIS HAIR, SHAKES HIS
HEAD SLIGHTLY AS THOUGH TRYING TO COME OUT
OF A NIGHTMARE.

BILL

SOMEWHAT HOARSELY

Look, fun's fun, but this is sort of overdoing it —
I'm willing to be a stooge, if that's what you
want, but there's a limit —
CUT TO CU OF FRED. HIS FACE IS SET, GRIM.

FRED

Shut up, Bassick!
CUT TO CU OF BILL

BILL

ASTONISHED

Bassick? Who's Bassick?
CUT TO LONG SHOT

FRED

You — you're Bassick! You're Carl Bassick!
Thought you were pretty wise, coming back here,
didn't you? Thought maybe we'd forget what
you look like after four years!
CUT TO CU OF BILL. FOR A MOMENT HE STARES AT
FRED AND THE OTHERS IN STUPEFACTION, THEN
SUDDENLY HE RELAXES AND BEGINS TO LAUGH,
LEANING BACK AGAINST THE COUNTER AND REALLY
ENJOYING HIMSELF.

BILL

So that's it — why, sure, that's it!
LAUGHS
Simple, isn't it? Explains the whole thing.

STOPS LAUGHING, BUT STILL AMUSED, HE LEANS
TOWARD FRED

Who did you say I was supposed to be — a guy
by the name of *Bassick?*

CUT TO LONGER SHOT. FRED LOOKS AT BILL
SILENTLY FOR A MOMENT, THEN:

FRED

Go ahead. Have your laugh. Probably your
last one.

MARCIA

STEPPING TOWARD FRED

Uncle Fred, I don't know what this is all about,
but you must have made a mistake —

FRED

WHIRLING ON HER, ANGER HIGH

You keep out of this! I told you to keep out!

BILL

MOVING SLIGHTLY FORWARD IN PROTEST

Look, Mr. Lennon, Marcia's only trying to —

AT THIS INSTANT, CHESTER, WHO HAS BEEN EYEING
BILL THREATENINGLY, FLIES AT HIM, PINNING HIM
AGAINST THE COUNTER.

CHESTER

I'll kill him! I'll kill him! I'll kill the —

FRED

TRYING TO PRY CHESTER LOOSE

Chester — let loose! Let loose, you hear me?
Bennie — Hal — help me get him off —

FRED, BENNIE AND HAL SEPARATE THE TWO MEN.
BILL IS NOW PLENTY MAD.

BILL

RIGHT FIST COCKED

Let him come if he wants to! Let him try it!

FRED, BENNIE AND HAL STAND BETWEEN BILL AND
CHESTER.

FRED

Cut it out, Chester! You'll have your chance —
don't do anything here!

PAUSES, TURNS AGAIN TO BILL

You trying to tell us you're not Carl Bassick?

BILL

HOTLY

Carl Bassick? Sure, I'm Carl Bassick! Only I'm
better known as Mary, Queen of Scots. My father
was King Henry The Eighth. I got a brother
named Napoleon.

FRED

Okay, Bassick. If that's the way you want it —

RETURNS TO THE OTHERS, AS THOUGH ABOUT TO

ORDER THEM TO GRAB BILL AGAIN.

MARCIA

COMING FORWARD, SPEAKING DECISIVELY

Wait — listen to me! Uncle Fred, I want you to
listen to me!

FRED

FACING HER

I told you —

CUT TO CU OF MARCIA

MARCIA

I don't care what you told me — I've got a right
to be heard the same as anybody else! You're
making a mistake. You think Mr. Guernsey is
somebody else. I don't know who this Bassick is
supposed to be —

CHESTER

VOICE – MAINTAIN CU OF MARCIA

I'll tell you who he's supposed to be!

MARCIA

But whoever he is, I'm sure he isn't Mr. Guernsey!

CUT TO CU OF BILL

BILL

If you'll calm down a second, instead of everybody
going crazy —

CUT TO MEDIUM CU OF CHESTER

CHESTER

RUSHING AT BILL

Let me get at him!
BENNIE AND HAL GRAB CHESTER. HOLD HIM.
CUT TO CU OF FRED AND MARCIA.

FRED

LOOKING AT MARCIA
How do you know so much about this feller,
Marcia?

MARCIA
I don't know so much about him — I only met
him today.

FRED
And you're trying to say you know him better than
we do, better than Chester does, and he lived in
Chester's house almost a month . . . .
CUT TO CU OF BILL. HE STEPS FORWARD, RAISES
HIS HANDS.

BILL
Wait a minute — wait a minute, everybody!
CUT TO LONGER SHOT. BILL LOWERS HIS HANDS.
Let's start all over again. Let's get this whole thing
straight. First I thought you were kidding.
Okay, you're not. You really *do* think I'm
somebody named Bassick.
HE TURNS TO FRED
Suppose you tell me, Mr. Lennon. Who is this
Bassick? What did he do?
FOR A MOMENT THERE IS SILENCE. FRED STARES AT
BILL.

CHESTER
You murdered my sister, that's what you did.

BILL
Murdered . . . . !

CHESTER
You got away four years ago, but you're not going
to get away now.

BILL
Wait a minute! Wait a minute! I'm not Bassick.
CUT TO CU OF CHESTER, BETWEEN BENNIE AND HAL.

CHESTER

WILDLY

He's lying — He's Bassick! I know he's Bassick!
Bennie — Hal — you know Bassick.

BENNIE AND HAL NOD VIGOROUSLY.

CUT TO CU OF FRED AND BILL.

FRED

GRIMLY

Seems you're out-voted, Bassick. I remember you
pretty well myself. But we wanted to wait till
Chester got back from Weldon to make sure.

BILL

Look, this isn't funny — you're accusing me of
murder. Let's get this thing straight. I can prove
who I am.

REACHES IN INSIDE POCKET, TAKES OUT WALLET,
OPENS IT

Here's my driver's license. Here's the registration
license of the car. Here — look.

SHOVES THEM AT FRED

Guernsey. Like the cow.
William Guernsey. Address, 182 Center Street,
Montclair, N.J. Read it.

FRED LOOKS AT LICENSE. HIS FACE DOES NOT
CHANGE. HE HANDS THEM BACK TO BILL.

FRED

I read it.

BILL

IMPATIENTLY

Well? When do you start apologizing?

FRED

Anybody can get licenses. Give any name they
want.

BILL

INCREDULOUSLY

You mean you still don't believe —

DIGS INTO WALLET AGAIN

Here. Look. My Social Security card. See it?

SHOVES IT AT FRED

William Guernsey, employed by the Holly Smith
Company, Newark, N.J.

FRED

LOOKING AT CARD, HANDING IT BACK

Notice the date is 1949. Guess you already
changed your name by that time.

CUT TO LONGER SHOT

BILL

What do you expect me to do, carry a birth
certificate around with me?

CHESTER, BENNIE AND HAL ARE SLOWLY CLOSING
IN NOW. IRVING'S MOUTH OPENS A LITTLE WIDER.
SOMETHING IS ABOUT TO HAPPEN. MARCIA PUTS
A HAND OUT AS THOUGH TRYING TO STOP IT FROM
HAPPENING.

FRED

ALSO STEPPING TOWARD BILL

You gotta be locked up.

BILL

Locked up? *Me?*

FRED

PUTTING A HAND ON BILL'S ARM

It'll be easier if you don't make any trouble.

CUT TO CU OF BILL AND FRED

BILL

LOOKING DOWN AT HAND

Trouble. Oh, no, I won't make trouble.

THEN, SUDDENLY WILD, FLINGING OFF THE HAND

I'm sick of this — sick of the whole crazy business!
My name's Bill Guernsey, you hear? — Guernsey,
like the cow! And I've never been in this crazy
town before, and you can bet your last dollar
I'll never —

CUT TO LONGER SHOT. CHESTER RUSHES AT BILL.
IN HIS HAND HE HAS A METAL CONTAINER FOR
STRAWS. HE RAISES IT, BRINGS IT DOWN ON BILL'S

HEAD. BILL FALLS. CUT TO CU OF MARCIA. SHE
STARTS FORWARD FRANTICALLY.

MARCIA

Bill! Bill! —

CUT TO CU OF CHESTER. HE IS STANDING OVER THE
BODY OF BILL.

CHESTER

Guernsey. Like the cow.

FADE OUT

END OF ACT ONE

ACT II

ANNOUNCER

We continue with the second act of *The Inn* by
Roger Garis.

SCENE IS THE HORMUTH JAIL. THERE IS A SMALL
OUTER ROOM, WITH A TABLE, A FEW CHAIRS, AND,
AGAINST THE WALL, A DESK. THIS LEADS TO THE
INNER ROOM WHERE THERE ARE THREE CELLS. A
BARRED DOOR IS BETWEEN. AT OPENING WE SEE A
LONG SHOT OF OUTER ROOM. A MAN SITS AT THE
TABLE, A THERMOS OF COFFEE AND A CUP NEAR HIM.
DOLLY UP FOR MEDIUM CU. THE MAN, DAN, IS THE
JAILER; HE IS READING A MAGAZINE, AND IS SIPPING
COFFEE. HE FLIPS OVER A PAGE OF THE MAGAZINE.
EARL KENT WALKS INTO PICTURE. STANDS OVER
DAN. DAN LOOKS UP.

DAN

Morning, Earl.

EARL

So you got Bassick in here again.

DAN

Yep. Same cell he had four years ago.

EARL

Is he up yet?

DAN

Wouldn't rightly say *up*. He's awake.

EARL

Chester must have hit him a good one.

DAN

Bled a lot. I put a bandage on it.

EARL

More than he deserves. Well, let's have a look at him.

DAN RISES, GOES TO DESK, TAKES LARGE KEY RING WITH SEVERAL KEYS ON IT. HE AND EARL WALK TOWARD BARRED DOOR, WHICH DAN UNLOCKS. CUT TO SHOT OF TWO ENTERING CELL BLOCK. THEY PROCEED TO A CELL, STAND OUTSIDE. CAMERA DOLLYING UP FOR MEDIUM CU. WITHIN CELL CAN BE SEEN A COT, ON WHICH BILL IS LYING.

Rattle him up.

DAN RASPS KEY RING ALONG BARS OF CELL. CUT TO CU OF BILL ON COT WITHIN CELL. WE HEAR EARL RATTLE THE KEY RING AGAINST BARS AGAIN. BILL MOVES, SITS UP SLOWLY. HIS HEAD IS BANDAGED; HE LOOKS PRETTY BAD. HE RAISES HIS HEAD, STARING OUT AT DAN AND EARL. CUT TO SHOT OF DAN AND EARL, WITH BILL, SITTING ON COT, SEEN THROUGH THE BARS.

EARL (CONTINUED)

TO DAN

It's him all right.

TO BILL

Hello, Bassick.

CUT TO CU OF BILL. HE STARTS TO RISE, FALTERS, PUTS OUT A HAND TO STEADY HIMSELF ON COT, THEN GETS TO HIS FEET AND COMES FORWARD. CUT TO SHOT OF BILL, DAN AND EARL.

Remember me, Bassick?

BILL LOOKS FROM ONE TO THE OTHER

BILL

Should I?

EARL

I'm Earl Kent.

BILL

VAGUELY

Earl Kent.

EARL

So you thought we wouldn't remember what you look like, hey, Bassick?

BILL

DULLY

Bassick. Bassick. I'll begin to believe it myself pretty soon.

HE TOUCHES HIS BANDAGE, THEN GRIPS BARS OF CELL

Look, mister — you the sheriff?

EARL

Your memory's comin' back real good, Bassick.

BILL

Well, look, Sheriff — what did you say the name was?

DAN

VOICE . . . . MAINTAIN CU OF BILL

Kent. Earl Kent.

BILL

Mr. Kent — I want to get word to my boss, Robert Cooper, in Newark. Newark, New Jersey. The Holly Smith Company. Air Conditioning. I want to call him on the phone.

CUT TO SHOT OF THREE.

EARL

Sure puts on a good act, don't he, Dan?

BILL

He'll straighten this out for you. I suppose I ought to get a lawyer and sue this town for a million bucks, but —

HE SWAYS, GRABS AT BARS AGAIN

I just want to get away from here.

EARL

Hear that, Dan? He wants to sue us!

DAN

WITH KINDNESS

I wouldn't talk like that, son.

BILL

LOSING CONTROL FOR AN INSTANT

Talk like that! You wouldn't talk like that, after —

WITH AN EFFORT HE REGAINS CONTROL

Just do me one favor. Just get Robert Cooper, in
Newark, New Jersey. The number is Market Two
Eight Four Hundred.

EARL

Sure, Bassick — anything you say. I'll call anybody
you want. How about San Francisco? Got a
girl in San Francisco?

BILL

Don't kid. Just get Mr. Cooper for me.

EARL STEPS CLOSE TO CELL BARS, SO THAT HE IS
FACE TO FACE WITH BILL. DOLLY UP FOR CU OF EARL
AND BILL.

EARL

Okay, Bassick, I won't kid. What did you come
back for?

BILL

Come back —

EARL

You must have known you'd be recognized —
that you couldn't get away with it — Why did you
come back, Bassick?

BILL

I didn't come back — I've never been here
before —

EARL

HIS VOICE RISING

You came back for a reason! What is it, Bassick?
What's your reason?

BILL

HOARSELY

I'm not Bassick — my name's Guernsey. I live
in Montclair —

EARL

ALMOST SHOUTING

You think you can fool us into believing you
didn't kill Norma —

BILL

Name's Guernsey — like the cow —

EARL

They didn't wait for a trial last time, Bassick —
and I don't think they will this time, neither. We're
respectable folks in this town — and when they
catch a murderin' rat like you they know what to
do with him —

HE REACHES THROUGH BARS SUDDENLY, SHOVES
BILL'S FACE WITH HIS HAND. BILL STAGGERS BACK,
FALLS ON COUCH, CAMERA PANNING, HOLDING BILL.
THERE IS THE SOUND OF THE OUTER DOOR CLANGING
SHUT. DOLLY UP FOR CU OF BILL ON COT, WHERE
HE HAS FALLEN. FOR A MOMENT HE IS STILL, UNABLE
TO MOVE. THEN SLOWLY HE PUSHES HIMSELF UP
WITH HIS HANDS, AND STARES AT BARS. HE SHAKES
HIS HEAD SLIGHTLY, AS THOUGH TO CLEAR IT.
FADE OUT
FADE IN ON CU OF MARCIA. SHE IS AT HOTEL DESK,
LISTENING TO MRS. BUTTERWORTH, A TOWN
BUSYBODY, GIVE HER VIEWS ON THE ARREST OF
"CARL BASSICK."

MRS. BUTTERWORTH

VOICE — MAINTAIN CU OF MARCIA

I think it was so clever of Bennie Rutledge and
Hal Jones to recognize him! Just seeing him come
in the hotel! My dear, weren't you *horrified*
when you found out?

MARCIA

FLATLY

No, Mrs. Butterworth, I wasn't.

PULL BACK FOR SHOT OF MARCIA AND MRS.
BUTTERWORTH.

MRS. BUTTERWORTH

Weren't you frightened when you knew that the
man you were talking to was a *murderer?*

MARCIA

I don't think he is a murderer, Mrs. Butterworth.

MRS. BUTTERWORTH

Well, really! You mean Earl Kent, and Bennie,
and Hal, and Chester Harper, and your own
uncle, and all the other people who recognized
him don't know what they're talking about?

MARCIA

WEARILY

I don't know what to think, Mrs. Butterworth.
But I'm sure the man they've got in jail never
killed anyone.

MRS. BUTTERWORTH

OFFENDED

Well, I must say, Marcia, you seem mighty strange
to me!

SHE TURNS HUFFILY AND EXITS.

MARCIA GAZES AFTER MRS. BUTTERWORTH.

MARCIA LOOKS AT REGISTER, THEN TAKES PHONE.

MARCIA

Hello . . . Give me long distance, will you? . . .
Yes, I want to speak to the . . .

CHECKING REGISTER

Holly-Smith Company in Newark, N.J. and I want
to talk to the manager. I don't know his name. . . .
yes, yes, I'll be here.

SHE HANGS UP.

HER FACE IS DRAWN, TIRED. FRED COMES INTO
PICTURE. HE WEARS HAT AND COAT.

FRED

I'm going over to the post office.

MARCIA

All right, Uncle Fred.

FRED

LOOKING AT HER KEENLY

You still thinkin' about that feller?

MARCIA

Yes.

FRED

Don't. He's not worth it. Put him out of your
mind.

MARCIA

TURNING TO HIM, PLEADING

But, Uncle Fred — I know he didn't do anything
wrong — and he *could* be who he says he is —

FRED

DECISIVELY

Not a chance. Chester Harper would never make
a mistake like that. Bassick lived with Chester
for a solid month.

MARCIA

But that was four years ago.

FRED

Then all the others recognized him.

MARCIA

Yes — *you!* Are *you* so sure he's Bassick?

FRED

Sure enough.

MARCIA

But you're not *positive*, are you?

FRED

I never knew Bassick too well. But I seen him a
couple of times. We got the right man.

MARCIA

PUTTING A HAND ON HIS ARM URGENTLY

But if you're not absolutely certain — think what
it would mean if you were wrong!

FRED

GAZING AT HER A MOMENT ALMOST AS THOUGH
INCLINED TO ADMIT TO SOME DOUBT. THEN
CHANGING HIS MIND AND DRAWING HIS ARM FROM
HER GRASP

You romance too much. Just because he ain't bad lookin' —
HE STARTS AWAY
Got to get over to the post office.
FRED EXITS. DOLLY UP FOR CU OF MARCIA. THE
PHONE RINGS. SHE TURNS, GOES TO TELEPHONE,
CAMERA PANNING. DOLLY UP FOR CU OF MARCIA
AT PHONE.

MARCIA

NERVOUSLY
Hello — Hello — yes — Hello! The Holly Smith Company? I want to speak to the manager — I want to find out something — can you tell me whether a man named William Guernsey is employed by the Holly Smith Company — he is? Well, can you tell me what he looks like — no, I'm not exactly a customer — I think I used to know him — yes — yes — I see — yes —
CUT TO SHOT OF CHESTER ENTERING HOTEL.
HE LOOKS AROUND.
CUT BACK TO MARCIA AT PHONE.
SHE HAS SEEN CHESTER ENTER AND IS FRIGHTENED
LEST HE DISCOVER WHAT SHE IS DOING.

MARCIA (CONTINUED)

SPEAKING QUICKLY AND NERVOUSLY
Thank you very much — no — no, that's all I wanted to know — thank you — good-by. . . .
SHE REPLACES RECEIVER, TURNS, GOES TOWARD
DESK, CAMERA PANNING. DOLLY UP FOR MEDIUM CU
OF MARCIA AT DESK. CHESTER COMES INTO PICTURE.

CHESTER

Where's Fred?

MARCIA

TRYING FOR CALMNESS
He went over to the post office.
SHE BUSIES HERSELF WITH SOME PAPERS ON COUNTER.
CHESTER IS GAZING AT MARCIA SARDONICALLY. HE
IS ONE OF THOSE WHO ASKED HER OUT AND WHOM

SHE REFUSED. CHESTER WOULD LIKE TO GET BACK AT
HER.

CHESTER

SOFTLY AND MEANINGLY
Been to see Bassick at the jail yet?

MARCIA

NOT LOOKING AT HIM
No.

CHESTER
Thought you'd be there bright and early this
morning.

MARCIA

RESENTING THIS — LOOKING UP
Did you? Why?

CHESTER

SMIRKING
Oh, I don't know — seemed like you took sort
of a fancy to him —

MARCIA

LOOKING AT HIM STEADILY
Is that why you hit him so hard?

CHESTER

STARTLED OUT OF HIS COMPLACENCY
Hey, wait a second!

MARCIA

POINTING
If you want to wait for my uncle, wait over there.

CHESTER

DISCONCERTED
Oh, yeah — sure —
HE WALKS AWAY, CAMERA PANNING, LOOKS BACK
UNCERTAINLY AT MARCIA. DISSOLVE TO CU OF
LUNCH TRAY ON TABLE. DAN'S HANDS ARE
POURING COFFEE INTO A CUP FROM A THERMOS. HE
ADDS SUGAR. THERE IS A SANDWICH ON TRAY. PULL
BACK FOR SHOT OF DAN LIFTING TRAY. HE WALKS
TOWARD BARRED DOOR, UNLOCKS IT, GOES TO BILL'S
CELL, CAMERA FOLLOWING. HE PEERS IN. CUT TO SHOT

OF BILL LYING ON COT, SEEN THROUGH BARS. CUT TO
DAN OUTSIDE CELL. HE HOLDS TRAY WITH ONE
HAND, UNLOCKS CELL, WALKS IN.

DAN

Hello, son.

CUT TO CU OF BILL ON COT. HE MOVES HIS HEAD,
SEES DAN, SITS UP SLOWLY. PULL BACK FOR LONGER
SHOT OF TWO IN CELL.

BILL

SITTING ON COT

What do you want?

DAN

I brought you something to eat.

BILL

BITTERLY

You mean you feed prisoners in this town?

DAN

Now, son, take it easy.

HE WALKS FORWARD, PUTS TRAY ON COT NEAR BILL.
MOVE IN FOR MEDIUM CU

It's afternoon. You ain't had any breakfast.

BILL

LOOKING AT TRAY THEN LOOKING UP AT DAN WHO
PERHAPS ISN'T AS BAD AS THE REST OF THEM.

Thanks.

DAN

Coffee'll make you feel better.

BILL

Yeah.

HE LIFTS CUP, DRINKS.

DAN

How's the head?

BILL

Dandy. What did he hit me with, a lead pipe?

DAN

Guess I'm not so hot as a doctor.

BILL

You put this bandage on?

DAN

Yep.

BILL

TAKING UP SANDWICH, PAUSING

Much obliged.

BITES INTO SANDWICH

DAN

That's all right.

HE LEANS AGAINST SIDE OF CELL WATCHING BILL EAT

BILL

AFTER A MOMENT

How long am I supposed to stay in here?

DAN

Don't know. Arraignment will be tomorrow, or
the next day.

BILL

Arraignment?

DAN

Sure, you got to be arraigned. A charge has got to
be made against you.

BILL

BITTERLY

You are hereby charged with stopping at a town
called Hormuth. I plead guilty.

DAN

It'll be murder, I guess.

BILL

LOOKING UP AT DAN, TAKING ANOTHER DRINK OF
COFFEE, PUTTING CUP DOWN.

Don't I even rate a lawyer?

DAN

Don't know. Sheriff Kent arranges those things.

BILL

SARCASTICALLY

I'll bet he does. I'll bet he's some arranger.

TAKES ANOTHER BITE OF SANDWICH

Look, Mr. —

DAN

Dan.

BILL

Look, Dan. What about you putting through that
call to Newark for me?

DAN

SHAKING HIS HEAD
Can't do that.

BILL

RISING, URGENTLY
Why not? I'll pay you. I'll give you ten bucks.

DAN

Sorry, son.

BILL

Okay, twenty.

DAN

Nope. Sheriff Kent wouldn't like it.

BILL

Kent! I'd like to take Kent and . . . . .
HE CONQUERS HIS ANGER
You won't, then?

DAN

Sorry. Can't afford to.

BILL

MUTTERING, SITTING ON COT AGAIN
They stick you in jail and won't even let you
telephone — never heard of the Constitution of the
United States —
SUDDENLY, AS HIS ANGER FLARES, HE GETS TO HIS
FEET, AND STEPS TOWARD DAN
What would you do if I rushed you? The door's
open — what would you do if I knocked you
down — ?

DAN

REACHING IN HIS BACK POCKET AND DRAWING A GUN
BUT SPEAKING GENTLY
I wouldn't do it, son.

BILL

STARING AT GUN

No. Guess you're right.

HE SITS ON COUCH AGAIN, LOWERS HEAD IN HANDS.

DAN

REPLACING GUN

Things may not be so bad. You'll get your chance
to talk at the arraignment.

BILL

HEAD IN HANDS

Talk. Sure, I'll talk — but who'll listen to me?

HE RAISES HIS HEAD, STARES AT DAN

This fellow Bassick. Did he talk?

DAN

HUMORING HIM

You mean you forgot? Sure, Bassick talked.

BILL

Did he deny killing the girl?

DAN

Sure, he denied it.

BILL

But they didn't believe him.

DAN

STILL HUMORING HIM

Can't blame them, can you?

BILL

I don't know. Did they have any evidence against
him?

DAN

He was seen walking into the woods with the
girl . . . and walking out alone. She was found dead.

BILL

That's not even circumstantial. No jury would
convict on that.

DAN

They weren't exactly waiting for a jury.

BILL

You mean they were going to lynch him?

DAN

That's right. They broke the jail open, that's how he escaped.

BILL

But they didn't know whether he was guilty or not.

DAN

Everybody took it for granted.

BILL

Took it for granted. A man's life, and they took it for granted.

HE POUNDS WALL IN EXCESS OF ANGER

That's murder! You know that? That's murder!

DAN

Now, son, calm down —

BILL

APPROACHING DAN, AND GRABBING HIS ARM

Didn't they even bother to find out the truth — they didn't care — all they wanted was somebody to hang —

DAN

Take it easy, son! They found the girl — Doc Quinby said she'd been hit in the face —

BILL

But how did they know Bassick did it?

HE IS LEANING TOWARD DAN EXCITEDLY

It could have been anybody! A stranger — some tramp who came along —

DAN

PULLING HIS ARM FROM BILL'S GRASP

We don't have tramps around here. Don't let 'em near town.

BILL

You don't know! It was in the woods, wasn't it?

DAN

Sure, but —

BILL

Didn't anybody but Bassick ever go out with the girl? Was she pretty —

DAN

Awful pretty, Norma was.

BILL

Then didn't Norma have any other boy friends
except Bassick?

DAN

Oh, sure, plenty. Norma liked to gad. Over to
Weldon, sometimes to Riverdale, Hoxley,
Muncton, to dances, parties — why, even Earl
Kent used to take her out once in a while — him
being a bachelor —

CUT TO CU OF BILL

BILL

Okay! Then it could have been *anybody*, couldn't
it? She walks into the woods with Bassick — all
right.

HE HAMMERS POINTS HOME WITH GESTURES

Then they had a quarrel. Oh, about — another
girl Bassick was seeing. Or maybe another boy
friend of Norma's. Anything. Bassick gets mad
and leaves. Norma stays behind. Then this other
fellow comes along. Maybe he sees Bassick —
sees Norma with him and *he* gets mad. They have
a fight. He socks Norma. Norma falls. The guy
is scared. He runs away. Norma's brother finds
her. This other fellow — you think he's going
to come forward, when he finds out he killed
Norma?

CUT TO SHOT OF BILL AND DAN

DAN

That's all guess-work.

BILL

Sure it's guess-work! Saying that Bassick killed
Norma is guess-work, too!

DAN LOOKS AT BILL A MOMENT WITHOUT SPEAKING.
HE DOESN'T AGREE WITH BILL, BUT HE SEES THAT
BILL IS VERY SERIOUS, AND HE RESPECTS HIM FOR IT.
HE ALSO FEELS SORRY FOR BILL, SORRY THAT A

NICE-TALKING FELLOW LIKE HIM SHOULD KILL A GIRL.

DAN

You better finish your food.

HE STARTS OUT OF CELL.

BILL

Wait a second. Tell me something. When they brought Bassick in — what did he say happened between him and Norma?

DAN

SLOWLY

Well — as I recollect he claimed he left Norma in the woods because he remembered all of a sudden that he was supposed to do something over to the saw-mill and had to get there in a hurry.

BILL

He didn't say they had a quarrel?

DAN

Nope. Claimed he and Norma were good friends like always.

BILL

Well, *did* he have something to do at the saw-mill?

DAN

Don't know. Sounded pretty fishy.

BILL

Didn't anybody check on it, to see?

DAN

Nope. Don't think they did.

BILL

You mean to say —

A WILD GESTURE

What kind of people are you, accusing a man of murder without —

DAN

It would have come out at the trial.

BILL

RAMMING IT AT HIM

But you weren't going to give him a trial! You

wanted to lynch him, hang him without a trial!
DAN
Not everybody. But — well, I guess everybody
got sort of aroused all of a sudden — like
spontaneous combustion.
BILL
And who got them all aroused?
DAN
I dunno as there was anybody in particular. Like
I say, it was sort of spontaneous combustion.
BILL
Who was leading the mob?
DAN
Well, there was her brother, and Fred Lennon,
and —
BILL
And where was Sheriff Kent all this time?
Couldn't he have stopped them?
DAN
I dunno. He was away on business some place, I
guess. He wasn't here, anyway.
BILL
No. He wouldn't be. He's one of them! See here —
DAN
TURNING FROM HIM
I can't talk no more now. You finish your food.
HE GOES OUT, NOT LOOKING AT BILL, LOCKS THE CELL
DOOR BEHIND HIM, CAMERA PANNING, AND
DISAPPEARS. CUT TO CU OF BILL. SOUND OF OUTER
DOOR CLANGING SHUT AND BEING LOCKED. BILL
WALKS TO BARS, GRASPS THEM, STARES OUT. HE IS
AGITATED BY WHAT HAS JUST DEVELOPED. HE
TURNS, AND SLOWLY GOES BACK TO COT AND SITS
DOWN. HE IS IN DEEP CONCENTRATION. HE TAKES
COFFEE CUP AND SIPS IT ABSENTLY. HE RAISES
SANDWICH TO HIS MOUTH, BUT DOES NOT EAT. HE
LOWERS HIS HAND AGAIN, SITS THERE STARING,
THINKING OF THE MAN HE IS SUPPOSED TO BE, THE

MAN WHO WAS ALMOST LYNCHED FOR A CRIME HE
MIGHT NOT HAVE COMMITTED. CUT TO MEDIUM CU
OF MARCIA BEHIND COUNTER IN HOTEL. SHE IS
TENSE, EXCITED. A MOMENT, AND FRED COMES INTO
PICTURE, WEARING HAT AND TOPCOAT. HE CARRIES
SEVERAL LETTERS.

MARCIA

EXCITEDLY

Uncle Fred — I've got to talk to you. I telephoned
Newark — where Bill said he worked. I got the
manager of the company —

FRED

Thought I told you to stay out of this?

MARCIA

I had to find out! The manager said they did have
a William Guernsey working for them — and he
described him, and it was exactly like Bill —

FRED

FORCIBLY

Now you listen to me. Don't mess into this — at
all. Understand?

HE SEIZES HER ARM

You mind your own business!

MARCIA

But if what he says is true — if he isn't Bassick —

FRED

He *is* Bassick! You hear?

HE THRUSTS HIS FACE INTO HERS

He *is* Bassick!

MARCIA

But the manager in Newark — I talked to him —
he described Bill —

FRED

Keep quiet! You hear me? *Keep quiet!* You
already shamed yourself enough by bein' seen in
public with that murderer.

THE TWO ARE FACE TO FACE WITH EACH OTHER.

THEN, AS MARCIA RECOGNIZES THE USELESSNESS OF
FURTHER ARGUMENT . . .

                    MARCIA
QUIETLY

All right, Uncle Fred.

HE DROPS HIS ARM, STARES AT HER, MOVES BACK.
AFTER A PAUSE

Will you be here for a while? I have to go out —

                    FRED

I'll be here.

MARCIA EXITS. DOLLY UP FOR CU OF FRED, HE STARES
AFTER MARCIA. HE TAKES OUT A HANDKERCHIEF,
WIPES HIS FOREHEAD, HIS LIPS, HE TRIES TO COMPOSE
HIMSELF. HE TURNS, AND BEGINS TO PUT LETTERS
IN PIGEON-HOLES BACK OF DESK, CAMERA FOLLOWING.
HE FUMBLES BADLY AND ONE OF THEM DROPS. HE
PICKS IT UP, PLACES IT IN BOX. CUT TO MEDIUM
CU OF DAN. HE IS SITTING AT TABLE IN JAIL, PLAYING
SOLITAIRE. A MOMENT AND MARCIA ENTERS. DAN
LOOKS UP.

                    MARCIA

Dan —

                    DAN

Hello, Marcia.

                    MARCIA

Can I see Mr. — the man you've got here?

                    DAN

You mean Carl Bassick?

                    MARCIA

Yes.

                    DAN

Don't think I could let you do that.

                    MARCIA

Please, it's important —

                    DAN

I got orders not to let anybody see him.

                    MARCIA
PLEADING

Just for a few minutes — no one will know! I just
want to talk to him — you know me, Dan, you
know I wouldn't do anything wrong —

DAN

SHE IS CONVINCING HIM

I guess you wouldn't at that, Marcia —

HE MAKES UP HIS MIND, RISES, TAKES HIS KEYS
FROM DESK

Okay. Only a few minutes, though.

MARCIA

Thank you —

HE UNLOCKS OUTER DOOR, THE TWO WALK THROUGH.
CUT TO SHOT OF TWO ENTERING CELL BLOCK.

DAN

You'll have to talk to him through the bars.

HE LEAVES MARCIA THERE, RETURNS TO HIS SOLITAIRE,
CAMERA FOLLOWING. CUT TO MEDIUM CU OF BILL
SITTING ON COT. THE TRAY HAS BEEN TAKEN AWAY.
BILL IS THINKING HARD. ONE HAND HAMMERS INTO
THE PALM OF THE OTHER. AT THE SOUND OF THE
OUTER DOOR BEING UNLOCKED HE LOOKS UP
QUICKLY. AFTER A MOMENT

BILL

Marcia!

HE RISES, STRIDES FORWARD. CUT TO SHOT OF MARCIA
OUTSIDE CELL, BILL COMING TOWARD HER. DOLLY
UP FOR CU OF MARCIA AND BILL. HE'S SEEN
THROUGH THE BARS.

MARCIA

Bill —

THEN AS SHE SEES HIS HEAD IS BANDAGED

Oh, Bill, they did hurt you —

BILL

ALL THAT MATTERS AT THIS MINUTE IS THAT
MARCIA IS HERE

It's not important — Marcia, it was good of you
to come —

MARCIA

Is your head very bad? Did you have a doctor?
Can I —

HER HANDS CLASP THE BARS. BILL COVERS THEM
WITH HIS OWN.

BILL

Don't worry about it.

HE MOVES CLOSER TO HER

Why did you come?

MARCIA

Bill — listen to me! I called your office in
Newark —

BILL

Mr. Cooper?

MARCIA

I think that was his name. I told my uncle what
he said, but my uncle wouldn't believe me.

BILL

Why didn't he talk to Mr. Cooper?

MARCIA

He didn't seem to want to know anything about it.

CUT TO CU OF BILL

BILL

SLOWLY

There's something queer about this whole thing,
Marcia. I don't mean just — mistaking me for
Bassick. I'm not worried about that. That'll
get straightened out, even if Mr. Cooper has to
come here to identify me. But the way they tried
to railroad Bassick —

CUT TO SHOT OF BOTH

MARCIA

Everybody takes it for granted he killed Norma
Harper.

BILL

TURNING, PACING, RETURNING TO MARCIA

Sure — they take it for granted. Why? You
know why?

MARCIA

They saw him go in the woods with her —
CUT TO CU OF BILL

BILL

That's not it. That's not the real reason.
WITH IDEA

Marcia, tell me, was this Harper girl supposed to
be kind of wild?

MARCIA

I don't know. You see, I wasn't here then. But
I've never heard anything against her.

BILL

Dan says she used to gad around a lot. Suppose
she used to go out with some of the married men
in this sanctimonious little backwoods town.
Maybe she went with more than a few of them.
Maybe they were scared that they'd be found
out if it ever came to trial. Maybe they'd be ready
to do anything about Carl Bassick as long as they
could convince themselves that he was guilty.
They might even work themselves up to that
lynching party.

MARCIA

Bill, you're just imagining things.

BILL

Yes, I suppose so. But I do know there's something
strange and wrong about all this. Marcia, listen.
Can you do something for me? Can you find out
all you can about Bassick?

MARCIA

Find out —

BILL

It's a big order. But there might be someone
who'll tell you.

MARCIA

But you've got to prove who you are — get out
of here — I'll telephone Mr. Cooper again —

BILL

No. Don't telephone Mr. Cooper.

MARCIA

They'll keep you in jail! You'll be accused of the murder —

BILL

I already am. I got a feeling I'd like to see this thing through.

MARCIA

Bill — it's dangerous — the people in this town —

BILL

I know the people in this town. Bassick knew them, too. I figure he rates a fair show. I'm just going to sub for him, that's all.

DOLLY BACK FOR LONGER SHOT AS DAN CALLS

DAN

Time's up, Marcia.

MARCIA

TURNING

Yes . . .

CUT TO CU OF BILL. HIS FACE IS CLOSE TO BARS.

BILL

Marcia — you'll do it?

CUT TO CU OF MARCIA. SHE HAS STOPPED, IS LOOKING BACK AT BILL.

MARCIA

SLOWLY

I'll do it — if you want me to —

BILL

VOICE

I want you to.

MARCIA

I'll try — good-by, Bill . . .

CUT TO CU OF BILL

BILL

So long, Marcia.

BILL WATCHES MARCIA LEAVE. SOUND OF METAL DOOR CLANGING SHUT. PAUSE. BILL CALLS.

BILL

Dan!

A MOMENT AND THE SOUND OF OUTER DOOR OPENING
AGAIN. DAN ENTERS WITH KEYS. PULL BACK FOR
SHOT OF BOTH.

DAN

You want me?

BILL

How well did you know Bassick?

DAN

Seen him around town. And while he was in here.
SUDDENLY REALIZES HE IS ADMITTING BILL ISN'T
BASSICK.

Hey! *You're* Bassick! What are you trying to —

BILL

Would you say he was the kind of a guy who would
commit murder?

DAN

I ain't answerin' any more questions.

BILL

INSISTENTLY

Tell me, Dan — was he?

DAN

GRUDGINGLY

No. Surprised me, all right.

BILL

And while he was in here — did he talk to you?

DAN

Sure. Listen, I told you I ain't —
CUT TO CU OF BILL

BILL

Dan — *do you think Bassick killed Norma Harper?*
CUT TO CU OF DAN. HE RAISES HIS HEAD DEFIANTLY.

DAN

No! I never did think so!

THEN, ANGRILY

And that's the very last word I'm goin' to say!
CUT TO CU OF BILL

BILL

One more thing, Dan — how did Bassick act, when
they were taking him out to lynch him?

DAN

He was awful scared. All the time he was here
he was scared.

LOOKS UP SUDDENLY

You ain't scared. Why ain't you scared like you
was before?

HE CUTS OFF AS THERE IS THE SOUND OF BREAKING
GLASS IN THE OUTER OFFICE

BILL

VOICE . . . . MAINTAIN CU OF DAN

What was that, Dan?

DAN

UNCERTAINLY

Don't know . . .

HE TURNS AND HURRIES TOWARD OUTER OFFICE.
CUT TO CU OF BILL. HE IS LOOKING THROUGH BARS,
PUZZLED. A MOMENT, AND DAN REAPPEARS WALKING
TOWARD BILL'S CELL. PULL BACK FOR SHOT OF
BOTH. DAN CARRIES A ROCK IN HIS HAND.

DAN

This — came through the window —

BILL

Somebody threw a rock?

DAN

Yeah — somebody threw a rock —

BILL

Must have real playful kids around here.

DAN

STARING AT ROCK

That's the way — the other started —

BILL

What other?

DAN

Before they came in — to take Bassick out —

CUT TO CU OF BILL

BILL

You mean before they tried to lynch him?

CUT TO CU OF DAN. HIS FRIGHT SHOWS MORE PLAINLY.

DAN

That's right . . . they threw rocks, and after a while they came in. . . .

PULL BACK TO SHOT OF BOTH.

BILL

Don't worry. They won't lynch me.

CUT TO SHOT OF MARCIA, ENTERING DOOR OF JAIL. SHE IS AGITATED. SHE RUNS TOWARD DAN AND BILL, CAMERA PANNING.

CUT TO SHOT OF DAN AND BILL AS MARCIA RUNS TOWARD THEM

MARCIA

Bill — Bill!

SHE GOES TO THE CELL, GRASPS BARS. DOLLY UP FOR CU OF BILL AND MARCIA.

BILL

Marcia — take it easy! What's the trouble?

MARCIA

PANTING

Men — outside — in the street — they're gathering — talking —

BILL

Nothing's going to happen.

MARCIA

CLOSE TO THE BARS

You've got to get out of here! You've got to get out quick! They'll come after you —

BILL

No, they won't.

MARCIA

But they're talking about it! I heard them!

SHE TURNS HER HEAD

Dan — you've got to let him out — they'll hang him —

CUT TO CU OF BILL. HIS FACE IS GRIM.

BILL

I don't think they'll hang me, Marcia. I never did
like mobs. They try to scare you, and if you don't
scare, they're licked.

SOUND OF ANOTHER ROCK THROUGH THE WINDOW.
BILL'S HEAD JERKS AROUND. HIS EXPRESSION DOES
NOT CHANGE. FROM OUTSIDE A MAN'S VOICE.

MAN OUTSIDE

SHOUT

Bassick!

CUT TO CU OF MARCIA, SHE IS STARING AT BILL,
THE FEAR SHE FEELS FOR HIS SAFETY STRIKING AT HER.
FADE OUT

END OF ACT II

ACT III

ANNOUNCER

We continue with Act Three of *The Inn,* by Roger
Caris.

OPEN ON ACTION AS IN END OF ACT TWO. MARCIA,
BILL AND DAN. DAN IS VERY NERVOUS. SUDDENLY
HE TAKES HIS GUN FROM HIS POCKET AND HOLDS IT
TOWARD BILL

DAN

Here. Take this.

BILL

LOOKING AT IT. SPEAKING WITH KINDNESS

Thanks, Dan. You're a good guy. But I won't
need a gun.

DAN

If they come in —

BILL

Even if they come in.

DAN

URGING THE GUN ON HIM

Take it — I'll unlock the cell — you go out the
back way —

MARCIA

Bill — please —

BILL

No, thanks, Dan.

DAN

If they come in, they'll hang you! Take you out
and hang you! You won't get away this time!

BILL

I'm not going to try to get away.

DAN

That's crazy! You don't want to be hanged —

CUT TO CU OF BILL

BILL

SLOWLY

No. I don't want to be hanged. But you see, this
is kind of a funny situation. In the first place I'm
not the guy they claim I am — I'm not Bassick.

CUT TO SHOT OF THREE

DAN

It won't make any difference. . . .

BILL

In the second place even if I was Bassick, I don't
think he did it. At least I don't think they can
prove he did it.

DAN

I'm offerin' you a chance to get away —

BILL

And I thank you for it. But I think I'll pass it up.

MARCIA

Bill —

STEPS TOWARD HIM

You've got to — you can't stay here —

MORE YELLS FROM STREET. DAN IS TENSED, LISTENING.
SUDDENLY HE TURNS AND RUNS TOWARD OUTER
OFFICE. IN A MOMENT HE RETURNS WITH KEYS.
HE UNLOCKS CELL DOOR, THROWS IT OPEN.

DAN

Get out of here — out the back way — through the

cellar — I ain't goin' to have your blood on my
conscience —

> BILL

What was on your conscience, Dan, the last time
you let them take him?

> DAN

I dunno, I dunno, I dunno. I was just glad you got
away. I used to dream every night about how
they was hanging you. Now you get out of here!

> BILL

No.

> DAN

EXCITED, IN PANIC

You're crazy — they'll hang you — they're comin'
in —

SOUND OF YELLS, LOUDER

— they're comin' in!

> BILL

Not quite yet, Dan. From the sound of them it'll
take them quite a few minutes until they've yelled
enough courage into themselves to charge the jail.

> MARCIA

What do you mean?

> BILL

I've had a little experience in that kind of thing.

TO DAN

Those poor Jap troops in New Guinea used to
have to work themselves up into quite a fury
before they gave us the old banzai. You could
always tell by the sound of their yelling when
they were going to come. These people aren't
quite ready yet. Hold your horses, Dan.

TO MARCIA

So listen to me a second, Marcia, before I shoo
you out that back way.

> MARCIA

I won't go out the back way.

BILL

Oh, yes, you will. Now listen to me.

CUT TO CU OF BILL. HE TAKES OUT A CIGARETTE
AND LIGHTS IT

SOFTLY

You see, Marcia, when I was a kid I used to have
crazy ideas. Dreams of glory, I guess you'd call 'em,
where I was battling all alone against a mob that
had some little kid down and was punching and
kicking him . . .

CUT TO CU OF DAN

DAN

FRANTICALLY

Listen to 'em —

YELLS

CUT TO CU OF BILL. HE TAKES A PUFF OF THE
CIGARETTE

BILL

— of course when I got older, it was a girl the
mob was after. Joan of Arc, usually. I must have
rescued Joan of Arc from being burned at the stake
a thousand times.

DAN

VOICE, HOARSELY

They're comin' across the street —

BILL

I used to be sort of ashamed of those dreams.
Because I was afraid I'd never be that way, really,
if it came to a showdown.

PAUSE

Of course it never did come to a showdown . . .

YELLS

CUT TO CU OF DAN. HE TAKES GUN OUT OF HIS
POCKET, FACES AROUND

DAN

I won't let 'em take you —

CUT TO CU OF BILL

BILL

. . . . . until now. Put the gun away, Dan. And
when I go out front, see that Miss Lennon gets out
that cellar way.

DAN

But where does that leave you, Mr. — Mr. —
whoever you are?

BILL

Here. But with an open door.

HE DROPS CIGARETTE, STEPS ON IT, STRAIGHTENS,
MOVES TO CENTER OF CELL DOORWAY, STANDS
THERE, READY.

CUT TO SHOT OF THREE

MARCIA

Bill — Bill, please . . . . come with me!

MOVE IN FOR CU OF BILL AND MARCIA. BILL PUTS
HIS HANDS ON MARCIA'S SHOULDERS

BILL

GENTLY

No can do! Marcia — listen to me.

MARCIA RAISES HER FACE TO HIS

I want to explain something to you and I'm not
sure I know the right words.

YELLS

CUT TO CU OF DAN. HE HAS THE GUN OUT. HE RUNS
TOWARD THE OUTER OFFICE

DAN

RUNNING

I won't let 'em!

CUT TO CU OF BILL AND MARCIA. HIS HANDS ARE
ON HER SHOULDERS

BILL

Whenever I read a story about anybody pulling
this hero stuff — you know, risking his life when
all he has to do is just go away from there, or call
the cops — I always figure it's a phony.

MARCIA

Bill, you've got to —

BILL

WITH MORE URGENCY

Listen, Marcia. I'm scared now. I'll admit it.
I wasn't before. I am now. But those guys out
there —

MARCIA

You can still get away —

BILL

No. I can't get away. And maybe I'm not scared.
I feel lots of different ways all at once — the only
thing I know is, I'm not going to run!

MARCIA

Bill, you've got to! Once these people get an idea
in their heads there's no reasoning with them!

BILL

Idea in their heads? Those people are too worked
up to have any ideas left in their heads. Marcia,
before what's going to happen, happens, I'd like
to tell you something.

IMPATIENT

Oh, the devil! There isn't time to tell you. But,
Marcia, you know that I love you, don't you?

MARCIA

I hoped you did.

BILL

Do you love me?

MARCIA

Yes, I love you, Bill.

BILL

If I ever get out of this, will you marry me?

MARCIA

Yes.

BILL

Thank you, Marcia. Now I think this calls for —
something — something like this.

HE KISSES HER VERY THOROUGHLY. THERE IS ANOTHER
SHOUT "BASSICK." WHEN HE RELEASES HER HE
TAKES HER FACE IN HIS HANDS VERY TENDERLY.

I'll bet that was the shortest love scene in history.
MARCIA
It was a beautiful love scene.
PAUSE
But, Bill, what are you going to do?
BILL
I'm not sure. I guess I would know if I were the
hero type. What do heroes do in a case like this?
I don't know. But I know one thing for absolute
sure. I'm not going to wait for them to break in
here and grab me like a cornered rat.
ANOTHER SHOUT
MARCIA
Bill!
BILL
I'm going out there and face them.
MARCIA
You can't do that!
BILL
But I am. Marcia, get going *now!* Out the back
way. I don't want you mixed up in this. Promise.
MARCIA
LYING
All right, I promise.
BILL
Okay.
EXITING
Well, here goes!
CUT TO THE MOB AND WE SEE THEIR TENSE AND
WAITING FACES. ONE MAN CARRIES A ROPE. THEY
SHOUT "BASSICK"
(NOTE: It is suggested that the following be played
on an exterior so that when Bill appears he is on
the jail set)
THE MOB MOVES FORWARD A LITTLE. THE MOB
CONSISTS OF ALL PREVIOUSLY SEEN MALE CHARACTERS
EXCEPT EARL. THERE ARE ALSO MANY EXTRAS,
INCLUDING PETE AND HORACE HASKINS, WHO HAVE

BEEN MENTIONED BEFORE. DAN IS STANDING A LITTLE
TO ONE SIDE OF THE DOORWAY AS HE FEEBLY WAVES
HIS GUN.

DAN

Stand back, you!

DAN IS JUMPED AND DISARMED

CHESTER

All right! Let's go in and get him.

SO SUDDENLY THAT EVERY ONE FALLS BACK A STEP,
BILL APPEARS IN THE DOORWAY. HIS COMPLETE
CALMNESS AND LACK OF FEAR IS NOT WHAT THE MOB
EXPECTED AND IT CONFUSES THEM

BILL

MILDLY

Was someone calling for me?

HE TAKES OUT CIGARETTE AND PUTS IT IN HIS MOUTH

Anybody got a light?

WE, BUT NOT THE MOB, REALIZE THAT BILL'S
NONCHALANCE COVERS A FEAR THAT GOES DOWN
TO HIS TOES. HIS FOREHEAD SWEATS, PERHAPS, BUT
HIS HANDS AND VOICE ARE STEADY. HE IS A VERY
BRAVE LITTLE MAN.

CHESTER

TO THE OTHERS

Well, there he is! Why don't we go git him?

BILL

ADVANCING TOWARDS THEM

Nobody got a light?

BILL ADVANCES TOWARD THEM AND THEY DRAW BACK
A LITTLE AS IF EACH INDIVIDUAL WERE CURIOUSLY
RELUCTANT TO BE THE FIRST TO SEIZE HIM

CHESTER

SOTTO VOCE TO PETE HASKINS

We don't have to wait for the rope. Get him with
your shotgun!

PETE RAISES HIS SHOTGUN

FRED

GRABBING MUZZLE OF GUN

No! You'll hit her, too!
NOW WE SEE THAT MARCIA HAS STEPPED INTO THE
DOORWAY BEHIND BILL

> FRED

Marcia, you get out from behind there.

> BILL

Marcia, go to your uncle.

> MARCIA

I'm staying right here!

> BILL

Then I'll have to go to him.
HE DOES
Got a light?

> CHESTER

Grab him, Fred.

> FRED

Hold it, Chet! I want to ask him something first!

> BILL

CLOSE TO FRED
I'm right here. What is it?

> FRED

Do you admit you're Bassick?

> BILL

When a guy is going to be either shot or hanged,
it doesn't matter what his name is, does it?

> FRED

I asked you a question.

> CHESTER

He murdered my sister! What are you all standing
around for!
OTHERS HOLD HIM BACK

> FRED

TO CHESTER
Hold it, Chet!
TO BILL
Why don't you admit it?

> BILL

Before I do any admitting, will you grant me one
request, before you string me up?

HORACE

Why should we?

BILL

It's generally granted to the condemned before
execution.

FRED

That seems fair enough.

HE LOOKS AT THE OTHERS AND SOME ASSENT AND
SOME SHOUT "NO." BUT THE "AYES" HAVE IT

BILL

Do I get your solemn promise, then, that I'll get a
final request even if I am Bassick?

FRED

You get it.

BILL

Okay. Then let's say I am Bassick! Have it your
way — I'm Bassick.

MARCIA'S INTERCEPTION IS PUSHED ASIDE

MARCIA

He's not Bassick, he's not —

FRED

TO ONE OF THE MEN

Take her away.

THE MAN PULLS MARCIA TO ONE SIDE. THEY
SURROUND BILL. THEY SAY SUCH THINGS AS "HE'S
ADMITTED IT!" — "THAT'S GOOD ENOUGH FOR ME"
— "LET'S FINISH IT THIS TIME" — ETC. ETC.

CHESTER

SHOUTING OVER THE OTHERS' MENACING MURMURS

Take him! Take him! He murdered my sister!

FRED

INTERVENING

Hold back!

BILL

TO FRED

You promised a last request, didn't you?

FRED

All right, what is it?

BILL

All I want to do is to show you people that you've got no proof that Bassick committed this murder. No proof at all! I'm going to ask a few questions, and I'm going to trust you to give me honest answers. And I'm in a tough spot because I don't know much about this murder. But when I'm finished, if you want to hang me, go ahead. I want ten minutes. Okay?

FRED

Okay.

BILL

LOOKS AT HIS WRIST WATCH

Ten minutes to life . . . or death.

HE WALKS INTO THE HEART OF THE MOB, THEY DRAW ASIDE FROM HIM.

DURING THE FOLLOWING SCENE THERE IS PROBABLY A SERIES OF CLOSE-UPS OF THE FACES OF THE MEN

BILL

First question . . . since you're sure I did it, will you tell me how it happened?

CHESTER

You know how it happened. You took my sister out for a walk in the woods, and when she wouldn't have anything to do with you, you killed her.

BILL

Did anybody see me go in the woods with her? How do you know?

PETE HASKINS

STEPPING TO HIM

I saw you go in the woods with her. And so did my son.

HORACE HASKINS

That's right! I remember! I was cuttin' wood near the slashin' and Pa was carting it up to the yard.

Both of us saw you and Norma go in the woods together.

BILL

TO HORACE

Was Norma a pretty girl?

HORACE

Sure she was.

BILL

Did anybody else ever go walking with her? Did you?

HORACE

LOOKS AROUND AND SWALLOWS

Well, sure, once in a while.

MEMBERS OF THE MOB BEGIN TO EYE ONE ANOTHER WARILY. THE CAMERA CATCHES THEM AT IT IN THE FOLLOWING SEQUENCES.

BILL

Anybody else?

HORACE

Joe Gaines took her out lots more than I did. And so did Bob Jones.

BILL

I see. Joe Gaines? Bob Jones? Either of you two here?

JOE GAINES

PUSHING FORTH

Sure, I used to go out with her once in a while. What of it? That was four years ago. I wasn't married then.

BILL

I guess Bob Jones isn't here?

ALL EYES TURN TO WHERE HE IS

BOB JONES

I never — I never took her out at all.

ALL THE EYES LOOK AT HIM

I never did, I tell you!

LAMELY

I used to see her in the woods once in a while when

I took the short cut home from work — just to
say hello. But I never — look, I got a wife and
four kids. I wouldn't —

HE TRAILS OFF

CHESTER

SEIZING BILL

Look here, you! What are you insinuatin' about
my sister?

BILL

Nothing! Nothing at all! Except that she seemed
to be very fond of going out with different men.

CHESTER

I'll kill you if —

FRED

Let him alone, Chet.

TO BILL

Go on.

BILL

MILDLY TO HORACE

So when it happened, you were cutting wood and
your father was carting it away. Right. That
means he left you alone while he took the wood
away. What did you do then?

HORACE

I cut more wood. What d'ya mean?

BILL

Nothing. Except I thought perhaps you might
have gone into the woods.

HORACE

That's a lie! I never went into the woods that day!

BILL

Can you prove it?

HORACE

Well — I — no!

BILL

So you could have done it. I didn't say you did,
I said you could have. You had the opportunity.
Just as much as Bassick.

TO JOE
What about you? Did you take a walk?

JOE

I was in my barber shop the whole day.

FRED

PUZZLED
Wait a minute, Joe. It happened on a Wednesday.
Your shop's closed Wednesday afternoons.

JOE

Well, maybe it was! So what?

BILL

So how do we know you didn't do it? You can't
prove it!
TO BOB
How about you?

BOB

SULLENLY
How do I know where I was four years ago?

FRED

TO BILL AS HE LOOKS AT WATCH
You haven't got much time left. What're you
trying to prove?
DOUBT IS IN FRED'S MIND

BILL

I'm not sure yet. Just that you haven't got any
more on Bassick than you have on a lot of other
people.

FRED

We know them.

BILL

Yeah, I know. It's a crime to be a stranger. I'd
like to know something else. How did you
identify me so fast? Chester here knew me
because I lived in his house. For one month —
four years ago.

CHESTER

Come on, what are we waiting for?

BILL

I still have a little more time, haven't I?

FRED

Yeah.

BILL

TO CHESTER

Chester, it doesn't look as if anybody about here had an alibi. How about you?

CHESTER

I found her body.

BILL

So you found the body. That proves something. That proves you were there. How do we know you didn't kill her?

CHESTER

She was my sister.

BILL

People have killed their sisters before. You could have done it. You were there. There were no witnesses. You had a fight with your sister.

CHESTER

Who says so?

BILL

Let's say *I* say so. You've got a hammer in your pants. You could have killed her with that hammer.

CHESTER

She wasn't killed with a hammer.
It was a stone.

BILL

How do you know it was a stone?

CHESTER

Well . . .

BILL

The coroner's report?

CHESTER

Yes.

BILL

Couldn't the coroner be mistaken?

DAN

Wait a minute. I read the coroner's report. He didn't say stone. He just said blunt instrument.

BILL

How do you know it was a stone, Chester?

CHESTER

Maybe it wasn't . . .

BILL

You were pretty sure a minute ago. You said stone. Didn't he?

CHESTER

I said it might have been a stone.

BILL

You said it was a stone. And the only person who knows what it was is the murderer. You murdered your sister, didn't you?

CHESTER

FEELING TRAPPED

No, I didn't . . . I swear I didn't!

BILL

Can you prove it? Why did you do it, Chester, why? Why did you go out in the woods that day, anyway? You went out there because you knew you'd find her with one of her boy friends, didn't you?

CHESTER

Come on, we've had enough of this, let's get him.

FRED

Wait a minute, Chester. Why did you go out in the woods that day?

CHESTER

You don't think I did it!

BILL

Why did you go, Chester?

CHESTER

What difference does it make?

BILL

Why did you go, Chester? Why did you hit her with the stone?

CHESTER

I didn't hit her, she fell.

DAN

How do you know that?

FRED

Yes, how do you know that, Chester?

BILL

You murdered her, didn't you?

CHESTER

No! No, I didn't!

BILL

Then who did?

CHESTER

You did — and you — and you — if it wasn't for
people like you who made her what she was, she
wouldn't be dead.

BILL

But you're the one that hit her.

CHESTER

I only hit her twice. And the second time she fell
down and hit her head against the stone. She
died right there in my arms. It don't matter now,
you all know all about her anyway. Nothin' don't
matter no more.

HE SINKS DOWN ON THE JAIL STEP OR IN A CHAIR.
(Note set)

HE WEEPS BITTERLY INTO HIS ARMS. WE REALIZE
THAT HIS SOBBING COMES FROM A DEEP AND BITTER
GRIEF. IT IS THE KIND OF CRYING WHICH DEMANDS
THE PRIVACY OF SILENCE. THE CROWD RECOGNIZES
HIS SORROW AND THEY STAND QUIET AND STILL
FOR A LONG TIME. HE IS UTTERLY FORLORN. AFTER
A TIME, AND IN DEAD SILENCE, HE RAISES HIMSELF TO
FACE THE OTHERS

I guess you wouldn't understand. Ma and Pa
both died off in that same year and they left her
to me to bring up, my little sister. I tried my best,
she was only six then. She had hair wavy and

silky and yellow like on corn. But there ain't no
need my telling you what she looked like. You
knew her and she weren't never no trouble. Mrs.
Lewis said — you remember Mrs. Lewis who
used to look after Norma while I was working —
Mrs. Lewis, she said she'd never seen a more
beautiful and well-behaved child. It was after
Mrs. Lewis died the trouble all started. She was
about fourteen or fifteen then, or maybe even a
little more. I came home from work early and
found her — he was a foreigner like this fellow
Bassick. I darned near killed him before he could
get out of the house, then I whopped her till my
arm got tired. But it didn't do no good. After
that I had to watch her all the time. Sometimes I
couldn't believe it. You know what she was like
with those blue innocent sort of eyes and all that
yellow hair. You wouldn't believe it, would you?
I guess I spent most of my life between then and
now keeping you from believing that she was
anything else but a good girl. I couldn't stand
seein' her shamed. I loved her so much. I guess
that's why I hit her so hard that day in the woods.
She was alone when I saw her. But I knew she'd
gone there with Bassick. So I accused her of a
lot of things — maybe they was true and maybe
they wasn't — and when she stood up to me I hit
her, and when she didn't go down I hit her again.
That's when she died. And after that I couldn't
think of nothing else except nobody musn't
never know she was anything else but a good girl.
NOBODY SAYS ANYTHING.
If you boys got that rope ready — I guess it
belongs on me.

FRED

Well, boys, we got our murderer. Any of you
feel like stringing him up?
THEY LOOK AT ONE ANOTHER. THERE IS NO REPLY

Then maybe you better get on home.
THE CROWD MELTS AWAY. CHESTER REMAINS
COMPLETELY STILL AS FRED GOES TO THE LITTLE
GROUP OF DAN, MARCIA AND BILL.

FRED

TO DAN
I guess you better lock him up, Dan. This time
we'll have a regular trial. Even if he has confessed.

DAN

ACQUIESCING
I don't like to do it.
HE MOVES OFF CAMERA TOWARD CHESTER.
FADE OUT
FADE IN HOTEL LOBBY. BILL ENTERS. HE HAS HAT
AND COAT ON, AND CARRIES HIS BAG. A STRIP OF
ADHESIVE SHOWS BENEATH THE HAT. HE IS CHEERFUL.
HE SETS BAG DOWN IN FRONT OF COUNTER. FRED
CROSSES TO HIM BEHIND COUNTER.

BILL
Mr. Lennon, how much do I owe you for the room?

FRED
Nothin'. Not a cent.

BILL

CHEERFULLY
Now, that's not right. I can't let you do that. I
had the room. I'll pay for it. Of course I didn't
sleep in it, but that doesn't matter.
PUTS HAND IN POCKET
How much?

FRED
Two dollars.

BILL
Two dollars. Here you are.

FRED
I don't suppose there's much use sayin' "come
again."

BILL
Oh, I don't know. This town doesn't seem so bad

when you're leaving. So long.

HE WALKS TOWARD DOOR. NEAR DOOR HE IS JOINED
BY MARCIA. SHE IS ALSO IN HAT AND COAT, CARRYING
A BAG. SHE LINKS HER ARM IN HIS, AND HE KISSES
HER. THEY EXIT THROUGH THE DOOR.
CUT TO EXTERIOR. THEY PASS UNDER SIGN WHICH
SAYS "HORMUTH INN." IT SWINGS IN THE WIND.
PAN UP TO SIGN.
FADE OUT

THE END

TECHNIQUE OF TRANSITIONS IN "THE INN," ACT I.

There would be a minimum of three CAMERAS required on a "live" production like *The Inn*. All sets would be built and standing at the same time, in the most practical juxtaposition to allow actors to move physically from one set to another. Four cameras may have been used, but not required.

From Opening Shot to Lobby Interior

One CAMERA would be CU on the highway sign, would DISSOLVE OUT as a second CAMERA would DISSOLVE IN on large swinging wooden sign of the Inn. Through a CUT, third CAMERA would pick up FULL SHOT of lobby as Bill enters. The first two CAMERAS are now released to be moved into position for whatever variation of SHOTS the television director may conceive during the long scene in the lobby.

From Lobby to Bill's Bedroom

Waving to Marcia, Bill walks out of the scene. The CAMERA MOVES IN for a CU of Marcia, who looks in the direction Bill has gone. By the expression on her face, we know that Bill has aroused her interest, an important detail of the story. Equally important, the few seconds that we see Marcia in CU are enough to permit Bill to walk (or perhaps run) to the bedroom set, where the next scene takes place. Thus, the transition is achieved by the CAMERA's *excluding* everything but the CU of Marcia, a technique basic to transitions in "live" television production.

From Bedroom to Lobby

Bill walks out of the bedroom. Through a CUT, we change to the desk in the lobby, where we meet a new character, Fred Lennon, Marcia's uncle. The few seconds in which we study his face permit Bill to walk (or run) from the bedroom set to the hotel lobby.

From Lobby to Garage

Bill walks out of the scene. Fred goes to the telephone, makes a call which advances the story and increases the suspense, and which allows Bill time to reach the garage set. This sort of transition is the most valid, because the "cover scene" of Fred's telephoning is indispensable to the plot, and is not merely a trick to provide the time required for Bill to reach the garage set.

From the Garage to Hotel Lobby

Once again, the mechanic's telephone call is the valid "cover scene" allowing time for Bill to return to the lobby set. This "cover scene" greatly increases the suspense, also.

From Hotel Lobby to Exterior, Bus Stop

As part of the action, Fred makes another telephone call which we see but do not hear. Therefore, when Bill walks out of the scene to catch the bus, and the CAMERA MOVES IN to a CU of Fred, for the length of time Bill requires to reach the exterior, bus stop set, the suspense is heightened by Fred's inscrutable expression, covering action we do not yet know. You will recognize the technique of the transition as that of the CU *excluding* everything else.

Exterior, Bus Stop to Lobby

Bill walks out of the exterior set. CAMERA PICKS UP Fred, behind desk, waiting for Bill, purposefully. Now we suspect that the strange behavior of the mechanic in the preceding scene was prompted by Fred's telephone call which we saw but did not hear. So, Fred's attitude of tense waiting increases the suspense, and the SHOT on him holds for the time required for Bill to walk back into the lobby set.

From Lobby to Taxi Office

Bill walks out of the lobby set. Once again, Fred's telephone call serves as the necessary "cover scene"; and this telephone device of the author takes on impressive suspense value. Suspense is increased also by having Marcia hear Fred's strange telephone call (after Bill has left the lobby set).

From Taxi Office to Exterior of Inn

Bill walks out of the taxi office set, and the CAMERA MOVES IN for a CU of the dispatcher reaching for the telephone, the telephone thus linking him with whatever train of thought Fred is following. Additional time is provided for Bill to go from the taxi office set to the exterior set through having the following scene — exterior, the Inn — open on Marcia, before Bill walks into it.

From Exterior, the Inn, to Interior Drug Store

Bill and Marcia walk out of the shot, and through a DISSOLVE we go to the drug store, opening MEDIUM CLOSE on the soda clerk, Irving, with whom we STAY for a few seconds, to start characterizing him. It is valid to set Irving's character, because the nice relationship between Marcia and him increases our interest in her as an attractive person whom we want to "win," in the story. This long scene is played through to the END OF ACT I. All three CAMERAS would be used in this scene, since maximum visual variety is called for, to break up the "talkiness," to handle the rather unusually large number of characters playing the scene together, and for dramatic emphasis through CLOSE SHOTS and CLOSE-UPS of individuals.

TRANSITIONS, ACT II

From Interior Jail (which is an elaborate but unit set of two rooms, so that action can go back and forth easily through camera manipulation) *To Lobby Set*

We FADE-OUT on Bill, shaking the jail bars in despair, and FADE-IN on Marcia. Since Bill is not in the scene with Marcia, the transition is simple. In the progress of the story, however, it is important to "keep action on the principals," and this the transition does.

From Lobby Set to Jail Set

The transition is no problem, since we DISSOLVE from Chester and Marcia in the hotel lobby, to the jail set. Neither Chester nor Marcia is in the following scene, so no "cover scene" is required.

From Jail Set to Lobby Set

The action in the jail ends on Bill, and begins on Marcia, in the lobby set. Therefore, the transition is simple, and, through being done in a CUT, conveys the fact that the action is continuous. from jail to lobby.

From Lobby Set to Jail Set

Marcia has to be in this scene, about to be played. Therefore, she walks out of the lobby set, while the CAMERA MOVES IN for a CLOSE SHOT of Fred, using the device of the CAMERA'S EXCLUDING all but one actor (Fred). This "cover scene" is valid, because, from Fred's jittery behavior, the tension is increased. Now, through a CUT, we open the scene in which Marcia must appear on a CU of Dan, the jailer, playing solitaire, a device to indicate that he is alone. Here is the CAMERA'S EXCLUDING used in reverse, so to speak. Marcia walks into this set, the few seconds of the CU on Fred and on Dan being enough to allow her to move physically from the lobby set to the jail set. This long scene is played out to the END OF ACT II.

TRANSITIONS, ACT III

From Jail Interior to Jail Exterior

Dan has left the jail interior some time before the scene ends, so that when we CUT to the jail exterior, showing the mob, Dan has had plenty of time to move to the exterior scene; and the action involving him is a valid "cover scene" for Bill to leave the jail interior and reach the jail exterior, when his presence is required by the story.

From Jail Exterior to Lobby Set

We FADE-OUT on the jail exterior, and FADE-IN on the lobby set, a process which allows a few seconds of "black screen." These few seconds, plus the additional few gained by FADING-IN on Fred, behind the hotel desk, showing him chagrined and hang-dog, are sufficient for Bill to move from the jail exterior, put on a hat and coat (held waiting and ready for him by a costume technician), pick up a traveling bag, have the makeup technician slap a strip of adhesive tape on his forehead, and enter the lobby set for the scene with Fred. Fred himself (who was in at the end of the preceding scene, jail exterior) had time to reach the lobby set through the technique of the CAMERA'S EXCLUDING: at the end of the preceding scene, the CAMERA MOVES IN on Dan (jailer) and Chester (the revealed murderer), as Dan arrests him. For the satisfaction of the audience, in seeing the guilty man caught, and innocence vindicated, this CAMERA EXCLUDING scene would hold for several seconds before the FADE-OUT, FADE-IN, adding up to perhaps ten seconds, during which the fleet-footed actor playing Fred could reach the lobby set. Marcia has had plenty of time to put on a hat and coat, and pick up a traveling bag, because she does not appear in this final scene until after Bill and Fred have played their scene. Here ends Act III, and the play. Elapsed time of the story: about twenty-four hours.

13

Adaptations

THE GOAL of the adaptation of any work into television play form is to tell the original basic story in as full detail as time and dramatic structure (as contrasted with narrative structure) permit; and to present the characters richly, recognizably and believably — faithful to the original author's concept.

Dramatic structure frequently demands the elimination of many "fine touches" of prose writing, usually descriptive passages which create mood and atmosphere and which describe the locale in greater or lesser detail. Minor characters who do not fit inextricably into the basic situation and/or who do not advance the plot also have to go. Suspense must be created in the dramatic structure, the sooner the better; and once created it must be maintained and, ideally, increased, as the drama progresses toward its climax and denouement.

Motivation must be clear beyond question. Styles cannot be mixed. The singleness of purpose, of intent, of the television drama must be so plain that it is understood by the viewer without his realizing it, as he watches your story, meets and understands your characters, and lives with them their time of conflict and resolution. The intensity of television drama which we have talked about so much in this book hones a razor edge on the sharpness of impact on the viewer.

If we are not permitted fine detailed prose writing, we are given in its stead the CAMERA, which shows us at a glance what paragraphs may have been written to tell us in the prose work. "One picture is worth a thousand words," the saying goes. When the

361

television playwright is undertaking the job of condensing a long prose work or a long stage play into a television form, he must think first of what he can show *visually* before he considers what words his characters are to speak. Sight is the short-cut in your task of condensation, of distilling the essence of the drama from the story you have selected.

In Chapter Seven, discussing "On Borrowed Time" as presented in five media, a technique is used which is recommended for any adaptation of a prose or stage dramatic work into television form.

1. First write out the basic story, using *only those characters* who cannot be dispensed with.

2. Break the *original work* down into Master Scenes. Having done this, select the scenes which *actually tell the basic story*.

3. Using the scenes you have selected in (2), write a basic story based on these scenes. Does this basic story form (2) match the basic story of (1)? If it does, you may be ready to start work on your television play. We say "may be ready" because your scenario consisting of Master Scenes *as arranged by the original author* can still be in prose or narrative form and not in dramatic form. And, this scenario may require too much time for the telling of the basic story, more time than you, the television playwright, are allowed for your television play.

4. Therefore, examine the scenario you have prepared (3), and see which basic Master Scenes can be condensed — one scene made to do the work of two or three — without damaging the story. An example comes to mind: In a first draft, *Billy Adams, American,** opened with a scene in a doctor's office, in Hamburg. A middle-aged man is told by the doctor that he has only a short time to live. End of scene. Second scene: the man's living room. His young son is introduced, and we are told the man's great longing is to have the boy somehow get to America so that he can grow up and become an American citizen. End of scene. Third scene: a park. The man and his son meet an American soldier who tells them that in America a child abandoned on the streets eventually would find a good home, as there is more demand for children than there are children. Now we know the intent of the play; the middle-aged man somehow will get his son to America. But it has taken three scenes to reach this suspenseful situation.

* See complete script of *Billy Adams, American,* pp. 197–222.

As re-cast, the three scenes were combined into one. The setting was a park, in Hamburg. The middle-aged man, the doctor and the son are seen. The father sends the son away to play for a little while. He protests to the doctor that he (the doctor) should not leave his office at such a busy time. The doctor replies that there are times in life when human consideration and old friendship are the most important things. So, with a nostalgic and portentous mood set, we hear the doctor's news that the father is soon to die, news having more impact on the viewer of the play because of the special circumstances of its being revealed. The father slumps on the bench; the boy returns; the doctor leaves. Unable to get his father into conversation, the boy starts playing with a marble, on the ground. At once the American soldier comes into the scene, sees the marble, shows the boy how to hold and shoot it correctly, and so provides the motivation for the stricken father's asking about the condition of children in America. One scene has done the work of three, and done it far more effectively, because the drama is *condensed*, sharpened, as events happen rapidly, one after the other, so that the basic situation is quickly established.

Now, the dramatic elements, the plot factors, of the original *three* scenes all are required for the story; it is the manner of their presentation which changed a narrative technique into a dramatic technique.

To repeat, examine your scenario from (3) and see which Master Scenes can be combined or rearranged to provide the most drama and save time.

It can be stated almost as an unbreakable law of television writing that any scene which does not accomplish more than one result is not a good scene. Television playwriting has got to "get 'em coming and going!"

When you have a scenario arranged which first of all conforms to your time limit, which tells the basic story and which uses dramatic structure establishing a situation at once, creating suspense immediately, and heightening conflict and suspense as the action progresses, you are ready to begin to write the actual dialogue.

II

We propose now to discuss a remarkable prose work which was

transformed into one of the best dramatic television plays this author has ever seen produced.

The prose work is *Rise Up and Walk*, by Turnley Walker, published 1950 by E. P. Dutton & Company, Inc. *Rise Up and Walk* is Mr. Walker's own story of his being stricken with polio, and of his experiences in hospital and in adjusting to the new life his illness imposed on him.

The television play, *Rise Up and Walk*, was adapted from Mr. Walker's book by Mr. Robert Anderson, and was produced on the dramatic program, "Robert Montgomery Presents."

We shall practice what we preach and first write the basic story of *Rise Up and Walk*. Since Mr. Walker did not use his own name, or the name of his wife, we'll use the names established in Mr. Anderson's television play.

STEP ONE — *The Basic Story*

Overnight, Ted Walker is stricken with polio, and is moved from the home he supports by his abilities as a writer and public relations executive to the Hospital for Special Surgery in New York City. His wife and two children are dependent upon him for their living, and his anguish as he contemplates his plight is indescribable.

Ted is cared for in a hospital room which shelters three other men, polio victims. Nurses and doctors make preliminary and very painful examinations to determine the extent of the damage. Ted's thoughts are equally painful, as are the thoughts of the other victims. Under the grim stress, the four become friends very quickly.

Worry about immediate financial difficulty is a little dissipated when Betty Walker, his wife, brings for Ted to read a letter from the National Foundation for Infantile Paralysis assuring him that his obligations will be cared for by the Foundation "until you are able to work again."

All the polio victims are waiting the arrival of a noted Swedish doctor, an authority on poliomyelitis. As he waits, Ted ponders about the manuscript of the novel he was writing — he cannot even remember where he left it.

Immediate treatment of Ted involves agonizing massage, and

visits to a tank where a crane lowers him into hot water. His pain-wracked body is "lifted, turned, packed, dried, tested, exercised."

The Swedish doctor arrives. He cannot tell much about Ted; it is too early. Ted tries his legs: In the left nothing happens, but in the right something does happen. Will it make Ted walk? The Swedish doctor can only say, "We'll watch it."

"He found a muscle in my right leg," Ted tells one of his friends, the lawyer victim. There is an atmosphere in the room now, of courage and a peculiar kind of confidence.

A social-service worker calls on Ted to reaffirm the concern of the National Foundation in him. She leaves a book about polio, which Ted reads aloud to the others. All discuss the way they contracted the disease, and declare their relief that they — and not their children — are afflicted. But they are scared.

The wives of the victims visit them, bringing news of home and children, and special treats of good things to eat.

As the days pass, strength returns to Ted's arms and shoulders. At night, in the dark, he struggles to sit up, in a battle which no one else can observe. Then the editor who has encouraged him to write the novel calls, with Betty in attendance. Ignoring Ted's helplessness, he talks briskly and in a businesslike way of Ted's continuing the novel. It is part of the "cure," although Ted cannot yet assimilate this fact. Pity is ruled out; the editor leaves after advising Ted to "write something about the way you feel in here, perhaps a few sketches."

Late that night, Ted starts reading the manuscript of his novel. He is, at the very least, working again. When, after three hours of reading, the nurse asks him to put out his light, he starts practising "sitting up." His efforts are rewarded when the doctor tells him next day that he may sit in a wheel chair an hour a day. Ted asks for a place to work on his writing; he is given the tank-room for an hour, after treatment time.

One day, Ted clenches the muscle of his right leg, and the knee lifts the fraction of an inch. He shouts the news to the other victims in his room; all respond eagerly — it is the most wonderful thing they ever heard of. Now the question is — will Ted walk again? He ponders on the miracle of walking, observes the wonderful legs of well men and women. Eventually the Swedish doctor returns, to look at the revivifying right leg. "Doctor, will I walk again?" But the doctor doesn't know; it is a strange disease.

"Day after day you think about your children." Betty is with Ted every visiting period, but children are not allowed. Ted's birthday is at hand, his pleading is rewarded; his children may be brought to the hospital lecture room, where he will go himself in the wheel chair. But he has no clothes; his own clothes were taken from him and, naked, he was wrapped in a blanket before the hospital garments were put on him.

Miraculously, a friend presents him with a handsome sports jacket. One of his other friends, a polio victim, sends an attendant out to buy Ted a shirt. Thus dressed, and with his helpless legs wrapped in a blanket, Ted goes to meet his children on his birthday.

They are fearful of him. The little son backs away. The little daughter, slightly older, begs for reassurance that her Daddy can walk. Betty turns the conversation onto other things, but the end of the party is the little girl sobbing out, "Daddy — please walk, please!"

Betty hurries away with the children.

A friend calls on Ted, a friend who is a corporation lawyer. As a lawyer, he is impatient — or pretends to be — with Ted's helplessness. But he has brought a "job of work" for Ted, the public relations counsel, to perform, and so he is an angel of mercy whose sternly controlled face does not reveal the pity he feels for Ted.

In a few days, when Betty is visiting him, Ted proudly shows her a bill for services rendered he is sending to the lawyer. Betty grips Ted's hand hard. "We're going to be all right," she says.

Ted grows stronger, and is allowed more time in his wheel chair. He visits from bed to bed, in other rooms of the hospital. The one patient he cannot make friends with is Droopy, a twenty-two-year-old boy who must receive psychiatric treatments as well as hot packs. They learn that Droopy's wife has had a miscarriage when he was stricken with polio. The baby died.

In the gymnasium, where Ted goes for exercise, a little boy is trying to walk, his legs in braces, along the two bars of the parallel bars. He tells Ted he is only three. The nurse whispers that actually he is six, but because "boys six years old can walk," the little victim has decided that he is only three, still a baby. So does his mind adjust to his infirmity. Furiously, he shouts to Ted that "everybody can walk!" and his courage is an inspiration.

At Christmas, many months after he was first stricken, Ted is allowed to go home to his apartment. All the details are arranged by the National Foundation for Infantile Paralysis. All the men in Ted's room are to go; they make plans in "happy violence." Ted is carried from the car of friends, with his wheel chair, to his apartment. Christmas morning, the little family has its Tree — only the little daughter again says, "Daddy, please stand up."

"Walking is only a trick." The time comes when the doctor orders two attendants to stand Ted on his feet. Ted resists; he is not sure he can do it. But the two therapists stand him upright, and leave him there, unassisted. At least, Ted can stand. Then, as the doctor insists, Ted takes one step, with his right leg. The therapists lower him into a chair. Next he will be fitted with a brace for the still inert left leg. A steel brace, very heavy.

With crutches jammed under his arms, and with the brace on, Ted is ordered to walk. Without mercy, the doctor drives him on. Ted walks.

He can leave the hospital now for Warm Springs. His "right leg is terrific." He will have return of muscle strength for a year. He must keep working. His friends, victims like himself, compliment him on his walking. "In the morning, you will walk back through the doorway into the firm world you knew, and you will make that passage without fear."

END OF BASIC STORY

STEP TWO

Master Scenes in the Book as Established by the Original Author

1. What polio is like, "right after it hits you like a hammer in the head." Exposition of Ted Walker's whereabouts in the hospital, his private feelings, his shock at being stricken, some indication of treatment, building to the hope of a visit from his wife, Betty. (NOTE: the book, *Rise Up and Walk*, is written largely in "interior monologues," as if the protagonist were talking about himself to himself, a form of writing most difficult to dramatize, because there is no confidante for the protagonist to talk to. We

shall see that the television playwright uses pre-recorded "thoughts" as an invaluable technique in reproducing this interior monologue dramatically.)

2. Ted's fellow victims are introduced; his wondering about them is a bridge to exposition of his own career as a novelist and public relations counsel.

3. Treatments are indicated when the spasms of polio bring pain, and in turn Ted's thoughts turn darkly to the dark future.

4. Betty, Ted's wife, brings a letter from the Foundation for Infantile Paralysis, giving news that the Foundation will handle all financial needs "until you are able to work again."

5. Treatment, pain, symptoms, hope described in considerable detail, tied-in with the growing friendship between Ted and his fellow victims.

6. The Swedish doctor is introduced, and Ted and his friends discuss the chances of this authority's being able to help them. The Swedish doctor "finds a muscle in my right leg," arousing Ted's wildest hopes.

7. A social worker brings a book about polio, and Ted reads it aloud to his fellow victims. They discuss the way each was felled by polio. In the end, they are "scared."

8. The wives of the victims visit their husbands. Talk is all of how they're going to get well.

9. Ted's novel is on his mind, and he is visited by the two editors who encouraged him to write it. They toast the prospective novel with a bottle of sherry the editors have brought.

10. Late that night, Ted starts reading the manuscript of as much of his novel as he has done. After several hours of reading, the nurse asks him to put out his light.

11. The light out, Ted practices "sitting up," alone in the dark of the early morning hours. He tells the doctor, next day, that he can sit up, and asks for a place to work, to write. The doctor arranges for Ted to use the tank-room, after treatment time.

12. One day, in great excitement, Ted discovers that he can lift the whole of his right leg very slightly from the bed. It is the biggest single event of Ted's hospital stay, although the therapist does not get very excited about it. But Ted is excited; in his wheel chair, he visits other hospital rooms, the solarium, watches people performing the miracle of walking on their good legs,

trying to figure out how they do it. Then later when the doctor arrives, Ted announces his great news. But the doctor will say only that he thinks the right leg will grow stronger; he doesn't know positively.

13. Ted's thoughts are on his children. His birthday is at hand; his wife may visit him, but not his children. Then, miraculously, the hospital chief agrees to let Ted's children visit him briefly in the lecture room. The necessary clothes are provided; Ted wheels himself to the lecture room. But the party is a tragic event, because his children are afraid of him.

14. A friend, a corporation lawyer, visits Ted, and, concealing the pity he feels, brusquely gives Ted a "job of work" in public relations to do. When next Betty visits Ted, he shows her a "bill for services rendered" he is sending the lawyer. He is back at work again, at last, and they "will be all right."

15. Ted visits in other rooms, meets other patients. Tragedies in various form are revealed to him.

16. The scene is the gymnasium. Ted, there for exercise, sees Ralph, the six-year-old boy who pretends to be only three, dragging himself along the parallel bars. "Everybody can walk," shouts Ralph, after he has dragged himself near Ted.

17. Ted is allowed to go home for Christmas. It is a joyous time, although his little girl once again demands, "Stand up, Daddy!" — and Ted cannot.

18. "Walking is only a trick." So the chief therapist assures Ted. Helped by other therapists, Ted is lifted, in fear and doubt, onto his feet, made to stand upright. Then he takes one step, with his good right leg, and is congratulated by the doctor and the therapists. Now Ted is to get a brace for the still inert left leg.

19. Ted is fitted with his heavy steel brace. "Walk," orders the doctor. With crutches jammed under his arms, Ted slowly obeys. Now he may leave for Warm Springs, next day, if he wants to.

20. Ted tells his friends, his fellow victims, goodbye. For the last time, he hoists himself onto his high, narrow, white bed. "In the morning you will walk back through the doorway into the firm world you knew, and you will make that passage without fear."

END OF MASTER SCENES IN THE ORIGINAL BOOK

Master Scenes of Television Play
(For brevity, in this case adaptor's basic story and scenario are combined.)

NOTE: In the book, *Rise Up and Walk*, the actual settings were never clearly defined as to number and variety, because it was not necessary. Neither was the number of characters specified. "Patients, therapists, visitors," etc., etc., were mentioned as needed. But in the television play, actual sets and actual characters must of course be specified. Therefore we start with a list

of settings and characters.

Sets

1. Main set is a hospital room with three beds in it . . . and little else . . . tables . . . hook-neck lamps on bed . . . windows.
2. Another hospital room where the birthday party is held.
3. The tank-room . . . a corner of it, where Ted goes to work.
4. The hall of Ted's apartment house . . . and a part of his living room, with large Christmas Tree.
5. Part of gymnasium or exercise room in hospital, with parallel bars for a little boy to walk through . . . using the bars as supports.
6. A hall connecting the main set and the tank-room.

Characters

Ted Walker	Donald Davidson
Ralph Webber	Betty Walker
Carol Davidson	Sarah Webber
Dr. Swanson	Miss Carlson
Miss Thornton	Harry
Therapist	Ralph, a small boy
First Doctor	Second Doctor
First Webber Brother	Second Webber Brother
Attendants (two)	Tommy Walker
Tiny crippled girl in walking harness	Peggy Walker

General Description of Characters

The three polios, Ted, Davidson and Webber, are all in their thirties . . . Webber the oldest (39) . . . Ted the youngest . . . maybe 31. Davidson is probably the most sensitive, takes things the hardest. Their wives, Betty, Carol and Sarah, are the girls you might expect the men to marry. . . . Betty is probably a Dorothy Maguire sort of girl (actually played by Kim Hunter). . . . Sarah is large to go with her husband, Webber . . . and Carol is sweet and more reserved than the others.

Dr. Swanson . . . is described as not an old man, but with white hair.

Harry . . . is blustering, stocky, energetic, smokes a cigar constantly.

Miss Carlson . . . is a very pleasant nurse.

Miss Thornton . . . is an older nurse who tries to be gruff, but doesn't succeed too well with it.

Ralph . . . is a little boy six years old . . . a polio.

Therapist . . . is a very nice young woman in her twenties . . . with the gentle way necessary to work with this kind of child.

The Brothers of Webber are both large . . . they must be, to carry Ted and the wheel chair.

Master Scenes

1. Ted's bed in the hospital room. In a pre-recorded monologue, Ted gives the exposition of his illness and of where he is, as he lies in bed.

2. Then, as Miss Carlson enters in response to Ted's ringing, a scene is played between Ted, Miss Carlson, Davidson and Webber, in which the men exchange confidences about their outside lives and their illness. As the conversation turns to the cost of polio, in a CLOSE SHOT on Ted, we hear his pre-recorded monologue on this subject. Back in a direct scene, a continuation of the previous scene, it is established that they're all waiting for the Swedish authority, Dr. Swanson, to arrive.

3. Time Lapse of Several Days. Ted notes this time lapse in pre-recorded speech. Dr. Swanson arrives. Examining Ted, he finds a "good muscle" in Ted's right leg. The suspense of Ted's recovery is established.

4. A Series of Montage Shots, Covering Details of Treatment. The hot-water tub with the wringer for the hot applications . . . . the stretching process, etc., etc. This action is covered by a pre-recorded monologue of Ted describing what is going on. This montage covers an indeterminate time lapse.

5. Back in the Hospital Room. Visiting time for the wives. This is the first time the wives are introduced. Action is concentrated on Ted and Betty, his wife, who brings the letter from the National Foundation for Infantile Paralysis. Note that this is *story progression,* after the suspense of Ted's recovery or non-recovery and the technical details of treatment for polio have been covered. In addition, Betty tells of their children, who "hate her," because she "won't bring Daddy home." Then, the letter motivates Ted's thinking of his novel, and he asks Betty to bring him the manuscript. This scene is a fine example of one scene's accomplishing several objectives: the financial part of Ted's dilemma, the attitude of his children toward him, the pointing forward of his determination to start work again. The scene ends with Betty's steadfast declaration that Ted will walk again.

6. Again an Indeterminate Time Lapse. Late at night in the hospital room. In a pre-recorded monologue, Ted talks about his novel. Davidson is attracted by Ted's night light, and they talk about being able to work again. When the nurse asks Ted to put the light out, he complies; but then he begins, in the dark, to practise "sitting up" for the first time. Note: this is story progression along the suspense-line established: will Ted walk or not?

7. The Next Morning. Dr. Swanson has just seen Ted sitting up. He arranges for Ted to use the tank-room so that he can work.

8. Indeterminate Time Lapse. The tank-room. In a pre-recorded monologue, Ted tells of having been there several times, trying to work. But the words won't come: he cannot write. Miss Carlson arrives, tells him that his children are downstairs (tremendous surprise) for his birthday party, which had been kept secret in order not to excite him. Miss Carlson wheels Ted back to his room, where he is dressed in the new shirt and sports coat Webber and Davidson have given him. Miss Carlson then wheels

Ted to the small room where his children are to meet him. FADE OUT.

9. Fade In, a few minutes later. Ted is sitting quietly in his wheelchair, waiting for his children and his wife. His deep concern is revealed in a pre-recorded monologue. The children arrive. The party, with presents and a cake, is underway. The time goes happily and quickly; but the party ends in sadness when the little girl bursts into sobs, demanding that her Daddy "walk." As the children leave with their mother, it is the

END OF ACT I

10. The Hospital Room. Indeterminate Time Lapse. In a pre-recorded monologue, Ted sets the exposition; he is lying awake nights trying to clench the muscle above his right knee. Then, in direct action, Ted and Davidson weigh Ted's chances. Some simple, dramatic, tragic discussion of the behavior of polio as a disease follows, logically enough, as it intensifies the drama of Ted's struggle. Then Ted, Davidson and Webber discuss what happened when polio attacked them, a scene deeply dramatic and full of tension because by now these three men have been so fully characterized that what happens to them is of the greatest concern to us, the viewers. In other words, with the basic situation strongly established, and with suspense high, there is time for this sort of deeper insight into the principal characters of our drama; insight fulfilling television's major ability to reveal character. The scene ends with a *forward movement in the plot:* Ted suddenly can move his right knee, just a little bit. At this climactic moment, Dr. Swanson arrives and Ted demonstrates the new-found strength in his right leg. Will he walk, Doctor? The Doctor refuses to commit himself. Ted becomes dejected, and replies to the Doctor's questions about progress on his book, that he cannot write . . . no need to save the tank-room for him any longer. But the Doctor refuses to accept Ted's attitude, makes him promise to try the tank-room and writing just once more. FADE OUT.

11. Fade In. The Tank-Room. Indeterminate Time Lapse. Ted, alone, shuffles listlessly through his manuscript, then gives up and lays his head on the typewriter. The outside door opens, and Harry, the corporation lawyer, enters. He has come to give

Ted a "job of work" in Ted's capacity as a public relations counsel. NOTE: Technically, plot-wise, at the instant our protagonist is farthest down, a new development in the plot arrives, and the story is carried forward thereby. Overriding Ted's self-doubt, Harry sets a time limit of three days for the finishing of the work he has brought Ted. Harry leaves, and Ted picks up the assignment, with interest and enthusiasm starting to grow. FADE OUT.

12. Fade In. The Hospital Room Again. Indeterminate Time Lapse. Ted, Davidson and Webber are discussing Christmas plans. Davidson reveals that he can write a little (sub-plot development), and so he is writing a surprise letter for his wife's present. Then the wives arrive . . . and in Ted's case, he shows Betty the bill he is sending to Harry "for services rendered" on the job of work. Then, Miss Thornton, the tough-tender nurse, arrives with news that all the men are to go home for Christmas. FADE OUT.

13. Fade In. Indeterminate Time Lapse. The hallway outside Ted's apartment. Betty and the two children are waiting for Ted's arrival. He comes, carried by Webber's two stalwart brothers. Left alone with his little family, Ted starts Christmas, symbolized by the big tree ready to be trimmed. His joy at being home is tempered by his little girl's asking him to stand up and put the trimming on the tallest part of the tree. This is the

END OF ACT II

14. Fade In. The Gymnasium. Time Lapse of Several Weeks, Indicated in Ted's Pre-Recorded Monologue. Ted has come for exercise. The action is centered on the little boy, Ralph, pulling himself along on the parallel bars. Ted's discouragement is dissipated by the pathetic youngster's refusal to give up, although he has been afflicted for a long time. In the face of such courage in so small a human being, Ted can only renew his determination to walk. FADE OUT.

15. Fade In. The Hospital Room Again. Davidson is now sitting in a chair (more sub-plot development, accomplished visually). Webber is still in bed. Ted is waiting for Dr. Swanson and the two attendants who will stand Ted on his feet in his first attempt to stand alone since he was stricken. Panicky, Ted is left

standing. The Doctor commands him to take a step. Finally, Ted does. Now he is ready for his brace. FADE OUT.

16. Fade In. The Gymnasium. The little boy is walking on the parallel bars. Then a tiny little girl appears, held upright by a harness controlled by the therapist. Then Ted is seen, walking along the parallel bars. This action is covered by Ted's pre-recorded monologue. If children can learn to walk, so can he. DIS-SOLVE.

17. Dissolve. The Hallway. Dr. Swanson, an attendant, and Ted, who is practising walking on crutches, with a brace on his inert left leg. Now Ted may leave for Warm Springs. Ted's deeply-felt, awkward attempts to thank the Doctor are brushed off by the Doctor's brisk "Next patient." The Doctor also is covering his deep emotions. Ted walks into the hospital room, *without* a CUTAWAY FROM THE CAMERA, to tell Webber and David-son that he will leave the next day for Warm Springs. FADE OUT.

18. Fade In. That Night, Moonlight. Ted alone is seen. As the Camera Stays on Ted, his pre-recorded thoughts are heard . . . " . . . you relax, and the softness of the moonlight takes you gently into a dream in which your victory continues forever."

END OF ACT III

END OF TELEVISION PLAY.

STEP FOUR

Comparing Breakdown of Master Scenes in Original Book with Master Scene Breakdown in Television Play.

Your author is cheating a bit, and acting from hindsight, in making this comparison. He has omitted the recommended adaptor's basic story written out in narrative form, and has gone directly to a breakdown of the master scenes of the television play, as produced on the air. This way seems the best to make the most lucid comparison between the structure of the book and of the television play.

Mostly the difference is in a rearrangement of the plot elements, to create suspense in the television play, and to separate and spot the progressions in the story in order to maintain and increase suspense — and to have "something happening" at intervals spaced out more in the play than in the book.

There are twenty master scenes in the book, eighteen in the play, as analyzed by your author. The comparison will be made from the point of view of the play.

SCENE ONE uses about the same material in play and book.

SCENE TWO uses material from Scene Two, Scene Six and Scene Seven of the book. From the book's Scene Six, comes the element of the Swedish doctor's pending arrival. This element was moved up in the play in order to establish immediate suspense: "Will Ted recover? Will the Swedish doctor be able to help him?"

SCENE THREE concentrates on the Swedish doctor's arrival (Scene Six in the book), when the doctor finds a "good muscle" in Ted's right leg. So, Scene Three is a logical continuation of Scene Two; the element of the Swedish doctor is used for full story value and for increased suspense, which is being heightened by arousing hope in Ted.

SCENE FOUR is a montage showing the nature of the treatments administered to polio victims. This is Scene Three and Scene Five in the book. Spotting this material in earlier in the play covers the point about treatment, once and for all. The play will hold at this point because strong suspense has been established at the end of the play's Scene Three. (In other words, factual data will hold our interest at this point when it might not later on in the story. The montage also satisfies our natural curiosity about how treatments are given; and it serves as a time lapse device.)

SCENE FIVE brings in the poignant human element strongly, when the wives visit their victim-husbands. This scene uses material from Scene Four and Scene Eight of the book, and is an example of condensation. In Scene Four of the book, Ted's wife only is the visitor. The other wives don't arrive until Scene Eight. But *visually*, the arrival of *all* the wives (in the play) brought an emotional response that was overwhelming, as each wife first hesitated, then went to her husband. Now more than ever we want Ted to recover; in short, the suspense established by the end of the play's Scene Three is once again heightened almost unbearably. For we have now been through what Ted must endure in the form of treatments (the montage), and we know that he has been given hope when the doctor found the "good muscle in my right leg" (Scene Three).

Here also an additional story element is introduced: Ted's wife brings the letter from the Foundation for Infantile Paralysis which increases hope as it relieves worry about finances. In the book, this letter arrives in Scene Four, too soon for our dramatic purpose of spacing out the story elements in order to wring the situation dry. If worry about money is relieved, hope, being increased, increases the suspense.

To put it another way — don't squander all the story elements — the weapons and ammunition you have to hold suspense and build story — all at once! Rather than one wild assault, a steady, spaced pounding, increasing in intensity, will create the utmost emotional reaction from your audience.

SCENE SIX combines material from Scenes Nine, Ten and Eleven of the book. We are now deep into the story, and Ted's magnificent courage and his efforts to get well in themselves constitute a development of the plot, as does also his awakened interest in completing his novel. Please note that the *new* story elements of Ted's practising sitting up, and of his novel, are introduced for the first time, at a moment in the structure when a story development is needed.

SCENE SEVEN is a logical outgrowth of the play's Scene Six (Scene Eleven in the book).

SCENE EIGHT follows good dramatic practise and shows Ted, the protagonist, temporarily defeated. The story development, in the form of a surprise to us and to Ted, is the presence of his children for his birthday party (Scene Thirteen in the book). At once, Ted's spirits soar, but in a logical development. . . .

SCENE NINE his heart is broken again, when his children are afraid of him (Scene Thirteen in the book). This scene ends Act One, and, once again in good dramatic practise, shows our protagonist utterly sunk. But the introduction of the various story elements (1) Recovery (2) Ted's Work (3) Ted's Family Relationships — these elements have built a taut suspense to "hold over" interest for the Second Act.

ACT TWO

SCENE TEN continues the "down" mood of our protagonist, heightened by the use in the scene of Ted's roommates, whose stories also are furthered at a place in the story structure when suspense is still holding strong, and so we can include action other than that directly on Ted. The sudden, electrifying plot development is Ted's discovery that he can move his right knee, just a little bit (Scene Twelve in the book). The Swedish doctor arrives at this climactic point, increasing suspense by refusing to commit himself on the importance of Ted's new-found ability to move his right kneecap. Ted is plunged into gloom, following good practice again of bringing your hero up a little, then dashing him down again, on an ever-ascending plane of rising action, however. The doctor, in making Ted promise to try his writing once more, makes us feel Ted's futility — we are enmeshed in Ted's problem.

SCENE ELEVEN (Scene Fourteen in the book) furthers the story by introducing the corporation lawyer with his "job of work" for Ted. Ted's successful accomplishment of this "job" deserves a scene by itself, when his wife visits him again, and this is

SCENE TWELVE of the play (Scene Fourteen of the book). The forward movement of the plot comes from the nurse's arrival with the news that Ted and all his friends are to go home for Christmas (Scene Seventeen of the book, and near the end of the book, in fact, while the play still has its Third Act to play out). Clearly, the rearrangement of the material has provided *more story* for the play, although the play uses exactly the same material as the book. Once again, it is a matter of spacing the story elements so as to wring the most out of them. Suspense is heightened here, too, because we remember how Ted's children reacted at his birthday party; and we are filled with apprehension about their behavior toward him during the holy Christmas season, most beloved of family holidays.

SCENE THIRTEEN plays out the Christmas visit home; and its poignancy, when Ted's little girl asks him to "stand up and put the star on the tree," and he cannot, creates a natural climax for the end of Act Two.

Act Three

SCENE FOURTEEN, set in the gymnasium, takes place after an indeterminate time lapse, in which Ted's slow improvement can be assumed from what has gone before. The poignancy of his effort is sharply highlighted by his scene with the little boy, Ralph, Scene Sixteen in the book, a scene in the book set even before the Christmas visit. The little boy's courage inspires Ted to greater determination, thereby increasing suspense along the main story line: will Ted recover?

SCENE FIFTEEN shows the development of this determination: Ted is stood upright, and commanded to walk (Scene Eighteen in the book). Now he is ready for a brace, although he is fearful of being able to use it.

SCENE SIXTEEN carries the plot development that Ted is trying out his brace (Scene Nineteen in the book). The setting of this scene in the gymnasium gives another opportunity to use little Ralph, legitimately enough from a dramatic standpoint, to point both Ted's struggle with the brace and his resolution that he will master its use.

SCENE SEVENTEEN brings the climax and denouement of the play (Scene Nineteen of the book). Ted may leave for Warm Springs. We, the audience, feel that he is on his way to recovery and as normal a life as may be possible. But we know that, spiritually, Ted has won — he is a bigger, better, more confident man than he was before. We love him deeply, because we have been through his struggle with him.

SCENE EIGHTEEN uses the material of Scene Twenty in the book. Our belief that Ted has conquered spiritually is confirmed . . . We know that his "victory continues forever."

To summarize:

PLAY SCENES	use	BOOK SCENES
One		One
Two		Two, Six and Seven
Three		Six
Four		Three, Five
Five		Four, Eight

Six	Nine, Ten and Eleven
Seven	Eleven
Eight	Thirteen
Nine	Thirteen
Ten	Twelve
Eleven	Fourteen
Twelve	Fourteen, Seventeen
Thirteen	Seventeen
Fourteen	Sixteen
Fifteen	Eighteen
Sixteen	Nineteen
Seventeen	Nineteen
Eighteen	Twenty

Scene Fifteen in the book is not used in the television play, except as it may have been drawn on for atmosphere and details.

Pre-Recorded Monologues

Since the television play, *Rise Up and Walk*, leans heavily on translating the book's "interior monologues" into "pre-recorded monologues," it seems only fair to give you samples for comparison of a passage from the book with the corresponding dialogue for the play.

Prose Passages from the Book

Chapter I. The regulation hospital bed is thirty-four by seventy-four inches. In the beginning that much space is allotted to each *polio* — the new name you get after Infantile Paralysis slugs you. Forever after you will be known as *a polio*. That thirty-four-by-seventy-four inch area is a place that poliomyelitis allows you, and even though you have been a much-traveled man in the outside world, you learn to live in it.

At first it's a very quiet life. You lie flat on your back, stretched out as far as you will go, and nothing about you moves — if you are a serious case — except the wheels inside your head. Those wheels grind out a terrible pressure of fear and pain and loneliness. Very suddenly you have been yanked out of the relaxed, marvelous, commonplace world and set down in a tiny flat white jail. Polio is always so unexpected. . . .

Chapter II. You spend a considerable part of your time estimating small but important distances. By the hour, you stare at the
open doorway of your room. Somehow, some day, you must walk
to that doorway from the faraway pit of helplessness in which
you lie. . . .

On the other bed a man lies full length on his back. The day
before you watched them roll him into the room and turn him
from the stretcher into this permanent position. Their hands
touched him tenderly, but he screamed in rage, and under your
breath, you cursed their hands in his behalf. You did not know
his name, you had not seen his face because a high table cut it
off from view, but he was a friend of yours. He groaned and
called out for the nurses in an exasperated voice. He was afraid.
To the depths of your soul, you understood him. Now you watch
his bare feet in their tight position on the footboard. . . .

These two excerpts from Chapters I and II became the opening of the television play; with the television playwright making
certain changes and additions:

ACT I

FADE IN ON TED'S BED IN THE HOSPITAL
ROOM. . . . AS HE TALKS ABOUT IT, PAN
SLIGHTLY TO COVER ALL PARTS OF THE
BED.
MUSIC, AS WE FADE IN, A LOVELY PLAINTIVE
SINGLE INSTRUMENT (ALTO FLUTE) STARTS . . .
IT WILL BE USED TO BACK ALL THE
NARRATIONS. . . .

TED (PRE-RECORDED)

The regulation hospital bed is thirty-four
by seventy-four inches . . . In the beginning
that much space is allotted to each polio . . .
the new name you get after Infantile
Paralysis slugs you. That thirty-four-by-
seventy-four inch area is a place that
poliomyelitis allows you, and even though
you have been a much-traveled man in the
outside world, you learn to live in it. . . .

At first, it's a very quiet life, the minutes,
hours and days ticked off by the three-dollar
watch you've had tied to your bed. . . .
PAN TO A TIGHT SHOT OF WATCH,
HANGING ON A STRING FROM HEAD
OF BED. . . .
You lie flat on your back, stretched out as
far as you will go, and nothing about you moves,
except the wheels inside your head. And those
wheels grind out a terrible pressure of fear
and pain and loneliness. . . .
You spend a considerable part of your
time estimating small but important
distances. By the hour you stare at
the open doorway of your room. Somehow, some day, you must walk through
that doorway from the faraway pit of
helplessness in which you lie. . . .
PAN ALONG THE FLOOR BETWEEN
THE BED AND THE DOORWAY, SLOWLY,
AS IF MEASURING THE DISTANCE.
AND END UP ON THE DOORWAY . . .
On the bed next to yours a man lies full
length on his back. The day before you
watched them roll him into the room and
turn him from the stretcher into this
permanent position.
Their hands touched him tenderly, but he
screamed in rage, and under your breath,
you cursed their hands in his behalf. . . .
Now you watch his bare feet in their tight
position on the footboard.
PAN TO THE SECOND BED . . . DONALD
DAVIDSON LYING THERE, FLAT ON
HIS BACK. . . .
COME IN FOR TIGHTER SHOT OF
DAVIDSON'S FEET ON FOOT BOARD.
HE TRIES TO MOVE THEM, BUT

THERE IS NO MOVEMENT. . . .

(Author's note: Now live action begins.)

TED

(REACHES OUT WITH RIGHT HAND AND TRIES TO
MOVE ASIDE TABLE BETWEEN HIS BED AND NEXT.
. . . CAN'T. REACHES UP AND PUSHES THE
BUTTON SUMMONING THE NURSE. . . . WHILE HIS
HAND IS UP THERE, HE TAKES A LOOK AT THE
WATCH HANGING THERE. . . .)

MISS CARLSON (NURSE)

(COMES IN) Yes?

TED

(LOOKING TOWARDS OTHER BED)

Hello, there.

Etc., etc., etc.

Chapter VII. The book which you have written is not yet a book at all. It is nearly five hundred sheets of typewriting in a brown legal folder, heavily disfigured with pencil markings. But, with the sponsorship of the two well-known editors, a front-rank publishing firm has given you a cash advance against possible future royalties.

The book lies on the high narrow table near the head of your bed, and with your stronger hand you touch it timidly, not wanting to examine its pages. You are not yet physically able to do the added writing which is needed.

You remain smothered by the fact that with you writing must be done sitting upright, with active hands, a typewriter before you — a position and activity now impossible.

Recently, however, strength has been rushing back into your arms and shoulders. Each day, the muscle re-education exercises discover new and stronger movements. You flex your fingers and ponder their efficiency on typewriter keys. At night you struggle to sit up in your bed. All through your body the muscle spasms are lessening, and the pain is fading with it. Your mind is gaining space to think.

Thinking has always been the work you do. You think about problems and events and situations, and then you write messages which seem appropriate.

Now you are thinking about the book's needed reconstruction, and this work provides the first important relief from the paralyzing depression which polio brings with it.

From Act I of the television play:

FADE IN ON WEBBER'S BED. . . . AND DURING
NARRATION PAN TO DAVIDSON'S AND THEN
FINALLY TO TED'S. . . . WEBBER'S LIGHT
IS OUT. HE IS SLEEPING. DAVIDSON HAS
HIS LIGHT OUT, BUT HE IS AWAKE, WATCHING
TED OUT OF THE CORNER OF HIS EYE.

TED (PRE-RECORDED)

Then one night, some time later, your wife
brings the book, which is not a book at all
yet, but just five hundred typewritten pages
in need of organization and re-writing. . . .
And after visiting hours, while Webber sleeps
and Davidson lies thinking of his wife, you
start to look at your work.

TED

(LYING FLAT ON HIS BACK, HE PICKS UP PAGE
AFTER PAGE, AND GLANCES AT IT. . . . AS NARRATION
GOES ON. . . .)

TED (PRE-RECORDED)

You are afraid because you are not physically
able to do the work that must be done on it.
Reworking and re-organizing a long work of
fiction is a tough job under the best of circumstances. Lying flat on your back, unable
to bring your mind to bear on any one thing
for more than a short time, it's an almost
superhuman task. But you dream of its selling
a million copies, ridding you of your financial
worries, and you try to work on.
(Author's note: Now into live action)

DAVIDSON

What are you up to?

TED
My book. I'm working.
        Etc., etc., etc.

From all that has been written and illustrated, you will see that
the job of adapting is a job of condensation, of rearranging, of
emphasis on dramatic climaxes, of capturing the essence of the
original author's story.

So, the book, *Rise Up and Walk,* about 25,000 words long, was
adapted as a powerful and successful television play, running
time between 52–55 minutes.

It is regretted that the limitations of space prevent reproducing
the television play in full. That space, it was decided, might
better be reserved for a summary (plus important excerpts given
in dialogue) of the television script of *Wuthering Heights,* the
classic novel, an adaptation which offers in addition to problems
of structure, the problem of writing dialogue for a period remote
from ours, dialogue which must convey the flavor of that period
and yet be composed so that a modern audience would accept it.

We proceed to a study of *Wuthering Heights,* classic novel and
successful television play.

II

ADAPTATION OF A CLASSIC NOVEL: *Wuthering Heights,*
BY EMILY BRONTË

The distinguished "live" presentation of *Wuthering Heights* on
Studio One, the famous, successful and pioneer hour-length dra-
matic program of CBS Television, was produced by Worthington
Miner, directed by Paul Nickell, from the adaptation by Lois
Jacoby.

If *you* had been assigned the job of adapting *Wuthering
Heights,* the first thing you would have done would be to read the
novel.

Therefore, as a student of adaptations, you must read the novel
in connection with your study of the television script by Lois
Jacoby, following. Obviously, it is impossible to print the whole
of the novel in this book. So, pretend that *you* are the adaptor
instead of Miss Jacoby, and take the first step any adaptor has

to take: read, study the source material. Your author chose *Wuthering Heights* not only because it *is* a classic, but because the book surely is available to everyone.

Comment and comparison between the novel and the television play appear at the end of the television script.

So you've read the novel, *Wuthering Heights?* Now read the condensation of the television play:

WUTHERING HEIGHTS *

A Play for Television adapted

by Lois Jacoby from the novel

by Emily Brontë

SETS

1. Wuthering Heights: Kitchen, Living Room, Exterior Door
   (one unit)
2. Wuthering Heights: Bedroom (separate unit)
3. Peniston Crag
4. Thrushcross Grange: Living Room, Hall, Exterior Door,
   Exterior Garden (one unit)
5. Thrushcross Grange: Cathy's bedroom (separate unit)

Characters

HEATHCLIFF	CATHERINE EARNSHAW
HEATHCLIFF AS A CHILD	CATHERINE AS A CHILD
HINDLEY EARNSHAW	LOCKWOOD
HINDLEY AS A CHILD	EDGAR
NELLIE DEAN (ELLEN)	ISABELLA
MR. EARNSHAW (FATHER)	JOSEPH
	DR. KENNETH

EXTRAS (MEN AND WOMEN) AT THE GRANGE PARTY

WUTHERING HEIGHTS

Part One

THE TITLES ARE SUPERIMPOSED OVER A SILHOUETTE
OF HEATHCLIFF, STANDING TALL AND GAUNT AGAINST
THE SKY AT PENISTON CRAG. AS WE COME OUT
OF THE TITLES, SNOW BEGINS TO FALL. WE COME

* *Wuthering Heights.* Copyright Columbia Broadcasting System. Inc., 1953.

IN CLOSER TO SEE THAT THERE IS A GRAVE AT
THE FOOT OF THE CRAG. WE SEE THE NAME ON THE
HEADSTONE: "CATHERINE EARNSHAW LINTON".
HEATHCLIFF KNEELS AT THE SIDE OF THE GRAVE.

HEATHCLIFF

Cathy, it's fitting your name should be carved
in the rock, for this was you — part wind, part
stone. And my name shall be carved beside yours!
For all time we shall be bound together — here
by the rock, by the wind. Over the moors.
(SLOWLY HE RISES AND STARTS TO GO DOWN FROM
THE CRAG) I envy you, Cathy, locked in your
eternal sleep, while for me there is only the living
death at Wuthering Heights — the nights without
sleep, the days without rest. How long, Cathy,
how long, before we can be together — forever?
DISSOLVE TO A STILL PICTURE OR DIORAMA OF
WUTHERING HEIGHTS WITH SNOW FALLING IN THE
FOREGROUND. DOLLY IN: THEN DISSOLVE TO A
PAIR OF BOOTS TRUDGING THROUGH THE SNOW.
THEN A VIEW OF A BLEAK, STONE EXTERIOR WITH
A ROOFED-OVER COBBLESTONE FLOOR . . . A SORT
OF PORTE-COCHERE, CONNECTING HOUSE AND
STABLE. TO THE RIGHT, THE DOOR TO THE LIVING
ROOM, WITH AN INTERIOR STAIRWAY TO THE
ROOMS ABOVE. THIS ALLOWS THE KITCHEN TO BE
USED AS AN ALCOVE TO THE LIVING ROOM, PARTLY
DIVIDED FROM IT. THE FEET WE HAVE SEEN
TRUDGING THROUGH THE SNOW BELONG TO MR. LOCK-
WOOD, WHO IS NOW SEEN, FULL-LENGTH, KNOCKING
AT THE DOOR TO WUTHERING HEIGHTS. NELLIE
DEAN ANSWERS HIS KNOCK AND LETS HIM INTO
THE HOUSE. THE SCENE IS ONE OF UNBEARABLE
SQUALOR. HINDLEY EARNSHAW, SULLEN AND
DRUNKEN, IS SEATED AT THE TABLE, A BOTTLE RIGHT
BESIDE HIM. ISABELLA IS SEATED IN A CHAIR
BESIDE THE FIRE. ALTHOUGH SHE IS ONLY FORTY,
SHE LOOKS LIKE A HAG OF SIXTY. THEY BARELY
ACKNOWLEDGE THE PRESENCE OF THE STRANGER.

Summary of Action: Lockwood asks lodging for the night. Hindley and Isabella warn him against staying in "this haven of damned souls", but when Lockwood persists, agree to take him up to "Cathy's old room", although Hindley declares that Heathcliff will be enraged.

Nellie leaves Lockwood in "Cathy's old room". Lockwood sits on the single bed, shivers. The window is open. As he rises to close it, he hears a cry, "No! No! No!". He opens the window again, sees carved in its wood frame the names: "Catherine Earnshaw, Catherine Heathcliff, Catherine Linton". The crying has stopped. As Lockwood starts again to close the window, Heathcliff rushes in.

HEATHCLIFF
Who are you? What are you doing here?

LOCKWOOD
I was on my way to the Grange. But the storm was rising, and your servant brought me to this room —

HEATHCLIFF (IN A RAGE)
And so now you want to close this window? Didn't you hear her cry? Don't you know this window is never closed?

LOCKWOOD (IN SOME FEAR)
I did not know —

HEATHCLIFF
Fool! Would you leave my Cathy wandering the moor?

HEATHCLIFF BECOMES LIKE A MAN POSSESSED. HE RUSHES OVER TO LOCKWOOD, TAKES HIM BY THE SCRUFF OF THE NECK AND PRACTICALLY THROWS HIM OUT THE DOOR. THEN HEATHCLIFF COMES BACK AND OPENS THE WINDOW WIDE. THERE IS NO SOUND BUT THE HOWLING OF THE WIND, THE RUSTLE OF THE BRANCHES IN THE STORM.

HEATHCLIFF (SOBBING)
Come in! Cathy! Cathy! Come in! Once more come in! Oh, my heart's darling — hear me this time! Catherine, at last! Come as you were that

first moment I saw you. How long is it? You were only a child!

HE LOOKS OUT INTO THE DARKNESS AND SEES ONLY A BLURRED IMAGE OF WUTHERING HEIGHTS. THE SNOW IS FALLING AND AT THE WINDOW NEXT TO THE DOOR, A CHILD'S FACE BEGINS TO APPEAR, PRESSED AGAINST THE WINDOW PANE. THEN THE CHILD RUNS OUT THE DOOR, INTO THE SNOW. IT IS CATHY AS A LITTLE GIRL. HER BROTHER, HINDLEY, RUNS AFTER HER AND TRIES TO PULL HER BACK INTO THE HOUSE.

CATHY

Leave me be. I shall be the first one to see father.

HINDLEY

Nellie says you are to come in at once.

CATHY

I won't come in. I love the storm.

HINDLEY

You are a foolish girl! The fire is much nicer and it is warm and snug inside. Come!

HE IS BIGGER THAN SHE; HE PULLS HER INDOORS BY THE HAIR, WHILE SHE SHRIEKS IN PROTEST. THEN WE SEE THE KITCHEN-LIVING ROOM AT WUTHERING HEIGHTS AS IT WAS 35 YEARS BEFORE. THE ROOM IS CHEERFUL WITH BRIGHT CURTAINS AND FLOWERS AND FRESHLY SHINED BRASS. JOSEPH IS BUSY WITH THE SUPPER PREPARATIONS

Summary of Action: Inside, Cathy and Hindley fight . . . their row is stopped by the arrival of their father. He distributes their presents, until their attention is directed to the carriage the father has traveled in.

A LITTLE BOY IS COMING OUT OF THE CARRIAGE. HE IS VERY DIRTY, PERHAPS A LITTLE OLDER THAN CATHY AND HINDLEY. A DARK CHILD WITH BUSHY EYEBROWS. HE TALKS BUT ONLY SOME WEIRD GIBBERISH ISSUES FROM HIS MOUTH.

JOSEPH

Master! Who is this?

HINDLEY

He's filthy! (PINCHING THE BOY, WHO LETS OUT A
YELL) I'll get rid of him!

CATHY (SURVEYING THE CHILD)

Where did he come from?

MR. EARNSHAW

It's a long story, and I am far too fatigued to tell
it. 'Tis enough that he was starving and homeless
on the streets of Liverpool. I could not leave him!

HINDLEY

He shall sleep in the stable.

CATHY

I shall teach him to speak as we do.

HINDLEY

I don't want him here. I'll run away. I hate him!
I want no other boy here!

CATHY

And I *do!* I do want him! When his face is
washed, I think he will be quite nice. What is
his name?

MR. EARNSHAW

We will give him the name of your little brother
that died. He shall be called Heathcliff!

FADE OUT. FADE IN . . . THE KITCHEN, SOME MONTHS
LATER. NELLIE IS AT THE STOVE. SHE CROSSES DOWN
TO SEE SOMETHING ON THE TABLE, AS JOSEPH
ENTERS.

Summary of Action: Joseph reveals that a deep bitterness has
grown up between Hindley and Heathcliff in the last three months
(which gives us the elapse of time). Hindley enters and rages
against Cathy and Heathcliff, who are "off again on the moors".
Thus, attitudes of major characters towards each other are given
in this scene.

CROSS FADE TO CATHY AND HEATHCLIFF ON
PENISTON CRAG

HEATHCLIFF

It is late, Cathy. Should we start back?

CATHY

No. I never want to leave. And as long as we
both shall live, this will be our place!

HEATHCLIFF

Yes! The sun is going down!

CATHY

Stay a moment longer!

THEY STAND GAZING OFF AT THE SETTING SUN. WE
PAN DOWN TO THEIR HANDS. HERS IS HELD TIGHTLY
IN HIS. SLOWLY WE DISSOLVE TO ANOTHER PAIR OF
HANDS, OLDER, STRONGER HANDS. WE PULL BACK.
THE CHILDREN ARE GONE. IN THEIR PLACES STAND
CATHY AND HEATHCLIFF, FULL GROWN NOW. HE
IS TALLER THAN SHE BY A FULL HEAD.

CATHY

How many sunsets have we watched from here,
Heathcliff?

HEATHCLIFF

Too many to count! This is the only time it has
made me sad.

CATHY

Yes! I wish once we might have brought father
here with us.

HEATHCLIFF

It will be different now he's gone. Why did he
die? He was good.

CATHY

Perhaps he is better off. He was ill for so long.

HEATHCLIFF

He loved us too much to want to leave us.

CATHY

I think he loved you better than he did Hindley
and me — his own children.

Summary of Action: Heathcliff declares that Hindley hates him.
"He hates me, too," replies Cathy, "but it should make no difference, even if he is now master of Wuthering Heights."

Hindley arrives, and quarrels with Cathy and Heathcliff. He orders both back, for "there's work to be done". They defy him, here on "their place", Peniston Crag. Hindley leaves when Heathcliff threatens him with violence. "But then, Cathy, he will get you away from me." She declares she will never leave Heathcliff, and he responds that she is his "excuse for being".

"Oh, Heathcliff, nothing can part us now! I'll find a way for us to be together always! Come! We shall get back home!"

As they start to leave the Crag, Cathy sprains her ankle. The nearest house is Thrushcross Grange, home of Edgar and Isabella Linton, whom Cathy considers snobbish.

But Heathcliff carries Cathy to the Grange, where the young Edgar is reading, while Isabella plays the spinet.

Cathy is received graciously, and it is arranged that she stay there until her ankle heals. Heathcliff is antagonistic, and finally leaves, further enraged when he sees that Cathy has begun to be charmed by the beauty and comfort of the Grange. FADE OUT.

FADE IN, Wuthering Heights. It is five weeks later. Nellie is cleaning the room, as Hindley watches. He is contemptuous of her efforts. They give us the exposition that Edgar has fallen in love with Cathy, while Cathy is strongly attracted to him and to his luxurious way of life. When Hindley talks of Cathy's interest in Edgar, Heathcliff attacks him violently. Hindley taunts him that Cathy will marry Edgar, because he is a gentleman, while Heathcliff is a "beast". Heathcliff, however, is positive that once she is home, Cathy will accept things with him on the old basis.

Very much dressed up as a lady of fashion, Cathy arrives, with Edgar. Her first request is for Heathcliff.

HEATHCLIFF ADVANCES TO HER SIDE. HE IS A SORRY PICTURE NEXT TO THE DAPPER AND ELEGANT LINTON. BUT CATHY KISSES HIM. THEN SHE DRAWS BACK.

CATHY

Why, how black and cross you look, Heathcliff!

HINDLEY

Shake hands with her, man! That is permitted —

HEATHCLIFF (SNATCHING AWAY HIS HAND)
You needn't have touched me! I shall be as dirty
as I please! I like to be dirty, and I will be dirty!
HINDLEY (LAUGHING)
At last, you see him as he is — more animal than
man!
HEATHCLIFF RUSHES FROM THE ROOM. CATHY
LOOKS AFTER HIM.
CATHY
Do not dare to call him an animal. For all you
know, he may be a prince in disguise. His father
may well have been the Emperor of China, his
mother an Indian Queen!
HINDLEY (LAUGHING)
My horse needs shoeing. If you don't mind, I
shall go and have your prince attend to this royal
task. (HE EXITS)

Summary of Action: Cathy sends Nellie to get a bit of lace as a
present for Isabella. Edgar proposes marriage to her, but she asks
that she not be required to answer at once. Nellie returns with
the lace. Edgar leaves.

CATHY RUSHES TO NELLIE AND KNEELS BESIDE HER.
CATHY
Oh, Nellie, Nellie! He has asked me to marry
him! And I must give him an answer! What shall
it be?
NELLIE
Do you love him?
CATHY
Who can help it? Of course I do.
NELLIE
Why?
CATHY
Well, because he's handsome, and pleasant to be
with.
NELLIE
Bad.

CATHY

And because he's young and cheerful.

NELLIE

Worse!

DURING THIS LAST SPEECH OF NELLIE'S, HEATHCLIFF
HAS COME INTO THE ROOM, AND STANDS IN BACK OF
THE BENCH WHERE THE TWO ARE SITTING. AND SO
HE HEARS EVERYTHING THAT CATHY SAYS.

CATHY

And he will be rich. I shall be the greatest woman
in the neighborhood! I shall be proud of having
such a husband.

NELLIE

Worst of all! And now, say how you love him!

CATHY

As anybody loves! You're silly, Nellie.

NELLIE

Not at all! Answer!

CATHY

I think he will make me happy! I think I can
make him happy!

NELLIE

Then where is the obstacle?

CATHY

Here! (ONE HAND STRIKES ON HER FOREHEAD AND
THE OTHER ON HER BREAST) And here! In which-
ever place my soul lives. In my soul, and in my
heart, Nellie, I know it is wrong!

NELLIE

But why, child? Why?

CATHY

It should be heaven for me to marry Edgar
Linton. And yet I've no more business to accept
him than I have to be in heaven! I belong to
Heathcliff! And yet it would degrade me to marry
him now —

CU OF HEATHCLIFF'S FACE DISTORTED WITH GRIEF
AND ANGER. HE TURNS AND LEAVES.

CATHY

He's more myself than I am. Whatever our souls
are made of, his and mine are like one flame!
Edgar's is as different as a moonbeam from
lightning! I am Heathcliff! He's always, always
in my mind! Not as a pleasure, any more
than I am always a pleasure to myself, but as
my own being! And yet, if he and I were
married, we should be beggars! But, if I marry
Edgar, I can aid Heathcliff to rise and place him
out of my brother's power.

NELLIE

That is the worst motive yet for you to marry
Mr. Linton.

Summary of Action: A storm has risen. Hindley rushes in, in a
maniacal fury. Heathcliff has gone on Hindley's best horse! Cathy
collapses, crying "Oh, Heathcliff! I cannot live without you —
now and forever!"

FIRST COMMERCIAL BREAK

Part Two

Summary of Action: FADE IN: Wuthering Heights Room, Three
Years Later. The place is in terrible condition, dirty, run-down.
Nellie greets Joseph as he returns from an attempt to buy food,
on credit, which has been refused him. Hindley enters, an empty
liquor bottle in his hand. It is revealed that Cathy has married
Edgar Linton, and lives in luxury at the Grange.

At the moment of ignominy, Heathcliff returns. He is hand-
somely dressed. Hindley shouts that he is not welcome at Wuthering Heights. But Heathcliff says, "The fortune I carry with me
may compensate for my unwelcome!" The debauched Hindley
agrees to let Heathcliff stay in return for Heathcliff's financial
support. As Heathcliff pulls out a full bottle of wine and offers
it to Hindley, we CROSS FADE to the drawing room at Thrushcross
Grange.

Here we see a calm domestic scene. Edgar is reading. Cathy,

now his wife, works at embroidery. Isabella plays on the spinet.

The scene set, Nellie enters in great agitation. Asking to see Cathy alone, she reveals that Heathcliff has returned, with great wealth. Her words are scarcely spoken when Heathcliff himself arrives. He is let into the house by Isabella (a significant detail, in view of their future relationship). Isabella, who has not recognized the "new" Heathcliff, is instantly attracted to him.

Cathy has rushed Nellie away before Heathcliff's entrance into the drawing room, and now she asks Isabella to leave, so that Cathy and Heathcliff are alone together.

They embrace passionately, as if they had never been parted. There are mutual recriminations, but the final result is the inference that they will keep loving each other, although Cathy is "not free." Heathcliff leaves on a vow not to wait much longer for Cathy.

Isabella has watched Heathcliff's departure, crouched on the stairs, looking through the bannisters. She runs to the distraught Cathy, asking "Do you not find him fascinating? I do!"

Cathy's reply maintains the suspense: "Yes! I always have!" FADE OUT.

FADE IN, the kitchen at Wuthering Heights. Heathcliff and Hindley are playing at dice. Hindley is drinking heavily. In a final throw, Heathcliff wins Wuthering Heights from the debauched Hindley. In his rage, Hindley — taunting Heathcliff — gives us the exposition that months have passed since Heathcliff's return, and that his and Cathy's behavior with each other has become an open scandal. Angered, Heathcliff warns Hindley not to extend his "spying" to Peniston Crag.

Through a FADE OUT, FADE IN we are at Peniston Crag. Cathy is climbing to the summit, calls back to Heathcliff, who soon appears. (Technically, Cathy is shown first in order to give the actor playing Heathcliff time to move from the kitchen set to the Crag set.)

Cathy and Heathcliff exchange bitter reproaches. Hers are that Heathcliff is cynically out to marry Isabella, a naïve little thing bewitched by the magnificent Heathcliff. His are that Cathy learned to "love" Edgar Linton, so why shouldn't he "love" Isabella Linton? They work themselves up to a declaration of passionate love.

HEATHCLIFF WHIPS A KNIFE OUT OF HIS POCKET.
HE MAKES A CUT ON HIS ARM UNTIL HE DRAWS BLOOD.
HEATHCLIFF

See! If you love me, let your blood flow along
with mine, and stain the heather at our feet, so
that we are joined together forever, here, for
always! (HE TAKES HER ARM, TRIES TO CUT HER)
CATHY

No! No! (SHE IS FRIGHTENED AND RUNS AWAY)
HEATHCLIFF

So you can't bear it after all, can you, Cathy?
You cannot bear the thought that love is pain
and desolation and despair. Well, you will know,
as I have known!
IT IS ALMOST DARK NOW ON THE CRAG. ALL WE CAN
SEE IS THE DIM OUTLINE OF HEATHCLIFF AGAINST
THE SKY, AS WE FADE OUT.

Summary of Action: FADE IN, Wuthering Heights, night. Hindley,
in a drunken stupor, prays for strength to kill Heathcliff. Heathcliff enters, dressed for a ball at the Grange, where he is to be the
guest of honor, at Isabella's invitation.

DISSOLVE to the Grange, where Heathcliff and Isabella are dancing, among other guests. Isabella is fascinated by Heathcliff.
Cathy, dancing with Edgar, is profoundly disturbed, and tries to
warn Edgar of Heathcliff's sinister intentions.

The scene moves into the garden, where Cathy, alone with
Isabella, warns her against Heathcliff. Isabella accuses Cathy of
jealousy. At once, Heathcliff enters. Cathy speaks to him, jests
that Isabella has boasted she can win him, and destroy Cathy's
memory in Heathcliff's heart. Isabella denies this vehemently.
Cathy grabs her arm, and Isabella scratches Cathy. Edgar enters;
Cathy appeals to him to control Isabella. Then she leaves, in
anger, followed by Edgar.

Left alone with Isabella, Heathcliff settles the fact that they two
will marry, in a manner which is clearly brutal to us, the audience,
but which goes unobserved by Isabella, infatuated with Heathcliff. We know that Heathcliff still loves Cathy with a tormenting
passion. FADE OUT.

FADE IN. Cathy's bedroom, that night. Cathy upbraids Edgar for his lack of control of Isabella. When he mildly reproves Cathy for her behavior, she flies into a rage, a rage which reveals to us that she still loves Heathcliff. They quarrel, and at the quarrel's height, Nellie enters. She brings a letter from Isabella. Isabella and Heathcliff have eloped! Catherine falls fainting, crying "No! No!"

SECOND COMMERCIAL BREAK

Part Three

Summary of Action: FADE IN, Cathy's bedroom at the Grange. It is some months later. Cathy has been ill ever since Isabella's elopement with Heathcliff. Finally she sends Nellie to Wuthering Heights, to bring back personal word of Heathcliff and Isabella.

At Wuthering Heights, Nellie is horrified to find Isabella aged, unkempt, slatternish. For such has been Heathcliff's effect on Isabella, who tells Nellie, "The single pleasure I can imagine is to die!"

Heathcliff corners Nellie, demands word of Cathy. Nellie says, "She wants only to forget you!" Heathcliff refuses to believe this. The scene ends with Heathcliff saying, "I must see her! I shall come to her of my own!"

Later that night, Edgar consults the doctor about Cathy. The doctor is pessimistic: "It is a sickening of the soul that she has."

In Cathy's bedroom, Cathy receives in horror Nellie's report about Wuthering Heights. "How much was *I* to blame for this?"

When Edgar comes to bid her good night, she sends him away almost at once. A strange excitement possesses her. She feels she is going to die.

Edgar is scarcely gone, when Cathy hears a noise at her window. Looking out, she sees Heathcliff in the garden, cries to him: "Stay where you are! I'll come to you!" She goes, over Nellie's protest.

HEATHCLIFF TAKES HER IN HIS ARMS AND KISSES
HER PASSIONATELY.

HEATHCLIFF

Oh, Cathy! Oh, my life! How can I bear it?

CATHY

You have broken my heart, Heathcliff. You have
killed me — and thriven on it, I think. How
strong you are! How many years do you mean to
live after I am gone?

HEATHCLIFF

Cathy, don't!

CATHY

I wish I could hold you, till we both were dead.
Will you forget me? Will you be happy when I
am in the earth? Will you say, twenty years
from now, that's the grave of Catherine Earnshaw?
I loved her, long ago, but it is past. Will you
say that, Heathcliff?

HEATHCLIFF

Don't torture me! Is it not enough for your
infernal selfishness, that while you are at peace,
I shall writhe in the torments of hell?

CATHY

I shall not be at peace, and I'm not bequeathing
you to torment! I only wish us never to be
parted. I shall take you with me, Heathcliff,
within my soul!

HEATHCLIFF (HE HOLDS HER MORE TIGHTLY)
Why did you betray your own heart, Cathy?

CATHY (VERY FAINTLY, SHE IS FAILING NOW, HE
HAS TO HOLD HER UP)

It's always been too late for us! Remember me,
Heathcliff! Be near to me in my death! I loved
you, and I lost you, and now you've lost me!
Surely there must be some place — where we can
be together — in peace!

THE LAST WORDS ARE MERELY SIGHED. SHE DIES.
HE FEELS HER DEAD WEIGHT IN HIS ARMS AND LAYS
HER GENTLY ON THE GROUND. HE STANDS SUDDENLY,
GAZING DOWN AT HER.

HEATHCLIFF

Who talks of peace? May you wake in torment,

Cathy! (WILDLY) Catherine Earnshaw, may you
not rest, as long as I am living! You said I killed
you! Haunt me, then! Let your ghost be with
me always! Let it drive me mad! Only do not
leave me in this abyss, where I cannot find you!
Oh God, it is unutterable! I cannot live without
my life, I cannot live without my soul!
HE KNEELS, CLASPING HER TO HIM, AS WE FADE OUT.
FADE IN, WUTHERING HEIGHTS, AS IT WAS IN THE
FIRST SCENE. HINDLEY DRUNK AT THE TABLE,
AGED AND DISSIPATED. ISABELLA AN OLD LADY.
NELLIE VERY, VERY OLD. IT IS SNOWING OUTSIDE.
HINDLEY (TO ISABELLA)
I remember, dear sister, when Nellie, here, looked
like your mother. But now see what time has
done — time and Heathcliff, our mortal enemy!
Nellie could be your sister.
ISABELLA
And you my father!
HINDLEY
But *he* does not age! The devil in him keeps him
young! For twenty years we have waited, but
he'll never die. . . .
JUST THEN, JOSEPH COMES RUSHING IN, TERRIFIED.
JOSEPH
I've seen him! Up at Miss Cathy's grave on the
Crag! Digging away at it with all his might.
NELLIE
He's mad! He must have been out all night in
this storm! We must go to him, Joseph!
HINDLEY (LAUGHING)
It won't kill him.
ISABELLA
Maybe this is it. Perhaps she's got him at last.
Let's drink on it, Hindley!
SHE TAKES A DRINK FROM HIS BOTTLE. THEY BOTH
LAUGH HYSTERICALLY AS NELLIE AND JOSEPH
RUSH OUT.

FADE IN ON PENISTON CRAG. IT IS SNOWING VERY
HARD. THE WIND IS HOWLING. HEATHCLIFF IS
KNEELING AT CATHY'S GRAVE TRACING HER NAME
CARVED ON THE STONE WITH HIS FINGERS. HE IS
MOANING LIKE AN ANIMAL, SAYING HER NAME OVER
AND OVER AGAIN.

HEATHCLIFF

Cathy! Cathy! Cathy! It's been a long time!
You've come to me often, but why haven't you
taken me with you? The nights I've left the
window open for you, why didn't you lead me out
after you? Oh, my darling, take pity on me!
There has not been a day when I have not felt
you near me. But now, tell me I can rest my cheek
against yours at last, that we are together for
always! Oh, Cathy, my love, my love!

AND HE DOES LAY HIS HEAD AGAINST THE STONE, AS
IF IT WERE A LIVING BEING. HE GASPS, AND FALLS
LIFELESS ON THE GRAVE.

WE CUT TO THE FACES OF JOSEPH AND NELLIE,
TERRIFIED BY WHAT THEY SEE. NELLIE WANTS TO
RUSH FORWARD, BUT THE OLD MAN STOPS HER.
IT IS TOO LATE.

AND THEN WE SEE IN PLACE OF THE HEADSTONE
AND THE FIGURE OF HEATHCLIFF ON THE GRAVE, TWO
SILHOUETTES ON THE CRAG . . . HEATHCLIFF AND
CATHY, HAND IN HAND, FACING A GREY SKY.

THE END

COMMENT ON ADAPTATION OF *Wuthering Heights*

The adaptor's first job is to determine the basic story, which is:
the love between Heathcliff and Catherine Earnshaw from their
first meeting as children until their reunion in death (as conceived
by Emily Brontë). Anything not relevant to this basic story must
be discarded.

The second job is to cast the *story for television* within the time
limits (at most, fifty-five minutes), and under the conditions of a
"live" production as opposed to one on film. Inseparable from this

second job is the determining of the sets in which the basic story must be told, and *can* be told. For instance, the incident in the novel of Catherine's being chased by the bulldog and finally seized by the ankle is impossible in "live" television, obviously. Yet this incident motivates Catherine's being introduced to the Lintons and to her staying at the Grange for five weeks. This motivation is indispensable to the basic story. The adaptor substituted the incident of Catherine's spraining her ankle and of being carried to the Grange by Heathcliff, which incident fulfills the need *in essence*.

Similarly, the incident Emily Brontë uses of Heathcliff digging up Catherine's coffin, opening the lid, and looking at the long-dead body of Catherine is too horrible for a general television audience. It shows, however, the indissoluble bond between Heathcliff and Catherine, dead or alive. To convey the feeling of this bond, the adaptor uses (at a different and, for television, a more suitable spot in the story) the incident of Heathcliff's slashing his wrist, in his desire to mingle his blood with Catherine's as a symbol of their soul-union. The essence of Heathcliff's burning desire is conveyed.

Perceiving that the love story of Heathcliff and Catherine is the basic story, and working under the knowledge of "live" television and time limitations, the adaptor dropped entirely the story of the second Catherine, the daughter of Catherine Earnshaw and Linton, because, strictly speaking, this whole second section of the novel has *nothing to do* with the love story of Heathcliff and Catherine. It is, in a sense, merely a delaying of the fulfillment of the love story, in the death of Heathcliff and his reunion in spirit with Catherine. (Those who remember the motion picture version of "Wuthering Heights" will recall that it, too, ended with the death of the first Catherine, Catherine Earnshaw.)

From a practical production and time limitation standpoint, it would be impossible to present *the entire novel* as an hour-length (fifty-five minutes) "live" television play.

The adaptor's all-over job, therefore, is to present the *essence* of the novel, the basic story, to repeat, which begins with the meeting of Heathcliff and Catherine and ends with their reunion after death.

Part of this essence is re-creating the spirit, the atmosphere of the supernatural, of doom and high tragedy, which pervade the novel. As you have read the television script, it is hoped that you did so, bearing in mind the contribution that sets, costumes, and lighting and sound effects (including music) make.

It is impractical, for modern audiences, to reproduce the dialogue of the novel, with its high-flown "literary" style, and with the unintelligible (to us) dialect of, say, the character Joseph. At the same time, the adaptor must not write in a strictly modern idiom, which would impair the "feeling" of the time, historically, in which the novel is set. The adaptor, therefore, avoided all modern expressions, all modern contractions of speech, any possible anachronisms which destroy the "believability" of the play on its own terms as set forth by the original author, Emily Brontë. Brontë's dialogue was meant to be read, not spoken. The spoken dialogue must convey the feeling, the sense, the atmosphere and the fact — rapidly, succinctly, and characterizing-ly.

Ever so much more than in a novel, in a play, and particularly in a television play, the mood and style must be set *at once*. Therefore, the first thing we see on our television screen is a "mood" scene which also acts as a "narrative hook", when Heathcliff, at Catherine's grave at the foot of Peniston Crag, soliloquizes and states the theme (thereby creating suspense) of the story: When will he and Catherine be re-united, in death? Note that the location of Catherine's grave is at the foot of the crag instead of in the churchyard, a dramatic license which adds very much pictorially, and which ties-in with the later development of the story when the most intense love scenes between Heathcliff and Catherine are played on Peniston Crag. Practically, the locating of the grave at the foot of the crag saves another set — the churchyard — which in the television play would serve no other purpose than to show the grave as it was in the novel. The process of *condensation* is at work, heightening the dramatic effect of the love story, and, practically, cutting down the cost of production.

Emily Brontë herself used the flashback technique in telling her story, so it is natural and logical that the television play should be told — in one long flashback. And Brontë also used the "narrative hook" which set the mood, and at greater length, in her scene with Lockwood at the window of Catherine's former bedroom at Wuthering Heights, when the ghost of Catherine pleads to be let into the room. In fact, only in this scene does Lockwood justify his presence in the television play, for he disappears thereafter, having served the purpose of motivating the flashback into the story. You will recall that in the novel, Lockwood serves throughout as the listener to whom the story is told by Nellie Dean, until the final chapters, in which, back in contemporary time, he appears again as an active participant.

Let's examine the more interesting transitions in the television script, in the light of what we have read in previous chapters of this book. At the same time, this progress through the television script will give us a chance to comment on major differences and condensations from the story as it is presented in full length in the novel. (The first DISSOLVE, to a *diorama*: A diorama is a miniature three-dimensional set which when photographed in a tight, close shot, seems to be full-scale.)

To make the transition back in time, the adaptor used Brontë's "obscurely, a child's face looking through the window", seen by Lockwood. The adaptor's use is different from Brontë's use of this device; but the TV play use is valid and in the spirit of the story. Here is an example of the original author's ideas used differently, but legitimately and effectively.

Into the next scene, Mr. Earnshaw's arrival by carriage is more pictorial and also more believable than Brontë's device of having had Mr. Earnshaw carry the child Heathcliff all the way from Liverpool. Possibly the size of the child actor playing Heathcliff was a consideration, also, for "believability". Note that at once, in this scene, emphasis is placed on the attraction between Cathy and Heathcliff, with Hindley's antipathy also established.

At the end of the scene between Joseph, Hindley and Nellie, when the dialogue is about Heathcliff and Cathy, the DISSOLVE (or CROSS FADE) is into the first of the scenes between Heathcliff and Cathy played on Peniston Crag, their "place". The adaptor took the dramatic license of establishing this "place", based on the frequent talk in the novel about the children's running wild over the moors. Visually the crag will always be identified with Cathy and Heathcliff, from now on. And at the end of their first scene, when they clasp hands, the MATCHED DISSOLVE into another pair of hands serves to establish a long elapse of time, from the childhood of Heathcliff and Cathy to their maturity. The scene continues; and into it, conflict in the form of Hindley is introduced very soon. In a few pages of dramatic dialogue, many pages of the novel are condensed. When Hindley leaves, in anger, after having given us the exposition that with his father's death, he is master of Wuthering Heights, the story moves forward swiftly to the introduction — through the sprained ankle — of Cathy and Heathcliff into the Linton household.

Note that in the TV play, the Hindley-Frances-Hareton story is dropped completely. This story is a sub-plot pointed toward the latter portion of the novel, when Hareton grows up to marry Catherine Earnshaw Linton's daughter, by that time the widow of Linton Heathcliff.

The next plot step in the Heathcliff-Catherine story is the Linton household complication, which follows immediately. Isabella and Edgar Linton, major characters both, are introduced. The transition into the following necessary scene, back at Wuthering Heights, is a "normal" one of FADE OUT, FADE IN.

The next plot step in the basic story is to marry Catherine to Edgar Linton. Edgar proposes at once, in the Wuthering Heights scene, and leaves Catherine to discuss the eventualities with Nellie. Here the adaptor has taken the Brontë dialogue between Cathy and Nellie fairly literally, although with some cutting. And out of this scene (when Heathcliff overhears Cathy's remark that to marry him would "degrade" her) develops the next plot step, Heathcliff's disappearance, a disappearance lasting three years.

Consider how undeviatingly the adaptor is carrying forward the basic story, omitting *all* elements of the novel which do not so carry forth the story.

The knowledge that Heathcliff has fled closes the first act of the three-act structure, with the emphasis on Catherine's despair — despair even in the face of her determination to marry Edgar Linton.

ACT II. The adaptor had a choice: to open the new act with a scene at the Grange, showing Catherine married to Edgar; or to bring Heathcliff back, as a menace to the marriage which we can assume (from the First Act) has occurred. However, the first new *additional* development is Hindley's financial near-ruin. Therefore, the adaptor opened the new act at Wuthering Heights, establishing Hindley's desperate state; then into this situation Heathcliff comes, rich, after a three-year absence. This arrangement of the scenes increases the suspense, for now a new, formidable Heathcliff must be reckoned with.

We can now enter the Linton drawing room, into a peaceful domestic scene between Isabella, Catherine and Edgar, knowing that a powerful new force is about to be exerted against the tranquility of the Grange.

It is interesting to note that at this point, in time, the story is about halfway finished, *both* in the novel and in the TV play, showing that television playwright and novelist are moving ahead at the same pace on a sure story line. (The story in the novel, that is, ending with the death of Catherine Earnshaw, which is also the ending of the TV play.)

When Heathcliff arrives at the Grange, Isabella's great interest in him is at once planted, since out of that interest will come, a little later on, another major plot step.

At this point, too, let it be pointed out that the characterizations are so firmly set in the likeness of the novel's originals, that though incident may differ greatly vis-a-vis play and novel, the essential story is firmly adhered to. The *essence* is being portrayed dramatically!

Now we have Catherine again declaring at the end of a major scene that she finds Heathcliff "fascinating", yet she is married; we have Isabella beginning to fall in love with Heathcliff; and we have Edgar bitterly opposed to everything connected with Heathcliff. Since all the action and suspense are centered in Heathcliff, the logical next step is for him to take. Through a "normal" FADE OUT, FADE IN, we move back to Wuthering Heights, to watch Heathcliff take that step. (And may your author point out the exactness with which the adaptor has followed the *unbreakable* rule: "Keep your action on the principals!")

Heathcliff is completing the winning of everything Hindley possesses, including the house, Wuthering Heights. Heathcliff takes a great step forward in his mad determination to dominate everything and everyone associated with Catherine. Hindley, half-crazed by his losses, points the way toward the next important "must scene": a meeting between Catherine and Heathcliff, with Heathcliff in his new role as master of Wuthering Heights. Naturally, this meeting takes place at Peniston Crag.

Through a "normal" FADE OUT, FADE IN, we move to Peniston Crag. Combined with a fierce love scene between Cathy and Heathcliff is the threat that he intends to marry Isabella. The adaptor took dramatic license in the incident of Heathcliff cutting his wrist to mingle their blood, but such license is justified in your author's opinion, as was discussed earlier: it is the swift, dramatic visual device to indicate the intensity of Heathcliff's passion.

FADE OUT, FADE IN. At Wuthering Heights, Hindley has grown more desperate, while Heathcliff dresses for a ball at Thrushcross Grange. (In the novel, he was never invited to a ball, which did not take place; but the next plot step demands that Edgar, Isabella, Catherine and Heathcliff play a climactic scene together.) A ball is the most sensible device to bring them together. The music, the festive atmosphere of the dance, heighten the quarrel between Catherine and Isabella over Heathcliff, and give action to what in the novel is a static scene, visually. The ball scene ends, in the garden, with the unmistakable implication that Heathcliff will marry Isabella. The transitions in these various scenes are "normal" FADE OUT, FADE IN and CUT.

It is logical to show the effect of the quarrel on Catherine. As she relates her side of it to Edgar, in her bedroom, Nellie arrives with Isabella's letter announcing her elopement with Heathcliff. It is the only possible plot development. Catherine's reaction, closing Act II, is a dead faint, as she screams "No . . . No!"

There remains the Third Act, which in both novel and TV play is one long death scene, with Catherine dying as a result of the elopement. In the novel, she dies in giving birth to a daughter, the "second Catherine"; but the TV play omits this birth in view of the end of the play. (One can only surmise that the virginal Emily Brontë was interested only in the result, never in the cause and process of the arrival of a baby, for one is forced to wonder when — in the midst of their extravagant language, and wild scenes together — the characters were in the mood to produce children.)

The plot step demanded is for Cathy and Heathcliff to confront each other. In the novel, Brontë gives many, many pages to a letter written by the repentant and suffering Isabella to Nellie Dean, telling what has happened to her. Since it is necessary, however, to finish off the Isabella story showing what happened to her, in the TV play the scene is acted out. After an opening scene establishing Cathy's mortal illness, through a "normal" FADE OUT, FADE IN, we move to Wuthering Heights and see the wreck that is Isabella, in relation both to Hindley and Heathcliff. However, this scene serves a double purpose: Nellie's news of Cathy's plight will send Heathcliff to Cathy.

FADE OUT, FADE IN, and we are back in Cathy's bedroom, where she is revealed as being much worse. Edgar's story is finished off: we see him faithful and grieving, to the end. He leaves; Heathcliff is heard outside. Dismissing Nellie, Cathy goes to Heathcliff, through a normal DISSOLVE. The death scene is played in the garden, perhaps for greater pictorial effect, but possibly also because the TV Code would frown on a presumed lover being in a married woman's bedroom. In content, this powerful scene uses much of the Brontë dialogue. It ends with Cathy's death and Heathcliff's lamentation over her body; and, technically, it runs long enough for the actors portraying Hindley, Isabella, Joseph and Nellie in the following scene to assume the make-up of advanced age. The age indicated visually (and the inferred passage of time) is talked about, also, further to point up the elapse of time; and Heathcliff's current actions are described by the rushing entrance and excited words of Joseph (in the role of the messenger in Greek plays). Hindley and Isabella ignore Joseph's news; thus, their story in relation to Heathcliff is ended. Joseph and Nellie rush out to find Heathcliff.

FADE OUT, FADE IN. Heathcliff is seen at Peniston Crag, at Cathy's grave, for the climactic action. In a wild monologue addressed to the dead and buried Catherine, a monologue which clarifies completely his action throughout the play, including the reason for his keeping open the window of Catherine's former bedroom at Wuthering Heights, Heathcliff works himself into a passion, and dies, on Cathy's grave.

Nellie and Joseph arrive; it is too late. We CUT to their faces, a technical CUT excluding Heathcliff, to allow the actor portraying Heathcliff time to move from the grave to the top of the Crag, where the actress portraying Catherine waits for him. The final shot of the play shows Heathcliff and Catherine silhouetted on top of the Crag; and the play is over. The structure completes its harmonious form with this final shot, which was also the opening shot, save only that in the opening, Heathcliff was alone.

The final shot is completely motivated by the passage in the novel, in which — after Heathcliff's burial — a little blubbering shepherd boy tells of seeing Heathcliff and "a woman, yonder, under t'nab". In short, Heathcliff and Catherine, united in death.

THE END

The basic story of a classic novel between 120,000 and 125,000 words long has been told in 50-odd minutes, through the skill of a television playwright using the technique peculiar to the medium.

ADAPTING THE SHORT STORY AND LONG STAGE PLAY

It would seem needlessly repetitious to go further into the technique of adaptations. What has been written in great detail in this chapter applies exactly to adapting the short story, except that it is inevitable that the number of master scenes will be less for the half-hour (22–24 minute) play; about the same, obviously, for the longer short story or long stage play adapted into the hour (52–55 minute) television play as for "Rise Up and Walk" and "Wuthering Heights."

Time is the controlling factor, without exception.

The fundamental procedure is to determine the basic story, then break it into master scenes; see which master scenes can be eliminated or condensed; arrange the final breakdown of master scenes which will still tell your story and also fit your time limit. Then write the dialogue.

By plan, the book, *Rise Up and Walk*, was broken down into master scenes in order to compare these with the master scenes of the television play. For contrast and to approach the problem from a different angle, for clarity, you are asked to read the novel, *Wuthering Heights*, then read the condensed television script for comparison.

SECURING MATERIAL FOR ADAPTATIONS

Special Note

The first draft of this chapter was submitted to Mr. Ross Donaldson, Supervisor of Literary Rights & Story Division for the National Broadcasting Company, Inc., New York. With complete graciousness, Mr. Donaldson and his assistant, Miss Mary Shea, read the chapter; then Mr. Donaldson listed certain qualifications to the original chapter. After serious consideration, I decided upon the plan of letting the chapter stand as it was written, with Mr. Donaldson's qualifications printed immediately following the section where each qualification applies. Some of the qualifications fit special cases only, as you will note. The intention is to supply you with the most complete information possible. If there seems to be contradiction, *both* sides of the contradiction may be true, as they apply to different circumstances. In other words, it is impossible to generalize on each aspect of the tangled copyright situation, national (American) and international. Each piece of material can be said to be a "special case," with its status vis-a-vis copyright to be determined under its own unique conditions.

Public Domain

Material "in the public domain" is what it says: public property. Any one can make any use of it he wants. "Wuthering Heights" is in the public domain, for instance.

Material enters the public domain in the United States at the end of the 56-year period of the American copyright. An author can copyright his work first for 28 years, then for a second and continuing 28-year period.

According to American law, every copyrighted work must state on its flyleaf (if published) that it *is* copyrighted, and give the year of the copyright. Unpublished material should also state on its title page that it is copyrighted, with the year; or that copyright has been applied for.

Therefore, you are reasonably safe in assuming that any published book which does *not* carry a copyright notice is in the public domain and so can be used by you without asking the permission of any one.

Mr. Donaldson's qualification

Some books published outside of this country bear no copyright date, but, under certain conditions, the material may not be in the public domain since it may have been published under other auspices in this country and be properly copyrighted. In this connection also: writers might find a story of Edgar Allan Poe (public domain) published in an anthology copyrighted 1954. The publisher has copyrighted this copy in order to protect new material or other material which is not in the public domain. The real test is to locate a copy of the material more than 56 years old, or to establish, through the copyright office in Washington, D.C., that it is "free."

For your guidance, the U.S. Copyright Office will undertake to search a copyright for you at the cost of an hourly fee. Inquiries should be addressed to the Register of Copyrights, Library of Congress, Washington, D.C.

In estimating the time when a copyrighted work enters the public domain, calculate 56 years from the date published, *and then add one year, to be safe* (unless you choose to have the copyright searched as described above). For instance, assume that a book carries the notice, "Copyright, 1898". Adding 56 years, we logically should say that the copyright expires in 1954. BUT — and it's a large *but* — the book may have been copyrighted *December 19, 1898,* so that the copyright would not expire until December 19, 1954. Suppose you assumed that on January 1, 1954, the book is in the public domain and wrote a television play based on it. If you offered your play for sale *before December 19, 1954,* you would be violating the copyright, and you would be legally vulnerable for your violation. Of course, there's no reason why privately you shouldn't write a television play on a copyrighted book at any time; the point is, you cannot offer it for sale without being liable to prosecution by the copyright owner.

Of course, the simplest and most sensible way is to secure permission from the copyright owner to adapt his material still protected by copyright.

International laws on copyrights and copyrights of countries other than the United States of America are heavily complicated. There are lawyers who do nothing else but function on copyright matters. A book or work which is in the public domain in the United States may not be in the public domain in another country. At present writing (1953), for instance, the works of Gilbert and Sullivan are in the American public domain, and the music (tragically enough) is being used for singing commercials. But in Great Britain, Gilbert and Sullivan are still protected by copyright, so that any television play based on their works might be sold and telecast in the United States, but not in Great Britain or the British Commonwealth, where the copyright has several years to run.

Mr. Donaldson's qualification

British copyright protection extends for 50 years, after the *death* of the author. This protection, of course, does not extend to British works copyrighted in this country (the United States). However, a television show produced in the United States which is to be distributed on Canadian television stations must give attention to the fact that material may be public domain in the United States but still protected in Commonwealth countries. The complication of international copyright law begins to be suggested by the fact that the French government has, by decree, given *perpetual* copyright protection to certain members of the French Academy and the profit therefrom goes either to the family or to charities, scholarships and the like.

For the television playwright unfamiliar with the intricacies of foreign and international copyright laws, it is suggested that he might stick to material on which the copyright and public domain status can be easily and quickly established beyond question. (Of course, it must be recognized that any American publication of a foreign work must be copyrighted under American law; the warning given above applies to the chance book or work which might be used, in a foreign edition or publication, as the basis for a television play.)

The field of public domain material has been thoroughly researched by readers and editors and established television playwrights. Therefore, unless you know for a *positive fact* that material you may be planning to adapt has not already been used, it is earnestly recommended that you check with the Story Departments of the networks, to find out if your proposed material is "free."

You may say that in asking a network Story Department executive about a public domain property, you risk losing it — that the Story Department executive will "take over" the material which you have found. The answer to this is that all such network personnel are persons of good will and integrity who are extremely unlikely to "betray" your request, your confidence.

However, if you don't share this opinion, you can take such protective measures as sending yourself a registered letter in which the whole transaction is described, *before* you write asking the network about the public domain material you wish to adapt. Then, if necessary, the registered letter could be opened in court as evidence of your prior claim (which is perhaps an ethical rather than a legal one). The Authors League of America and the Writers Guild of America have effective protection devices available to their members.

Mr. Donaldson's qualification

The device of posting a registered letter to oneself is fair protection of a program suggestion or other original idea. However, it seems to be of doubtful safety in the case of a person who suggests material for adaptation, and would likely hold up only if the submitter could prove that the network editor could not have known about the material except through his (the prospective adaptor's) communication.

I believe that trust propagates trust, and I believe equally strongly that it's better to find out ahead of time, whether or not your proposed public domain material is "free," rather than to write a television play which will represent a total waste of time and energy — when you discover that your material has already been used.

Mr. Donaldson's qualification

As suggested, both public domain and copyrighted material is thoroughly searched by television editors. Should the (prospective) writer stumble over an outstanding piece of material which has not been used on television, there may be good reason from the network point of view why it was not used. Somerset Maugham's story, from which the play and motion picture *Rain* were made, has not been presented on network television. Most motion picture companies acquire exclusive film rights when buying the material, with the result that, while we might obtain permission to do *Rain* on one station or by interconnected stations, we cannot acquire the necessary rights to distribute a kinescope to non-interconnected stations. (A kinescope is a film reproduction of a "live" telecast made in the network laboratories at the time of the "live" telecast.)

Copyrighted Material

The television playwright must secure permission to use any copyrighted work as the basis for a television play, or for any use whatsoever. (In preparing this book, I secured permission in writing from each author or publisher for every example taken from a published or performed work. These letters of permission were given to the publisher of this book for his permanent files. In some cases, the exact wording of the "permission" was dictated by the copyright owners, as in the case of Metro-Goldwyn-Mayer Studios and *On Borrowed Time,* and the Columbia Broadcasting System on the *television play* of *Wuthering Heights,* which, being a new and original work, can be copyrighted. You could write *your* version of the novel *Wuthering Heights,* as long as you did not use the copyrighted CBS script in any way whatsoever, except by permission.)

During the years of the growth of television, almost all material published has been examined minutely for possibilities of television adaptation. Every issue of practically all magazines is read as soon as it comes out, to see if it contains material suitable for adaptation. In short, you've got to be quick on the draw to beat some other aspirant to the best material, which usually is controlled by a literary agent or a publisher, as far as adaptation rights are concerned.

If you find a story you want to adapt, write to the editor of the publication in which it appears and ask him who controls the television rights and how this controller or owner can be reached. Ninety-nine times out of a hundred you will be referred to a literary agent.

If you read a book you want to adapt, write to the publisher and secure the same information.

After you've made contact with the owner or controller of the rights, it becomes a matter of negotiation, and, importantly, of your qualifications as adaptor. Always, of course, you can gamble, make an adaptation, send it to the owner of the material — and run the risk of acceptance or rejection. At any rate, *you will own no rights whatsoever in your adaptation,* if it has been made *without permission.* As has been said, the one virtue a speculative adaptation has, is that it *might* tip the scales in favor of the owner's granting you permission, on the strength of the excellence of your unsolicited work.

Mr. Donaldson's qualification

If a writer receives permission from an author or agent to adapt a work and offer it for sale, he still may not have an exclusive right of adaptation. Some authors have been free granting permission for their stories to be adapted for another medium and have given away the same rights to various people. Not long ago, I made all arrangements to acquire an adaptation of a story by a best-selling writer, being assured that the first writer was agreeable to granting us the necessary basic rights. A few days before rehearsal, we found that another network proposed to do the same story on the same evening as our (NBC) scheduled broadcast and that they had engaged a cast. Author number one had given another adaptor permission to sell his work and was aware of both productions but was unaware that he would be asked for exclusive license to his material for the purpose of our (NBC) broadcast.

While many editors and readers for television programs are searching published material of all kinds for possible television material, the field cannot be said to be covered completely. It is common practice for a television playwright to unearth a short story or an old play or a new novel he wants to adapt and to bring his new-found material to a program editor, and so secure the job of making the adaptation. In fact, in the early days of television, your author knew positively that one hour-length program was kept on the air by material discovered and brought in on a speculative basis by the eventual adaptor. In short, the television playwright was acting both as reader and playwright for this particular program, a condition which made the program's script editor's work infinitely lighter.

This practice is still followed, perhaps not on so great a scale as to keep one-hour-length programs running.

It is not necessary that you secure the original author's permission *to bring his material to the attention* of a script editor. All the networks, and all the big producing agencies and units maintain staffs of one or more persons who engage in "securing literary rights," and, since they are the ones to set the price to be paid, both to the original author and to you as playwright, they are the logical ones to negotiate for permission to use the original material — you are then assigned as playwright. The universal practice is to pay the original author so much for the right to use his material, and so much to you as the television playwright.

The question of ownership of a television play adapted from another author's material usually is a matter of negotiation between the original author and the adaptor. Or, ownership may be determined in accordance with the Minimum Basic Agreement between the networks and producing organizations and the Writers Guild of America (see Chapter 15, Selling). If you are a member of the Writers Guild of America, you will of course be subject to the contractual arrangements of the Minimum Basic Agreement. If you are not a member, your arrangements conceivably will be the matter of a private contract between you and the original author.

Mr. Donaldson's qualification

If all parties are acting in good faith and fairly, the problem of the "ownership" of the adaptation becomes academic. If the writer "owns his adaptation" he cannot use it without the permission from the owner of the basic work. Some agents have maintained that they must own all adaptation in order not to complicate a future motion picture or dramatic sale. This argument would have more strength if the "ownership" of an adaptation included any right to use it on the air — which it does not.

One final word: adaptations from other literary forms into television plays will always be with us; and the fees paid for them have supported many a television playwright.

But in an adaptation, there are *two* authors to be paid; the program's writing budget must be split two ways; original author and adaptor. Why not write an original television play, then, and collect the *entire fee?*

Your author admits it: if this book ever serves any one purpose, the purpose he desires most above all others is to stimulate the writing of *original* works for television, for they are the best hope for the growth of our miraculous medium of communication, education and entertainment.

14

The Documentary
Television Play

DOCUMENTARY DRAMATIC WRITING has as its purpose the presenting of the facts about a given situation or circumstance in dramatic
form, that is, with sound dramatic structure requiring a beginning, a middle and an end; identifiable characters; suspense, climaxes; and a clear resolution of the situation or circumstance —
all just like the plays you make up out of your own head. Sometimes the resolution (or denouement) can do no more than pose
a question: for instance, a documentary play on the hydrogen
bomb of necessity would end by asking, "What happens now, on
the basis of all the facts you have been given?" So, perhaps the
definition of a "documentary" should include the qualification that
the play (or motion picture or whatever) presents a *picture* (in
the sense of a study) of a factual situation or circumstance.

The newsreel of motion pictures, with its spoken commentary,
is the most elemental type of documentary. During the nineteen
thirties the Federal Theatre developed The Living Newspaper
technique for writing a stage play. One such play considered the
question and problems of the Agricultural Aid Administration,
under the title, *Triple A Ploughed Under*. "The March of Time,"
an elaboration of the newsreel technique, was in its concept and
execution entirely a documentary. From "The March of Time"
evolved such full-length documentary motion pictures as *The
Ramparts We Watch* and *The House on 92nd Street*. These two
motion pictures were full dramatic entertainments, meeting all
the structural demands of good drama listed above. They had

characters whom we followed through a story with a beginning, a middle and an end; and there was a clear and final resolution of the fate of these characters. Yet all the material was *factual*, and this material was made into a play by the skill of the playwright.

One successful documentary television play, *The 1000-Yard Look*, was based on the dispatches filed from Korea by the Associated Press foreign correspondent Hal Boyle, during the latter half of 1950 and the first half of 1951. This documentary television play was written by Don Ettlinger and Nelson Gidding, and was produced on the Pulitzer Prize Playhouse program.

First of all, naturally, the playwrights read all the dispatches Mr. Boyle had filed in the period stated. They also had the great advantage of being able to talk personally with Mr. Boyle. Their primary need was to decide upon the character or characters whom they would follow in a story which would present an accurate picture of the fighting American soldier in Korea.

The playwrights read the following dispatch, filed from Korea. This dispatch provided the title for the play, the principal character, and fundamental action.

SEPTEMBER 25, 1950.
THE SUPPLY TRUCK WAS LOADED WITH BADLY NEEDED GASOLINE. BUT AT ONE POINT ALONG THE RUTTED ROAD IT PAUSED WITH THE UNDEVIATING COURTESY OF THE BATTLE-FRONT TO PICK UP A SOLITARY, HITCHHIKING SOLDIER.

HE WAS A PRIVATE FIRST CLASS AND HE LOOKED LIKE A TIRED BATTLE STRAGGLER LOST FROM HIS COMPANY.

HE WAS A STOCKY YOUTH OF ABOUT 22 WITH BLUE EYES AND A STARE THAT COMBAT SOLDIERS CALL THE THOUSAND-YARD LOOK. IT IS AN EXPRESSION MEN OFTEN GET AFTER SUDDEN BATTLE SHOCK OR LONG EXPOSURE TO DANGER.

THE PRIVATE'S FACE WAS PALE BENEATH ITS TAN. HE WORE STAINED DUNGAREES AND THERE WAS NO HELMET OVER HIS FATIGUE CAP. HE CARRIED NEITHER WEAPON NOR CANTEEN, AND THAT WAS UNUSUAL, TOO, IN A FIGHTING ZONE.

HE CLIMBED LABORIOUSLY INTO THE BACK OF THE TRUCK. AS IT SWUNG SLOWLY ON UP THE HEAVY YELLOW ROAD HE SAT DOWN WEARILY AMONG THE GASOLINE CANS NEXT TO ANOTHER HITCHHIKER, AN A.P. CORRESPONDENT.

THE TWO SOON FELL TO TALKING. THE PRIVATE WAS
NERVOUS AND KEPT CLUTCHING HIS SIDES WITH BOTH ARMS
AS HE SPOKE. HE SAID THAT HE WAS ONE OF THE ENGI-
NEERS WHOSE JOB HAD BEEN TO STEER THE ASSAULT BOATS
THAT CARRIED THE DOUGHBOYS ACROSS THE NAKTONG.
"I WAS IN THE SECOND WAVE," HE SAID. "THEY SHOT
UP OUR BOAT WITH MACHINE GUNS AND IT WENT DOWN.
THEN A MORTAR SHELL HIT IN THE RIVER BY ME AND IT
SEEMED LIKE THE WATER WAS SQUEEZING ME TO DEATH."
THE PRIVATE HELD HIS CHEST AND COUGHED PAINFULLY
AND SPIT OVER THE SIDE OF THE TRUCK. HE SHOOK HIS
HEAD WHEN OFFERED A CIGARETTE.
"I BLACKED OUT AND I GUESS I WOULD HAVE DROWNED IF
SOME OF MY BUDDIES HADN'T PULLED ME INTO ANOTHER
BOAT," HE SAID. "DON'T REMEMBER ANYTHING ABOUT THE
NEXT 12 HOURS, EXCEPT STANDING IN A CHOW LINE SOME-
WHERE. THEN I CAME TO IN A HOSPITAL.
"THEY SAID I HAD CONCUSSION AND OUGHT TO STAY
THERE FOR AT LEAST A COUPLE OF DAYS. BUT I DIDN'T
WANT TO DOPE OFF ON MY OUTFIT -- NOT AT A TIME LIKE
THIS. SO I WAITED UNTIL BREAKFAST AND THEN I TOOK
OFF."
THEY TALKED FOR A WHILE THEN ABOUT THE KOREAN WAR
AND THE PRIVATE SAID HE WASN'T SURE JUST WHAT IT IS
ALL ABOUT. BUT HE SAID HE HAS SERVED THREE YEARS OF
A SIX-YEAR HITCH IN THE ARMY AND PLANNED TO SIGN UP
FOR ANOTHER SIX. AND HE MADE THE USUAL FRONTLINE
SOLDIERS' GRIPE ABOUT THE BEER RATION.
"WE HAVEN'T HAD ANY FOR FOUR DAYS," HE SAID.
"NOW, THEY OUGHT TO BE ABLE TO DO BETTER THAN THAT."
WHEN THE TRUCK HALTED TO LET HIM OFF, HE CLIMBED
DOWN SLOWLY. HE GRIPPED HIS CHEST, BENT OVER AND
COUGHED AND SPAT BETWEEN HIS WIDESPREAD FEET.
THEN HE STRAIGHTENED, SAID "SO LONG" AND WALKED
OFF TO REJOIN HIS UNIT.
AS THE TRUCK PULLED AWAY THE CORRESPONDENT GLANCED
AT WHERE THE PRIVATE STOOD. IN THE GOLDEN DUST
GLEAMED SEVERAL BRIGHT DROPS. THEY WERE RED.
END OF THE DISPATCH

In the condensed documentary television play which follows,

Gil Evers is the principal character, modeled after the 22-year-old described in the dispatch you have just read.

The Thousand-Yard Look
Act One

VIDEO	AUDIO
	BOYLE
FADE IN:	It's been over two months
MED. SHOT — HAL BOYLE	since I returned from covering
AT DESK	the Korean war, but it's still
	very much with me. I re-
	member those ugly brown
	hills and the heat and the
	cold and guns and death.
	But most of all I remember
	the faces of the men who are
	fighting the war. Young
	faces — growing old fast.
	I remember fear on those
	faces and fatigue and courage
	and a grim determination
	to keep going somehow.
	And I remember faces with
	the thousand-yard look.
	(MUSIC . . . FADE INTO B.G.)
	That's a special look anyone
	who has fought in Korea, or
	reported the fighting, knows
	about. You'll know about
	it, too, after tonight because
	you are going to see a story
	of the G.I.'s in Korea —
DISSOLVE TO:	
(FILM) SHOTS OF MEN	
DEBARKING AT PUSAN,	
EQUIPMENT BEING UNLOADED,	
ETC.	

BOYLE'S VOICE
— some of the first soldiers who debarked in Pusan ten months ago, green, untried occupation troops from Japan. Back in July, 1950, the world was sure it was just a matter of weeks before 'the Korean situation' was cleaned up. The world was sure of it —

DISSOLVE TO:
(FILM OR LIVE)
AN ARMY TRUCK MOVING UP A DUSTY KOREAN ROAD. IN THE BACK OF THE TRUCK ARE ABOUT NINE SOLDIERS

BOYLE'S VOICE
— and so were the G.I.'s who were moving up toward the fighting —

CUT TO:
(LIVE) ANGLE ON THE SQUAD OF MEN IN THE BACK OF THE TRUCK AS IT BUMPS ALONG THE RUTTED ROAD. THEY ARE DRESSED IN FATIGUES, THEIR HELMETS PUSHED BACK ON THEIR HEADS IN THE HEAT.

BOYLE'S VOICE
— like squad number two in the third Platoon of B Company.

CAMERA STARTS TO PAN DOWN THE LINE OF MEN BEGINNING WITH WYOMING, AND MARCUM. WYOMING, CLEAR-EYED

WESTERNER, MARCUM, NERVOUS
AND YOUNG.

> BOYLE'S VOICE
> — pretty representative of the
> first troops that hit Korea.

CAMERA PANS TO
CORPORAL HASTINGS, LEAN,
TACITURN, EXPERTLY
ROLLING A CIGARETTE.

> BOYLE'S VOICE
> . . . The Corporal, the only
> vet in the bunch.

CAMERA PANS TO
MITCH, CALM AND
SERIOUS, PUFFING ON
PIPE, STEEL-RIMMED
GLASSES

> BOYLE'S VOICE
> . . . Mitch transferred from a
> desk job to the infantry.

CAMERA PANS TO
PETE, AN INTENSE ITALIAN
AMERICAN, INDUSTRIOUSLY
POLISHING HIS RIFLE

> BOYLE'S VOICE
> . . . Pete was an eager beaver
> — on his seventeenth birth-
> day down at the recruiting
> office before it opened.

CAMERA PANS TO ZUG,
AN ELONGATED ARKANSAS
HILLBILLY, CONCENTRATING
WITH SOME DIFFICULTY
ON A COMIC BOOK.

> BOYLE'S VOICE
> Zug — straight from a share
> cropper's farm in Arkansas.

CAMERA PANS TO
CORB. COCKY, BRASH,

TOUGH, BUT LIKABLE.
HE LIGHTS A LARGE CIGAR
AND FLIPS AWAY THE MATCH.

BOYLE'S VOICE (WITH A SMILE)
Corb. Caught in a raid in a
Chicago bookie joint and
given his choice of ninety
days or joining up.

CAMERA PANS TO JOE.
LATE TEENS. QUIET,
KIND, SLOW SPOKEN,
NICE-LOOKING. HE IS
STUDYING A USAFI
PAMPHLET.

BOYLE'S VOICE (FONDLY)
Joe Cecilwich — son of a coal
miner who had it all figured.
A hitch in the Army, then to
agricultural school under the
G.I. bill.

CAMERA PANS PAST AN EMPTY
SPACE IN THE BACK OF THE
TRUCK AND FINALLY TO GIL,
SEATED APART FROM THE
OTHERS, IN THE CORNER NEXT
TO THE CAB OF THE TRUCK.
ABOUT TWENTY, HE SITS GRIMLY
LOOKING OFF INTO SPACE AS
HE SMOKES.

BOYLE'S VOICE
And Gil. Gil Evers from
Iowa. Take a good look at
him. He's different from the
rest. Gil was drafted —
right out of college. It was
a pretty fast change for Gil —
almost too fast.
(MUSIC . . . THE MUSIC FADES
OUT)

Summary of Action: B Company moves up toward the front, with characteristic gripes and personal remarks, angled by the playwrights to show Gil in isolation from the camaraderie. Soon the MPs make the Company abandon the trucks and walk, because of the danger. This scene is all atmosphere and characterization of the principal characters, particularly of Gil and Joe.

Here we stop for a dispatch, dated August 30, 1950:

THE AMERICAN ARMY HERE IS BEING CAPTURED, ALMOST AGAINST ITS WILL, BY A YOUNGER AND MORE NUMEROUS FORCE.

IT IS SLOWLY BECOMING THE PRISONER OF THE CHILDREN OF KOREA.

IN EVERY COUNTRY IN WHICH THE GI HAS FOUGHT, HE USUALLY MAKES FAST FRIENDS WITH THE KIDS FIRST. TO THEM HE IS A MILITARY CROESUS WITH ENDLESS STORES OF CHEWING GUM, CHOCOLATE BARS AND CANDY MINTS, AND FEW COULD WITHSTAND THESE MAGIC BRIBES LAVISHLY DEALT OUT.

END OF DISPATCH

VIDEO	AUDIO
ANGLE ON A LITTLE KOREAN BOY AT THE SIDE OF THE ROAD, DIRTY, BAREFOOT, AND IN TATTERS. UNNOTICED, HE WATCHES THE SQUAD SOBERLY. HE TAKES A FEW TENTATIVE STEPS TOWARD THEM. ANGLE ON CORPORAL	
	CORPORAL Let's go, Zugsmith — let's go —
ANGLE ON ZUG, WHO IS FROWNING DOWN AT THE LITTLE KOREAN BOY WHO STARES UP AT HIM APPEALINGLY.	

ZUG

I think this here little tyke's
hungry. (HE REACHES IN
HIS SHIRT POCKET, BRINGS OUT
A CANDY BAR, AND HANDS IT
TO THE LITTLE KOREAN BOY,
WHO SOLEMNLY BOWS IN
APPRECIATION)

CORPORAL'S VOICE

What's a matter, Zugsmith?
You gone deef? Come on . . .
(UNHURRIEDLY, WITH A LAST
WORRIED FROWN AT THE BOY,
ZUG STARTS DOWN THE ROAD)

Summary of Action: We come in on the platoon command post,
before Company B arrives. An "old Army" sergeant talks on the
phone, tells his captain (not seen) that a patrol he sent out has
not returned, nor has B company arrived. But at this moment B
company does arrive. The sergeant receives from the newcomers
an account of their troubles in reaching the command post. In
turn, the sergeant goes more into detail about the patrol which
has not returned, having been out now, under command of the
lieutenant, for seven hours. He is worried. Gil's behavior attracts
the sergeant's attention: once again, the playwrights center interest on him in order to paint his isolation from his comrades (in
view of the very end of the play, when Gil has totally identified
with his buddies). There is more characterizing dialogue among
the men themselves, as in this quiet beginning there is time and
room — before the plot gets strongly underway. We are held
by the atmosphere, the characters, and by the one strong note of
suspense supplied by the missing patrol. We sense that soon *our*
characters will be out on a patrol, possibly lost, certainly facing
great and unknown dangers. The little Korean boy has followed
along, and his lack of shoes arouses the concern of Joe and Zug.
(The little Korean boy is used as a "running gag" for humor and
pathos, all through the play.)

Dispatch dated August 29, 1950

A SOLDIER HAS TO FIND SOME WAY TO KILL THE BOREDOM
OF BATTLE.

ONE DAY I VISITED A FORWARD COMMAND POST IN A
GULLY NEAR THE NAKTONG RIVER. THE POSITION HAD BEEN
HEAVILY SHELLED AND MORTARED ALL DAY. ONE SHELL—
BURST A HALF HOUR BEFORE HAD KILLED AN OFFICER AND
WOUNDED HIS DRIVER.

THOSE IN THE GULLY WERE HUNCHED AGAINST ITS SIDES
FOR PROTECTION AND THEIR EYES HELD A TENSE EXPRES-
SION. BUT ONE SOLDIER ACROSS THE WAY WAS LEANING
COMFORTABLY AGAINST THE BANK AND FROWNING INTENTLY
AT A PAPER—BOUND BOOK.

I STARTED TO WALK ACROSS TO HIM. A SHELL HIT SOME
HUNDRED YARDS OR SO BEHIND US JUST THEN.

THE GULLY SEEMED SUDDENLY WIDER AND BARER THAN A
SIX—LANE FREEWAY.

"WHAT ARE YOU READING?" I CALLED.

THE SOLDIER GOT UP, BRUSHED OFF SOME DUST, AND
STROLLED UNCONCERNEDLY OVER TO WHERE I CROUCHED.

HE HELD OUT A COMIC BOOK CALLED "THE BATMAN." I
ASKED HIM IF IT WAS VERY EXCITING.

"JUST SO—SO," HE SAID PLACIDLY. "BUT IT HELPS
FILL IN THE TIME."

THEN HE STROLLED BACK, LEANED AGAINST THE BANK AND
READ ON IN SEARCH OF ADVENTURE.

END OF DISPATCH

VIDEO	AUDIO
	ZUG
	I got a pretty excitin' comic book here if you care to look at it.
	(GIL RAISES HIS HEAD AND LOOKS AT ZUG UNCOM-PREHENDINGLY, AS ZUG PROFFERS HIS BATTERED COMIC BOOK.)
	ZUG
	It's called 'The Mars Men.'

You know — men from
Mars. . . .
(GIL FORCES A SMILE, TRYING
TO BE PLEASANT, DESPITE
HIS DEPRESSION.)
GIL
No — no thanks.

Dispatch dated January 6, 1951

THE AMERICAN SOLDIER IN KOREA IS GETTING MORE
AMERICAN EVERY DAY.

THE MORE AMERICAN HE GETS, THE MADDER AN AMERICAN
SOLDIER BECOMES AT FEELING HE IS BEING PUSHED
AROUND, OR THAT HIS COUNTRY IS BEING THREATENED.

UNDER THE BLUE AND WHITE FLAG OF THE UNITED NA-
TIONS HE FOUGHT HERE FOR MONTHS WITHOUT ANY REAL
IDEA OF WHAT IT WAS ALL ABOUT.

IN THAT RESPECT, THE AMERICAN SOLDIER WAS LIKE THE
AVERAGE AMERICAN CITIZEN. WHO AT HOME OR HERE
REALLY FELT IN HIS HEART WHAT THE WAR WAS ABOUT?

TO BE TOLD THEY WERE FIGHTING FOR THE PRINCIPLE OF
THE U.N. MEANT LITTLE TO THE FIRST AMERICAN TROOPS
HERE, BECAUSE TO THEM THE IDEALISM WASN'T CLEAR.

THE ARMY DID MAKE — AND STILL IS MAKING — AN
ATTEMPT TO INDOCTRINATE AMERICAN SOLDIERS INTO THE
WHYS AND WHEREFORS THAT BROUGHT THEM HERE, AND THE
REASONS FOR THEIR SACRIFICES.

VIDEO	AUDIO
REVERSE ANGLE ON MITCH WHO SITS IN THE B.G., PHILOSOPHICALLY PUFFING ON HIS PIPE	

MITCH
I believe in it.
GIL
In what?
MITCH
The idea of a police force —

an international police
force — to keep law and
order in the world — and
maybe peace — like you have
cops at home.

QUICK CUT OF CORB AS HE
PULLS HIS HELMET FURTHER
DOWN OVER HIS EYES AND
SLOUCHES INTO A MORE
COMFORTABLE POSITION

CORB
Oh — oh, the professor is on
the soap box again.

ANGLE SHOOTING PAST GIL
AND JOE ON MITCH

MITCH
No — no soap box. You
guys can think anything you
want. This is what I think.

MED. SHOT — A SOLDIER
WALKING IN SLOWLY FROM
THE SAME DIRECTION THE
SQUAD ARRIVED. HE IS YOUNG,
CLEAN SHAVEN AND WITHOUT
RIFLE OR HELMET. HE HAS A
SPECIAL STARE IN HIS EYES —
THE THOUSAND-YARD LOOK.
CAMERA PANS WITH HIM AS HE
WALKS SOBERLY UP TO THE
GROUP, PAYING NO ATTENTION
TO THE CLOWNING.

Author's note: The following scene sets the plot of this play,
as it will be carried out by the character, Gil Evers. Note that
the long speech of the Soldier is almost word for word the dispatch printed at the beginning of this chapter, telling the story
of The Thousand-Yard Look.

SOLDIER

Any of you guys know where the 26th Engineers is?

ANGLE FAVORING PETE, CORB AND THE OTHERS. THE GRINS FADE. CORB AND PETE STOP THEIR CLOWNING

CORB

Huh?

SOLDIER

I'm looking for my outfit — the 26th Engineers. I — I got to find 'em.

(NOW THE MEN CIRCLE AROUND HIM, SENSING SOMETHING WRONG WITH THIS SOLDIER.)

JOE

We just got up here ourselves.

SOLDIER

I gotta find 'em. (TO SERGEANT, O.S.) You know where the 26th is at, Sergeant?

ANGLE FAVORING THE SERGEANT AND THE CORPORAL. THE SERGEANT LOOKS AT THE MAN SYMPATHETICALLY

SERGEANT

No, I don't, soldier.

ANGLE ON SOLDIER SHOOTING PAST GIL, WHO WATCHES HIM WITH INTENSE INTEREST.

SOLDIER

Got to find 'em. (TELLING THE STORY ALMOST TO HIM-

SELF) I was steering one of the assault boats crossing the Naktong. Then they machine gunned it and I would've drowned if my buddies hadn't pulled me into the boat. Don't remember anything about the next twelve hours except standing in a chow line, then comin' to in a hospital. They said I had concussion and wanted to send me back to a rest camp, even talked about sending me home. So I just waited till breakfast this morning an' took off. I can't dope off on my outfit at a time like this. (CATCHING HIMSELF) You don't know where they are, huh? (HE LOOKS UP AT THE MEN)

REVERSE ANGLE ON MEN. THEY STARE AT HIM WITH SHOCKED INCREDULOUS EXPRESSIONS. NO ONE ANSWERS HIM. ANGLE BACK TO SOLDIER

SOLDIER

Well — maybe I'll find 'em up this way. Hope the beer rations is better than they was.
(STARTS WALKING, THE GROUP OF MEN BREAKING IN FRONT OF HIM.)

ANGLE ON GIL AS THE SOLDIER PASSES IN FRONT OF HIM. IMPULSIVELY GIL PUTS A HAND ON HIS ARM.

GIL

Wouldn't it be smarter to get
back to that hospital?

SOLDIER

Those guys are my buddies.
That's where I'm getting back
to. You can't be smarter than
that.

Summary of Action: At this instant, the overdue patrol returns,
filthy and exhausted, bearing some of their wounded. B Company
is horror-stricken . . . and our platoon is at once told to be prepared to go into action. The overdue patrol was ambushed. Three
enemy companies are pointing toward our perimeter of the battle
line. The sergeant telephones the captain that he will hold the
line as long as he can with the forces he has, chiefly our boys. The
actual plot is now underway.

Dispatch dated February 17, 1951

SUDDENLY HE (THE GI ON THE BATTLE LINE) SEES ENEMY
CAMPFIRES SPROUT IN THE DISTANCE ON EACH SIDE OF HIS
POSITION. THAT IS THE BEGINNING OF THE CHINESE
STRATEGY OF NOCTURNAL TERROR. STRANGE SOUNDS RING
OUT -- BLOWING WHISTLES, WEIRD CALLS, CLASHING CYM-
BALS. THEN A BUGLE CALLS SHRILLY. AND THROUGH THE
DARK, WAVE AFTER WAVE OF QUILT-COVERED CHINESE RUSH
TOWARD HIM FIRING BURP GUNS AND SCREAMING AT THE TOP
OF THEIR VOICES.

END OF DISPATCH

VIDEO	AUDIO

DISSOLVE TO:

THE PERIMETER. NIGHT. QUIET.
CAMERA MOVES IN TO MED.
CLOSE SHOT OF ZUG AND PETE,
PEERING OUT OF A FOXHOLE,
THEIR FACES STRAINED AND
TENSE. THERE IS COMPLETE
SILENCE FOR A LONG MOMENT.
THE ATMOSPHERE IS TENSE
WITH WAITING.

PETE (FRIGHTENED)
(A WHISPER) Ya hear something?

ZUG (COCKING AN EAR)
No . . . (PAUSE) . . . You hear something?

PETE (PAUSE)
I — I ain't sure. (PAUSE) You think they make noise?

ZUG
Who . . . ?

PETE
The gooks.

ZUG
I don't know. (PAUSE) (HOPEFULLY) Maybe — Maybe they ain't comin'.

PETE (SCARED)
They're comin' . . . You heard the lieutenant.

QUICK CUT TO:

MED. CLOSE — THE CORPORAL

CORPORAL
(SHOUTING) . . . They're comin! Don't push the panic button now . . .
(MORTAR AND RIFLE FIRE BEGIN)

CORPORAL
Here it comes. Keep down and keep firin'!

Summary of Action: Our platoon goes into action. We see how the individual men behave. Joe's hand freezes, he can't shoot his rifle. Gil fires automatically, not even seeing in what direction his rifle points. The corporal fires coolly. Corb holds his rifle, can't shoot. A mortar shell explodes nearby. Corb sobs, drops his rifle. The corporal gives him hell. Pete, in terror, starts to run away. Zug pulls him back into the shell hole where they're all crouched. This is our boys' first taste of battle. Gil behaves well, and the beginning of a special relationship between him and Joe (in view of future plot development) is begun by the playwrights. On this violent bit of action, the FIRST ACT ENDS.

ACT TWO

Summary of Action: Opening of ACT TWO, in the platoon command post. The area shows effects of having been fought over heavily. It is some weeks later. Our boys are shown as they rest, as weary, dirty, unkempt as the first patrol we saw. There is a replacement, a recruit, Miller. He asks questions fearfully, and is answered by Joe and Gil (now the center of our dramatic interest as a duo) in such fashion to show that they have become hardened battle veterans. Their boiled-down advice to him is to take what comes stoically. It turns out that Miller and Gil come from the same home town; they talk about it, nostalgically. Mail call sounds; our boys gather for their letters. Another scene of nostalgia. (Note: very carefully, the playwright begins "low", in order to build rising action, in this new act.) The atmosphere and the nostalgia hold us, for we anticipate new intense action. The dispatch dated August 23, 1950, gives the playwrights a chance for a moment with a Korean soldier who is given the name Kelly. This Korean also becomes a "running gag" through the rest of the play, as comic relief.

Dispatch dated August 23, 1950

THERE ARE SOME HARD ROKS WITH IRISH MONIKERS RATTLING AROUND WITH THE U.S. INFANTRY. THEY ARE GIVEN IRISH NICKNAMES IN HONOR OF THE KOREAN'S REPUTATION AS "THE IRISH OF THE EAST." THUS KIM HWAN ROW MAY BECOME A KIMMIE O'TOOLE OR A REILLY, AND HAK CHOO KANG ANSWERS TO THE NAME OF RYAN, OR KILROY, IN AN ACCENT NO SON OF ERIN WOULD EVER RECOGNIZE.

Summary of Action: As the mail call scene continues, the important plot detail introduced is that Joe has a girl who writes him faithfully every day, and about whom he is very secretive.

By now, Gil has become a favorite with his platoon. He is offered the corporal's stripes, and refuses them, because, while outwardly conforming to duty and doing his duty well, he inwardly is isolated and resentful of having been drafted. Mitch is made corporal when Gil refuses the stripes. The platoon is bitterly disappointed in Gil (the playwrights are still building for the emotional climax at the end of the play: namely, Gil's total identification with his comrades). In this scene, too, the little Korean boy is used for pathos and human interest: his relationship with Pete and Zug has deepened so that now they are like very worried parents toward him and his welfare. Then the platoon moves on to join the troops in combat on the battle line. This far-flung action is covered by Hal Boyle's narration, which follows next in sequence.

VIDEO	AUDIO
DISSOLVE TO:	
FILM MONTAGE (ARMY STOCK) OF BATTLE FOOTAGE, SUPERIMPOSED OVER IT A SIMPLE MAP SHOWING THE PROGRESS OF U.S. TROOPS NORTHWARD	
	(OVER THE ABOVE, NARRATION BY MR. HAL BOYLE DESCRIBING THE MILITARY ADVANCE. THE NARRATION WILL END WITH THE WORDS:)
	BOYLE
	Our offensive pushed on through Seoul, the capital of South Korea, through Penyang, the capital of North Korea. And the beaten North Korean Army fled through the hills. The Chinese entered the picture, and slowed our march to the Manchurian border, but by late November we re-grouped and started our famous 'win-the-war'

offensive. And the morale of
the third squad of the second
platoon of Company B was
high — held back in reserve in
Penyang (Pyongyang), the
North Korean capital —
Victory and home were in
sight . . . . .

Dispatch dated December 6, 1950

THERE ARE A FEW SORDID DIME A DANCE JOINTS WHERE
THE SOLDIER CAN JITTERBUG WITH KOREAN GIRLS AND
DRINK BEER AT 80 CENTS A CAN. BUT THEY SHUT DOWN AT
NIGHTFALL AND FEW OF THE GIRLS CAN SPEAK MORE THAN A
PHRASE OR TWO OF ENGLISH. THE SOLDIERS WHO PATRON-
IZE THESE JOINTS USUALLY LEAVE THEM FEELING MORE
LONELY THAN WHEN THEY WENT IN.

THERE ARE NO EXTENSIVE SERVICE RECREATION CENTERS
SUCH AS THE RED CROSS SET UP IN EUROPE WHERE THE MEN
CAN SHOWER, GET A CHANCE TO WRITE HOME AND FIND
BUNKS FOR THE NIGHT.
                    END OF DISPATCH

VIDEO	AUDIO
AS CAMERA MOVES IN ON WORD 'SEOUL' ON MAP, DISSOLVE TO: LARGE ROUND TABLE IN A CORNER OF A SEOUL RESTAURANT. MED. CLOSE SHOT — PETE, SEATED AT THE TABLE, HOLDING A COPY OF THE STARS AND STRIPES.	PETE (EXCITEDLY) Read it — read it! There it is! 'Home by Christmas.' They wouldn't say it if it wasn't true.

(INCREDULOUS) 'Home by
Christmas.'

AS PETE SPEAKS, CAMERA PULLS
BACK TO FULL SHOT OF TABLE.
ON EITHER SIDE OF PETE SIT
JOE AND CORB, CRANING OVER
HIS SHOULDER AT THE PAPER.
RANGED BEHIND HIM, LOOKING
OVER HIS SHOULDER ARE ZUG,
MITCH (NOW WEARING CORPO-
RAL STRIPES), CORB AND
MILLER.
SEATED AT THE TABLE NOT
LOOKING AT THE PAPER IS GIL.
A MEMBER OF THE SQUAD, BUT
NOT 'ONE OF THE BOYS' HE IS
QUIETLY SAVOURING THE NEWS.
ACROSS FROM HIM SITS BOLES,
THE G.I. GRANDFATHER, HIS
LOWER LIP TREMBLING IN
SLOPPY EMOTION.
ALSO AT THE TABLE, SEATED ON
THE SIDE NEAREST CAMERA, IS
MILLY THE MOUSE, A YOUNG
STUPID KOREAN DANCE HALL
GIRL, DRESSED IN A TATTERED
SEQUINNED 'EVENING DRESS'.
SHE IS COMPLETELY OBLIVIOUS
TO THE NEWS. SHE BEGINS
TALKING AT THE BEGINNING OF
THE SCENE AND GIVES THE
IMPRESSION OF TALKING
STRAIGHT THROUGH IT.
IN A CHAIR TIPPED BACK
AGAINST THE WALL IS THE
LITTLE KOREAN BOY,
SOUND ASLEEP.

JOE

Christmas! That's less than
a month! Oh, boy!

MILLY

(TO NO ONE IN PARTICULAR)

Talkee — talkee — no one pay
no attention to poor Milly
the Mouse . . .

PETE

I'm gonna spend Christmas in
the bathtub, only it's goin' to
be filled with beer and
mermaids!

ZUG (EXUBERANTLY)

Ya know how I'm goin' to
spend Christmas?

MITCH (GRINNING)

How, Zug?

ZUG

I don't know, but I'm sure
goin' to spend it.

MILLY

I want marry G.I. . . . go to
States, do jitterbug.

CORB

I'm just goin' to stroll into
Mac's Pool Parlor, corner
Cottage Grove and 61st, and
say 'Hi boys — Anybody for
snooker?'

MILLY

I think I go to Kalamazoo
where they got the sky-
scrapers. A G.I. tell me about
Kalamazoo. . . .

MITCH

Where's the wedding going
to be, Joe?

JOE

Well, we — ain't decided
yet. . . .

BOLES

I'll be there if it ain't on
Christmas. I'm goin' to play
Santa Claus for my grand-
daughter on Christmas.

MILLER

Hey, Gil, you and I can go to
Joe's wedding on our way
home to Cedar Rapids. How
about it?

ANGLE FAVORING GIL, HE LOOKS
UP ALMOST WITH AN EAGER
SMILE, FORCING SLIGHTLY,
KNOWING THAT HE IS SUBTLY
EXCLUDED.

GIL

Swell — And I'm going to give
the bachelor's party the night
before the wedding. Cham-
pagne and the works —

MILLY

Weddings, champagne, parties
— nobody invite Millie no
place . . . poor Millie . . .

CORB

(GETTING BACK INTO THE MOOD)
Boys, all I can say is good-bye
Korea and who wants it?

MILLY

Maybe I still marry G.I.
Maybe commies do Millie
good after all — Maybe I still
end up in States doing
jitterbug . . . (SMILING) Maybe
war go on for long, long
time. . . .

DISSOLVE TO:

FILM MONTAGE OF BATTLE
SCENES (ARMY STOCK) OF
THIRD PHASE OF WAR, THE
CHINESE COMMUNISTS' ENTRY
INTO THE CONFLICT.

OVER THE ABOVE WILL BE
NARRATION BY MR. HAL BOYLE
DESCRIBING THE ACTION, HIS
NARRATION ENDING WITH THE
WORDS:

BOYLE

. . . . . . And Milly was right.
The war did go on. And in
two days the great Allied
advance turned into the great
Allied retreat. The Chinese
had been coiled and waiting
for us . . . waiting to strike.
Across a carpet of their own
dead . . . this living yellow sea
. . . this great and resistless
flood of armed and heedless
flesh . . . drove us back . . .
back . . . back . . . through
Pyongyang . . . through Seoul.
"Home by Christmas" became
a joke instead of a dream. But
near Osan . . . the town where
it all began . . . the Allied
line stiffened and counter-
attacked . . . and the men of
the third squad of the second
platoon of Company B found
themselves fighting again . . .
harder . . . more desperately
. . . than ever before . . . .

Summary of Action: The platoon is in battle. Our attention is centered on Joe and Gil. Gil is wounded badly in the leg. Joe attempts to carry him back to their lines; they are captured by three Korean riflemen. As a cover scene, to allow the actors playing Joe, Gil and the Korean riflemen to get into place in the hut set (soon to follow), we play a scene back behind the American lines, where the lieutenant refuses to let our platoon go out in a rescue attempt.

Dispatch dated August 28, 1950
    "I NEVER SAW ANY ONE IN MY LIFE WHO WAS MORE
HEARTBROKEN THAN SERGEANT ———— WAS THE DAY THEY
BROUGHT IN OUR SOLDIERS WHO HAD BEEN SHOT TO DEATH
WITH THEIR HANDS TIED BEHIND THEM," SAID ONE OF HIS
MEN. "HE CRIED."
                        END OF DISPATCH

VIDEO	AUDIO
DISSOLVE TO:	
INT. KOREAN HUT. THE HUT IS	
LIT WITH THE BEGINNINGS OF	
DAWN. MED. CLOSE SHOT —	
JOE AND GIL, WRISTS WIRED	
TOGETHER AS THEY STAND BACK	
TO BACK. OVER THE SHOT IS	
HEARD THE GABBLE OF NORTH	
KOREAN SOLDIERS.	
CAMERA PULLS BACK TO REVEAL	
JOE AND GIL WIRED BACK TO	
BACK BEING STRIPPED OF ANY	
VALUABLES BY TWO KOREAN	
SOLDIERS, WHILE A THIRD WITH	
A GUN TRAINED ON THEM	
STANDS IN THE DOOR.	
GIL'S INJURED LEG IS PUSHED	
AWKWARDLY IN FRONT OF HIM	
WHILE HE SUPPORTS HIS	
WEIGHT ON THE UNINJURED	

LEG. HIS PANTS LEG IS STAINED
WITH BLEEDING AND HE IS
TENSED WITH PAIN WHICH HE
TRIES NOT TO SHOW.
THE FIRST KOREAN HOLDS UP
GIL'S WRIST WATCH HAPPILY TO
THE SECOND KOREAN.

> GIL (FORCED BRAVADO)
> If you take my watch, you
> stinking gook, how are Joe and
> I going to know the time.
> We gotta know the time, don't
> we, Joe.
>
> JOE
> (PLAYING UP) Yeah we got to
> know the time. Why we might
> get all mixed up if we didn't
> know the time!

AS JOE AND GIL TALK, EACH
KOREAN IS BUSY REMOVING
THEIR BOOTS.
ANGLE ON KOREAN AS HE TUGS
AT BOOT ON GIL'S INJURED LEG.

> GIL'S VOICE
> (THROUGH GRITTED TEETH) Yeah
> — we might get breakfast
> mixed up with dinner and get
> dinner mixed up with —

THE KOREAN GIVES A PARTICU-
LARLY VICIOUS JERK ON THE
BOOT.
MED. CLOSE SHOT — GIL. HE
BITES HIS LIP AND CLOSES HIS
EYES IN AGONY, ALMOST
FAINTING.

> GIL
> (TRYING TO KEEP ON) . . . dinner
> mixed up with — with —

(WITH TERRIFIC EFFORT) —
dinner. (HISSING IT ON HIS
BREATH) Take it easy, you
lousy crud — take it ea —
(ALMOST FAINTS AS BOOT IS
PULLED OFF — THEN RELIEF)
— sy . . . Yeah . . . (SWAYS,
FEELING FAINT)

ANGLE TO INCLUDE KOREANS,
JOE AND GIL. THE KOREANS
HOLD UP THE MEN'S BOOTS
HAPPILY. IN THE B.G. THE
KOREAN WITH A GUN BARKS A
COMMAND. THE KOREANS TEST
THE WIRE BINDING JOE'S AND
GIL'S WRISTS TOGETHER.
SATISFIED THEIR PRISONERS ARE
SAFELY TRUSSED, THE KOREANS
GO OUT THE DOOR, ALL
TALKING AT ONCE.
MED. TWO SHOT — GIL AND JOE,
STANDING BACK TO BACK, THE
GRADUALLY INCREASING LIGHT
FROM THE WINDOW HIGH-
LIGHTING THEIR FACES. SILENCE.
GIL SWAYS SLIGHTLY WITH THE
PAIN OF HIS LEG AND THE LOSS
OF BLOOD.

JOE
Gil, how's the leg?
GIL (SLIGHTLY DAZED)
Don't feel it any more.
JOE
Is it bleeding?
GIL
Can't see a thing. Can't feel
a thing.

JOE
Let's get down. It'll be easier
for you. Come on — lean
back on me —

Author's Note: Mr. Hal Boyle relates that this following scene is
based on fact, so that Joe's characterization also is grounded on an
actual relationship between an American G.I. and a Japanese girl.

VIDEO	AUDIO
	JOE (PAUSE — THEN QUIETLY)
	Yamashita, Gil. . . .
PAUSE AS GIL TURNS THE NAME OVER IN HIS MIND.	
	GIL
	Pretty — pretty name. . . .
	JOE
	You didn't hear me, Gil. I said it was Yamashita.
	GIL (HIS EYES HALF-CLOSED) Why don't more girls have pretty names like that?
	JOE
	Gil, listen to me. She's Japanese — and I'm gonna marry her.
ANGLE FAVORING GIL. HIS EYES FLUTTER CLOSE AND HIS HEAD BOBS TO HIS CHEST AS HE LOSES CONSCIOUSNESS. ANGLE FAVORING JOE. HE WAITS FOR AN ANSWER FROM GIL. WHEN THERE IS NONE, HE INTERPRETS IT AS MUTE CRITICISM.	
	JOE
	Oh, I know what you're thinking. That's why I never

told any of the guys — not
even you. But, Gil, I feel
about her like I never felt
about a girl before. I'm — I'm
happy with her, Gil . . . You
understand . . . . ?

ANGLE FAVORING GIL,

HIS EYES HALF-OPEN. HE IS

ONLY HALF-CONSCIOUS.

GIL

Yeah — yeah . . .

Summary of Action: You see now how important — back in the
mail call scene — it was to plant Joe's mysterious and faithful
letter-writer. For the whole emotional impact of this dramatic
scene with Joe and Gil bound together is the revelation of Joe's
love for his Japanese sweetheart.

As Joe keeps talking, Gil lapses into unconsciousness, pulls them
both to the floor. A Korean soldier rushes in, fires two shots at the
men. Joe is killed. However, both men seem dead to the Korean,
who rushes out again. The noise of the battle rises to furious pitch
outside; this is the END OF ACT TWO.

ACT THREE

Summary of Action: Behind the American lines, a hospital tent.
The doctor and a war correspondent are making the rounds of the
wounded. The correspondent is shown talking to the wounded,
taking names, addresses, data for his stories. Finally the correspondent reaches Gil, who sits on a bed, completely dressed, staring at nothing. The doctor is unable to get anything out of Gil.
The correspondent finally gets him to talk. Gil reveals that Joe
was killed, he himself was rescued. He talks dully, noncommit-
tally, in a state of apparent shock. But the correspondent finally
arouses Gil's great interest, as follows:

VIDEO

AUDIO

HARRIS

(TAKING NOTES) What's your outfit?

GIL

Twenty-fifth Division, B Company.

HARRIS

I was with the Twenty-fifth just yesterday.

GIL

(FOR THE FIRST TIME INTER-ESTED) You were?

HARRIS

Sure. They're outside of Waegwan. They've crossed the Naktong River again.

GIL

(MORE INTEREST THAN BEFORE) They did? Say, you didn't by any chance talk to any guys from the 3rd Platoon?

HARRIS

Could be. I'll look. (LEAFS THROUGH NOTEBOOK) Yeah, here's one. The 3rd Platoon, Company B. Corbett. Do you know him?

GIL (SMILING FONDLY)

Corb. Yeah — Still shooting off his mouth?

HARRIS

He had a lot to say.

GIL

Yeah, that's Corb. (EAGERLY) Did you talk to any of the other guys?

HARRIS

That's the only name I took
down.

GIL

It's a good outfit. A real good
outfit. You don't remember a
guy by the name of Mitchell,
do you? He wears G.I.
glasses. Or a sort of tall dumb
guy — he's not really dumb
— called Zug?

HARRIS

No, I'm afraid I don't. I see a
lot of men every day.

GIL

Yeah, sure. There was sort of
a little eager guy called Pete
— and the lieutenant — do
they still have a red-headed
lieutenant, Otis?

HARRIS

Gosh, soldier, I wouldn't know.

GIL

(CLENCHING AND UNCLENCHING
HIS FISTS) Yeah, sure.

HARRIS

(WALKING TO DOOR) Well, lots
of luck to you.

GIL

(THINKS, THEN SHOUTS) Hey —

HARRIS

(STOPS IN DOORWAY) Yes. . . .

GIL

If you write anything, try and
mention my platoon. They're
a great bunch of guys. You
won't meet another bunch like
'em any place. No kidding.

                                        Harris
                            (leaving) I'll see what I
                            can do.
                                        Gil
                            (persistently) They're —
                            they're really swell.

Author's note: The preceding scene, starting with the beginning
of Act III, and continuing (as far as Gil's actions are concerned)
until the time when Gil finds his outfit and rejoins it, is, as you
will of course recognize, a dramatization of the thematic dispatch
printed at the beginning of this play.

VIDEO	AUDIO
DISSOLVE TO:	(MUSIC . . . . FADES IN)
	GIL STANDING ON SIDE OF ROAD.
	HIS NEAT HOSPITAL UNIFORM
	IS ALREADY SHOWING THE
	EFFECTS OF HIS JOURNEY. HE
	HAS NO WEAPON OR EQUIPMENT.
	HE THUMBS A JEEP AS IT
	COMES DOWN ROAD WITH TWO
	SOLDIERS. THE JEEP STOPS.
	TWO SOLDIERS ARE IN FRONT,
	A CORPORAL AND PRIVATE. THE
	CORPORAL IS DRIVING.
	GIL NERVOUSLY ASKS DIREC-
	TIONS. ONE OF THE SOLDIERS
	ANSWERS AND POINTS DOWN THE
	ROAD IN THE OPPOSITE DIREC-
	TION THEY ARE GOING. GIL
	STARTS DETERMINEDLY AWAY.
	CAMERA HOLDS ON SOLDIERS
	WHO STARE AFTER HIM, SHAKE
	THEIR HEADS, THEN START
	AWAY.
	DISSOLVE TO:

ANOTHER SECTION OF THE ROAD.
MED. SHOT. MP, SITTING AT
SIDE OF ROAD.
IN A MOMENT GIL APPEARS,
DRAGGING HIS FEET, DEAD TIRED.
THE MP WATCHES HIM FOR A
MOMENT. GIL STARTS FOR A
MOMENT WHEN HE SEES HIM.
THEN HEAD DOWN, GUILTILY,
HE PLODS ON, MAKING HIMSELF
WALK FASTER AND FASTER.
DISSOLVE TO:
GIL TALKING TO TWO SOLDIERS
IN FULL FIELD EQUIPMENT AT
SIDE OF ROAD. HE IS TIRED AND
WEAK — BUT DESPERATELY
ANXIOUS. ONE SOLDIER NODS IN
ANSWER TO HIS QUESTION AND
POINTS DOWN THE ROAD. AT
THE INFORMATION GIL SMILES
AND STARTS OUT.

Summary of Action: With suspense established by Gil's flight from the hospital, there is time to pay-off the little Korean boy who has appeared throughout the picture. In a very affecting scene, he is shown preparatory to being flown to an orphanage on a Korean island. Pete and Zug are on hand to tell him good-bye; and no two parents ever suffered more from this leave-taking. This minor plot element finished off, we CUT TO

VIDEO

AUDIO

SQUAD, MITCH, CORB, KELLY,
THE KOREAN, BOLES, MILLER, IN
FULL FIELD EQUIPMENT, SOME
STANDING, SOME SITTING.

MITCH
Everybody all set?
CORB (GETTING UP WEARILY)
Yeah — yeah — all set.

PETE (COMING IN)
Well, we said good-bye to
Junior.

ZUG
Yeah — we said good-bye.

MILLER
Hey, look at that guy over
there . . . No gun or nothin'. . . .

THEY ALL TURN

PETE
He's sure got the 1000-yard
look . . .

MILLER
It's Gil!!

Author's note: In Korean War terminology, a "million-dollar
wound" is one severe enough to send the victim back to the U.S.A.

CORB
Now what would the boy with
that million-dollar wound be
doin' up here!

ZUG
No — that is Gil!

ANGLE FAVORING GIL AS HE
WALKS UP CASUALLY

GIL (QUIETLY)
Hi, you guys.

CORB STANDS BACK A BIT,
EYEING GIL CAREFULLY

(CHORUS OF LEISURELY,
UNEXCITED HELLOS)

MITCH
Finally kicked you out of the
hospital, huh?

GIL
Yeah. They kicked me out.
(LOOKING AROUND) Nothing's
changed, huh?

ZUG

All the same. Except we got
a new replacement. You
know — for Joe.

GIL (NOT WANTING TO TALK
ABOUT IT)

Yeah — Yeah.

ZUG

Gosh darn, I thought for sure
they'd send you home.

CORB

Yeah, we heard you had a
million-dollar wound.

GIL

Naw, nothing like that. I'm
all right.

CORB

(NARROWING EYES SUSPI-
CIOUSLY) Y'are, huh?

GIL (TEMPER GOING)

I said I was all right. Now,
lay off.

(WHISTLE BLOWS. SHOUTS FROM
SERGEANT. MASS OF MEN STIR
TO ACTION, GETTING INTO SOME
SEMBLANCE OF FORMATION
IN PREPARATION FOR MARCH.)

CORB, ZUG, PETE AND OTHERS
MOVE AWAY TO GET THEIR
EQUIPMENT.

SERGEANT'S VOICE

(OFF) . . . Let's go — let's go —
let's go.

TWO SHOT — GIL AND MITCH

MITCH (QUIETLY)

Gil — you should be in that
hospital. What did you come
back for?

GIL (TRYING TO REPRESS HIS
EMOTION)
To see your ugly face —
(LOOKING AROUND) — and all
the ugly faces of — of my
buddies — my — my friends.

Summary of Action: And so the play ends. Gil, of his own wish
and action, has returned to the battle, in order to be with and
share with his buddies the dangers and hardships. The circle has
come full turn. From a technical point of view, the playwrights
have fulfilled the task they set themselves when they took as their
premise the dispatch sent in by Hal Boyle telling about the soldier
who returned to his unit, the dispatch printed in full at the beginning of this condensed television play. No longer isolated from his
comrades, Gil is now one of them; and the emotional story of his
journey from isolation to full comradeship has been the theme of
this skillful and powerful documentary television play.

ADDITIONAL COMMENT ON "THE 1000-YARD LOOK"

As you no doubt have observed for yourself, there is a lot of
"playwriting" in "The 1000-Yard Look," meaning that the bulk of
the play is made up of fictional incident and dialogue, chiefly to
develop and deepen the characterizations of the principal players.

Yet the entire play is based on *fact;* and we believe that the
characters *could* be real, live men even if we know that they are
only the creations of skilled playwrights who are masters of their
material.

This story, then, *could* have happened, and these men *could* be
alive, because they are the prototypes of actual living men, fighting
under the conditions set forth in the play. Therefore, this play is
a *true story,* an authentic picture of the war in Korea. It is beyond
dispute a pure example of the documentary television play, which
in this particular case had the presence of the Associated Press
correspondent, Mr. Hal Boyle, to lend verisimilitude, when the
play was telecast.

The obligation of the playwright composing a documentary

television play, then, is to do a very thorough job of researching his material before he turns to the imaginative presentation of it in the form of a soundly constructed dramatic work.

Note that from their research, Messrs. Ettlinger and Gidding selected even the smallest items as clues to major and minor scenes. The one dispatch about the GI reading the comic book was used as the basis for a characterization of a principal player, for instance. The dispatch about the very young Korean boys who attach themselves to the GI troops provided a plot element which worked not only for great human interest, but for comedy relief, and, finally, in the end for pathos.

In addition, the playwrights assured your author that they watched newsreels of the Korean fighting for accurate details of the terrain; that they talked to veterans rotated from Korea; that they and Mr. Hal Boyle held many conversations; that they read all of Mr. Boyle's dispatches for general background and color, even if a particular dispatch did not provide a specific incident or character.

A documentary television play, then? *Research plus sound dramatic technique!*

15

Selling Your
Television Scripts

WRITING in the November 1952 issue of *Academy*, the magazine of the Academy of Radio and Television Arts and Sciences, Mr. Ross Donaldson, Supervisor of Literary Rights and Story Division for the National Broadcasting Company in New York, says:

> "I cannot believe that we are in danger of running out of material (for television). Perhaps both writers and editors have been somewhat lax in establishing methods of cooperation and communication.
>
> "Editors cannot sit alone in offices and wait for that perfect plot, devoid of all staging and talent headaches, replete with the finest dialogue.
>
> "Similarly, writers cannot write in a vacuum without careful attention to what a particular show can and must be.
>
> "Television has some very special (and, it seems everchanging) requirements. Could it be that, through the initial stages for a new artistic medium, writers have not had time to adjust themselves to these special production requirements and the framework in which we must operate?
>
> "More and more writers are becoming successful at slanting their material to a particular show and producer."

These are historic and pertinent words from the executive heading the department which would receive your television play manuscript if you mailed it in "blind" to the National Broadcasting

Company, New York, New York. They emphasize what has been written in this book; the tyro television playwright should watch and study television endlessly, and prepare his material for a particular program, while he hopes that that program will not suddenly be discontinued. Even if it is, chances are that another similar program will at some future time be presented, so that the playwright's work is not lost. For one thing, the network Story Departments will not let such work be lost; it is difficult to find *good* material and *good* writers; and if a script is not suitable for immediate telecasting, it will be remembered, or bought and kept in "inventory"; eventually *every good script* will find its market. The author speaks from considerable personal experience in making this unqualified statement. "Good" is a relative word, of course; what the author considers "good" may not be so considered by an editor, whose judgment in the end must be accepted by the playwright, who then can approach another editor for *his* judgment.

Let's follow the course of a television play you have sent in, unsolicited, to the National Broadcasting Company, New York, bearing in mind that all network practice is subject to change without notice. (However, while *details* may change, the general principles are not likely to.)

You will, eventually, receive a Release Form which you must sign before your television play will be read. Release Forms vary; two varieties of the NBC Release Form are printed in following, by special permission. Release Forms are apt to seem to "snarl" at you; they apparently take your script without payment, and you so agree when you sign. NBC's form even requires a witness to your signature, and asks that you write out a brief synopsis of your play or program idea. You are resigned to having "given away" a play you have worked long and hard on.

Nothing could be more untrue. The networks, the advertising agencies, firms producing "packages" for television independently of both, talent agencies and motion picture studios require a Release. It is standard operating procedure, as a protection against possible plagiarism suits on unsolicited material and ideas. Many authors think of the same story, write it out, send it in, as the author of this book knows from long experience.

Some stories, the same stories, *sometimes the same even in details,* come in regularly, from authors of unquestioned integrity who never heard of each other, and who write in entire innocence. If a network, or one of the other producers, bought one such story, and it could be proved even that he had had access to a similar story by a different author, a costly plagiarism suit might ensue. So it is simply for self-protection that the producers require a Release Form to be signed before material can be read. This author knows of not one case in which the author of unsolicited material has ever been treated unfairly. Let him say also that the more professional the writer, the less import he attaches to signing the Release Form; it is the amateur (and this is understandable) who fears that he will be "robbed." In the name of simple common sense, why should a reputable producer of television steal material, an act which might cost him thousands of dollars in litigation, when by paying for it at current rates he can acquire said material for an infinitesimal fraction of what litigation might cost?

The signing of a Release Form *in no way* gives legal control or ownership to the producer for whom you sign the Release. The question arises because this author has been asked countless times: "Do you own my play now?" Of course not! *You* own it, and *will,* until you sign whatever contract you may be agreeable to, conveying what rights you are willing to sell. In the end, you see, the Release Form is a detail required by the producers in the routine handling of many thousands of unsolicited scripts and program ideas.

So much for the Release Form. You have signed it, and returned it; or, better still, by writing ahead and asking for Release Forms, which will be sent on request, you have sent in a signed Release Form *with* your manuscript. (It is also good manners, but not obligatory, that you send with your manuscript a stamped, addressed envelope for the return of your material, should it be unsuitable for the present needs of the producing agent.)

If your material is unsuitable, and if your writing as such does not interest the editors, they will return your material with a printed rejection slip.

If the material is not suitable, but the writing shows promise, it may be that you'll get a personally-written encouraging letter expressing the hope that your future material will be submitted to the editors.

Best of all, if your material is to be bought, you'll get a telegram or a letter so advising you; and you will have started to arrive.

(It is essential that you firmly get in mind the fact that editors and story department heads are, just like you, human beings; that they are usually badly overworked, harassed, under pressure on all sides, and — like you too, perhaps — sometimes out of patience. The point is, don't expect a reply by return mail; give the editors and story heads enough time to climb out from under the mountain of mail which most of them have to face as a part of the daily task. It is *most valuable* also for you to grasp the fact that you are not the *only* writer in the world, and that it is likely you will have to await your turn for the editor's attention. In short, don't write, telegraph or telephone him to ask what he thinks of your material; and do not waylay him on the street or at the counter where he has fled for a cup of tea, to be alone for a moment. If you do, he is likely to spend half a day looking up your material so that he may send it back at once with a printed rejection slip, even though it may be a work of art comparable to Shakespeare. It is the *amateur writer* who is the *eager-beaver;* the professional knows what an editor must do and he waits for him to do it!)

If you live near a regional telecasting station, it is likely you will be able to get in to see the Program Director of such a station, and he can advise you on his local needs. But, *please,* write him first and ask for an appointment. Otherwise, sure as fate, you'll arrive unannounced at a moment of crisis and your visit will be a curse instead of a potential blessing.

It was stated previously that almost every program has a mimeographed Format Description or Market List which describes the kinds of material the editor and the producer are looking for, and which lists the programs open to the free-lance television playwright. This Format Description and/or Market List probably will be mailed to you, on request.

Will your television plays be read? Yes, if you conform to the stipulation, now general among the major networks, that your material be submitted *in television play form.* We quote Mr. Ross

Donaldson, manager of writing services for the National Broadcasting Company, writing in *The Writer* for March, 1956:

"The Story Department (of NBC) has made a rule: we will now read only those scripts submitted in teleplay form. While we are not concerned with which half of the page you type it on, we do want it in dialogue, constructed as a play. If you are really interested in writing for television, you will do this without being asked. The form in which you put it, the elements and technique you choose to tell your story, will be a reflection of your equipment as a writer. We are vastly more interested in writers than in plots!"

In December, 1956, all of the dramatic programs produced by the Columbia Broadcasting System were opened to the free-lance, unknown, unestablished playwright, with the stipulation that all material submitted *must be in teleplay form.* CBS no longer requires that a would-be television playwright have "professional writing credits"; *anyone* may submit material, if — to repeat — it be *in teleplay form.*

As of this writing, most of the half-hour programs are independently-produced "packages." Submissions for such programs should be made to the independent "package producers." This author knows of only one trustworthy, kept-up-to-date Market List for such independent television productions: it is the Ross Reports on Television Monthly Talent and Script Report, published by the Ross Reports on a monthly basis, at 551 Fifth Ave., Suite 417, New York City. This monthly Talent and Script Report costs one dollar (plus three per cent sales tax if you live in New York City). The Report lists names, addresses and telephone numbers in whatever city (New York, Chicago, Hollywood, Dallas, etc., etc.), for *all* independent, "package" producers and editors, together with the programs each one handles. Address a Query Letter to the script editor of a program you're interested in, and this editor will tell you whether or not your submissions will be received, read and considered. You're almost sure to have to sign a Release Form for these independent producers, same as for the networks. Typical of such independent productions are the Loretta Young show, the Jane Wyman show (as of February, 1957).

Let's start at the beginning: I have decided that I want to write for television. I have an idea for "Studio One," a CBS program. What do I do?

1. I write to the Story Department, Columbia Broadcasting System, 524 West 57th St., New York 19, N. Y., requesting a Market List and Release Forms. Then I wait.

2. In due time, I receive a reply (probably mimeographed), sending me the Market List and Release Forms. I note that my submission *must be in television play form,* an hour-long script.

3. I write the script, if my idea seems to be suitable for "Studio One" (general range of suitable ideas is described on the Market List), and then send it in. If my idea seems not suitable, I will look at other television programs on other networks for a market for my idea; and I will follow the same procedure with the other networks.

Of course, I will send in my script with the Release Form properly filled out, and, preferably, with a return envelope, addressed and stamped. Then I wait for acceptance or rejection; and, if I am sensible, I will at once begin work on *another* play, since I know that the job of the writer is to write and not to sit and wait for the mailman or for the telephone to ring. (Hollywood is filled with writers sitting and waiting for the telephone to ring.)

Or, again, I live in Texas, and watch television on a local station. This station may receive programs from several different networks and I do not know which one to write for information. So, I write the Program Director of the local station and ask him:

"On which network is 'Robert Montgomery Presents' telecast, and where do I address the Story Department of this network?" He will reply, "'Robert Montgomery Presents' originates over WRCA (NBC) in New York City, and you should address enquiries to the Story Department of this network in New York City."

Of course, if you have thoughtfully provided yourself with a copy of the Ross Reports Monthly Talent and Script Report, at the designated price of one dollar, all of the information you need to establish contact with whatever program or programs you're interested in will be available to you under one cover.

If you live in or near the big production centers — New York, Chicago, Hollywood — you may find it necessary to deal directly with advertising agencies, in some instances. The big corporations which sponsor television programs all have advertising agencies to handle their advertising, of which television is a part. Which advertising agency handles which corporation's advertising? There are three ways to find out: (1) ask the network; (2) write to the advertising manager of the corporation; (3) consult the *Standard Advertising Register,* which lists names and addresses of advertising agencies and their clients (the sponsor corporations).

(Lately, the trend has been radically away from production of television programs by advertising agencies, so that either the networks or the independent "packagers" produce the programs. This information about advertising agencies is included to cover the event of the trend's being reversed, as many television authorities think it may be, so that advertising agencies again would be television's producers.)

Undoubtedly, the best of all ways to get your scripts considered by purchasing editors is to have them handled for you by a reputable, established literary agent; or better than that, even, by a literary agent specializing in television.

There are hundred of literary agents of varying capabilities, as in any other profession. Their names may be found in the classified telephone directories of the large cities. But to be sure they are reputable it is probably better to write to the legally-constituted association of literary agents, governed by a constitution and by-laws: It is The Society of Authors' Representatives, Inc., 522 Fifth Ave., New York, N.Y.

For the services of a literary agent, you pay, usually, 10% or perhaps 15% of the total fee you receive for your script or for your services as a writer. There may be other special, private arrangements, but the percentages stated are usual.

Beyond any question, literary agents specializing in television earn their 10% cut. The market for sales of scripts changes almost daily; a good agent will watch this market as a stock broker watches the daily reports of the New York Stock Exchange. A market may go off the air without warning, or a new one may be quietly developing which has not yet been publicly announced. It is the duty of the television agent to keep posted about such changes and developments; it is also desirable for the individual writer to know about them — desirable, but not always possible. Many sources, public and private, must be consulted to keep completely informed on television markets; never has there been such a condition for the writer where "who knows whom and how well" has been so important.

The problem for the beginning writer is to get an agent to handle him. An agent's time, like every one else's time, is his stock in trade. He can read only so much, can advise on only so much, can talk only to so many editors in the course of his waking hours. It is not possible to state any firm principle as to how a writer acquires an agent: he can write to agents he has heard of; or he can call on those in cities where he and the agents happen to be, getting their names from the classified telephone directory. If, by his own efforts, he becomes established as a television writer, he will have the agents coming after *him* — and this, of course, is a delightful situation to be in.

It is sensible, both for the writer and for the literary agent, in the beginning, to work together on a one-script-at-a-time basis. The relationship between writer and agent is a sensitive one, in many ways more intimate than any other relationship, as time goes by, because the agent is dealing with the writer in his most important (to the writer) character, his creative character. Therefore, it may be foolish to rush into a contract before you find out if you and the agent are compatible and can be happy together. Literary divorces often are as painful and as messy as dissolving a marriage.

Having said all this, let us say finally that it is not necessary to have a literary agent to sell your television material. The networks will buy a good script from the writer just as fast as they will from his agent. Scripts identified as coming from a well-known agent may be *read* faster, because it will be assumed that any material such an agent handles will be quality stuff, else the agent wouldn't handle it.

It is to be hoped that you, the reader, will have realized by now that you will fight for the *chance* to sell your material as hard as you will strive in the writing of it.

Should you copyright your material? This is a matter of individual preference. One editor's experience is that not one television play in five hundred is copyrighted. If you choose to copyright, write to the Register of Copyrights, Library of Congress, Washington, D.C., for the necessary form: Copyright Form D, Unpublished Dramatic or Musical Work.

The fee, relatively, is considerable, and it is also required that you deposit a copy of your play with the Copyright Office. To a writer doing his own typing, this may be a considerable factor, a nuisance, since it takes one copy out of circulation among the markets.

Let it be said right here, that the practice of multiple submission of television plays — that is, sending a copy of a given play to each of several markets at the same time — is generally followed and is quite ethical.

The Writers Guild of America, Inc., provides protection by registration; but a writer must be a member in order to have the privilege of this registration service.

A writer may also send to himself by registered mail (which he then does not open) a copy of his play. If the need should ever arise, he has the priority date established by the postmark on the sealed envelope, which, if need arise, could be opened in court as evidence of authorship and ownership.

But I am honestly convinced that the high level of ethics of the editors and producers of television is of itself sufficient "protection" for the writer, known or unknown.

Now — you have sold a television play! What, actually, are you selling? A "one-time shot" around the circuit? *All* rights, in perpetuity? American rights only, or foreign rights as well? And so on, and on, and on; because the working out of the tangled problem of rights in material has taken years of negotiation between writers and purchasers of their material.

Negotiations continue on contracts between the television playwright and the purchasing-producers, as the scope of telecasting changes and increases. There is already a difference between "live" telecast contracts and those for film, for the producers are increasingly aware of world markets where filmed television plays may be telecast, vastly increasing residual returns. And, motion pictures are buying increasingly from "live" telecast plays, so that the sharing of motion picture sales between the playwright and the producer is a possibility for the future. As of this writing, it is impossible to lay down any hard and fast set of conditions; it is possible only to alert the television playwright to all possibilities and variations of contracts, so that he can drive a favorable bargain for himself. What he can rely on the most is the vigilance of the Writers Guild of America, which the television playwright inevitably will join as soon as he has had one play bought and/or telecast. The Writers Guild of America gets a copy of *every* contract involving one of its members, so that protection of this Guild is automatic for its members.

There has been evolved a basic Writers Guild of America contract, the details of which are too long and too complicated for inclusion in this book. But the following general information is important and pertinent; it was supplied to the author of this book by the executive director of the Writers Guild of America, East, Inc., and is reproduced by permission:

"The Writers Guild of America, an independent labor union, came into existence on July 18, 1954, as a successor organization, for representation purposes, to the Radio Writers Guild, the Television Writers Group, and the Screen Writers Guild, the first two of which had been part of, and the third an affiliate of, the Authors League of America. The purpose of the Writers Guild is to represent writers in the fields of radio, television and motion pictures. It has entered into basic contracts with employers in all three fields, covering compensation, working conditions, rights to material, etc.

"For administrative purposes the Guild is organized into two corporations: Writers Guild of America, East, Inc., and Writers Guild of America, West, Inc., but for all practical purposes membership is on a national basis.

"Offices of Writers Guild, East, are at 22 West 48th St., New York 36, and its executive director is Miss Evelyn F. Burkey. Offices of Writers Guild, West, are at 8782 Sunset Blvd., Hollywood 46, Calif., and its executive director is Miss Frances Inglis. National chairman is F. Hugh Herbert of WGA–West.

"In order to be eligible for membership, a writer must be either currently employed or have a contract for employment (or for a

production based on a free-lance sale) or have had material produced in one of our three fields of jurisdiction within the two-year
period immediately preceding the date of his application.

"There is an initiation fee of $35.00. The basic annual dues are
$10.00. The initiation fee includes the annual dues for the re-
mainder of the fiscal year during which a member joins the Guild.
In addition, there are quarterly dues of one per cent of gross income from writing in the covered media (radio, television and
screen). Among benefits to members, besides coverage under the
Minimum Basic Agreement now in effect, WGA provides members a registration service for non-copyrightable material (ideas,
formats, synopses, treatments), group hospitalization plans, and
business counsel on professional craft matters."

It is this author's understanding that, following a television
playwright's first sale and production, it is — if not obligatory —
highly desirable that the playwright join the branch of Writers
Guild of America, Inc., for which he is eligible, depending on his
geographical location. Note that addresses of both branches are
given in the text preceding. An enquiry surely will receive cour-
teous and prompt attention.

Television Commercials and Continuities

The writing of television commercials and continuities is so
much a matter of being employed in that special kind of job by
an advertising agency, a corporation's advertising department,
or a network, that this book's author never heard of a free-lance
commercials writer. A writer gets a job writing commercials or
continuities as another person gets a job as a salesman.

If you, a free-lance writer, get an *idea* for a commercial or a
continuity (the words joining together the separate parts of a
program: see Chapter Seventeen, which includes excerpts from
a "Your Hit Parade" script). . . . it would be handled the way a
dramatic script or idea is handled: you would go through the same
process, you would be asked to sign a Release Form; but you
might, also, get a staff job!

The following remarks about the writing of television commercials are so felicitously stated by Mr. Ira L. Avery that we reprint
them here:

The Television Commercial

The television commercial is a play, too — a complete little drama all by itself — with a provocative opening, a well-rounded middle, and a convincing, conclusive finish. Like a good play, a good commercial gets off to a fast start. Like a play, it is written, produced and performed with the best uses of the medium in mind. Television is a demonstration medium, a place where products can be shown in use — and where ideas can be graphically represented. Like plays, commercials should reflect the spirit and personality of the sponsor.

A good commercial should have a single theme — a message emphasized and clarified by pictures which tell the story along with the copy, by camera work which is imaginative but which never calls attention to itself; by smooth production; and by delivery of the spoken message — not at the speed at which people can talk, but the speed at which people listen.

We think it only fair to point out that every single thing said today (about television both as entertainment and as a sales medium — *Author*) may be contradicted as the shifting kaleidoscope of public taste changes and varies through the years and even months. But we are not content to shift and change from a sense of insecurity . . . a famous wit once said, "A leader is a man who sees where the crowd is going and steps in ahead of them." The entertainment business, like many others, is highly competitive and above all is fluid. And we find ourselves in this business at a time when there are more sources of entertainment available to the public than at any time in all history.

That is why we say that we have a greater responsibility (i.e., in Commercials — *Author*) than that of putting across a selling message and relaxing while TV follows the path of radio to the soap opera, the path of the theatre to restive, plotless meanderings, the path of Hollywood to the slick grade B movie.

There *are* new worlds to conquer.

RELEASE FORMS

Here is a sample Release Form required by an advertising agency. Reproduced by permission.

TITLE: .... DATE: ....

Batten, Barton, Durstine & Osborn, Inc.
383 Madison Avenue
New York, N.Y.

Attention: Mr. ....

Dear Sirs:

I am asking you to let me present an idea, suggestion, or uncopyrighted work which I think may be of interest to you or to some of your clients. This presentation is being made on my own initiative and not at your request.

I understand that the established policy of your company is to refuse to entertain or receive ideas, suggestions or uncopyrighted works except on the distinct understanding that they may be used by you or your clients without any obligation whatever to the person submitting them. Anything I submit to you or your company will be on that basis; disclosure by me of any idea, suggestion or uncopyrighted work is gratuitous, unsolicited, without restrictions and involves no confidential relationship between us.

Use by you and your clients of any ideas, suggestions or uncopyrighted works submitted by me, and the compensation, if any, that I may receive therefor, are matters resting solely in your discretion.

BRIEF DESCRIPTION OF IDEA, SUGGESTION OR UNCOPYRIGHTED WORK: MUST DESIGNATE PRINCIPAL CHARACTER OR CHARACTERS: STATE THEME, IF ANY; TELL STORY IN SUCH DETAIL AS TO MAKE CLEAR UNIQUENESS OF MATERIAL, IF ANY: ....

....

....

....

....

....

(continue on reverse side, if needed)

Signature in ink: ....

Name printed or typed: ....

Address: .... Telephone: ....

Here is a sample of one style Release Form for Scripts from a television network. Reproduced by permission.

NBC POLICY CONCERNING SUBMISSION OF IDEAS AND OTHER MATERIAL

The National Broadcasting Company, Inc., deeply appreciates the courtesy of many of its listeners and of people in the profession who submit ideas, suggestions and material for use in its activities. However, so many ideas and suggestions are offered to us which embody suggestions previously developed by members of our own staff, or submitted by others, that we cannot consider any material unless we receive a waiver of compensation therefor. Only in this way can we avoid the risks and uncertainties which often arise by reason of the use of ideas independently conceived and submitted to the Company by others.

Therefore, before considering any ideas, suggestions or material, it is the policy of the National Broadcasting Company, Inc., to require the signature of the release appended to this statement.

Title(s): ....

Date: ....

National Broadcasting Company, Inc.
30 Rockefeller Plaza
New York 20, N.Y.

Gentlemen:

I have received a copy of your policy in connection with the submission of ideas and suggestions to you. I understand that it is your established policy not to entertain or receive an idea or suggestion except on the distinct understanding that the person submitting the same is willing to rely entirely upon your good faith in determining the question of whether the submission is truly novel, whether it is actually used by you as a result of his having submitted it, and the amount of compensation, if any, to be paid if you should use it.

As an inducement to you to entertain my ideas and suggestions, I agree that they are submitted to you upon the conditions set forth above.

Name: ....

Address: ....

Witness: (Author or agent: Please write on the back of this form a short summary of the contents of the material being submitted.)

Here is a second Release Form for Ideas and Material used by a network. Its conditions and terms are self-explanatory. Reproduced by permission.

....

NBC POLICY CONCERNING SUBMISSION OF IDEAS AND OTHER MATERIAL

We appreciate the courtesy of our listeners and professional people who suggest material, including ideas, program formats, literary material, and other suggestions, for our use. However, we receive many suggestions which have been made previously either by our own staff or by others. Likewise, we may commence using material similar to yours which we receive after the date of your submission. It has therefore become necessary for us to adopt the policy of refusing to consider any material unless the person submitting it has signed the agreement appended to this statement and has specified the maximum payment to be made to him in the event of our use of his material. KINDLY DO NOT SUBMIT TO US ANY MATERIAL WHICH YOU DEEM TO HAVE A VALUE IN EXCESS OF THE LIMITS SPECIFIED IN PARAGRAPH 1 OF THE BELOW AGREEMENT BETWEEN US. There are two copies of this agreement; please sign in the space provided and return one copy to us.

....

National Broadcasting Company, Inc.
30 Rockefeller Plaza
New York 20, N.Y.   Attention: Story Division
Gentlemen:

In accordance with your NBC POLICY CONCERNING SUBMISSION OF IDEAS AND OTHER MATERIAL, I am today submitting to you my material summarized on the reverse side pursuant to the following agreement:

1. You agree to cause your appropriate employee having the duty of evaluating material of the type now being submitted by me to review my material. I agree that you may have my material or one or more of its features or components. If you commence such use, and provided it is original, novel and valuable, you agree to pay me as total compensation therefor such sum of money as we may subsequently agree upon in writing. If we have not attempted or are unable to agree upon the amount of such payment and you commence the use of such material, you will pay and I will accept as full consideration for all rights of every kind, the sum of $1,000.00 if the material is first used as the basis of a series of network broadcasting programs, $500.00 if the material is first used as the basis of a series of local programs, or $250.00 if the material is first used for any other purpose. I agree that I can suffer no damages in excess of the foregoing from your use of my material or for any other claim with respect thereto.

2. I declare that all of the important features of my material are summarized in the space provided and I have disclosed no other features to you. I warrant that the material is original with me and that no one else to my knowledge has any right to it. I believe my material and its features to be unique and novel. However, I recognize that other persons including your own employees may have submitted to you or to others, or made public, or may hereafter originate and submit, or make public, similar or identical material which you may have the right to use, and I understand that I will not be entitled to any compensation because of your use of such other similar or identical material.

3. Any controversy arising as to whether you used my material, or relating to this agreement, will be conclusively determined by arbitration as provided by New York law and the regulations of the American Arbitration Association and our arbitrator will be a person experienced in the broadcasting field mutually selected by us; if we cannot agree, we will accept as arbitrator any person designated by the President of the Association of the Bar of the City of New York who will agree to arbitrate the controversy, in accordance with the rules of the American Arbitration Association. The arbitrator's decision shall be controlled by the terms of this agreement and no award may exceed the appropriate amount specified in Paragraph 1. I agree that any action against you must be brought within six months after the date of your first use of my material.

4. I have retained a copy of my material submitted to you and release you from liability for, loss of or damage to such material.

5. This agreement constitutes our entire understanding. Any modification or waiver hereunder must be in writing, signed by both of us. The invalidity of any provisions hereof is not to affect the remaining provisions. This

agreement applies equally to any other material which I may submit to you, unless agreed in writing to the contrary.

Dated: ....195...... Name ....

Address ....

....

AGREED:

NATIONAL BROADCASTING COMPANY, INC.

By ....

(Author or agent: Write on the back of this form a short summary of the contents of the material being submitted.)

....

(End of Release Form, front side.
Reverse side not shown in this book.)

As one who has been forced to care for numbers of foundling scripts, scripts bearing no name, no identification whatsoever, I wish to place last, for emphasis, the following advice:

Be sure that the title of your play, your name, your address, and possibly your telephone number are *on the script itself*, inextricably a part of your script. You would be dumbfounded by the number of scripts which arrive on an editor's doorstep with *no identification whatsoever.* It is not enough to give this identification in a covering letter accompanying your script, or even on the Release Form: in the turmoil of an editor's office, in spite of his best intentions and scrupulous care, Things Can Happen. *Please!* The title, your name, your address, your telephone number *on your script itself!*

Since this book was first printed, channels for selling your television plays have changed in that the advertising agency as a producing unit has largely been eliminated, with the network itself taking on this function (including buying your script); and that the half-hour play market now largely is with the independent "package producers," located mostly in Hollywood, with half-hour television plays produced on film, rather than "live". Procedures of reaching all producing organizations (networks and independents) have been spelled out carefully in this chapter.

16

The Television Code

FOLLOWING are excerpts from the copyrighted official The Television Code of The National Association of Radio and Television Broadcasters, effective March 1, 1952. These excerpts apply particularly to the television playwright in his choice and execution of material. They are reprinted by permission of the copyright holder, The National Association of Radio and Television Broadcasters, 1771 N Street, N.W., Washington 6, D.C. Copies of the complete Code may be obtained at this address.

In addition to the broad general guiding principles of the Code, the playwright will find that each television program has its list of "taboos". One program will do no crime or mystery plays; another wants only crime or mystery; still another may refuse stories concerned with "career women", etc., etc. Only by familiarizing himself with the special requirements of each television program will the playwright be able to function successfully, as he learns each separate sponsor's "do's and don'ts". This problem was discussed fully in the preceding chapter.

Preamble

Television is seen and heard in every type of American home. These homes include children and adults of all ages, embrace all races and all varieties of religious faith, and reach those of every educational background. It is the responsibility of television to bear constantly in mind that the audience is primarily a home audience, and consequently that television's relationship to the viewers is that between guest and host.

The revenues from advertising support the free, competitive American system of telecasting, and make available to the eyes and ears of the American people the finest programs of information, education, culture and entertainment. By law the television broadcaster is responsible for the programming of his station. He, however, is obligated to bring his positive responsibility for excellence and good taste in programming to bear upon all who have a hand in the production of programs, including networks, sponsors, producers of film and live programs, advertising agencies and talent agencies.

The American businesses which utilize television for conveying their advertising messages to the home by pictures with sound, seen free-of-charge on the home screen, are reminded that their responsibilities are not limited to the sale of goods and the creation of a favorable attitude toward the sponsor by the presentation of entertainment. They include, as well, responsibility for utilizing television to bring the best programs, regardless of kind, into American homes.

Television, and all who participate in it, are jointly accountable to the American public for respect for the special needs of children, for community responsibility, for the advancement of education and culture, for the acceptability of the program materials chosen, for decency and decorum in production, and for propriety in advertising. This responsibility cannot be discharged by any given group of programs, but can be discharged only through the highest standards of respect for the American home, applied to every moment of every program presented by television.

In order that television programming may best serve the public interest, viewers should be encouraged to make their criticisms and positive suggestions known to the television broadcasters. Parents in particular should be urged to see to it that out of the richness of television fare, the best programs are brought to the attention of their children.

Advancement of Education and Culture

1. Commercial television provides a valuable means of augment-

ing the educational and cultural influences of schools, institutions of higher learning, the home, the church, museums, foundations, and other institutions devoted to education and culture.

2. It is the responsibility of a television broadcaster to call upon such institutions for counsel and cooperation and to work with them on the best methods of presenting educational and cultural materials by television. It is further the responsibility of stations, networks, advertising agencies and sponsors consciously to seek opportunities for introducing into telecasts factual materials which will aid in the enlightenment of the American public.

3. Education via television may be taken to mean that process by which the individual is brought toward informed adjustment to his society. Television is also responsible for the presentation of overtly instructional and cultural programs, scheduled so as to reach the viewers who are naturally drawn to such programs, and produced so as to attract the largest possible audience.

4. In furthering this realization, the television broadcaster:

    a) Should be thoroughly conversant with the educational and cultural needs and desires of the community served.

    b) Should affirmatively seek out responsible and account-able educational and cultural institutions of the com-munity with a view toward providing opportunities for the instruction and enlightenment of the viewers.

    c) Should provide for reasonable experimentation in the development of programs specifically directed to the advancement of the community's culture and educa-tion.

Acceptability of Program Material

Program materials should enlarge the horizons of the viewer, provide him with wholesome entertainment, afford helpful stimu-lation, and remind him of the responsibilities which the citizen has towards his society. Furthermore:

a) (i) Profanity, obscenity, smut and vulgarity are forbidden, even when likely to be understood only by part of the audience. From time to time, words which have been acceptable, acquire undesirable meanings, and tele-casters should be alert to eliminate such words.

   (ii) Words (especially slang) derisive of any race, color, creed, nationality or national derivation, except wherein such usage would be for the specific purpose of effec-

tive dramatization such as combating prejudice, are forbidden, even when likely to be understood only by part
of the audience. From time to time, words which have
been acceptable, acquire undesirable meanings, and tele-
casters should be alert to eliminate such words.

(iii) The Television Code Review Board ... shall maintain and
issue to subscribers, from time to time, a continuing list
of specific words and phrases which should not be used
in keeping with this subsection. This list, however, shall
not be considered as all-inclusive.

b) (i) Attacks on religion and religious faiths are not allowed.

(ii) Reverence is to mark any mention of the name of God,
His attributes and powers.

(iii) When religious rites are included in other than religious
programs, the rites are accurately presented, and the
ministers, priests and rabbis portrayed in their callings
are vested with the dignity of their office and under no
circumstances are to be held up to ridicule.

c) (i) Contests may not constitute a lottery.

(ii) Any telecasting designed to "buy" the television audience by requiring it to listen and/or view in hope of
reward, rather than for the quality of the program, should
be avoided.

d)   Respect is maintained for the sanctity of marriage and
the value of the home. Divorce is not treated casually
nor justified as a solution for marital problems.

e)   Illicit sex relations are not treated as commendable.

f)   Sex crimes and abnormalities are generally unacceptable
as program material.

g)   Drunkenness and narcotic addiction are never presented
as desirable or prevalent.

h)   The administration of illegal drugs will not be displayed.

i)   The use of liquor in program content shall be de-empha-
sized. The consumption of liquor in American life, when
not required by the plot or for proper characterization,
shall not be shown.

j)   The use of gambling devices or scenes necessary to the
development of plot or as appropriate background is
acceptable only when presented with discretion and in
moderation, and in a manner which would not excite
interest in, or foster, betting nor be instructional in

nature. Telecasts of actual sport programs at which on-the-scene betting is permitted by law should be presented in a manner in keeping with Federal, state and local laws, and should concentrate on the subject as a public sporting event.

k) In reference to physical or mental afflictions and deformities, special precautions must be taken to avoid ridiculing sufferers from similar ailments and offending them or members of their families.

l) Exhibitions of fortune-telling, astrology, phrenology, palm-reading, and numerology are acceptable only when required by a plot or the theme of a program, and then the presentation should be developed in a manner designed not to foster superstition or excite interest or belief in these subjects.

m) Televised drama shall not simulate news or special events in such a way as to mislead or alarm.

n) Legal, medical and other professional advice, diagnosis and treatment will be permitted only in conformity with law and recognized ethical and professional standards.

o) The presentation of cruelty, greed and selfishness as worthy motivations is to be avoided.

p) Excessive or unfair exploitation of others or of their physical or mental afflictions shall not be presented as praiseworthy.

q) Criminality shall be presented as undesirable and unsympathetic. The condoning of crime and the treatment of the commission of crime in a frivolous, cynical or callous manner is unacceptable.

r) The presentation of techniques of crime in such detail as to invite imitation shall be avoided.

s) The use of horror for its own sake will be eliminated; the use of visual or aural effects which would shock or alarm the viewer, and the detailed presentation of brutality or physical agony by sight or by sound are not permissible.

t) Law enforcement shall be upheld, and the officers of the law are to be portrayed with respect and dignity.

u) The presentation of murder or revenge as a motive for murder shall not be presented as justifiable.

v) Suicide as an acceptable solution for human problems is prohibited.

w)   The exposition of sex crimes will be avoided.

x)   The appearance or dramatization of persons featured in actual crime news will be permitted only in such light as to aid law enforcement or to report the news event.

y)   Treatment of Animals. The use of animals, both in the production of television programs and as a part of television program content, shall, at all times, be in conformity with accepted standards of humane treatment.

Responsibility Toward Children

1. The education of children involves giving them a sense of the world at large. Crime, violence and sex are a part of the world they will be called upon to meet, and a certain amount of proper presentation of such is helpful in orienting the child to his social surrounding. However, violence and illicit sex shall not be presented in an attractive manner, nor to an extent such as will lead a child to believe that they play a greater part in life than they do. They should not be presented without indications of the resultant retribution and punishment.

2. It is not enough that only those programs which are intended for viewing by children shall be suitable to the young and immature. (Attention is called to the general items listed under Acceptability of Program Materials, page 472.) Television is responsible for insuring that programs of all sorts which occur during the times of day when children may normally be expected to have the opportunity of viewing television shall exercise care in the following regards:

a) In affording opportunities for cultural growth as well as for wholesome entertainment.

b) In developing programs to foster and promote the commonly accepted moral, social and ethical ideals characteristic of American life.

c) In reflecting respect for parents, for honorable behavior, and for the constituted authorities of the American community.

d) In eliminating references to kidnapping of children or threats of kidnapping.

e) In avoiding material which is excessively violent or would create morbid suspense, or other undesirable reactions in children.

f) In exercising particular restraint and care in crime or mystery episodes involving children or minors.

Decency and Decorum in Production

1. The costuming of all performers shall be within the bounds of propriety, and shall avoid such exposure or such emphasis on anatomical details as would embarrass or offend home viewers.

2. The movements of dancers, actors, or other performers shall be kept within the bounds of decency, and lewdness and impropriety shall not be suggested in the positions assumed by performers.

3. Camera angles shall avoid such views of performers as to emphasize anatomical details indecently.

4. Racial or nationality types shall not be shown on television in such a manner as to ridicule the race or nationality.

5. The use of locations closely associated with sexual life or with sexual sin must be governed by good taste and delicacy.

Community Responsibility

A television broadcaster and his staff occupy a position of responsibility in the community and should conscientiously endeavor to be acquainted fully with its needs and characteristics in order better to serve the welfare of its citizens.

17

The Editor's Grab Bag

"Apparel oft proclaims the man". The Monday morning mail
. . . over the transom, as the saying goes, fly unsolicited manuscripts from the hopeful unknowns, tons of manuscripts, manuscripts tied with ribbon, manuscripts written on brown paper,
manuscripts held together with inadequate wire clips, which slip
off, scattering the pages in the welter as the editor scatters curses
against the well-meaning but inexperienced author. Then . . .
a manuscript calmly and securely put together, nicely typed,
clean, orderly, reflecting the mind of its author. *Well, the job of
reading must be done* . . . of course the editor reaches first for the
orderly manuscript. The disorganized manuscripts get pushed
down to the bottom of the heap. They will get read — conscience
will not allow otherwise — but they will have to wait . . . no one
likes an unappetizing and sloppy plate of food thrust at him, even
if it tastes delicious. Perhaps the orderly manuscript may be beautiful to look at, but empty of literary content . . . anyway, it will
get read first, because, like a clean and neat human being, it indicates good manners and consideration of the editor's problem,
his eternal problem of never getting caught up on his reading.

Funny thing . . . the more professional the writer, the more
physically attractive his manuscript. And angels among authors
always make sure that their names, addresses and telephone numbers *are on the title page of the manuscript itself*. The editor rue-
fully looks at the pile of manuscripts which are foundlings — left
on his doorstep with absolutely no identification — he keeps

them, against the day that the indignant letter comes in: "Where is my manuscript entitled *Aberration?* I sent it to you three years ago, and had no reply. I will sue you, have you fired by your boss, you thief, how do you hold your job, do you spend all your time in bars?"

And punctuation . . . The good dramatist knows how to punctuate. With periods, commas, exclamation marks, dashes, quotation marks, and all the rest of these common-sense tools . . . he *directs* his dialogue, as if he were the television director himself. It means to the editor — when a speech is correctly punctuated — that the dramatist is *hearing* his speech read by the actor, and since he knows the inflections, the emphasis he wants . . . he indicates his wishes by correct punctuation. He will *not* write: "How are you Harry darling get our guest a drink before you settle down Harry tell Charles and me the news from home Harry don't sit there sit here Harry."

He will write: "How are you, Harry? Darling, get our guest a drink before you settle down. Harry, tell Charles and me the news from home — Harry, don't sit *there* — sit *here*, Harry."

And directions for reading a given speech . . . Oh, eternal puzzle epitomized by

> "To be, or not to be; that is the question:
> Whether 'tis nobler in the mind, to suffer
> The slings and arrows of outrageous fortune;
> Or to take arms against a sea of troubles,
> And by opposing end them?"

Shakespeare left no directions as to how he wanted the speech read, except, in general, "trippingly on the tongue"; there have been as many styles of reading the speech as there have been Hamlets to read it.

But the dramatist *knows* how he wants a speech read. If the reading is not entirely clear from the context, from the characterization of the speaker, from what has gone before . . . the dramatist must indicate his desire. Consider the speech to Harry, above: It could be read "sarcastically", "gently", "crisply", "fearfully" — each style of reading giving a different significance. Only the dramatist knows how he wants the speech read; if it is a crucial speech, or an ambiguous speech suggesting several different readings, the dramatist must clearly indicate the correct reading.

The one-way telephone . . . oh, for this invention, sighs the editor! He recalls the unknown author who left an unsolicited manuscript at four in the afternoon, and who called at ten the next morning, demanding a report. He recalls the many authors who consider two days sufficient time for reading a manuscript, and who telephone when the 48 hours are up, on the dot. Oh, if only these authors were faced with the pile of manuscripts to be read; if only they understood the processes a television playscript has to go through! Sometimes as many as fifteen people must read a script before it is bought, or rejected; only the obviously unsuitable scripts are likely to come back home promptly. Please, dear dramatists, do not harass an editor with telephone calls. Let him call you, if you have been so considerate as to put your telephone number *on your script*. Do not call him long distance, either, to tell him a plot you have just thought of. You may be full of yourself, but he is not. He may be full, and probably is, but of other things you know nothing about. The editor's nerves are like your nerves: human nerves. He is more likely to hang up on you than to listen to your plot, especially if you start telling your story without first asking, considerately, if he has time to listen. Courtesy pays off in playwriting, as it does in every other human activity.

The well-traveled manuscript . . . it can be spotted at once by an editor. It is dirty around the edges, it is bedraggled, it has a musty smell; it has seen the world and has retired to a trunk. It has "rejected by everybody" written all over it. But if it is still good, in its author's judgment, for heaven's sake give it every chance by refurbishing it a bit; shine its shoes, tie its hair ribbons, clean and press its suit, wipe the egg off its mouth . . . before you send it out again. Even re-type it, if it's as good as you think it is; no doubt many a masterpiece which was offered to an editor in fourth-carbon-copy dress has gone back to its maker, since the editor was unwilling to risk eyestrain in an attempt to puzzle out the black smudges on the crinkled paper.

The poor-mouth author . . . "please buy my manuscript I am a little girl only eight years old with a harelip and crossed eyes

and nobody loves me so won't you please buy my story since I
am going blind and may not be able to write any more!" Ah, how
ruthless the editor can be with such a whimpering manuscript
— what joy, what savage pleasure, he derives from attaching the
rejection slip and flipping the pitiable mess into the out-going
mail box! Without exception, repeat, *without exception*, one editor has found such manuscripts unspeakably bad; their authors
know they are bad, and have the effrontery to try and make up
for the ineptness of their work by moaning to a stranger. There
have been authors with harelips, crossed eyes and going blind,
but their physical infirmities have been discovered after their
work has been revealed as whole, strong, beautiful and alive. The
authors themselves are whole, inside, and have self-respect, so
that they do not trade on their infirmities. So, please, dear dramatists, do not threaten suicide if your play is not bought; very likely
you will have to make good on your threat, as far as the editor
is concerned.

The sample-of-my-work author . . . He gets inside the editor's
office, and from some gargantuan container piles up on the editor's desk everything he has written since he learned to print the
alphabet. He is less interested in selling than he is in impressing
the editor with his genius. Volume, not quality, marks his output. Actually he is an insecure soul who wants to be told that
he is wonderful — wonderful, unappreciated, and capable of great
things he has no intention whatsoever of doing. He is first cousin
to the "poor-mouth" author. He is likely to telephone before the
week is out, and without asking the editor if he is free to talk, demand a detailed *favorable* criticism on each masterpiece.

He is also likely never to get inside a given editor's office more
than once. And his pile of rejection slips will grow.

It is a different matter if an author is *invited* to leave for reading samples of work which may show that he is capable of writing for a given television program. Oh, be not over-generous with
your samples, dear dramatists! Leave the editor panting for more.
Presumably he knows his job; he is probably more anxious to buy
than you are to sell, and he will recognize his own kind of material
(in your work) when he sees it.

"But it actually happened!" . . . the editor sighs when he hears

this argument, presented as an excuse for a rejected script's existence. Sure, the things that happen in life are stranger than fiction; but they don't always make good fiction, frequently because nobody will believe them. Within one editor's experience, this argument is silly: too often it is used as an excuse for a lack of skill in writing, for a lack of fundamental structure. Changed, adapted, made artistic in the true sense of that word — meaning that art in selectivity has chosen those portions of a true story which can be shaped into a dramatic pattern — true events can form the basis for wonderful plays, novels — whatever. It is generally believed that Charles Dickens wrote autobiographically in "David Copperfield" and "Oliver Twist"; certain portions of Maugham's "Of Human Bondage" are considered autobiographical; Samuel Butler's "Way of All Flesh" is no doubt based largely on his own life. The tyro playwright using a "true story" is apt to include *all* of it, so that the whole is cluttered and obscured by the tiny, meaningless, useless details. An unretouched photograph seldom resembles its subject truly, because small, unimportant blemishes and malformations are accented in the unretouched photograph, whereas in life they are not noticed. Wasn't it Oscar Wilde who said, in effect, that life imitates art — not art, life?

If "it actually happened", do your best to change it so as to make us believe that "it *could* happen". There is a tremendous difference! The difference is the art of the writer transforming his "material from life" into something that lives as an artistic entity.

The flip and/or smart-aleck unknown author . . . writes to an editor in the "show off" mood of a child trying to attract attention. Dear Dramatists, please don't do this! Honestly, do you like children who show off? Neither does an editor, especially when these children are supposedly adult. Believe one editor — said editor has all the advantage in such an attempted exchange; he has at hand the convenient rejection slip which will fix the smart-aleck writer's wagon *immediately*. Nothing gives speed to the rejection of a script like the supposedly witty personal remark addressed to an editor by a stranger. Be *impersonal* with an editor until such time as he invites your friendship; let your work make friends for you — it is the best intermediary of all, good work, that is, between editor and writer. You are not selling *yourself,* no matter how charming, intelligent, wise, beautiful, handsome you may be. And since senses of humor differ among human beings, what you think is funny, and so intend, may not be at all funny to the editor.

Seriously, these remarks, which may sound like scolding, are intended to save some possible well-intentioned but inexperienced playwright from a rebuff which might be really painful.

Writing for television is a business, too . . . that's what it all boils down to. We might as well face it. The literary work desirably is high art; the selling of it involves the courtesy, the consideration, the integrity ideally a part of any business affair. Would you send a jar of jelly through the mail without a lid? Well, then, don't send in your manuscripts lid-less, so to speak. Package them as efficiently and attractively (which means as simply) as you can. If, in poetic and creative mood when you prepare your manuscript for mailing, you have attached a snapshot of yourself, don't expect anything but a shrug from the editor as he sighs, "One more egomaniac" . . . . . and as he tosses the manuscript over into the "whenever I have nothing else to do" heap.

Take an editor's word for it . . . the things set down negatively in this chapter have happened, and continue to happen. He would only spare you heartbreak and sarcasm and the label of incompetence . . . and his sole intention is to help you sell your television plays.

II

The cliché stories . . . if one editor gets them in quantity every week or so, it is likely that other editors do, too; and you are wasting your time. There's the one about the blinded or scarred war veteran who won't look up his sweetheart when he returns, until he learns that during his absence she was in a wreck and is blind and/or scarred, too. The arrival of this tale brings screams of rage from one editor. Anyway, that story has been told rather well in "The Enchanted Cottage."

There's the one about the unappreciated elderly female member of the household, who retires to the attic at the end of the first act, emerging in the second as an artist of stunning genius who restores the family fortunes with her paintings. Well, ever hear of Grandma Moses? A lot of people have, and a lot of hopeful television playwrights are still writing her story for her.

There's the one about the starving young couple in Greenwich Village (or the local equivalent of it) who spend their last dollar for a murky painting they spot in a pawnbroker's shop and can't live without. It turns out to be a Titian, and its sale sets the young couple up for life . . . in not a single version one editor has read have the young people even intimated that part of the fortune might be given to the pawnbroker who was the means of their acquiring riches.

Another story worn down into the cliché groove is the one about the widow (or the widower) with children who object to her (his) marrying again. An amplification of this plot is when there are both a widow *and* a widower, each with children who object to their parents' marrying again. The ending is always the same: the children are reconciled, and the parent is happily married.

And adopted children! When one editor learns that a child has been adopted, he stops reading, even though the writing may be brilliant. Sometimes it is a war orphan brought back by the husband (or the wife) without any advance warning; sometimes the girl war orphan is described as being six years old, and then on arrival turns out to be sixteen, beautiful, and a menace to the integrity of the household. In the end, of course, every one is reconciled. How can there be any suspense in such a story? It has been told, or offered for sale, uncounted thousands of times, ever since *Daddy Long Legs* started this generic plot.

There is the boss who is invited home for dinner by the hopeful bridegroom, who is crassly after a big raise and an important promotion. The poor little bride does everything wrong; only, it turns out that the boss really dotes on burnt biscuits (which help his dyspepsia) and the bridegroom gets his raise, his promotion, and congratulations from the boss on having married such a clever, beautiful little girl.

There is the brilliant, scheming female newspaper reporter, who, in order to get a story, passes herself off on the unsuspecting widower as a baby-sitter or cook; she always falls in love with the trusting father, and the Big Scene is where she has to reveal both her treachery and her undying love.

There is the "Passing of the Third Floor Back" theme: a strange, unidentified man (or even child) who exhibits encyclopedic wisdom and understanding, who solves everyone's problems; and who then disappears, after unmistakable evidence that he is the Christ.

Conflicts over "expressing one's self"; between age and youth; between town living and country living; the tale of the misunderstood child who runs away at the end of the first act; the arbitrary separating of two sweethearts at the end of the first act (or the second, if it is a three act play); these and a hundred others are gross clichés, and you are warned against them, *as a practical matter*. True, great literary art can make any one of these cliché stories a masterpiece; but it is respectfully suggested that you be sure you are a great literary artist before you tackle these cliché stories and waste your time on material which has been glutting the television play market.

The hardest thing one editor has to do is to tell a television playwright, "Why did you write this? The material is so familiar that nobody will buy your play." Then, if challenged by the author, the editor goes on and cites chapter and verse.

What is left? *Plays revealing character*, the revelation of character being the unique quality of television; plays using situations which are unique and fresh and stories which may have been told before, but which you tell with a new approach . . . *through character*.

The cliché devices of exposition . . . there are certain phrases which make the editor's hackles rise: "You mean . . ." and "Just because . . . " are examples. Here is how inexpert playwrights use these phrases:

> FRED: (TO AMY) You mean you didn't know that
> I hit town last night at ten o'clock and
> have been burning up the wires trying to
> reach you?
> AMY: Yes, that's what I mean.

Poor Amy! She is made out something of a dunce because the author is one himself. He has put into Fred's mouth exposition that is vital, and he has done it by telling Amy things she already knows. Far better for Fred to come right out with it flat-footed and tell Amy that he hit town last night and has been trying to reach her, rather than for him to use the clumsy circumlocution "you mean." And here's another:

> FRED: Just because Father and Mother were
> separated when you were four is no
> reason for you to act crazy.

Just because as a springboard is followed inevitably by *is no reason,* in hundreds, no thousands, of scripts I have read.

If you can't think of smoother exposition, at least paraphrase the speech to avoid the "just because . . . . is no reason" shackles.

> FRED: You use the fact that Father and
> Mother were separated when you were
> four to justify your crazy behavior.

Or,

> FRED: Father and Mother were separated when
> you were four, and so *you* act crazy.

In these two examples, Fred's direct statement not only gives the needed exposition, but it also characterizes the person to whom he is speaking, as well as Fred, since it states his opinion of the person's behavior. It is submitted that in the "just because . . . is no reason" set-up, only the bald exposition is given, and awkward it is.

The climactic moment cliché. The author of this book admits that he is splitting hairs in mentioning the clichés of climactic moments — birthdays, special anniversaries, homecomings — but his conscience would hurt if he did not do so. Climax, climactic moments, crisis are the backbone of dramatic structure. Yet surely *all* plays do not have to be written with birthdays, anniversaries and homecomings as springboards for the playwright's attack on his material, his beginning point. These fairly arbitrary springboards are used so much that they have lost their freshness.

"Please don't kick me — it's my birthday!" "It's our anniversary — and you forgot to bring me roses." To one editor, no one should be kicked, birthday or not; nothing special is added to the dramatic tension because it may be an anniversary, since that tension has been stretched until it has been broken, in thousands and thousands of scripts, produced and unproduced. To use such cliché climactic moments is cheating a bit, like using springboards of deliberate violence to capture and hold attention, when the violence is not really a part of a character or the story.

III

THE MUSICAL VARIETY TELEVISION SCRIPT

The writing of a musical variety television script is such a highly specialized job that it is doubtful whether or not the freelance television writer can ever get a crack at it. A writer lands such a job as he would any other "expert's" job — such as directing a stage play, composing dances, playing first violin in an orchestra — by reason of his native talent, experience — and — importantly — his contacts.

Of course, the freelance television writer has the opportunity of selling skits or short dramatic pieces to those variety shows using such items; the sale of this kind of material is accomplished in exactly the same routine followed by the sale of longer television plays.

It is the writing of the continuity, the connecting passages, in a musical variety script which is handled like any other highly specialized job. That is, the singing and dancing numbers are joined together by brief passages of dialogue comprising the transitions. Sometimes these transition passages are spoken by an announcer, as in the case of "Your Hit Parade"; other shows employ a guest star to give the connecting dialogue, as on most musical variety programs. Still others present a permanent Master of Ceremonies, like Ed Sullivan in "Toast of the Town." All three shows mentioned are prototypes of television variety programs, and while the details vary, the general pattern remains the same in all three.

A variety show demands the utmost in cooperation among the

several departments accomplishing the final production: the over-all producer, the musical director, the dance director, the scene designer, the costume designer, the TV director, the lighting engineer, the sound engineer, and the playwright. In the excerpts of a TV variety script which follow, a short paragraph describing the scene to be played, danced and sung by the performers can give only the basic *idea* of the number: its execution is up to the collaborative efforts of those enumerated above. Yet the writer must manage to convey his *total* idea to the other technicians: for instance, in Song Number Four, even the mental attitude, the thoughts (which provide motivation for the action) are spelled out . . . "from the expression on the singer's face we surmise that the letter is from her beloved." This is only another way of saying what is said many times in this book: *as the playwright or librettist, you must at all times make your intention clear to the technicians who will produce your script.*

The following excerpts are from the script of "Your Hit Parade," as produced by the National Broadcasting Company, April 5, 1952.

Following the opening commercial announcement, which is on film . . .

CUT TO LIVE VIDEO

VIDEO	AUDIO
CUT TO OPEN BULL'S-EYE DOLLY IN FOR A CU OF DOROTHY COLLINS FOLLOWED BY EILEEN WILSON, SNOOKY LANSON, THE HIT PARADERS AND DANCERS. AND FINALLY WE SEE RAYMOND SCOTT AND THE ENTIRE LUCKY STRIKE ORCHESTRA WITH A LARGE PACK OF LUCKY STRIKES IN THE TOP CENTER PORTION OF THE PICTURE.	(MUSIC: DRUM ROLL UNDER) ANDRE BARUCH (ANNOUNCER) And now the Lucky Seven Songs of the Week with Dorothy Collins. . . . Eileen Wilson, Snooky Lanson . . . the Hit Paraders and Dancers . . . and Raymond Scott and the Lucky Strike Orchestra. (MUSIC: PLAYOFF)

INTRO TO FIRST NUMBER

VIDEO	AUDIO
OPEN ON A CU OF THE NUMBER 6 ON A RING BOX — THE BOX IS OPENED. AN ENGAGEMENT RING IS TAKEN OUT AND PUT ON DOROTHY COLLINS' FINGER. PAN TO A LARGE CAKE WITH THE TITLE: "BE MY LIFE'S COMPANION" ON IT.	BARUCH And off we go with Survey Song Number SIX! Dorothy Collins, Snooky Lanson and the Hit Paraders get together to bring us the bright tune that's Number six. . . . "BE MY LIFE'S COMPANION"

PULL BACK TO REVEAL DOROTHY
COLLINS AND SNOOKY LANSON
WITH FAMILY AND FRIENDS
AT AN ENGAGEMENT PARTY.
THE SCENE IS A LARGE FAMILY
RESTAURANT AND BEER HALL
OF THE EARLY 1900's.

MUSIC
(BE MY LIFE'S COMPANION) . . .
    DOROTHY COLLINS
    SNOOKY LANSON
    HIT PARADERS
    EXTRAS
DOROTHY COLLINS AND SNOOKY
LANSON SING TO EACH OTHER
IN HAPPY ANTICIPATION
OF THEIR LIFE TOGETHER.
THEIR FRIENDS AND FAMILY
JOIN IN THE MERRYMAKING.
THE NUMBER ENDS ON A NOTE
OF FRIENDLY WARMTH AND
HIGH SPIRITS.
(APPLAUSE)

INTRO TO FOURTH NUMBER

VIDEO	AUDIO
OPEN ON CU OF A LIGHTED PANEL ON THE WALL BESIDE THE ENTRANCE OF A RECORDING STUDIO. WE SEE THE WORDS: "RECORDING STUDIO." DISS TO THE INTERIOR OF THE STUDIO WHERE WE SEE A LABEL BEING APPLIED TO A RECORD THAT IS TO BE CUT. ON THE LABEL WE SEE THE NUMBER 4 AND THE WORD: "CRY."	(HARP GLISS) (MUSIC: HIT AND FADE) BARUCH Number FOUR on the Survey! Dorothy Collins and the appealing song that continues high in the favor of the nation . . . "CRY"

FOURTH NUMBER

MUSIC

(CRY) . . . .

      DOROTHY COLLINS

      HIT PARADERS

      EXTRAS

THE SCENE IS A RECORDING STUDIO WHERE DOROTHY COLLINS HAS JUST ARRIVED TO RECORD A SONG. SHE SITS ON A CHAIR AND, OPENING HER PURSE, TAKES OUT A FEW LETTERS SHE HAS RECEIVED IN THE MORNING MAIL. SHE STARTS TO OPEN ONE OF THE LETTERS — FROM THE EXPRESSION ON HER FACE WE SURMISE THAT IT IS FROM HER BELOVED — WHEN SHE IS SUMMONED TO THE MICROPHONE TO REHEARSE THE NUMBER SHE IS TO RECORD.

VIDEO

SHE BEGINS TO SING FROM THE
MANUSCRIPT OF THE MUSIC
WITHOUT MUCH EMPHASIS
ON THE DRAMATIC CONTENT
OF THE LYRIC. SHE IS
GRADUALLY CAUGHT UP BY
THE WORDS OF THE SONG
AND SUDDENLY IT OCCURS TO
HER THAT THE LETTER WHICH
SHE HAS LEFT ON THE CHAIR
MIGHT BE A COUNTERPART
OF THE LETTER IN THE SONG.
SHE LOOKS ANXIOUSLY AT THE
UNOPENED LETTER ON THE
CHAIR AND BECOMES MORE
AND MORE DISTRACTED BY THE
POSSIBILITY THAT IT MIGHT
CONTAIN BAD NEWS. AT THE
END OF THE SONG SHE RUSHES
TO OPEN THE LETTER, EAGERLY
SCANS IT AND A LOOK OF
HAPPINESS AND RELIEF COMES
OVER HER FACE WHEN SHE
FINDS THAT HER FEARS ARE
WITHOUT FOUNDATION.

These excerpts from "Your Hit Parade" present, in their physical setup, the choice of the producer to have the Video and Audio in two separate columns, with the matching sections directly opposite each other. We have remarked elsewhere that in dramatic scripts, this arrangement makes for hard reading; but here (firstly) it is the producer's choice, and (secondly) there is a minimum of Audio written into the script, so that it probably is even helpful to follow this arrangement.

Incidentally, the direction *harp gliss* is short for "glissando", a musical term which describes a sweeping chord on harp or piano.

IV

THE FUTURE OF TELEVISION

A shrewd man once remarked that it's impossible to predict the future, which he described as a combination of one's character and present circumstances. As these factors change and/or develop, the future is created as the present. On this basis, these remarks on the "future" of television are set down.

Whatever television's future, its artistic growth and fulfillment are up to you writers. The future is the great and precious responsibility of the new breed of artist, the playwright producing *original works* for television "which cannot be done as well in any other medium." Artists among scene designers will arise, artists of lighting; they still must have something for which to design a scene and something to light. Great actors will appear, needing, as always, great roles to play. Whether "live" or on film, or in a combination of these two techniques, television will come into its own as a mature art, as the greatest form of communication ever known, only as the creative writers give the full charge of their inspiration and talent to rooting and nourishing television's growth. Never has there been such a challenge (never such a market, to be practical about things) as television, when it hits its stride.

We can assume that out of the present "tinker toy" stage of television's mechanics will come the means to present "live" programs fluidly, smoothly, easily. A present-day television studio, when a program is in progress, has a jungle growth of sensitive, snarled cable on the floor; there are sound booms on pedestals ridden by one operator and shoved around by another; there are cameras similarly manually maneuvered; there are lights hanging from the grid, bolted onto sets, screwed onto stands which clang metallically when they're banged into through haste or carelessness or the presence of gremlins. There are sprawling, realistic sets which are built like stage sets; there are stands with clocks for indicating passage of time; stands with medallions of a play's "signature"; stands for all sorts of special effects; little tubs of water with toy boats to simulate storm-tossed craft; fog machines, cabinets for rolling titles; wind machines; rain machines; thunder sheets; improvised dressing rooms or perhaps just a clothes tree with the star's next costume hanging on it (the costume change will be made unashamedly, through necessity, in the presence of everybody, to the limit that decency allows and the script calls for); there are technicians shuffling their feet without knowing it; spectators coughing discreetly, unaware that they're standing near an open microphone which carries their catarrh to the ears of twenty million listeners; there are stagehands throwing nails and clips and paper wads at each other during love scenes, in the immemorial manner of stagehands; there is anxiety, peevishness, resentment, despair, joy, ulcers-in-the-making; there is the great fun of being a part of all this, of being, as it were, on the "frontier" of an unknown Promised Land.

Some day, through the growth of the mechanics of television in all its departments, all this confusion, cross purposes, crudeness, will be gone and "live" shows will be done with neatness and dispatch.

On that future day, television screens in the "television room" of future homes will be whatever size the owner desires. Positively there will be color television; possibly there will be television with "third dimension" or with such an illusion of depth that it amounts to "third dimension."

When that future day comes, the entrepreneurs of television will still be looking for great plays, which you playwrights will have to write. At least one man believes that these plays of the future will equal if not surpass the best plays the legitimate theatre has ever presented. A playwright will work a year, two years, three years on a full-length, two-hour or three-hour play which will be seen on a single telecast by fifty million viewers. And the royalties for such a telecast will be counted in tens of thousands of dollars. There will be original operas, musical comedies, revues on the same scale.

There will be such a revival of and sustained interest in drama and dramatic entertainment as the world has never known.

And it is good and valuable that some of us are attempting to learn now the technique of writing for television, however imperfectly we understand it, in order to be ready, to help and (it is devoutly hoped) to reap the reward, both artistically and financially.

Several important methods of letting the viewer pay for the television entertainment he may choose are being explored. These fall into two divisions: television in the home, and television in theatres, or in auditoriums which may be built in the future to present television to large audiences.

In home television with a "box office," where the family of viewers pay their money and take their choice, the desired programs may not be received until, through one of several devices, the money is deposited or a charge is made (through the family telephone bill, perhaps). In theatre television, the televised program is a part of the entertainment paid for in the usual way at the theatre box-office.

An important theatre chain is developing the presentation of "live" television in its theatres. Mr. Robert H. O'Brien, then secretary-treasurer of the then United Paramount Theatres, wrote in the *New York Times* of July 20, 1952, in part as follows:

"United Paramount Theatres has held from the beginning that closed circuit theatre television had its greatest potential in the field of commerce, industry and public service, in the off hours, morning or early afternoon, when the theatres are normally dark. . . . To this end, United Paramount has pioneered the field of off-hours use of theatre television by government, by public service organizations and by industrial and commercial concerns. . . . Closed circuit theatre television is rapidly becoming big business as far as capital outlay is concerned."

Further, "Other forms of entertainment via theatre television have yet to be tried. Many suggestions have been made and some pioneering work has been done in the Broadway opening night, the Metropolitan Opera, the ballet and the symphony orchestra field."

Mr. O'Brien, now financial vice president of American Broadcasting-Paramount Theatres, Inc. (the company resulting from the merger of Paramount Theatres with American Broadcasting), recently told your author that closed-circuit television has developed more for use in hotel ballrooms and auditoriums than it has for theatre use. However, Mr. O'Brien expressed the opinion that when color television becomes practical for use on the wide screens of theatres, theatres may well be put into service for the entertainment and business purposes outlined in his *Times* statement quoted on the preceding page.

In addition, Paramount Pictures is heavily concerned with the International Telemeter Corporation, as reported in *Sponsor Magazine,* for May 19, 1952. According to this source, Telemeter will erect a master telecasting aerial in Palm Springs, California, with seven Los Angeles channels via community antennae; then will test this pay-as-you-see system with new movies and special events programming over a closed circuit channel. The inserting of coins in a home meter permits viewer to see movies, sports activities or special programs. The device does not interfere with normal reception on regular commercial channels. *Sponsor Magazine* stated that the variation in price of shows to be seen on Telemeter will be from five cents to two dollars.

According to Mr. Paul Raibourn, vice president of Paramount Pictures, the experiment outlined in the preceding paragraph was carried out successfully; but certain legal difficulties were encountered. However, Mr. Raibourn told your author that in his opinion, economic pressures will eventually force telecasting into some sort of pay-as-you-see television.

The national and even international scope of the planning being made for pay-as-you-see television underscores the fact that in the future, the competition for the viewer's attention and money will be great, meaning in turn that the *quality* of the competing programs must be maintained, and increased, as time goes by. Once again, the *quality* must be provided by the creative artist completely at home in the technique of writing for TV.

In between the present time and this extravagant future lies much heavy, sober slogging. Television must free itself from its chains, which in addition to being mechanical are economic. The cost of producing television is unbelievable to the layman; one half-hour dramatic show can engulf forty thousand dollars a week. It requires a very large and very financially-sound and very brave corporation to pay this cost, and so win the right to be the sponsor and to advertise its wares. Since a given corporation, the sponsor, is paying the costs, naturally its management has the right to choose the kind of entertainment it is willing to be associated with. The unique quality of television, its immediacy, and the fact that it comes right into the family living room, act in reverse when it comes to the themes and subjects a writer may write about. Viewers can get extremely angry at a given brand of soap if the makers of the soap offend them with a play on a subject they happen not to approve of. A blight of "non-fan" mail can descend on this offending soap, and sales may drop to the point that the manufacturer will be forced off the air and conceivably out of business. A public apology by a sponsor to the viewing public has happened more than once, an apology usually made humbly, and implying, if not actually saying, "*Please* don't boycott us — please don't stop buying out product".

The millions in the viewing audience, therefore, are censors, each and every one of them, possessing a new, heady authority which becomes active and vindictive as the individual's prejudices are exacerbated and his realization of his power to retaliate grows.

No reasonable writer, therefore, will complain at the apparent timorousness of present-day sponsors in carefully avoiding certain themes and subjects. Writers should, on the other hand, be grateful to such sponsors for giving them the opportunity to experiment and to learn television technique, against the day when television will have the freedom of the novel and the legitimate stage in its choice of material. It is to be hoped soberly that the viewing audience similarly will grow in maturity, so that any material which is not actually indecent can become the material of the artist-playwright who writes with dedicated integrity. The future of television will be black indeed, dull, ugly, sordid, lifeless black, if *all* material must please *every one* and offend *no one,* not the nonagenarian, not the day-old infant. In that black future, television would be cursed for its dullness by the very ones who would prevent its growth through holding contracted the scope of themes and subjects. *It is a heavy and precious responsibility that the television playwrights of the future bear.*

As far as television playwrights are concerned, the anticipated new techniques are in the field of mechanics only; they cannot conceivably affect what you write for television or the basic techniques of television playwriting which this book attempts to set forth. It is fascinating to recall that George Bernard Shaw, in his monumental play, *Back to Methuselah*, published in 1922, and produced by the Theatre Guild in New York, used "live", face-to-face television in those future distant times.

The last act of *Back to Methuselah* is described as being laid in the future, "As Far as Thought Can Reach". So in this chapter, the author humbly has set down "present character and circumstances" as he sees them, hoping that his glance may be penetrating even a little bit into the future that will be created for itself by the electronic and artistic miracle of television, aided indispensably by the television artist-playwright who even now is beginning to emerge.

v

This chapter is the last in this book to be written. It is presented from the point of view of a practicing editor of a dramatic television program who has not the slightest wish to pose as a source of all-knowledge. He has instead tried to show you some of the obvious things to avoid in your dealings with editors, who are, as has been stated, human beings, too, and who have to cope frequently with unbridled and/or inexperienced creative talents. He knows that the budding creative individual more often than not is shy, unsure, and quivering with longing to succeed. These characteristics sometimes are masked by a cockiness, a bravado, a rudeness not at all truly a part of the creative individual's personality. In writing for television, particularly, there is not time for most editors to be gentle, tactful, understanding. They prefer that the *playwrights* be gentle, tactful and understanding. When they are confronted by a beginning playwright who is brash, loud and exhibitionistic, almost inevitably these harassed editors say, "Well, we can't bother with *him* — let him get his experience somewhere else".

Television playwriting is a new thing in the world, but good manners, tact, courtesy and plain old common sense are not new; and they are as important and necessary in our wonderful, exciting, provocative, strange universe of television writing as they always have been.

18

The Television Playwright
as an Artist

IT IS NOT THE PROVINCE of this book to discuss the nature of the material the playwright selects to write about. "A playwright is entitled to his own material." Of course, this freedom of choice carries with it the responsibility to make the material chosen acceptable and believable to the final judge: the audience. It has been said, lightly yet earnestly, by a great many masters, that *any* material, properly presented in artistic dramatic form by the playwright, may be used.

Yet perhaps the words of one great master, William Faulkner, may have meaning for you, the television playwright, in your choice of material, and so we are including here Faulkner's speech* on the occasion of his accepting the Nobel Prize for Literature.

And then, since all writers live under the lash of urgency, of the insatiable desire for successful achievement and recognition, this book is closed with some quiet remarks by another master, George Pierce Baker, who was not only a great teacher, but also a man who completely understood the nature of writers. Consider Mr. Baker's remarks and take them to heart, for they are a distillation of his decades of teaching and of his experience with the churning, erupting human being who burns "to write." You will not be the first one to find comfort and strength and courage to keep on in the face of apparent failure . . . in Mr. Baker's words, so gently spoken, and so right in their common sense.

---

* Reprinted by courtesy of Random House, Inc.

William Faulkner's Speech of Acceptance Upon the Award of the Nobel Prize for Literature, Delivered in Stockholm on the Tenth of December, Nineteen Hundred Fifty.

I feel that this award was not made to me as a man, but to my work — a life's work in the agony and sweat of the human spirit, not for glory and least of all for profit, but to create out of the materials of the human spirit something which did not exist before. So this award is only mine in trust. It will not be difficult to find a dedication for the money part of it commensurate with the purpose and significance of its origin. But I would like to do the same with the acclaim, too, by using this moment as a pinnacle from which I might be listened to by the young men and women already dedicated to the same anguish and travail, among whom is already that one who will some day stand here where I am standing.

Our tragedy today is a general and universal physical fear so long sustained by now that we can even bear it. There are no longer problems of the spirit. There is only the question: When will I be blown up? Because of this, the young man or woman writing today has forgotten the problems of the human heart in conflict with itself which alone can make good writing because only that is worth writing about, worth the agony and the sweat.

He must learn them again. He must teach himself that the basest of all things is to be afraid; and, teaching himself that, forget it forever, leaving no room in his workshop for anything but the old verities and truths of the heart, the old universal truths lacking which any story is ephemeral and doomed — love and honor and pity and pride and compassion and sacrifice. Until he does so, he labors under a curse. He writes not of love but of lust, of defeats in which nobody loses anything of value, of victories without hope and, worst of all, without pity or compassion. His griefs grieve on no universal bones, leaving no scars. He writes not of the heart but of the glands.

Until he relearns these things, he will write as though he stood among and watched the end of man. I decline to accept the end of man. It is easy enough to say that man is immortal simply because he will endure; that when the last ding-dong of doom has clanged and faded from the last worthless rock hanging tideless in the last red and dying evening, that even then there will still be one more sound: that of his puny inexhaustible voice, still talking. I refuse to accept this. I believe that man will not merely endure: he will prevail. He is immortal, not because he alone among creatures has an inexhaustible voice, but because he has a soul, a spirit capable of compassion and sacrifice and endurance. The poet's, the writer's, duty is to write about these things. It is his privilege to help man endure by lifting his heart, by reminding him of the courage and honor and hope and pride and compassion and pity and sacrifice which have been the glory of his past. The poet's voice need not merely be the record of man, it can be one of the props, the pillars to help him endure and prevail.

———————

George Pierce Baker, founder of the "47 Workshop" at Harvard College, and later Chairman of the Department of Drama at Yale University, was meeting his 1929 graduating class in Advanced Playwriting, Drama 47, for the last time. Mr. Baker spoke quietly. "Ladies and gentlemen," he said, "playwriting is a mature art. Give yourselves twenty years to get a play on. If you haven't gotten a play on in twenty years, you may not be a playwright."

The members of the class left quietly. They went out into the world, alone, as each artist and potential artist must, to realize his art or not to realize his art, but at least to try with all his heart, sustained by Mr. Baker's reminder that art is long.

George Pierce Baker did not live to see television, but it is the conviction of one of his pupils that if he had, he would have taught that writing for television must be brought to high art. Perhaps he would have revised his classic book, *Dramatic Technique,* to include for television writing the lucid, comprehensive, indispensable teaching that he gave to writing for the legitimate stage. Since, of course, he did not, I have attempted humbly to follow in his footsteps, and to apply, imperfectly at best but with the ideals instilled by Mr. Baker, the things learned from him, to the field of writing for television, the New Playwriting.

THE END

Appendix

Magnetic Tape Recording of Video — The Important New Technical Development in Television Playwriting

In television, there are milestone dates. Such a date is April 19, 1956, when Mr. Val Adams of the *New York Times* telegraphed a special story, with a Chicago dateline. We quote:

"The dramatic introduction of the video tape recorder turned out to be the biggest hit at the annual convention of the National Association of Radio and Television Broadcasters, which ended today.

"As of this morning, the Ampex Corporation, which developed the device, said it had taken orders for seventy-three recorders. This represented gross sales of $3,800,000.

"Four days ago, when the convention opened, most television station owners who have since placed orders did not know that a recorder ready for commercial use had been developed.

"The Ampex device records television pictures and sound on magnetic tape two inches wide. When the tape is re-wound by pressing a button, it can be played back immediately without being processed through a regular television system. Applications of the recorder in television, science and industry in the years ahead may prove to be almost unlimited."

In such brief words, a possible revolution in writing and recording for television and motion pictures was forecast.

Consider the possibilities: a dramatic scene may be "photographed" (actually, recorded) and then viewed immediately, without the elaborate and costly laboratory processes of developing and printing motion picture film.

500

If the scene isn't right, it can be "wiped off" the tape, and recorded again, immediately. The process can be repeated until the scene *is* right.

Thus, an entire dramatic program, or *any* program, can be taped in advance, and then telecast at the appointed time. Or, and this is very important to story structure and possibilities, *parts* of a dramatic program, or *any* program, can be taped in advance, and then can be *included* in a "live" telecast.

In essence, we have in the magnetic tape recording of video an infinitely faster, less expensive and possibly more satisfactory technique for "filming" programs.

It follows logically that any television playwright who can write film continuity, that is, in motion picture form, can also write for video magnetic tape recording. The heart of the matter is that — like filmed television plays — the time-on-the-air pressure is removed; costumes can be changed at will; scenes may be taped individually, literally anywhere in the world; a character can accomplish any desired makeup change, can grow from youth to age, or — in flashbacks — can regress from age to youth. *Writing for magnetic tape recording is exactly like writing for motion picture filming.*

The difference between video magnetic tape recording and motion picture filming is in *the time required for preparation of the telecast tape and film.* An entire television program, or parts of it, may be taped the morning before an afternoon or evening telecast (on the same day); in short, a few hours before the scheduled telecast.

But, it takes several days or even weeks to *film* a television program, or any part of it, although (through paying increased costs) short sequences (as in news reels) can be rushed through the film developing and printing laboratory.

The *cost* of magnetic tape video recording presumably will be *much less* than motion picture filming and processing; the entire operation should be simpler and involve fewer personnel.

The head of "live" television production for one of the large New York advertising agencies circulated a memorandum concerning the Ampex magnetic tape video recording. Portions of possible interest to the television playwright are quoted:

"Engineering vice-president of CBS television, William B. Lodge, said: 'We hope that use of this new equipment to overcome the three-hour East-West time differential will improve the technical quality of CBS television programs, and will enable our affiliated stations on the West Coast to deliver better quality pictures in the home.'"

And: "Perhaps even more important than the reproduction of recorded programs with 'live' telecast quality are the operational and economic advantages the Ampex Video Tape Recorder offers the television industry. Programs can be recorded directly from the TV camera, from a TV receiver, from television transmission lines, or from microwave relay systems. Just as with the Ampex Audio tape recorders, the program can be immediately replayed with no processing of any kind necessary. Considerable economy can be effected by erasing the recorded signal when it is no longer needed and re-using the tape to record another program. This is in contrast with photographic film which cannot be re-used after it has once been exposed.

"Once the equipment has been installed and adjusted, operation is as simple as that of an Ampex audio tape recorder. To record a program, the operator presses one button to start recording. To play a recorded program, he simply presses the playback button."

The first use of the Ampex system, therefore, would seem to be to replace kinescopes (a filmed recording of a "live" program, photographed in a laboratory from a receiving set while the program is actually on the air), in order to deliver a better picture on a delayed telecast than can be delivered with a kinescope. *Such a use has no effect whatsoever on the television playwright's story material and its dramatization.*

It is possible that there will be profound conflicts among labor unions over jurisdiction of the new magnetic tape video recording, when it comes into general use, not only in television but in motion pictures. Such possible conflicts could further delay general use of magnetic tape video recording.

A few days after the *New York Times* story quoted above appeared, the author of this book conferred at length with executives and technical personnel at two of the major networks, in New York. The consensus was that it would be at least two years minimum before the use of magnetic tape video recording became general. That would put its possible widespread use in late Spring, 1958; more likely in the Fall of 1958 — and this was a minimum estimate.

It will have to be enough for this edition of *Television Writing and Selling* to call the attention of the television playwright to the indefinite future general use of magnetic tape video recording, and to reassure him that if he can write television plays to be filmed he can also write television plays to be recorded — both video and audio — on magnetic tape.

There is also this factor to remember: as major motion picture films are telecast on coast-to-coast networks in preferred telecast time, those programs which are presented entirely "live" stress — one may even say "boast" — about the fact that their programs are "live", in contrast with the filmed programs. So, it would seem that in spite of the eventual availability of magnetic tape recording of the picture, that is, of "video", the proponents of live television will stick to their convictions about the superiority of live television, and will ignore magnetic tape recording of video.

But now we must record the first historic telecast of magnetic tape recording of video. In a news bulletin dated December 3, 1956, the Columbia Broadcasting System announced that on Friday night, November 30, 1956, the "Douglas Edwards with the News" program, which originates in New York, was received and recorded on magnetic tape at Television City in Hollywood, and then fed to West Coast CBS television affiliates. In the past, the bulletin stated, the problem of offsetting time differences between the East Coast and West Coast has involved the use of quick-processed filmed recordings. CBS Television hopes, according to the news bulletin, that use of magnetic video tape will eliminate the necessity for film processing, and will improve the picture quality of "delayed" programs seen by West Coast viewers.

The magnetic tape recording of video will be with us, without doubt; but, as we have said already in this book, those television playwrights who can write not only "live" but for motion picture filming will be well prepared for the inevitable scientific developments calling for a change in the techniques of writing for television.

SOME COPYRIGHT FACTS

Terms: A copyright is valid for 28 years. It can be renewed once for a like, continuing period.

Notice of Copyright: This should read, *on the title page,* COPYRIGHT (year) BY JOE BLANK

i.e., COPYRIGHT 1954 BY JOE BLANK (if 1954 is the year)

The word "copyright": This may be abbreviated to Copr. Do not use a "c" with a circle around it. Do not say "copyrighted".

Year of Copyright: The year must be used in which the copyrighted material is to be circulated or published. If you are preparing material in November that is to appear in February, use the February year. The date is determined by the time of distribution or publication.

Name of Copyright Owner: The full name of the copyright owner must be used, not the initials. "Copyright 1954 James Fulton Blank" is correct. The word "by" may be omitted.

Copyright applied for: Authors frequently put this notice on the title page of a work for which the copyright has not been finally secured, although it has been applied for.